Defence Industries in the 21st Century

Defence Industries in the 21st Century explores the transformation in the global defence industrial production through examining the interaction between international and domestic factors.

With the global defence industry and arms market likely continue to expand and mature, the ways in which this progression could influence international politics remain obscure. In practice, as the contents of this book show, the defence industrial bases and arms export policies of emerging states display significant variance. This variance is the result of a unique balance between domestic and international factors that has shaped the defence industrialization behaviour and policies of the less industrialized states. One of the most important conclusions of the book is that the interplay between domestic and international factors clearly influences the variation in the emerging states' defence industrialization policies, as well as their success or failure. While international factors create opportunities, they also limit the options available to emerging economies. Domestic factors also play an important role by shaping the policy choices of the states' decision-makers.

Exploring the balance between international and domestic factors and the ways in which they influence defence industrialization in emerging states, *Defence Industries in the 21st Century* will be of great interest to scholars of Defence Industries; Arms Manufacturing; and Defence, Strategic and Security Studies more generally.

The chapters were originally published in *Defence Studies, Comparative Strategy* and *All Azimuth*.

Çağlar Kurç is an Adjunct Lecturer at the Department of International Relations at I.D. Bilkent University, Ankara, Turkey. He was a Fulbright Fellow at the MIT Security Studies Program, and Visiting Post-doctoral Scholar at the Arnold A. Saltzman Institute of War and Peace Studies at Columbia University, USA. His work focuses on defense industrialization in the emerging powers.

Richard A. Bitzinger is a Visiting Senior Fellow with the Military Transformations Program at the S. Rajaratnam School of International Studies, where his work focuses on security and defense issues relating to the Asia-Pacific region, including military modernization and force transformation, regional defense industries and local armaments production, and weapons proliferation.

Stephanie G. Neuman is the Director of the Comparative Defense Studies Program and a Senior Research Scholar at the Arnold A. Saltzman Institute of War and Peace Studies at Columbia University, USA. Neuman has participated in study groups on the defense industry and arms control for both the Council on Foreign Relations and the Carnegie Endowment for International Peace.

Defence Industries in the 21st Century

A Comparative Analysis

Edited by
Çağlar Kurç, Richard A. Bitzinger and Stephanie G. Neuman

Routledge
Taylor & Francis Group
LONDON AND NEW YORK

First published 2021
by Routledge
2 Park Square, Milton Park, Abingdon, Oxon, OX14 4RN

and by Routledge
52 Vanderbilt Avenue, New York, NY 10017

Routledge is an imprint of the Taylor & Francis Group, an informa business

British Library Cataloguing-in-Publication Data
A catalogue record for this book is available from the British Library

ISBN13: 978-0-367-44453-2
ISBN13: 978-0-367-55435-4 (pbk)

Typeset in Myriad Pro
by codeMantra

Publisher's Note
The publisher accepts responsibility for any inconsistencies that may have arisen during the conversion of this book from journal articles to book chapters, namely the inclusion of journal terminology.

Disclaimer
Every effort has been made to contact copyright holders for their permission to reprint material in this book. The publishers would be grateful to hear from any copyright holder who is not here acknowledged and will undertake to rectify any errors or omissions in future editions of this book.

This volume could not have been possible without the considerable support and input of Dr. Stephanie Neuman, who sadly left us on April 15, 2020. She was, in the first place, the impetus behind the workshop series that ultimately resulted in this volume of essays. More than that, Stephanie was an inspiration and a true mentor, a muse that helped drive our work and challenge us to think creatively and imaginatively. The world is the poorer for her leaving, but richer for having had her in it.

Richard A. Bitzinger
Çağlar Kurç

Contents

Citation Information

The following chapters were originally published in the *Defence Studies*, volume 17, issue 3 (2017) and *Comparative Strategy* volume 37, issue 4 (2018). When citing this material, please use the original page numbering for each article, as follows:

Chapter 1
Commentary on The value of domestic arms industries: security of supply or military adaptation?
Marc R. DeVore
Defence Studies, volume 17, issue 3 (2017) pp. 242–259

Chapter 2
Israel's defence industries – an overview
Uzi Rubin
Defence Studies, volume 17, issue 3 (2017) pp. 228–241

Chapter 3
Between defence autarky and dependency: the dynamics of Turkish defence industrialization
Çağlar Kurç
Defence Studies, volume 17, issue 3 (2017) pp. 260–281

Chapter 4
Commentary on Assessing the Turkish defense industry: structural issues and major challenges
Arda Mevlutoglu
Defence Studies, volume 17, issue 3 (2017) pp. 282–294

Chapter 5
The Arab Gulf defense pivot: Defense industrial policy in a changing geostrategic context
Heiko Borchert
Comparative Strategy, volume 37, issue 4 (2018) pp. 299–315

Chapter 7
Asian arms industries and impact on military capabilities
Richard A. Bitzinger
Defence Studies, volume 17, issue 3 (2017) pp. 295–311

Chapter 8

State vs. market *in India: How (not) to integrate foreign contractors in the domestic defense-industrial sector*
Moritz Weiss
Comparative Strategy, volume 37, issue 4 (2018) pp. 286–298

Chapter 9

Armaments decision-making: Are European states really different?
Jocelyn Mawdsley
Comparative Strategy, volume 37, issue 4 (2018) pp. 260–271

Chapter 10

Defense industrialization in small countries: Policies in Czechia and Slovakia
Martin Chovančík
Comparative Strategy, volume 37, issue 4 (2018) pp. 272–285

Chapter 11

Brazil's defense industry: Challenges and opportunities
Raul Gouvea
Comparative Strategy, volume 37, issue 4 (2018) pp. 346–359

Chapter 12

Defense industrialization in Latin America
Patrice M. Franko and Mônica Herz
Comparative Strategy, volume 37, issue 4 (2018) pp. 331–345

Chapter 13

The puzzle: Multi-vector foreign policy and defense industrialization in Central Asia
Çağlar Kurç
Comparative Strategy, volume 37, issue 4 (2018) pp. 316–330

Contributors

Zeinab Abul-Magd Oberlin College, USA.

Richard A. Bitzinger S. Rajaratnam School of International Studies, Singapore.

Heiko Borchert Borchert Consulting & Research AG, Lucerne, Switzerland.

Martin Chovančík Department of International Relations and European Studies, Masaryk University, Brno, Czech Republic.

Marc R. DeVore School of International Relations, University of Saint Andrews, UK.

Patrice M. Franko Department of Economics, Colby College, Waterville, USA.

Raul Gouvea FITE Department, Anderson School of Management, University of New Mexico, Albuquerque, USA.

Mônica Herz Department of International Relations, Pontifical Catholic University Rio de Janeiro, Brazil.

Çağlar Kurç Comparative Defense Studies Program, Arnold A. Saltzman Institute of War and Peace Studies, Columbia University, New York City, USA.

Jocelyn Mawdsley School of Geography, Politics and Sociology, Newcastle University, UK.

Arda Mevlutoglu independent defense analyst, Ankara, Turkey.

Stephanie G. Neuman Director Comparative Defense Studies Program, Arnold A. Saltzman Institute of War and Peace Studies, Columbia University, New York City, USA.

Uzi Rubin The Rubincon Consulting Firm, Israel.

Moritz Weiss Geschwister-Scholl-Institute for Political Science, Ludwig-Maximilians-University Munich, Germany.

Introduction[1]

Çağlar Kurç, Richard A. Bitzinger and Stephanie G. Neuman

The Transformation in Global Arms Production

The global arms market experienced significant transformation after the end of the Cold War with the increasing amount of defence industrial cooperation among states as well as defence industry firms. The main driver of the transformation was the rising costs of military research and development, inadequate base markets, limited technological and industrial sources and rapid advances in production technologies, which incentivized defence companies to search for new markets beyond the national borders (Sköns 1993, p. 160, Sjolander 1999, pp. 122–31, Hayward 2000, pp. 116–7, Oudot and Bellais 2019, p. 169). Although operating in foreign markets was a second-best solution for defence companies in the major arms-producing states to maintain competencies, evolution into multinational corporations through mergers and acquisitions becomes the key feature in arms production (Oudot and Bellais 2019, p. 169).

Multinational defence corporations began to establish transnational networks of inter-firm relations that involved co-production/development, partnerships and sub-contacting agreements. As the inter-firm relations grew through establishment of joint-ventures and sub-contracting, "intricate international networks of research, production and information" (Sköns 1993, p. 165) emerged, thus making integration to the global production chains became a viable option (Bitzinger 2003). As the production relations changed, the arms cooperation practices also started to change. Increasingly formal, integrative and permanent systems of arms production between defence companies, largely in the West, slowly replaced inter-governmental ad hoc arms cooperation (Anthony 1993, Bitzinger 1994a, Sköns and Wulf 1994, Adams 2001). In the form of cooperative relations, the transfer of technology, technical data and industrial know-how became the new form of exchange between states and defence companies, thus transforming arms production into a more transnational endeavour (Bitzinger 1994a, p. 181, 1994b, p. 273).

The availability of military technology and production know-how transfer creates an opportunity for less advanced arms producers and non-arms producers to invest in defence industrialization. As the major defence companies sought for larger share in international military market, international competition intensified, thus increasing the market power of emerging countries (Oudot and Bellais 2019, p. 181). Emerging countries began systematically demanding technology transfer, technical data and industrial know-how to improve their defence industrial capabilities. Through the expansion of contractor and sub-contractor relationships, the emerging defence industries find the opportunity to become increasingly integrated into the transnational network of company-to-company exchange and so would be better positioned for shouldering the increased costs of arms production.

As a result, the number of arms suppliers in the global arms market increased. Should this transformation of the defence industrial market continue, the ways in which it will influence international politics remain obscure.

One school of thought expected that the transformation of the global arms market would lead to more integrative, liberalized and export-oriented arms production policies due to the increased cost of production and the need for sharing the cost. Other analysts disagree. They believe that domestic factors usually take precedence over international factors in the decision-making calculus of industrializing countries. Primarily concerned with protecting their country's indigenous industries, the leaders of these states are prompted to reject an export-oriented, integrative defence industrialization policy. Instead, according to these defence analysts, the emerging states choose to pursue self-sufficiency in arms production despite the financial burdens and weaknesses in their production capabilities.

Both sides of the debate actually capture some aspects of the global transformation. On the one hand, a group of emerging states choose to have limited defence industrialization that focuses on the niche markets and integrate to the global arms production networks. On the other hand, others continue to pursue self-sufficiency in arms production with limited international defence industrial cooperation. Thus, the breadth and the depth of integrative defence industrial relations show variation among states. The variation in state policies poses a challenge in understanding the implication of the transformation of global arms production for the international politics and security as the debate in the field did not resolve the issue.

In order to resolve some of the issues raised by these theoretical debates, we initiated an E-Workshop series at Columbia University and the Center for Foreign Policy and Peace Research. First, it is designed, through in-depth single case studies and comparative analysis, to shed empirical light on the defence industrial decision-making process in emerging states and the political, economic and military factors that have shaped it. Our focus is on the inner workings of the process: why certain policies have been adopted, what the production capabilities of selected emerging defence industries are and how they are changing in response to transformations in the global defence industrial system. We also hope to reach a deeper understanding of how these changes impact the national security interests of the arms-producing states and the ways in which they interact in the international political system. A second objective for the workshops is to digitally bring together arms trade analysts scattered all over the world. Through a series of workshops, we hope to create an ongoing, interactive community of defence industry specialists who will regularly interact and communicate with each other.

The Variation: Defence Industrial Policies of Emerging Defence Industries

Globalization of arms production, like globalization in general, is argued to be a process that pushes states to act in a similar fashion. Many analysts believe that less advanced states should follow an export-oriented defence industrialization. This means that states need to liberalize their defence markets and construct a beneficial investment environment for the multinational corporations. This should be done by withdrawing the state investments from arms production which would then prevent the preferential treatment of state enterprises. States should allow competition between private defence firms through dismantling protective laws and encourage local defence firms to form permanent relations with the multinational corporations. Consequently, states should not follow across-the-board military production strategies, but seek to invest in the production areas that they have a comparative advantage in. In the end, many analysts argue that the globalization of arms production would create an overarching production chain with the less advanced defence industries participating through integration. Yet, we observe that there are variances in development strategies, although inter-firm cooperation is increasing and the production is spreading.

Even if the states decide to integrate themselves to global production chains, their defence industry policies differ depending on their economic structures. Marc DeVore contends that although the global defence industrial transformation is limiting the options available to the states, the institutional structures of domestic political economies shape the nature of individual state and firm responses. In liberal market economies, we expect to see defence production centred on the private firms where contracts are distributed by competitive bidding and formal contracting, while state retains arms-length coordination through the market. Consequently, the system rewards companies that pursue radical innovation and fast moving technologies such as UAVs, missiles and defence software and electronics. On the other hand, in coordinated market economies, we expect to see direct state participation in defence production and negotiated contracting. Such systems encourage defence production that is capital intensive and allow only incremental innovations, such as aircraft, armoured vehicles and radar systems (DeVore 2015). Therefore, even if the states choose to integrate their defence industries to global production networks, the path and the development strategies show variance. However, others question the validity of globalization.

These analysts believe that domestic factors usually take precedence over international factors in the decision-making calculus of industrializing countries. Richard Bitzinger questions the validity of the globalization, the integrative drive in the global arms market, through referring the variations in the defence industrial strategies from one country to another. He contends that the integrative effect of globalization has not been reached the expected levels. In the core countries, integration remains limited and the cooperation between the United States and the Europe has not reached the anticipated heights. On the other hand, the emerging countries continue to seek defence industrialization with the goal of self-sufficiency despite the financial penalties and weaknesses in their production capabilities (Bitzinger 2010) because these countries have a different set of motivations for the defence industrialization.

Although it is generally agreed that arms production in all states is motivated by three main factors – the desire for power, wealth and prestige – these analysts argue that the motives for defence industrialization are ranked differently by many emerging states from those of the larger, more established arms producers. They believe that domestic factors usually take precedence over international factors in the decision-making calculus of less industrialized countries. Primarily concerned with protecting their indigenous industries, the leaders of these states are prompted to reject an export-oriented, integrative defence industrialization policy.

Emerging states, these analysts argue, seek to decrease their dependency on supplier states for access to high technology. Dependency on foreign suppliers, in the recipient's view, enables supplier to control which weapon systems and technologies they can acquire, and thereby gives a foreign state control over their military capabilities (Neuman 1988). Furthermore, from the recipient's perspective, the supplier state has the ability to shape the recipient's foreign policy through arms embargoes and restrictions on the usage of imported weapons systems (Kinsella 1998, Boutin 2009, p. 229). In the pursuit of increased power, therefore, emerging states perceive national defence industries as a tool for achieving a guaranteed and independent supply of arms (Evans 1986) and a measure of autonomy, while simultaneously decreasing the influence of supplier states.

Others, who focus on the pursuit of wealth as a policy motive, offer a complementary argument. They claim that because states have different economic capabilities they have different policy options. Emile Benoit, for instance, contends that national defence industries decrease the economic burden of procuring weapons systems from foreign suppliers. In his view, an import substitution policy is a logical choice for emerging states (Benoit 1973). Gansler and Bitzinger move beyond the argument of decreasing the burden on the economy. They assert that national defence industries can serve as a locomotive for the overall economy. National defence industries, they claim, help develop the state's technological base, modernize the overall economy and enable economic growth (Gansler 1982, p. 25, Bitzinger 2003, p. 73). Neuman, too, concludes that spin-offs from the defence sector foster economic development. Skills gained in military service can be transferred to the civilian sector by personnel rotating out of the military, such as technicians, mechanics, pilots and health-care personnel. Infrastructure such as roads, bridges, electrical lines and communication networks constructed for the military also benefit the civilian economy (Neuman 1978, 1994, p. 98).

These academics and policy analysts hold that emerging states can reap economic benefits, and perhaps some political power, by exporting domestically produced weapons systems (Sanders 1990). They point out that policy-makers in many emerging states apparently agree. The emerging countries, especially in Southeast Asia, continue to embrace the goal of defence industrial self-sufficiency (Bitzinger 2010). According to Bitzinger, a mix of desires for international prestige and the aspiration for an independent, strong and rich country are the main reasons why Southeast Asian states continue to pursue self-sufficient defence industries despite the high economic costs and the need for foreign technology (Bitzinger and Kim 2005, Bitzinger 2015).

Like Bitzinger, other analysts consider the pursuit of prestige to be an important policy consideration in emerging countries. Prestige denotes gaining status in the international arena by acquiring military might, becoming a regional power and demonstrating the technological/industrial capabilities of the state (Brozska and Lock 1992, p. 145). Arms production and transfers can also be used to augment national prestige by supplying and gaining influence over other regimes. As Bitzinger argues, 'an independent defence-industrial capability feeds directly into concepts of national power – not only by creating military power but also by demonstrating the country's industrial and technological prowess, thereby confirming its status as a great power in the broadest sense' (2003, p. 15). In emerging states, a national defence industry is a tool to create an image of a weighty state. It is the symbolic key to attaining international stature.

Even though states share the same end goal, self-sufficiency, their selected path differs from country to country. The first difference is how these countries establish cooperative relations with the foreign companies. On the one hand, as Bitzinger observes, the major arms-producing countries in Asia are very protective of their defence industries and direct investment of foreign companies in these countries remains limited (Bitzinger 2017). On the other hand, Turkey, which also aims to reach self-sufficiency, allows extensive participation of the foreign companies. It follows a more integrative approach and continues to encourage foreign partnerships through setting up joint ventures and establishing subsidiaries (Kurç 2017, pp. 270–2, Mevlutoglu 2017, p. 290). Second, these states approach to defence industries also shows variance. Tai Ming Cheung contends that international factors have shaped the policy choices of Asian countries. States, such as South Korea and Japan, place defence industrialization second to the "civilian techno-nationalism", because they enjoyed United States' security assurances during the Cold War. On the other hand, states, which felt insecure and threatened by the United States' position, such as China, focused on the "military techno-nationalism". Cheung also contends that changes in the global politics and technology production are pushing these two development strategies together (Cheung 2017). In the end, defence industrialization around the world shows a significant level of variance. Because of this variation in defence industry policies, we have not reach an agreement on how defence industrialization and cooperative relations would affect the international politics.

The Implications of the Global Defence Transformation on the International Politics and Security

The question – 'how does global defence industrial transformation affect the national security interests of states?' – is another source of disagreement among defence analysts. Not much is new in this regard. The effect of international commerce on the security of states has been debated for hundreds of years with little resolution. The debate revolves around the impact of economic interdependence and globalization on the relative power and foreign policies of the states. Robert M. Rosh, for example, contends that if emerging states continue to seek self-sufficiency and indigenous weapon systems, even if they require technology transfers from major suppliers, they could break their dependency either by increasing their production capabilities or by diversifying their sources of imports due to the opportunities created by the globalization of defence production (Rosh 1990).

Stephen Brooks, on the other hand, sees the globalization of defence production would make defence autarky impractical and very costly, even for the largest and most advanced powers, such as the United States. As the arms production become transnational, every states would become dependent on each other, thus reduces the influence of any hegemonic power in the system (Brooks 2005).

On the other side of the debate, Stephanie Neuman and Jonathan Caverley argue that the investments in defence production capabilities do not necessarily alter the continuing dependence on the major suppliers, especially to the United States. Neuman contends that while many emerging countries are capable of producing high-technology weapons, they are still dependent, to varying degrees, on foreign inputs (Neuman 2010, pp. 118–212). Major arms-producing countries continue to enjoy dominance in the global market due to their innovative capabilities, technological edge, resources and market power, which allows them to produce cutting-edge military technology and a full spectrum of weapon systems. Furthermore, the increased complexity of the state-of-the-art weapons increases the entry barriers for the production of these weapons, while increased significance of experience and tacit knowledge in the production hinders the diffusion of know-how necessary to produce advanced weapons (Gilli and Gilli 2019, p. 142). Consequently, especially the United States benefits from the spread of arms production by creating asymmetric interdependence among its partners and able to extend its power in the system (Caverley 2007, pp. 599, 607–8). Since the economic consequences of arms exports are secondary, the United States could utilize cooperative relations and arms transfers for the goal of maintaining the political influence abroad (Caverley 2007, p. 611), while adopting restrictive policies regarding the sale and the usage of its most advanced technologies to protect its technological edge (Caverley and Kapstein 2016, p. 171). In the end, cooperative relations in the defence production could still serve as a mean for political influence, despite the increased production capabilities.

Jonathan Kirshner provides a more nuanced view on the globalization and security and points out the variances in the system. He contends that the benefits and challenges of the globalization of production vary from one country to another. In overall, however, he argues that major powers are relatively empowered, even if their autonomy is reduced by the forces of globalization, while the weak states are left relatively weaker (Kirshner 2007, p. 596).

Despite the impressive research and careful reasoning of these and other scholars, there is still no agreement on the implications of the defence industrialization on the international politics. However, one issue is certain. The defence industrialization takes different characteristics in different states, and, therefore, has different implications on states' ability to pursue independent foreign policy. The continuing debate and the significant variance in the system point out the need for further in-depth case and comparative studies to reach a better understanding of the decision-making process in emerging states and to provide greater analytic attention of the proliferation of defence industrial capabilities and its consequences. This is what the E-Workshop series aim to do.

Defence Industries in the 21st Century: A Comparative Analysis E-Workshop Series

In order to reach a better and in-depth understanding of the transformation and how defence industrial policies in the emerging states had changed and what political, economic and military development caused these changes, we initiated an E-Workshop series. E-Workshop series is based on case studies and comparative analysis that focus on the inner workings of the defence industrialization in the emerging countries and ask which factors – domestic or international – have the greatest impact on the defence industrial and arms trade policies, what is the nature of the relationship with the foreign defence companies, how defence industrial partnerships affect the foreign policy and domestic industrial policy and what effect does the domestic decision-making process have on the defence industrial policies? In so doing, we aimed to reach a deeper understanding on the impact of the transformation of the global arms production practices and the ways in which emerging countries interact in the international political system.

In practice, as the contents of this symposium show, the defence industrial and arms export policies of the emerging states display significant variance. This variance is the result of a unique balance between domestic and international factors that has shaped the defence industrialization behaviour and policies of the less industrialized states. One of the most important conclusions of the symposium is that the dialogue between domestic and international factors clearly influences the variation in emerging states' defence industrialization policies, as well as their success or failure. While international factors create opportunities, they also limit the options available to emerging economies. Domestic factors also play an important role by shaping the policy choices of the states' decision-makers. It is this balance between international and domestic factors and the ways in which they influence defence industrialization in emerging states that we plan to explore in the future. Unfortunately, for a variety of reasons, interest in the defence industrialization of states has diminished since the end of the Cold War. We hope this symposium is just an initial step in the study of defence industrial transformation and arms proliferation, and their implications for the national security interests of countries around the world.

Note

1 This article is mostly the combination of the articles below:
Çağlar Kurç & Stephanie G. Neuman (2017). Defence Industries in the 21st Century: A Comparative Analysis, *Defence Studies*, 17 (3), 219–227, DOI: 10.1080/14702436.2017.1350105.
Çağlar Kurç & Richard A. Bitzinger (2018). Defense Industries in the 21st Century: A Comparative Analysis—The Second e-Workshop, *Comparative Strategy*, 37 (4), 255–259, DOI: 10.1080/01495933.2018.1497318.

References

Adams, G., 2001. Fortress America in a Changing Transatlantic Defence Market. *In*: B. Schmitt, ed. *Between Cooperation and Competition: The Transatlantic Defence Market*. Paris: Institute for Security Studies, Western European Union, 3–50.

Anthony, I., 1993. The 'Third Tier' Countries: Production of Major Weapons. *In*: H. Wulf, ed. *Arms Industry Limited*. Oxford & New York: Oxford University Press, 362–383.

Benoit, E., 1973. *Defense and Economic Growth in Developing Countries*. Lexington: Lexington Books.

Bitzinger, R.A., 1994a. The Globalization of the Arms Industry: The Next Proliferation Challenge. *International Security*, 19 (2), 170–198.

Bitzinger, R.A., 1994b. Customize Defense Industry Restructuring. *Orbis*, 38 (2), 261–276.

Bitzinger, R.A., 2003. *Towards a Brave New Arms Industry*. New York & London: Routledge.

Bitzinger, R.A., 2010. Globalization Revisited: Internationalizing Armaments Production. *In*: A.T.H. Tan, ed. *The Global Arms Trade: A Handbook*. London & New York: Routledge, 208–220.

Bitzinger, R.A., 2015. Defense Industries in Asia and the Technonationalist Impulse. *Contemporary Security Policy*, 36 (3), 453–472.

Bitzinger, R.A., 2017. Asian Arms Industries and Impact on Military Capabilities. *Defence Studies*, 17 (3), 295–311.

Bitzinger, R.A. and Kim, M., 2005. Why Do Small States Produce Arms? The Case of South Korea. *The Korean Journal of Defense Analysis*, 17 (2), 183–205.

Boutin, K.J.D., 2009. Emerging Defense Industries: Prospects and Implications. *In*: R.A. Bitzinger, ed. *The Modern Defense Industry: Political, Economic, and Technological Issues*. Santa Barbara, Calif.: Praeger Security International/ABC-CLIO, 227–240.

Brooks, S., 2005. *Producing Security: Multinational Corporations, Globalization, and the Changing Calculus of Conflict*. Princeton, NJ: Princeton University Press.

Brozska, M. and Lock, P., 1992. *Restructuring Arms Production in the Western Europe*. Oxford & New York: Oxford University Press.

Caverley, J.D., 2007. United States Hegemony and the New Economics of Defense. *Security Studies*, 16 (4), 598–614.

Caverley, J.D. and Kapstein, E.B., 2016. Who's Arming Asia? *Survival*, 58 (2), 167–184.

Cheung, T.M., 2017. Commentary on Asian Arms Industries and Impact on Military Capabilities. *Defence Studies*, 17 (3), 312–316.

DeVore, M.R., 2015. Defying Convergence: Globalisation and Varieties of Defence-Industrial Capitalism. *New Political Economy*, 20 (4), 569–593.

Evans, C., 1986. Reappraising Third World Arms Production. *Survival*, 28 (2), 99–118.

Gansler, J.S., 1982. *The Defense Industry*. Cambridge, MA: MIT Press.

Gilli, A. and Gilli, M., 2019. Why China Has Not Caught Up Yet: Military-Technological Superiority and the Limits of Imitation, Reverse Engineering, and Cyber Espionage. *International Security*, 43 (3), 141–189.

Hayward, K., 2000. Globalization of Defense Industries. *Survival*, 42 (2), 115–132.

Kinsella, D., 1998. Arms Transfer Dependence and Foreign Policy Conflict. *Journal of Peace Research*, 35, 7–23.

Kirshner, J., 2007. The Changing Calculus of Conflict? *Security Studies*, 16 (4), 583–597.

Kurç, Ç., 2017. Between Defence Autarky and Dependency: The Dynamics of Turkish Defence Industrialization. *Defence Studies*, 17 (3), 260–281.

Mevlutoglu, A., 2017. Commentary on Assessing the Turkish defense industry: Structural Issues and Major Challenges. *Defence Studies*, 17 (3), 282–294.

Neuman, S.G., 1978. Security, Military Expenditures and Socioeconomic Development: Reflections on Iran. *Orbis*, 22 (3), 569.

Neuman, S.G., 1988. Arms, Aid and the Superpowers. *Foreign Affairs*, 66 (4), 1044–1066.

Neuman, S.G., 1994. Arms Transfers, Military Assistance, and Defense Industries: Socioeconomic Burden or Opportunity? *The Annals of the American Academy of Political and Social Science*, 535, 91–109.

Neuman, S.G., 2010. Power, Influence and Hierarchy: Defence Industries in a Unipolar World. *Defence and Peace Economics*, 21 (1), 105–134.

Oudot, J.-M. and Bellais, R., 2019. Defence Companies in the Age of Globalisation: French Defence Industry as a Case Study. *In*: R. Matthews, ed. *The Political Economy of Defence*. Cambridge University Press, 169–194.

Rosh, R.M., 1990. Third World Arms Production and the Evolving Interstate System. *Journal of Conflict Resolution*, 34, 57–73.

Sanders, R., 1990. *Arms Industries: New Suppliers and Regional Security*. Washington, DC: National Defense University Press.

Sjolander, C.T., 1999. The Politics, Economics and Ethics of Arms Exports: Making Sense of (Canadian) Soverignty in a Post-Westphalian World. *In*: D.G. Haglund and S.N. MacFarlane, eds. *Security, Strategy and the Global Economics of Defence Production: How Much of What?* Montreal: Published for the School of Policy Studies, Queen's University by McGill-Queen's University Press, 119–134.

Sköns, E., 1993. Western Europe: Internationalization of the Arms Industry. *In*: H. Wulf, ed. *Arms Industry Limited*. Oxford & New York: Oxford University Press, 160–190.

Sköns, E. and Wulf, H., 1994. The Internationalization of the Arms Industry. *Annals of the American Academy of Political and Social Science*, 535, 43–57.

The value of domestic arms industries: security of supply or military adaptation?

Marc R. DeVore

ABSTRACT
Few issues are more important yet less understood than how the domestic production of armaments impacts military power. Scholars generally explain states' drive to develop defense industries in terms of a quest for supply security. Technological changes are, however, rendering an "autonomy preference" increasingly unaffordable. This raises the question of whether states can still derive strategic value from their defense industries. This study addresses the issue by examining whether Israel's and Serbia's defense industrial bases contributes to either the traditional goal of supply security or the alternative objective of military adaptability. To preview the conclusion, the strategic value that most states can extract from domestic defense firms lies in enhanced military adaptability. This advantage is far from negligible. Since war is unpredictable, it is often the side that adapts most rapidly to unexpected circumstances that prevails. Domestic defense industries contribute significantly to adapt both because of their technical capabilities and their patterns of routinized cooperation with a states' armed force. Supply security, by way of contrast, is today unattainable for all but the largest states.

Introduction

Few issues are more important to the distribution of military power yet less understood than the role of defense industries. Even small and developing states invest considerable resources into developing domestic defense industries in the belief that such industries contribute to national security. The need to guarantee a secure supply of military equipment has long served as such policies' primary justification. Technological changes are today, however, arguably rendering security of supply unattainable for all but the largest states. This raises the question as to whether and how smaller states derive benefits from their defense industries. One explanation may be that domestic defense industries enhance armed forces' capacity to adapt to unanticipated military challenges. This study addresses this issue by examining to what degree the Israeli and Yugoslav/Serbian defense-industrial bases contributed to security of supply and military adaptation.

Security of supply has long been the primary justification for states to develop domestic defense industries. According to this reasoning, states are more secure when they meet their armament needs with the products of domestic industry even when imported weaponry is more cost-effective. The reason for this is that arms importers are highly vulnerable to having their weaponry supplies threatened or cut-off by exporting countries. Domestic arms production is, therefore, often considered a prerequisite for an independent foreign policy. Many states historically achieved this objective through import substitution policies that ascended a metaphorical "ladder of production" from simple activities like maintenance to the indigenous development of major weapons systems.

While security of supply is one justification for domestic defense industries, another rationale lies in military adaptation. Technological and tactical surprises are common in contemporary warfare. The difference between military success and failure therefore frequently hinges on armed forces' ability to adapt to unanticipated challenges. The international arms market rarely offers adequate solutions for these eventualities because either satisfactory products do not exist or cannot be imported in a reasonable period of time. Domestic defense industries, contrarily, can logically enhance states' ability to adapt to unanticipated military challenges thanks to their cadres of engineers and technicians habituated to cooperating with military organizations.

This study tests whether small and medium states today derive national security benefits from domestic defense industries via either enhanced security of supply or military adaptiveness. To this end, two states will be examined – Israel and Yugoslavia/Serbia – that recently experienced repeated and prolonged bouts of warfare. These two cases both possess domestic defense-industrial bases, but these differ substantially in terms of their size and technological sophistication. Israeli defense industries are, as demonstrated by Uzi Rubin's contribution to this volume, comparatively large and innovators at the technological frontier. Yugoslav/Serbian industries are, by way of contrast, distinctly smaller and medium-tech.

To preview my conclusions, concerns over security of supply initially drove both states to invest heavily in developing domestic defense industries. At first each state achieved significant progress toward this objective, with Israel achieving 44 % and Yugoslavia 75 % self-sufficiency late in the cold war. Armaments' increasing cost and complexity thereafter undermined both countries' security of supply efforts over the course of the 1980s. Israeli leaders officially abandoned security of supply as a goal and Yugoslav planners de facto reduced their attempts to source weapons domestically in the late-1980s.

Military adaptation and the provision of secure command-and-control systems subsequently emerged as new justifications for domestic armaments industries. Israeli and Serbian defense firms played critical roles enabling national armed forces to adapt to technological surprises and unforeseen battlefield conditions. Israeli defense technologists adapted armored vehicles to withstand new anti-tank weaponry and hurriedly developed anti-rocket systems to defeat Hezbollah's and Hamas' unguided rocket attacks. Serbian armaments engineers, meanwhile, sustained the states' armed forces during conflicts that stretched much longer than hitherto anticipated and spearheaded the development of countermeasures that blunted NATO's 1999 air campaign's effectiveness. Domestic defense industries also developed secure command-and-control systems, employing civil and imported technologies, to ensure each state's strategic sovereignty.

Domestic defense industries, in sum, no longer provide meaningful levels of supply security, but they nonetheless enhance states' military power through improved military adaptiveness. The optimal size of states' domestic defense industries may therefore be considerably smaller than hitherto considered the case because even relatively large defense industries, such as Israel's, cannot deliver security of supply while even modest ones, such as Serbia's, provide substantial adaptation advantages.

Security of supply

Access to secure supplies of weaponry has long been the primary rationale for states to promote domestic defense industries. Even Adam Smith argued that government should actively cultivate arms industries rather than leaving them to the mercy of laissez-faire markets. Smith postulated that arms factories should be protected from market forces – particularly foreign imports – because states need reliable sources of weaponry in order to remain secure (Coulomb 1998). In many respects Smith prefigured latter generations of defense economists who argue the primacy of security of supply (Kapstein 1992, pp. 1–11). Although differing on details, proponents of security of supply suggest that domestic arms production: permits greater foreign policy autonomy, provides superior military capabilities, and is economically feasible for a wide-range of states.

Defense planners promoted domestic defense firms because they believed such industries contributed directly to national security. In foreign policy terms, states that export armaments can threaten to cancel or suspend deliveries as a means of coercing importing states into adopting their favoured policies. Contemporary examples of this dynamic abound, with Iran, Israel, and Pakistan all having been embargoed by their principle arms suppliers (Sampson 1977, pp. 311, 312). Armaments production can, therefore, be regarded as a prerequisite for pursuing an independent foreign policy, while dependence on imports is associated with an inferior international position (Gupta 1997).

Analysts argue that defense-industrial self-sufficiency provides military advantages in addition to these foreign policy benefits. Great powers oftentimes refuse to export cutting-edge weapons. During the cold war the superpowers followed symmetrical policies of selling only older and less sophisticated weapons to most clients (Le Roy 2002). Soviet technologists were particularly derisive, referring to export variants as "monkey models" (Suvorov 1982, p. 215). Great powers also frequently renege on commitments to export cutting-edge weaponry. The British state, for example, commandeered battleships being built for export clients during the First World War and the United States banned aircraft exports as it began to prepare for the Second World War. Thus, producing a weapon domestically is often regarded as the only guaranteed manner of acquiring a system.

High levels of defense-industrial self-sufficiency were long considered attainable by even small and medium states (Krause 1992, pp. 153–171). Expert opinion postulated that states could progress from importing armaments to autonomously producing them by ascending a metaphorical "ladder of production." States ideally proceeded through an incremental process of import substitution: first focusing on domestically maintaining imported weapons, then on manufacturing foreign-designed systems, before finally developing indigenous weaponry. Economists long anticipated that such policies could contribute to economic growth through technological spin-offs from defense industries to the broader civilian economy (Benoit 1973, 1978).

Security of supply's perceived benefits spurred states to invest in domestic defense industries during the cold war. The value of arms produced by non-great powers therefore quadrupled between 1970 and 1990, and the number of arms producers in the developing world increased from four to 50 between 1945 and 1985 (Rosh 1990, Krause 1992). Uzi Rubin's contribution to the present volume, indeed, demonstrates that considerations such as these drove Israel's initial investment in defense industries (2017). Although some producers subsequently exited the arms market, many continue to strive for high levels of supply security (Sen 2000, Moon 2015).

Nevertheless, defense economists are increasingly sceptical of this quest for security of supply. Both the nature of armaments and the firms that produce them are arguably evolving in ways that render high levels of defense-industrial autonomy illusory for most states. Technological progress is driving the costs of producing major weapons systems upwards at a rate of 6–10% per annum, which exceeds the growth rates of two percent sustained by mature economies (Kirkpatrick 2004). The smaller numbers of these more expensive weapons that small and medium states produce are inimical to adequate scale economies.

Defense firms in larger states merged to form conglomerates diversified enough to thrive under such circumstances. Limited by the size of their domestic markets, firms in small and medium states cannot follow this lead (Struys 2004). Thus, while policy-makers in smaller states continue aspiring to climb the "ladder" of arms production toward the goal of achieving supply security, structural economic and technological changes may be rendering that objective ever more difficult to achieve (Bitzinger 2003, Mawdsley 2008).

Military adaptation

Despite security of supply's popularity, another rationale for domestic defense industries lies in the military flexibility they provide. Frenetic technological change renders surprise frequent in warfare. Indeed, most conflicts feature unanticipated technological and tactical challenges. Domestic arms industries arguably enhance states' ability to adapt to such challenges. Domestic defense firms' engineers, technologists, and skilled workers possess technical skills and have experience cooperating with military professionals. They are therefore well-equipped for collaborating with domestic armed forces to develop technological solutions to unanticipated military challenges.

Technological surprise is a crucial and growing feature of contemporary warfare. Rapid technological change means that weapons systems' performance parameters change constantly and new types of military equipment appear with increasing regularity. The pace of contemporary military-technical change renders the character of future warfare inherently unpredictable. To make matters worse, bureaucratic biases shape how armed forces evaluate new weaponry, increasing the likelihood of their misperceiving technical developments. Indeed, as Thomas Mahnken (2002) demonstrates, military organizations frequently fail to appreciate the technical innovations pursued by their rivals for precisely these reasons.

Armed forces find military-technical change inherently difficult to evaluate. Technological surprise is the ineluctable result. Every recent conflict featured some degree of technological surprise, whether America's armed forces' being surprised by improvised explosives devices (IED) or Russia's surprise by Georgian air defences and unmanned aerial vehicles (UAV) (Pallin and Westerlund 2009). Armed forces' ability to respond to wartime surprises is therefore as important to national military power as their peacetime capacity to develop doctrine judiciously and make sound procurement decisions (Finkel 2011).

Two distinct forms of adaptation to technological surprise are critical to military power. The first such form is *intra-conflict adaptation* and refers to measures enacted over the course of a conflict. The United States' production first of armored HUMVEEs and then Mine-Resistant

Ambush Protected (MRAP) vehicles to counter Iraqi insurgents' IEDs is an example of intra-conflict adaptation (Lamb 2009). The second form of adaptation is *inter-conflict adaptation* and involves measures taken between distinct conflicts. Hezbollah's development of bunker complexes with multiple rocket launchers between its 1996 and 2006 rocket campaigns against Israel is a case in point (Cook 2000, Lambeth 2001, pp. 105, 106).

Close cooperation between military professionals and defense technologists is critical to both forms of adaptation.[1] Technological surprises disrupt the syntheses of tactics and equipment that undergird military doctrines. Countering technological surprise therefore requires military personnel to collaborate closely with engineers and scientists on new technological/tactical syntheses. Collaboration between such distinct groups of professionals requires, however, distinct forms of tacit knowledge about one-another's organizational logics and ways of communicating. Efficient cooperation between these groups should therefore occur logically most frequently in states that possess domestic defense industries. Because domestic firms routinely cooperate in peacetime with national armed forces, which are generally the firms' largest clients, both groups are well-equipped to jointly adapt to urgent requirements (Dombrowski and Gholz 2006).

Although foreign firms may offer more cost-effective products, they cannot provide these adaptation advantages. Commercially, most states' modest domestic defense markets provide few incentives for foreign firms to provide customized and timely solutions. Rather, arms exports generally consist of off-the-shelf weaponry originally developed to meet the producing states' requirements. Worse yet, geographic distances and the absence of long-standing cooperative routines render it more difficult for the foreign firms to cooperate with domestic armed forces to provide such solutions even when they wish to. Access to international defense markets is therefore most likely to contribute to military adaptation when states already possess their own domestic defense industries capable of integrating and modifying imported sub-systems to meet national requirements.

Hi-tech civil industries are also unlikely to lead the way in technological adaptation. Civil firms lack the deep relationships with military organizations and the knowledge of defense acquisition procedures that constitute defense firms' core competences (Dombrowski and Gholz 2006). Warfighters and civil industry therefore lack the institutionalized interactions whereby defense industries learn about warfighters' needs. Domestic defense firms are therefore better positioned to serve as systems integrators when it comes to military adaptation and civil industries are only likely to contribute in a subsidiary role, as subcontractors or component suppliers. This role is, however, significant insofar as broader-based civilian industries provide more technologies and components that can be used for military adaptation (Caverley 2007).

In sum, domestic defense industries can enable armed forces to better respond to technological surprises. This adaptation advantage provides a powerful rationale for states to support domestic defense industries even when those industries cannot provide meaningful levels of supply security.

Case selection

The plausibility of two competing arguments – security of supply and military adaptation – for domestic defense industries raises the question of which plays a larger role today. These hypotheses' relative value can best be assessed by examining states whose defense industries are representative of non-great power arms producers as a whole and which also possess contemporary combat experience. Proper case selection, furthermore, demands that governments of both countries have plausible motives for desiring both security of supply and military adaptation. Israel and Serbia collectively meet all of these criteria.

While these two states are similar in terms of population, with Israel's 8.7 million inhabitants only barely eclipsing Serbia's 7.0 million, they differ significantly in terms of their defense-industrial capabilities. The key quantitative criteria upon which states' defense industries can be compared are their size, as measured by employment, and the size of their domestic markets, as measured by defense budgets. Judged according to these criteria Israel and Serbia represent opposite ends of the spectrum of non-great power arms producers. Altogether approximately 60 states, nearly one-third of United Nations member states, invest scarce financial and human resources on domestic defense industries (Berman and Leff 2008).

Apart from a handful of great powers possessing defense industries with over 100,000 employees, most states' defense-industrial bases encompass tens of thousands of personnel (Brzoska 2005). Israel's 50,000 defense-industrial employees and $17 billion defense budget therefore statistically place it within the top quartile and top tier of each respective category (Dobbing and Cole 2014). Serbia's 15,000 defense-industrial employees at the end of the Yugoslav Wars and defense budgets that have fluctuated from $0.7 to $1.2 billion since the late-1990s place Serbia, meanwhile, in the bottom half in terms of employees and bottom quartile in terms of budget (Watkins 2001). Israel's defense industries are, in sum, representative of the world's premier non-great power producers, while Serbia's are illustrative of states that possess modest defense-industrial capabilities.

While Israel and Serbia differ substantially in terms of their defense-industrial capabilities, they are similar in that they have substantial post-cold war combat experience. This experience renders it possible to assess defense industries' contribution to military adaptation. Israel fought prolonged counterinsurgencies against Hezbollah (1985–2000) and Palestinian groups (2000–2005), and waged short campaigns against Hezbollah (2006) and Hamas (2009, 2012 and 2014). Yugoslavia/Serbia, meanwhile, fought wars against Slovenia (1991) and Croatia (1991–92); supported proxy Bosnian Serb and Krajina Serb armies during civil wars in Bosnia (1992–95) and Croatia (1993–95); and fought Albanian rebels in Kosovo (1998–99) and Southern Serbia (1999–2001). These conflicts generated unanticipated military challenges in response to which the Israel and Yugoslav/Serbian armed forces needed to adapt.

Both states, likewise, had strong incentives for privileging security of supply. Israel was embargoed by its principle suppliers after the 1967 Arab-Israeli War and the United States subsequently attempted to use arms transfers to shape Israeli policy. Yugoslavia, meanwhile, was embargoed by its primary arms supplier – the Soviet Union – in 1948. Thereafter, Yugoslav governments faced problems with suppliers' reliability, be they Soviet, American, or European. Yugoslavia/Serbia was then twice embargoed during the Yugoslav Wars, in 1991–1995 and 1998–2001. Israel's and Serbia's experiences being embargoed furnished both states with powerful reasons for seeking security of supply through indigenous defense industries.

Israel and Serbia are, in sum, powerful cases for comparatively testing the security of supply and military adaptation hypotheses. Collectively these cases represent the spectrum of non-great power arms producers, from the most capable (Israel) to the more modest (Serbia). Both states also, through their experiences of warfare and embargo, have powerful motives for pursuing both security of supply and military adaptation. The following sections therefore examine how each state derived national security benefits from its defense-industrial base.

Israel

The multifarious threats Israel faced since independence drove the state to develop robust defense industries. Although Israeli leaders originally sought high levels of security of supply, subsequent shifts in the nature of arms production forced them to reassess their defense-industrial policy. Consequently, Israeli policy-makers came to the painful recognition that even a state with defense industries as large as Israel's can no longer aspire to defense-industrial autonomy and that many indigenous weapons programs were severely inefficient. They, however, also concluded that a much reduced defense-industrial base could furnish substantial benefits in terms of military adaptation and secure command-and-control systems.

Israel's defense-industrial base is a product of the country's tumultuous history, with the first arms factories being established clandestinely during the 1920s. After Israel's 1948 declaration of independence, Israeli leaders built on this modest base by producing French-designed weapons under license (Barnett 1992, pp. 165–169). Later, the 1967 Arab-Israeli War's aftermath convinced Israeli leaders to build a broad-based defense-industrial complex. After winning a stunning victory with imported French and British weapons, Israel found itself embargoed by its principal suppliers. Although the United States filled the void, the American government's efforts to leverage arms shipments to compel Israel into policy shifts emphasized to Israeli leaders the lesson that an embattled state cannot afford to depend on imported weaponry (Rodman 2007, pp. 27–75).

Israel's government therefore launched a range of domestic weapons projects to improve the country's supply security. Israel developed its defense-industrial base with phenomenal speed thanks to its extensive military experience and the United States' willingness to transfer key technologies. Israel's defense-industrial base therefore expanded fivefold between 1967 and 1973, and another fourfold between 1974 and 1984 (Klieman 1998, p. 114, Hoyt 2007, pp. 83–93). Throughout this period, the share of Israel's procurement budget devoted to domestic defense firms rose from 20 to 40 % and the defense-industrial labor force grew from 14,000 to 80,000 (Klieman 1998, p. 113, Barnett 1992, p. 198). Soon Israeli industry was fulfilling 44 % of the state's weapons needs and Israel was producing even such sophisticated items as fighters (the Kfir), tanks (the Merkava), and warships (Sa'ar missile boats) (Tzalel 2000, pp. 43–80, Hoyt 2007, p. 83).

However, structural changes in the production of armaments then began to threaten Israel's defense-industrial base. This became apparent during Israel's second-generation fighter project. Having successfully developed the Kfir in the 1970s, Israeli policy-makers sought to produce a lightweight fighter – the Lavi – comparable to the American F-16. However, despite American technology transfers, the escalating technical and financial challenges of developing combat aircraft proved more than Israel could overcome. By the early 1980s the Lavi project was consuming 15 % of Israel's defense budget and occupying a quarter of its defense-industrial workforce, yet seemed destined for failure as inadequate domestic scale-economies rendered the final product overpriced (Steinberg 1998, pp. 121–123, Hoyt 2007, pp. 97–99). Although the Lavi was particularly taxing, other Israeli programs suffered from similar problems (Tzalel 2000).

Defense Minister Yitzak Rabin responded to the problems plaguing Israel's major weapons projects by replacing three costly endeavors (the Lavi fighter, Sholef self-propelled artillery system, and next-generation warship) with cheaper imports (Hoyt 2007, pp. 97–104). The only domestic weapons platform to survive this culling was the Merkava tank and that survived largely due to General Israel Tal's lobbying (Rubin 2017). All of the canceled projects were plagued by cost overruns and not one was considered as cost-effective as foreign systems sold by states whose larger production runs generated better scale- and learning-economies (Naaz 2000, pp. 2082–2084). However, these programs had been the centerpiece of Israel's defense-industrial strategy and their cancellation signaled Israel's abandonment of security of supply.

From the wreckage of Israel's self-sufficiency policy, Israeli policy-makers developed policies better adapted to changing realities. Recognizing that Israel would never achieve self-sufficiency in major weapons systems, they accepted their dependence on foreign systems for the indefinite future. Israeli policy-makers, however, increased the proportion of the budget spent on defense R&D even as they cut spending on weapons production because they concluded that domestic defense R&D contributed to national security in three ways (Sherman 1997, p. 34, Eilam 2011, pp. 207–219).

Firstly, Israeli leaders calculated that although they could rely on the United States for most weapons, they could not afford to count on even their closest ally for systems critical to the Israeli government's independent decision-making capacity. Secondly, Israeli policy-makers calculated that they could compel the United States to transfer weapons and technology to them if they could credibly claim that Israel would otherwise develop similar systems. Third and finally, Israel's unique and swiftly changing security environment convinced decision-makers that Israel needed to cultivate scientific and engineering skills for improvising solutions to unanticipated military needs.

Israeli leaders avoided relying on the United States for equipment they considered critical to strategic sovereignty – such as command-and-control and intelligence systems – even though they understood that their political leverage enabled them to access many American capabilities. Israeli policy-makers regarded domestic technical intelligence capabilities essential for independent decision-making because they suspected the United States of manipulating the technical intelligence they transferred in order shape Israeli decisions. For this reason, Israel's new defense-industrial policy prioritized the development of reconnaissance satellites (the Ofek), UAVs and electronic data collation (O' Sullivan 1999, p. 18, Eilam 2011, pp. 219–237). Israeli leaders, for similar reasons, entrusted their defense command-and-control infrastructure – including the armed forces' digitization – to Israeli companies (Ben-David 2008b, Eilam 2011, pp. 253–254).

Besides guaranteeing strategic sovereignty, Israeli leaders view indigenous defense industries as critical to accessing American technologies. The American government only reluctantly exports weapons that might destabilize the Middle East or further enhance Israel's technological advantages (Rodman 2007). Israeli policy-makers believe, however, that the United States will provide certain systems if Israel demonstrates that export restrictions will not prevent Israel from developing domestic alternatives (Opall-Rome 2000, Anderson 2008). As Israel's Weapons Development Administration's director admitted,

> They (the Americans) would agree to provide us with technologically advanced weapons only if we could prove that we either already possessed the technologies in question or that we were at an advanced stage of acquiring them. (Eilam 2011, p. 301)

Israeli policy-makers also envisaged their defense-industrial base as a reservoir of engineers and scientists capable of developing technological solutions to urgent military challenges. Hostile states and non-state actors regularly present Israel with unanticipated weapons and tactics. Since the cold war alone, Israel has faced: ballistic missile attacks, roadside bombs, urban guerrilla warfare, suicide attacks, rocket attacks, and cross-border commando raids. Israel pioneered "factor creating" policies for cultivating the type of highly qualified workforce needed to provide technical solutions for these urgent military problems (Breznitz 2002, Perman 2005).

Building on Israel's military service obligations, the Defense Ministry runs programs to inculcate high-school graduates with the technical skills defense firms need. The most exclusive of these is the Talpiot program, which channels technically gifted youth into scientific training at Hebrew University and service with the military's R&D establishment (Eilam 2011, pp. 278, 279). Because of Talpiot's small size – 50 students per year – the Ministry operates other programs, including the School for Computer Related Professions (MAMRAM) and Unit 8200's electronic intelligence training program (Breznitz 2002, Perman 2005).

Domestic defense industries staffed by graduates of these programs enable Israel's armed forces to rapidly adapt to unforeseen challenges. Hezbollah's innovative use of anti-tank weapons, for example, led Israeli engineers to develop inexpensive means of up-armoring existing armored vehicles and converting surplus tanks into heavily armored personnel carriers (Gelbart 2004, Pengelley 2008). Likewise, Hezbollah's long-range rocket offensive of 2006 drove Israel to engage in a crash program to shield urban areas with anti-rocket defenses (Ben-David 2008a, 2008b). Iron Dome, a system capable of shooting down these rockets, was improvised in barely five years and reportedly intercepted 80–90 % of Hamas' rockets in 2012 and 2014 (Rubin 2015). Finally, Israeli technologists collaborated with military commanders to render data from hovering UAVs instantaneously available to units engaged in urban warfare (Farquhar 2009, pp. 22–30, 90–94).

Policy-makers acknowledged that Israeli producers needed to conquer new export markets to sustain industries capable of fulfilling the above roles. Israel fulfills roughly 80 % of its military needs with imported products ever since abandoning the production of most weapons systems in the mid-1980s (Naaz 2000, p. 113). Israeli industries since then have needed to export approximately 75 % of the arms they produced, compared to 30 % previously to sustain an adequate defense-industrial base (Hughes 2003, Cook 2013).

Achieving such a high volume of arms exports required substantial adjustment in both Israeli technological and foreign policies. Rather than producing a wide gamut of military goods, the defense industry refocused on niches where Israel could compete in world markets. These niches existed in domains where development cycles are short ("fast innovation") and production runs short (limited scale-economies) (Kagan *et al.* 2010, pp. 238, 239). Such characteristics are common for homeland security systems, guided missiles and UAVs, which became the backbone of Israel's contemporary defense-industrial base. Homeland security systems, indeed, today constitute 43 % of Israeli defense exports, guided missiles 25 %, and UAVs 10 % (Gordon 2009, Dobbing and Cole 2014).

Although Israel eventually established a commanding position in these markets, transitioning from a broadly based defense-industrial base to one specializing in niches was accompanied by widespread lay-offs, as the state closed assembly lines in industries considered globally uncompetitive. Israel's artillery manufacturer – Soltam – therefore downsized from 2400 employees to 400 between 1987 and 1990, while its producer of armored vehicles – Israel Military Industries – shed 65 % of its labor force (Office of Technology Assessment 1991, pp. 96–99, Dvir and Tishler 2000). Overall Israeli defense-industrial employment shrunk from 80,000 to 49,000 in the 1990s (Naaz 2000, p. 2083). Vigorous exports enabled firms to halt this decline, however, and subsequently the industry rebounded thanks to growth in new niches (Gordon 2009, Dobbing and Cole 2014).

In sum, arms production's changing character rendered Israel's self-sufficiency policy obsolete. However, policy-makers nevertheless preserved a smaller, but hi-tech defense industrial base capable of: providing technologies critical to its strategic sovereignty and enhancing the armed forces' ability to meet unanticipated challenges. To this end, Israel's government implemented sweeping reforms of its defense procurement processes, prioritized R&D, and encouraged industry to specialize in niches where they could compete internationally.

Serbia

Between 1991 and 2001, Serbia (or the rump state of Yugoslavia) confronted one of the most demanding situations that a state can face. Serbia's leaders plunged the state into a series of wars that lasted for much of the 1990s and Serbian armed forces fought multiple opponents while cut off from significant arms imports. Serbia's modest domestic defense industry, however, enabled the armed forces to adapt to the many unanticipated requirements that the war generated and to repeatedly rebound from military surprises. They did this by enhancing the armed forces' adaptation capacity through such expedients as modifying existing weaponry and improvising secure command-and-control systems out of civil and imported components rather than manufacturing complete weapons systems. The extraordinary efforts Serbian governments have taken to preserve domestic defense industries since the Yugoslav Wars illustrates the strategic value they attach to them.

Non-alignment during the cold war meant that Yugoslav policy-makers never felt confident in their ability to import weaponry. Yugoslav President Josip Broz Tito's 1948 political rupture with the Soviet Union meant that Yugoslavia had to simultaneously prepare to defend itself from Soviet invasion and find alternatives to the arms previously supplied by the Soviet Union. Tito prioritized the development of an indigenous arms industry in response to this Soviet embargo (Mangasarian 1993, p. 236). Tito persevered in his drive for a secure domestic supply of weaponry despite the slow progress he initially achieved and his *in extremis* acceptance of American military assistance in 1951 (Dimitrijevic 1997).

Yugoslav leaders' quest for security of supply persisted throughout the cold war. Political events, indeed, continually reinforced this belief. The United States halted arms exports to Yugoslavia in 1958 as a result of Tito's pursuing a closer relationship with the Soviet Union. Cut off from American weaponry, Tito also failed to secure Soviet arms deliveries until 1962, meaning that the Yugoslav armed forces went four years without new armaments. Yugoslavia's relationship with this new arms supplier suffered again after 1968 when the Soviet Union's invasion of Czechoslovakia worried Tito lest Yugoslavia become its next target. This event gave increased impetus to Tito's defense industrialization drive. As Yugoslavia's Deputy Defense Secretary observed in 1973,

> The supply of armaments on the world market has always been uncertain: political conditions, demands for political concessions, even blackmail, have always been possible. Therefore we decided to build our own arms industry. (Roberts 1975, p. 195)

Yugoslav authorities devoted considerable resources to realizing this objective by purchasing foreign licenses and building factories (Mangasarian 1993, pp. 216, 217).

This policy yielded significant results throughout the 1970s. Yugoslav civilian companies established separate production lines for weaponry and expanded defense-industrial employment until it reached the figure of 70,000 personnel (Brzoska and Ohlson 1987, p. 111). These factories manufactured a wide-range of foreign-designed weapons and even developed domestic lightweight attack/training aircraft, long-range rockets and armored vehicles (Rajić *et al.* 2008). Good workmanship and competitive prices also meant that Yugoslav weapons sold well, rendering Yugoslavia a net arms exporter from 1977 onwards and ensuring that arms comprised 10.7 % of Yugoslav exports in 1981–1990 (Kusovac 2000). By the mid-1970s Yugoslav officials regarded their security of supply policy as a success and claimed that Yugoslavia fulfilled 75 % of its armaments needs domestically (Roberts 1975, p. 195).

Nevertheless, the level of supply security achieved lagged behind optimistic government assessments. Complex Yugoslav weapons, such as the Orao attack aircraft and Sava submarines, contained many imported electronics that Yugoslav industry could not produce autonomously (Mangasarian 1993, pp. 247–249). Worse yet, technological developments undermined the Yugoslav weapons development process throughout the 1970s and 1980s. Foreign states refused to sell licenses for sophisticated missiles and Yugoslav industries struggled to domestically develop such systems (Maurer 1988). Yugoslavia's government thus found itself obliged to de facto abandon its security of supply policy and import growing quantities of weaponry toward the cold war's end.

Yugoslavia's 1991–1992 collapse then disrupted major weapons systems' supply chains and definitively curtailed the country's pursuit of supply security. Yugoslavia's aerospace sector, for example, was headquartered in Bosnia and damaged in heavy fighting (Jandric 2012). Production of the Yugoslav M-84 tank likewise ceased because its assembly in Serbia depended on parts from Croatia and Bosnia. Indeed, disrupted supply chains interrupted production of all major Yugoslav weapons systems and successor states were left with the fragmented remnants of Yugoslavia's defense-industrial base. Even Serbia's 40 % of Yugoslavia's defense-industrial base swiftly declined from 30,000 to 15,000 defense industrial employees (Watkins 2001).

Serbia's residual defense-industrial base would, however, play a critical role during the wars of Yugoslav succession. This role was not, as Tito had anticipated, one of producing major weapons in wartime, but rather helping the armed forces adapt to unforeseen wartime challenges. The first such challenge was that of sustaining Serbia's armed forces and those of the allied Republica Srbska and Republic of the Serbian Krajina. Yugoslav strategists had long planned for a war lasting weeks or months, and had stockpiled equipment accordingly. Now, however, Serbian planners found themselves embargoed by the international community and mired in conflicts that stretched over a decade. Serbian ammunition stockpiles dwindled and equipment wore out through intensive use.

Serbian armaments engineers and technologists swiftly improvised ways to meet these urgent needs. They set up four new ammunition, powders, and explosives production lines, which comfortably met Serbia's ammunition requirements throughout the Yugoslav Wars (Beaver 1993). Serbian defense firms also extemporized measures for sustaining Serbian military equipment. They developed an armored vehicle maintenance facility at Cacak and developed hot cast techniques for refurbishing tank gun barrels (Beaver 1993). Domestic technologists likewise sustained Serbia's air force by improvising pyrotechnic cartridges for aircraft ejection seats and upgrading obsolescent Russian-built Vympel R-60MK (AA-8) air-to-air missiles (Gyürösi 2007, Rajić *et al.* 2008).

Defense firms then set about meeting unexpected military challenges after they had assured the armed forces' sustainability. Yugoslav military units suffered grave command-and-control problems at the wars' onset. Serbia's Military Technical Institute resolved these problems by rebuilding all-terrain vehicles as mobile command posts (the VK-0.75) and developing a portable digital communications system (the DISC system) (Rajić *et al.* 2008, pp. 10–15). They also improved combat helicopters' firepower by improvising hard points permitting helicopters to employ rocket pods built for jet fighters (Beaver 1993). Improvisations such as these enabled Serbia and its allies to stave off defeat and obtain a beneficial settlement to the Bosnian War even as the strategic balance shifted in favor of more numerous and increasingly better supplied Bosnian and Croatian forces.

Serbian arms' relative success was, however, discomfited by Serbian commanders' exposure to sophisticated NATO air power (Tomislav and Roland 2010). NATO accurately pinpointed enemy positions, suppressed air defenses and precisely destroyed Bosnian Serb assets during NATO's 12-day bombing campaign in 1995 (Owen 2000, pp. 257–296). Serbia's armed forces were initially powerless against NATO air power because the latter relied on different technologies – sophisticated air defense suppression and precision guided munitions – than those that Yugoslav commanders had prepared to meet. Serbian defense engineers therefore struggled to develop technological countermeasures to NATO's capabilities as soon as the Bosnian War ended. Between 1995 and 1999 Serbian defense firms extemporized two types of responses: passive countermeasures to blunt an air offensive's effectiveness and active measures to enable Serbia's air defenses to inflict damage.

Perhaps the foremost passive measure Serbian engineers developed was a fiber-optic network linking military units and air defenses, which thwarted NATO's efforts to destroy command nodes and jam communications (Lambeth 2001, pp. 105, 106). Other Serbian engineers, meanwhile, cooperated with military commanders to develop decoys from plastic sheeting and logs capable of tricking aircraft into wasting expensive guided weapons. They also improvised small gas furnaces to spoof NATO's aerial infrared sensors at nighttime and experimented with using old farm machinery placed around radar sites to reflect radiation and thereby confuse anti-radar missiles (Anon 2002). Serbian defense industries' program management and systems integration expertise was critical to these adaptations. Although civil industries helped and Serbia imported many dual-use components to build the decoys and fiber-optic network, Serbia's modest defense-industrial base provided the expertise and collaborated with the armed forces to integrate these components into a lethal ensemble.

Domestic defense firms played an even larger role with Serbia's active measures, including upgrades to air defenses, to complement the passive measures for limiting NATO's lethality. Technicians, for example, modified Serbia's Russian-built air-to-air missiles to be fired from the ground by adding rocket boosters and installing them on armored vehicles (Gyürösi 2008). Serbian technicians likewise added fuel cells to old SA-3 missiles to hit American spy planes flying at altitudes above the existing Serbian missiles. They also jury-rigged electro-optics to SA-6 missile systems for launching missiles without activating their targeting radars (Anon 2002). Defense engineers and military technicians cooperated on tactics to complement these equipment modifications. Radar operators, for example, learned to employ radars for 20 s intervals to avoid being targeted by anti-radar missiles and experimented tweaking old long-wavelength radars to detect stealth aircraft (Lambeth 2001, p. 108, Anon, 2005).

These efforts by defense firms prepared Serbia well for NATO's 1999 air offensive. Serbia's fiber-optic networks prevented NATO from decapitating the armed forces' command-and-control. Serbian missile crews' upgraded equipment and new tactics, meanwhile, threatened NATO aircraft throughout the war – destroying two manned aircraft and 25 drones – while preserving all but three of Serbia's 25 mobile missile batteries (Lambeth 2001, pp. 108–111). Serbian crews even downed one F-117 stealth fighter and damaged a second (Anon, 2005). As a result, the US Defense Department rated Serbian defenses in 1999 as three times more effective than Iraq's in 1991 despite Iraq's larger quantities of more modern weaponry (Cook 2000).

Serbian air defenses forced NATO aircraft to routinely fly at altitudes above 5 km where they mistook decoys for actual targets because of both the decoys' verisimilitude and high altitudes rendering target identification even more difficult (Anon 2002). NATO therefore only succeeded in destroying 14 Serbian tanks and 20 artillery pieces. Realistic decoys, however, misled NATO planners into believing their aircraft had destroyed 120 tanks and 450 artillery pieces (Lambeth 2001, pp. 129–131). With Serbia's air defenses and ground forces largely intact, NATO was no closer to military victory after two months of bombing than on the offensive's first day. Only NATO's superior resources and political solidity convinced Serbian leaders to capitulate to most of NATO's demands after 78 days of bombing (Posen 2000, pp. 60–66, Lambeth 2001, pp. 67–86).

The Yugoslav Wars convinced Serbian leaders of defense industries' strategic value. Post-war governments therefore legally protected the state's six (later nine) defense industries and encouraged exports to all possible clients, including Saddam Hussein's Iraq, Charles Taylor's Liberia and Muammar Gaddafi's Libya (International Crisis Group 2002). Serbian governments then gradually shifted their export drive's focus to less contentious customers as the country shed its pariah status. As Defense Minister Dragan Sutanovac observed, "we took out the [order] books from the past" because countries with pre-war ties to Yugoslavia would be well-disposed to Serbian weapons' "tradition and good quality, at a good price (MacDonald 2010)."

Serbian arms exports burgeoned beginning in 2002, growing annually by 30 % and rendering Serbia's arms industries the country's second-fastest growing economic sector. Serbia's defense industries have expanded 10 % in terms of employment, to 11,000, within the past five years and currently generate four percent of Serbian exports (Anon n.d.). Serbia's government views defense industries as strategic and anticipates that they will generate 800 new jobs and $200 million more a year in exports by 2020 (Anon 2017). Serbian leaders are therefore seeking to restore the sector's competitiveness, targeting the country's R&D resources on low-cost projects in booming market segments, such as small UAVs and counterinsurgency aircraft (Rajić *et al.* 2008, pp. 5–20, Jandric 2013, p. 17, Mladenović *et al.* 2013). Serbia's successful conclusion of a $236 million arms deal with Iraq, including 20 training aircraft, illustrates Serbian success at reestablishing indigenous R&D capabilities (Anon 2008).

Serbia, in sum, demonstrates that the value of possessing a domestic defense industrial base in wartime can be disproportionately large compared to its defense industries' size or economic competitiveness. Although Serbia's modest defense-industrial base failed to manufacture a single weapons system after the UN embargo disrupted its supply chains, it nonetheless contributed substantially to military effectiveness by adapting existing equipment for new circumstances and improvising secure command-and-control systems. Nowhere are the adaptation advantages provided by a small defense-industrial base more apparent than during the 1999 Kosovo War when Serbian air defense crews used tactics and missiles modified by domestic defense industries, networked by a domestically developed command-and-control system, to significantly degrade NATO's air offensive.

Conclusions

This study of the Israeli and Yugoslav/Serbian cases demonstrates that domestic defense industries' primary contribution to national security lies in how they enhance armed forces' capacity to adapt to unforeseen battlefield conditions. In addition to this adaptation advantage, both states' governments relied on domestic defense industries for command-and-control systems because they considered foreign involvement in such systems prejudicial to their strategic autonomy. Neither Israel's large, hi-tech defense-industrial base nor Serbia's smaller, lower-tech one provided, however, a meaningful level of supply security.

The finding that domestic defense industries cannot provide the vast majority of arms producing states with a meaningful level of supply security is a robust one. Israel's and Serbia's defense-industrial bases occupy significantly different positions in the international hierarchy of arms producers. Israel's defense industries were more than three times larger than Serbia's during the period in question and significantly more sophisticated. The medium-tech Serbian defense-industrial base, meanwhile, had deliberately been built-up during the cold war with security of supply in mind. Despite their vastly different sizes and capabilities, neither defense-industrial base furnished the states' armed forces with a secure supply of weaponry.

Israeli leaders concluded that security of supply was unviable in the 1980s and Yugoslav policy-makers retreated from their self-sufficiency policy at approximately the same time. Serbia, later, failed to produce a single major weapons platform during the Yugoslav Wars after international embargos and Yugoslavia's fragmentation disrupted defense firms' supply chains. Although a score of states possess defense industries more extensive than Israel's, there is no guarantee that even these possess an adequate degree of supply security. Considerable recent research, indeed, highlights defense-industrial supply chains' increasing globalization, which arguably undermines even great powers' pursuit of self-sufficiency (Dowdall 2004, Brooks 2005).

Although domestic defense firms provided neither Israel nor Serbia with security of supply, these same industries proved essential to both states' ability to adapt to unexpected battlefield conditions. Israeli defense firms, for example, assisted the armed forces in adapting to the threats posed by insurgents' rockets and anti-tank missiles by developing the Iron Dome anti-rocket system and by converting tanks into heavily armored infantry carriers. Serbia's defense industries, meanwhile, modified equipment and improvised tactics between 1995 and 1999 for frustrating NATO's anticipated air offensive. Domestic defense industries enhanced military adaptation to such a degree, regardless of the defense industries' absolute size, through their ability to weaponize civil technologies and exploit imported sub-systems. Many of the defense industries' concrete contributions to adaptation, meanwhile, centered around modifying existing equipment for new missions and assisting the armed forces in assessing and countering threats.

Israeli and Serbian leaders likewise called upon domestic defense industries to provide battlefield command-and-control systems, which they considered essential to their strategic sovereignty. Serbia's fiber-optic air defense network differs from Israel's tactical data links in terms of technological sophistication, but both systems have in common their integration of foreign and civil technologies into robust military networks. Both systems also centralize data and securely distribute commands from headquarters to frontline units. Such command-and-control systems are, however, highly vulnerable to espionage and disruption should an opponent know where critical nodes are situated and what communication protocols are used to connect them. The Israeli and Serbian governments, for this reason, considered it too risky to entrust command-and-control systems to foreign contractors and instead relied on domestic industry.

The fact that both Israel's cutting-edge defense-industrial base and Serbia's more modest one provide these military adaptation and strategic sovereignty benefits suggests that most other arms producing states enjoy them as well. A defense-industrial base's sheer size may therefore be less indicative of the military advantages it provides than hitherto considered the case. A good case can indeed be made that the marginal advantages generated by increasing a defense-industrial bases' size diminish rapidly since even comparatively large defense-industrial bases fail to provide security of supply and even relatively modest ones augment armed forces' capacity for battlefield adaptation and furnish them with secure command-and-control solutions.

Many states may therefore maximize their national security benefits by maintaining modestly sized defense-industrial bases. Within this context, maintaining overly large defense-specific industries can detract from states' security since, once established, defense firms become powerful lobbying groups that seek government contracts to maintain their technological and manufacturing capabilities. Such firms frequently make politically potent, if empirically contestable, arguments about preserving jobs in marginal constituencies and developing technologies that can be spun-off into the civilian economy. Adverse selection is the outcome when defense firms capture the public policy-making process in this manner and armed forces will be saddled with domestically produced weaponry that is either overpriced or underperforms compared to exports. Israel and Yugoslavia/Serbia, indeed, experienced precisely this dynamic in the 1970s and 1980s, which led both states to downsize their defense industries.

Even small defense industries are, however, strategically valuable because they cultivate engineers that understand weapons-related technologies and are experienced in helping armed forces solve battlefield problems. The second skill-set, the tacit knowledge needed to work with a states' military officers to address battlefield needs, is uniquely obtainable through domestic defense industries. Once such human capital exists, however, a small cadre of technologists can have a disproportionately large military impact by drawing on foreign imports and civilian industry for the components and sub-systems they need. Many of the 60 states that devote scarce resources to their moderately sized domestic defense industries are thus rationally investing in military power.

Note

1. The term defense technologist is used throughout this study to signify the nexus of managers, engineers, scientists and skilled workers who develop or produce weaponry.

Acknowlegement

I would like to thank the tireless help of my two research assistants, Amy McCudden and Oz Adari, whose efforts contributed greatly to this manuscript. I would also like to thank Caglar Kurc and Stephanie Neumann for organizing a stimulating series of online workshops that gave rise to this special issue. Finally, I would like to thank the anonymous reviewers for their invaluable feedback.

Disclosure statement

No potential conflict of interest was reported by the author.

References

Anderson, G., 2008. Bharat and Rafael move on plans for missile technology joint venture. *Jane's missiles & rockets.*, 12 (4).

Anon., 2002. NATO attack on Yugoslavia gave Iraq good lessons. *The Globe and Mail*, 20 Nov.

Anon., 2005. Air defense: how to take down an F-117. *Strategy Page* [online]. 21 November. Available from: www.strategypage.com/htmw/htada/articles/20051121.aspx [Accessed June 2016].

Anon., 2008. Report: Iraq in big arms deal with Serbia. *United Press International* [online]. 12 April. Available from: www.upi.com/Top_News/2008/04/12/Report-Iraq-in-big-arms-deal-with-Serbia/UPI-86821208050364/#ixzz2lQ23qz8L [Accessed May 2016].

Anon., 2017. Ambitious plans: Serbia ramping up defense production. *Sputnik News*, 1 May. Available from: sputniknews.com/europe/201705011053162269-serbia-defense-production/ [Accessed June 2017].

Anon. n.d. Serbia-defense industry. *GlobalSecurity.org*. Available from: www.globalsecurity.org/military/world/serbia/industry.htm [Accessed June 2017].

Barnett, M., 1992. *Confronting the costs of war: military power, state, and society in Egypt and Israel*. Princeton, NJ: Princeton UP.

Beaver, P. 1993. Yugoslavian defence industry re-grouped and rejuvenated. *Jane's Defence Weekly*, 28 Aug.

Ben-David, A. 2008a. Iron dome advances to meet Qassam threat. *Jane's Missiles and Rockets*, 7–8 May.

Ben-David, A. 2008b. Israel develops comprehensive defences against varied missile, rocket threats. *Jane's International Defence Review*, Jan, p. 60–64.

Benoit, E., 1973. *Defense and economic growth in developing countries*. Boston, MA: D.C. Heath.

Benoit, E., 1978. Growth and Defense in Developing Countries. *Economic development and cultural change*, 26 (2), 271–280.

Berman, E. and Leff, J., 2008. Light weapons: products, producers and proliferation. *In*: E. Berman, *et al.*, eds. *Small arms survey 2008*. Cambridge: Cambridge UP, 7–41.

Bitzinger, R., 2003. *Towards a brave new arms industry*. Oxford: Oxford UP.

Breznitz, D., 2002. *The military as a public space – the role of the IDF in the Israeli software innovation system*. Cambridge: MIT IPC.

Brooks, S., 2005. *Producing security*. Princeton, NJ: Princeton UP.
Brzoska, M., ed., 2005. *Conversion survey 2005 – global disarmament, demilitarization and demobilization*. Bonn: Bonn International Centre for Conversion.
Brzoska, M. and Ohlson, T., 1987. *Arms transfers to the third world 1971–85*. Oxford: Oxford UP.
Caverley, J., 2007. United States hegemony and the new economics of defense. *Security studies*, 16 (4), 598–614.
Cook, N., 2000. Survival of the smartest. *Jane's Defence Weekly*. 1 Mar.
Cook, J., 2013. Israel's thriving arms trade is a setback to peace agreement. *The national* [online], 23 July. Available from: www.thenational.ae/thenationalconversation/comment/israels-thriving-arms-trade-is-a-setback-to-peace-agreement [Accessed April 2016].
Coulomb, F., 1998. Adam smith: a defence economist. *Defence and peace economics*, 9 (3), 299–316.
Dimitrijevic, B., 1997. The mutual defense aid program in Tito's Yugoslavia, 1951–1958, and its technical impact. *The journal of slavic military studies*, 10 (2), 19–33.
Dobbing, M. and Cole, C., 2014. *Israel and the drone wars: examining Israel's production, use and proliferation of UAVs*. Oxford: Drone Wars UK.
Dombrowski, P. and Gholz, E., 2006. *Buying military transformation*. New York: Columbia UP.
Dowdall, P., 2004. Chains, networks and shifting paradigms: the UK defence industry supply system. *Defence and peace economics*, 15 (6), 535–550.
Dvir, D. and Tishler, A., 2000. The changing role of the defense industry in Israel's industrial and technological development. *Defense analysis*, 16 (1), 33–51.
Eilam, E., 2011. *Eilam's arc: how Israel became a military technology powerhouse*. Brighton: Sussex AP.
Farquhar, S., 2009. *Back to basics: a study of the second Lebanon War and operation CAST LEAD*. Fort Leavenworth: CSI.
Finkel, M., 2011. *On flexibility: recovery from technological and doctrinal surprise on the battlefield*. Stanford: Stanford UP.
Gelbart, M., 2004. *Modern Israeli tanks and infantry carriers, 1985–2004*. London: Osprey.
Gordon, N., 2009. *The political economy of Israel's homeland security/surveillance industry*. Beer-Sheva: Ben Gurion University NTC.
Gupta, A., 1997. *Building an Arsenal: the evolution of regional power force structures*. Westport: Praeger.
Gyürösi, M., 2007. Serbian factory offers to extend service life of Vympel R-60MK. *Jane's missiles & rockets*, 11 (9).
Gyürösi, M., 2008. Yugoimport offers infrared-guided SAM. *Jane's Missiles & Rockets*, 11 (5).
Hoyt, T., 2007. *Military industry and regional defense policy: India, Iraq, and Israel*. London: Routledge.
Hughes, R., 2003. Israeli defence industry: in the lion's den. *Jane's defence weekly*, 26 February.
International Crisis Group, 2002. *Arming saddam: the Yugoslav connection*. Brussels: International Crisis Group.
Jandric, M., 2012. One hundred years of the Serbian air force. *Scientific technical review*, 62 (1), 8.
Jandric, M., 2013. Seventh decade of the military technical institute (1948. – 2013.). *Scientific technical review*, 63 (2), 17.
Kagan, K., et al., 2010. Defence structure, procurement and industry: the case of Israel. *In*: S. Markowski, *et al.*, eds. *Defence procurement and industry policy: a small country perspective*. London: Routledge, 228–254.
Kapstein, E., 1992. *The political economy of national security: a global perspective*. New York: McGraw-Hill.
Kirkpatrick, D., 2004. Trends in the costs of weapon systems and the consequences. *Defence and peace economics*, 15 (3), 259–273.
Klieman, A., 1998. Adapting to a shrinking market: the Israeli case. *In*: E. Inbar and B. Zilberfarb, eds. *The politics and economics of defence industries*. London: Frank Cass, 111–134.
Krause, K., 1992. *Arms and the state*. Cambridge: Cambridge UP.
Kusovac, Z., 2000. Business: Serbia diversifies for survival. *Jane's Defence Weekly*, 5 Jan.
Lamb, C., 2009. *MRAPs, irregular warfare, and pentagon reform*. Washington, DC: National Defense University.
Lambeth, B., 2001. *NATO's air war for Kosovo: a strategic and operational assessment*. Santa Monica: RAND.
MacDonald, N., 2010. Serbia celebrates arms industry revival. *Financial Times*, 23 Mar.

Mahnken, T., 2002. *Uncovering ways of war: U.S. intelligence and foreign military innovation, 1918–1941*. Ithaca: Cornell UP.
Mangasarian, L., 1993. *Independence or dependence? the arms industries in Israel, South Africa and Yugoslavia during the Cold War*. Thesis (PhD). London School of Economics.
Maurer, P., 1988. Defence and foreign policy: Switzerland and Yugoslavia compared. *In*: M. Milivojevic, *et al.*, eds. *Yugoslavia's security dilemmas*. Oxford: Berg, 97–125.
Mawdsley, J., 2008. European union armaments policy: options for small states? *European security*, 17 (2), 367–385.
Mladenović, D., Jovanović, D., and Denić, N., 2013. Open source solutions in the development of military unmanned aerial systems. *Scientific technical review*, 63 (1), 36–46.
Moon, C.I., 2015. Military self-reliance, the big push, and the growth of the defense industry. *In*: *Korea and the world: contemporary history and its implications*. Seoul: National Museum of Korean Contemporary History, 205–238.
Naaz, F., 2000. Israel's arms industry. *Strategic analysis.*, 23 (12), 2077–2087.
O' Sullivan, A., 1999. Facing reality. *Armed forces journal*, 136 (9), 18.
Office of Technology Assessment, 1991. *Global arms trade*. Washington, DC: USGPO.
Opall-Rome, B., 2000. U.S. nixes Israel tomahawk plea. *Defense News*, 20 Aug.
Owen, R., 2000. *Deliberate force: a case study in effective air campaigning*. Maxwell Air Force Base Air UP.
Pallin, C. and Westerlund, F., 2009. Russia's war in Georgia: lessons and consequences. *Small wars & insurgencies*, 20 (2), 400–424.
Pengelley, R., 2008. Volatility in the Middle East drives Israeli defence industry innovation. *Jane's international defence review*, July, 56–57.
Perman, S., 2005. *Spies, Inc. Business Innovation from Israel's Masters of Espionage*. Upper Saddle River: Pearson.
Posen, B., 2000. The war for Kosovo: Serbia's political-military strategy. *International security*, 24 (4), 39–84.
Rajić, D., MAKSIMOVOĆ, S., and Jandrić, M., 2008. Six decades of military technical institute. *Scientific technical review*, 58 (3–4), 8–14.
Roberts, A., 1975. *Nations in arms*. New York, NY: Praeger.
Rodman, D., 2007. *Arms transfers to Israel: the strategic logic behind American military assistance*. Brighton: Sussex UP.
Rosh, R., 1990. Third world arms production and the evolving interstate system. *Journal of conflict resolution*, 34 (1), 57–73.
Le Roy, F., 2002. Mirages over the Andes: Peru, France, the United States, and military jet procurement in the 1960s. *Pacific historical review* 71 (2), 269–300.
Rubin, U., 2015. *Israel's air and missile defense during the 2014 Gaza War*. Ramat Gan: BESA.
Rubin, U., 2017. *Israel's defence industries – an overview*. doi:https://doi.org/10.1080/14702436.2017.1350823.
Sampson, A., 1977. *The arms bazaar*. London: Hodder and Stoughton.
Sen, S., 2000. *Military technology and defence industrialization: the Indian experience*. New Delhi: Manas.
Sherman, J., 1997. Niche carving: subsystem upgrades catapult Israeli defence industry to new heights. *Armed forces journal*, 134, 34.
Steinberg, G., 1998. Israel. *In*: R. Singh, ed. *Arms procurement decision making, volume 1*. Oxford: Oxford UP, 91–130.
Struys, W., 2004. The future of the defence firm in small and medium countries. *Defence and peace economics.*, 15 (6), 551–564.
Suvorov, V., 1982. *Inside the soviet army*. New York: Macmillan.
Tomislav, D. and Kostić, R., 2010. Yugoslavs in Arms: Guerrilla Tradition, Total Defence and the Ethnic Security Dilemma. *Europe-Asia Studies*, 62 (7), 1051–1072.
Tzalel, M., 2000. *From ice-breaker to missile boat: the evolution of Israel's naval strategy*. Westport: Greenwood.
Watkins, A., 2001. Yugoslav industry revival: fact… or fiction? *Jane's Defence Weekly*, 25 Jul.

Israel's defence industries – an overview

Uzi Rubin

ABSTRACT
Israel is currently one of the world's leading exporters of defence goods and services. Its defence industries originated in the covert workshops of the Hagana and other resistance groups in the pre-independence era of the 1930s, supplying the pre-state armed forces with light weapons. Mainly relying on imported weapons, the French arms embargo in 1967 came as a shock to Israel's leadership and public, causing a shift in policy towards self-sufficiency in major battlefield platforms (combat aircraft, armoured vehicles and warships) through indigenous research, development and fabrication. This policy of self-sufficiency was later modified to apply only to such weapons or systems that could not be obtained from abroad either for political or technical reasons. It can be expected that Israel defence industries now will focus more on sophisticated PGM's and battlefield robotics, whilst the Government will strive to fully privatize the remaining state owned defence industries. How successful this will be remains to be seen.

Introduction

Israel's defence industries are one of the main pillars of Israel's national security, whilst at the same time comprising essential components of Israel's high tech industry and a source of export revenues. This paper offers an overview of the defence industries – their origins, evolution and roles as security enhancers and economic players. To appreciate the scope of Israel's current defence industry – its size, policy and areas of specialization requires a historical perspective. One cannot understand the present without comprehending the complex history of Israel's various defence industries, both as part of the defence establishment, as well as commercial and business ventures. Accordingly, this paper will describe the evolution and consolidation of Israel's defence industry through the four successive eras of its history:

(1) The pre-state era. The underground munition industries of the Jewish community in British-Mandated Palestine.
(2) The formative era. From the establishment of Israel in 1948 to the Six-Day War in 1967.
(3) The "munitions independence" era. From the Six-Day War in 1967 to the termination of the Lavi fighter aircraft programme in August 1987.
(4) The Current Era. 1987 to present time.

The purpose of this paper is to outline the evolution of Israel's defence industry from an afterthought into national security and economical mainstays. Hence, it is descriptive rather than analytical or argumentative. The paper will concisely trace the evolvement of Israel's defence industry during each era, the basic rationale of its product lines, and its ownership and business policy. It will complement this description with a short discussion of the Israeli Government's defence export legislation, regulation and disclosure policy. Finally, it will offer a forecast for the future evolvement of Israel's defence industry.

For reliability purposes, all the information used in this paper is traceable to officially released information.

The pre state era: 1933–1948[1]

The growth of the Jewish community in the post-first World War British Mandate of Palestine, stemming from the Balfour Declaration of 1917 and energized by the Zionist movement, was accompanied by a growing conflict with the local Arab Palestinian community. To better defend itself, the Jewish community established an underground armed militia, the "Hagana." Initially equipped with whatever the light weapons that could be illegally purchased locally or smuggled from abroad, the Hagana was compelled by the growing level of intra-community violence to establish its own light weapon manufacturing facilities to complement its meager armoury. Its first underground workshop, which was established in 1933, manufactured hand grenades and explosives. This rapidly expanded into a covert factory system comprised of seven industrial plants producing mortars, submachine guns and ammunition.

After the Second World War, the Jewish community's increasing agitation for the end of the British Mandate and the establishment of an independent state brought the Jewish community into armed conflict with the British administration. This, and the growing perception that independence would be forcefully resisted by the local Arab community and neighbouring Arab states, increased the pace of the Hagana's arms production and broadened the portfolio of its nascent industrial plants to include the production of light and medium mortars, land mines and even primitive torpedoes.

During the late 1930s, the complex political struggles within the Jewish community caused a splinter group to leave the Hagana and establish its own underground armed militia, the Irgun, which splintered further to create the Stern Organization. Both splinter groups set up their own munitions workshops with the Irgun's production capability becoming almost as sophisticated as the Hagana's factories by the eve of the 1948 war. However, soon after the state of Israel was established, both the Irgun and the Stern Organization were absorbed by the Hagana to create the Israel Defense Forces (IDF). The separatists' arms factories were either closed down or absorbed by the Hagana factories.

In the pre-state era, the role of the incipient defence industries was to contribute to the armed struggle, initially against the local Arab irregulars, later against the British administration, and finally against the regular Arab armed force's intervention in 1948. The end of that war marked the end of the pre-state era.

The formative era 1948–1967

In its early days, Israel was faced with the immense task of nation-building. A flood of refugees from Europe, the Middle East and North Africa poured into the state in the wake of the 1948 war and required gainful employment. The statist policy of the then socialist government was to establish government-owned industries optimized for job creation rather than profits. The Hagana military industries were consolidated into a new entity, the Israel Military Industry, which was seen as more of a job creating enterprise than a response to a clear defence requirement.

At the same time, the early architects of Israel's economy strove to enhance the country's technological capabilities in both the civilian and military industries. The first major step in this direction was the establishment of Bedek Aviation in 1953, an aircraft maintenance, repair and overhaul (MRO) facility designed to serve the Israel Air Force as well as commercial air carriers (For the history of Israel Aerospace Industries see IAI and the Security of Israel 2016). The new venture was quite successful in creating thousands of jobs for new immigrants. And Bedek Aviation quickly broadened its product line to include the licence manufacture of a French jet trainer. Initially set-up as a department of the Israeli Ministry of Defense, the rapidly expanding Bedek Aviation was re-formed in 1965 as a government-owned commercial company and re-named Israel Aircraft Industries (IAI – today Israel Aerospace Industries).

The ambitious new company set its sights on becoming a full-fledged system house in aeronautical engineering. One of its main undertakings to achieve this goal was the design, manufacturing and marketing of its own indigenous aircraft. Its first product was the light transport aircraft (the "Arava"). It first flew in 1969, served in the Israel Air Force, and was moderately successful as an export item. Another major step towards the status of a full system house was the consolidation of its avionics repair shops, in 1967, into a modern electronics and radar affiliated company dubbed Elta Systems.[2] Typical of the period, Elta was built in the newly established immigrant town of Ashdod to provide jobs for the local workforce. This experiment turned out to be a successful commercial enterprise as well. Today Elta is a leader in avionics warfare systems and radars of all kinds (airborne, naval and terrestrial) whose products now serve in dozens of foreign armed forces.

Further progress towards technological ascendency was the transformation, in 1958, of the obscure Ministry of Defense Department for Scientific Advancement into an independent government authority, Rafael (Hebrew acronym for "Authority for Development of Weapon Systems").[3] The new "Authority" focused on advanced missile design. Its first product – a manually guided ground-to-ground missile – later evolved into the Gabriel, one of world's earliest anti-ship missiles, which defeated the Egyptian and Syrian navies in 1973 and was a major Israeli export for a time. Rafael further broadened its portfolio by developing air-to-air missiles. Today Rafael is a leader in the production of advanced weapon systems and has gained wide renown for the performance of its short-range missile defence system – the Iron Dome.

During this initial era, the IDF purchased its main weapon platforms from abroad, often with great difficulty due to the Arab League's objections to the arming of Israel. The fledgling IDF was initially equipped with fighter aircraft from the Eastern bloc, salvaged British tanks, and refurbished illegal immigrant ships. Its first jet fighters and major warships (WWII vintage destroyers) came from Britain. The massive armament purchases by the neighbouring Arab states (chiefly Egypt, Syria and Iraq) from the Soviet Union starting in late 1955 (SIPRI Arms Transfers Database 2016) triggered an arms race in which Israel initially clearly lagged behind. This changed in the later during that decade when France (with tacit US support) agreed to become Israel's primary weapons supplier. Germany also agreed to sell Israel a fleet of relatively modern US-made tanks. Other than modern air defence systems that were acquired from the US in 1965 (SIPRI Arms Transfers Database 2016), the IDF became reliant on French-made weapons, mainly fighter aircraft and light tanks. This reliance on foreign suppliers, which in turn was predicated on the shifting interests of the Western powers in the Middle East, was a source of concern among Israel's leaders. Proposals to embark on self-development and the manufacture of jet fighters, warships and main combat tanks were made in the mid-1960s by the Ministry of Defense. The IDF, however, preferred to rely on the purchase of ready-made major weapons rather than wait for indigenous products without proven performance. (For the internal debate within the Israel's defence establishment on the pros and cons of the armaments independence, see Greenberg 2002, pp. 175–194.)

The IDF's attitude was dealt a crushing blow on the eve of the 1967 Six-Days War. At a time when the IDF and the nation were striving to win what Israelis perceived to be a war for national survival, French President Charles De Gaulle proclaimed an arms embargo on Israel, completely severing Israel's access to advanced armaments. The ensuing shock compelled Israel's leadership to re-evaluate its former course and formulate a policy of "munitions independence," i.e. self-sufficiency in major weapon systems. This ushered in the next era in the history of Israel's defence industries.

The era of munitions independence: 1967–1987

The shock of the French Embargo of 1967 revived the Ministry of Defense's (MOD) aspiration for self-sufficiency in main weapon platforms; it also softened the IDF's preference for ready-made weapons from abroad. Israel, during this period, embarked on the indigenous design and manufacturing of combat aircraft, main battle tanks and warships.

Israel's navy was in the middle of re-equipping itself with an all missile fleet based on French-made patrol boats still in construction at the time of the embargo. The boats were smuggled out of Cherbourg shipyards and inducted into Israel's Navy under the class name Saar-3 (Rabinovich 1988) The balance of the planned fleet of Saar 3 boats was manufactured in the Israel Shipyards, a government-owned company established in 1955 as a naval MRO similar in concept to Bedek Aviation (Company History at a Glance 2016.). Like Bedek, Israel Shipyards quickly expanded into other related lines of business. Once it was tasked to build the Saar-3 boats, it matured into a ship design facility, providing the Israeli Navy with larger and more advanced boats of the Saar-4 and Saar- 4.5 classes, as well as small fast patrol boats of the "Zivit" class that were also supplied to foreign customers.

The land battles of the 1967 and 1973 wars were fought with refurbished and upgraded US and British tanks. Israel pinned its hope for a modern main battle tank (MBT) on the UK with whose armed forces it cooperated in designing the "Chieftain" MBT. The UK, however, refused to sell the jointly designed tank because of the strong protest from its Arab weapon buyers. As a result, Israel designed and manufactured its own MBT, the "Merkava" ("Chariot") which first rolled out in 1974 and entered the service of the Israel Army in 1979 (A Brief History of the Merkava Tank 2006.) Whilst this tank's main subassemblies are manufactured by dozens of Israeli contractors, it is distinguished by being assembled by the IDF's own tank shops – an anomalous situation which drew criticism from Israel's Government Comptroller.[4] Repeated efforts to transfer the "Merkava" production line to one of the existing defence industries failed to date, due to the institutional objections of the IDF. Even so, the basic

Merkava design evolved in time to the current Merkava Mk. 4, considered by some experts to be the best MBT of its generation.

It was in the air, though, where the policy of munitions independence was given its severest test and where it suffered a major reversal. As described above, IAI was already producing light jet aircraft and advancing the design of turbo prop transports well before the 1967 French arms embargo. At the time of that embargo, Israel had on order from France about 50 ground attack versions of the Mirage fighter, the Mirage 5. With the French embargo in place, however, Israel decided to manufacture those fighters in IAI. Either with the mute cooperation of the French aircraft manufacturer or by covert means (or by both) Israel managed to acquire the detailed plans of the aircraft which was duly manufactured locally on a specially built production line. The Israeli made Mirage 5's, named the "Nesher" ("Eagle") by the IAF, acquitted themselves well in the war of 1973 and were later exported to several overseas customers, most notably to Argentina where they fought against the RAF in the Falkland War (Huertas and Briasco 1987, p. 29). With a maturing cadre of experienced aircraft engineers and a fighter aircraft production line in place, IAI now proceeded to its next objective: a major upgrading of the basic French design of the Mirage 3, but with more powerful US made engine and significantly improved aerodynamics. This necessitated a major redesign of structures and systems resulting in what was in effect a new, indigenous combat aircraft. The new fighter dubbed "Kfir" ("Young Lion") closed an acute gap in Israel's fighter fleet. The avenue to advanced French fighters was now blocked by the French Government's embargo, and the new generation of US fighter aircraft was not yet available for sale to Israel. The "Kfir" with its superior performance to the Mirage filled this gap in Israel's inventory. It was accepted by the IAF and entered its service in 1975. "Kfir" like its predecessor the "Nesher" proved its mettle in the air battles of the era, and achieved some success in the international arms market. "Kfir" fighters are currently still in service with several air forces in the world and are being used by the US Navy for air combat training.

Buoyed by the success of the "Kfir" the IAI proceeded to its next fighter project, the "Lavi" ("Lion"). By the end of the 1970s Israel was already receiving the excellent US – made F16 fighter aircraft, but the Israeli munitions independence policy was still in force, and the IDF was still smarting from the 1967 embargo. Originally, the "Lavi" was planned as a light attack aircraft to complement the F16, but soon the specifications were changed and the "Lavi" design became even more ambitious than the US fighter. This caused concern in the US administration, which did not appreciate a competitor in the fighter aircraft market. Accordingly, the American administration did its best to undermine the "Lavi" by tempting Israel's leadership with offers for the local production of the F16 and financial assistance in modernizing Israel's navy (with US-made corvettes and German-made submarines) whilst at the same time refusing to underwrite the cost of the "Lavi"programme. The "Lavi" made its first flight in 1986, but by August 1987 Israel's government, bowing to strong US pressure, decided to abandon the programme (Zakheim 1996).[5] By doing so, Israel's arms industry bowed out of the fighter aircraft business and the policy of munitions independence was largely abandoned (Although the "Merkava" MBT programme was continued.) This caused a crisis in IAI which had to shed about 30% of its work force and its local suppliers. Israel Shipyards too went into a decline which eventually led to its sale and privatization.

The current era – 1987 to the present

The termination of the "Lavi" programme was strongly supported by the then Minister of Defense, Yitzhak Rabin. Rabin objected not only to the "Lavi" programme, but to the entire policy of munitions independence. Whilst being on the whole very supportive of Israel's defence industry, Rabin rejected the notion of self-reliance in major platforms. He correctly saw that the advertised self-reliance was illusory: All three major programmes of the munitions independence doctrine – the fighter aircraft, the tank and the missile boats – were critically dependent on the supply of US or European engines and other key components, and thus susceptible to future arms embargoes. Instead, Rabin formulated a policy of "focused self- reliance" which tasked the Israel defence industries to develop only such "force multiplier" systems that are uniquely tailored for the IDF and thus do not yet exist elsewhere, or such systems that are denied to Israel due to political impediments. As for major weapon platforms, Rabin preferred to purchase them from abroad, mainly from the US. (Why he allowed the "Merkava" MBT programme to proceed remains a mystery. Perhaps he was reluctant to quarrel with General Israel Tal, the father of the "Merkava"). Otherwise he saw the defence industries as business ventures, promoting their privatization and encouraging them to generate export revenues.[6]

And indeed, Israel's defence industries found their hands full with providing the IDF with weapons tailored to its unique requirements. The heavy losses of Israeli combat aircraft in 1973 by Soviet-made ground-based air defences (GBAD) forced it to seek innovative technologies and tactics to defeat these defences. The solution combined UAV's with air-launched Precision Guided Munitions (PGM). Both families of weapons hardly existed at the time. Air-to-Ground PGMs were first used in the Vietnam War and were still cumbersome and very expensive at the time. UAV's simply didn't exist. To satisfy the IDF's requirements, Rafael developed a series of free-fall and rocket propelled air-launched PGMs which later also became lucrative export items. Indigenous UAV systems were developed by IAI (and subsequently by a new defence contractor, Elbit Systems (on which more later). The combination of real-time reconnaissance from UAV's and pinpoint precision attacks by airborne stand-off weapons was first employed during the 1982 Lebanon war with spectacular results, eliminating Syria's GBAD systems with no losses to the Israel Air Force. This success enshrined UAV's into the IAF's order of battle creating a whole new industry and generating large export revenues.[7]

We have already mentioned Elbit Systems as the recent addition to the roster of the Israel's defence industries. The company originated from a partnership between the Ministry of Defense and a private contractor in 1966. Later on the company was fully privatized and expanded its product line to include high tech medical systems. In 1996, the parent company was divided into two separate companies, one dealing with civilian technologies and the other – Elbit Systems– specializing in defence products. Through the selective purchase of smaller defence contractors, Elbit System's portfolio includes today (among other items) UAV's, airborne avionics systems, automotive systems and light artillery. Its UAV's, like those of IAI, are serving today in many foreign air forces worldwide. Its innovative computerized Pilot Helmet is being used in the latest US combat aircraft, the F 35 Lightening II.[8]

Denied access to foreign intelligence data and facing a growing threat to its airborne reconnaissance capabilities, Israel developed a modest but capable space surveillance capability of its own, orbiting its first IAI made satellite by an IAI made Launch Vehicle in 1988.

Currently Israel is periodically replenishing its small constellation of Low Earth Orbit optical and radar reconnaissance satellites (see Eilam 2011, pp. 219–237.)

Since the 1973 Yom Kippur War, Israel has faced a threat from rockets and missiles. This threat grew more acute in the 1980s due to the large increase in WMD missile arsenals in Syria and Iraq. During the 1990s, Iran added to this threat by fielding long range Shahab missiles specifically designed to hit Israel. In response, Israel teamed up with the US in developing several types of missile defence systems, initially against long-range missiles from Iran and Syria, and later against shorter range rockets from Lebanon and Gaza (see Rubin 2001). Both IAI and RAFAEL participate in this ongoing effort, with the latter focusing on the defence against the shorter range threats. RAFAEL's latest product, the Iron Dome rocket defence system, gained world renown due to its remarkable success against rocket attacks from Gaza in 2012 and 2014. Israel's missile defence programmes are in aggregate the largest defence industrial programme since the "Lavi." They are currently ongoing at a rapid rate of development and production.

A corollary to missile defence is point defence of high value targets such as armoured fighting vehicles against anti-tank weapons. The losses to Israel's armour in the 2006 Lebanon War prompted the industrial development of active defence technology for vehicles. Rivalry between RAFAEL and Israel Military Industries (IMI) resulted in the design and production of two different systems: RAFAEL's "Trophy" and IMI's "Iron Fist." "Trophy" performed satisfactorily in Gaza and is now installed in a growing proportion of Israel's armour. According to media reports, "Iron Fist" is to be installed in the next generation of Israel's armoured personnel carriers (APV).

As in much of Israel's history, the exigencies of the battlefield have dictated the direction of its defence industrial progression. Some of the expertise needed for missile defence was gained by Israel's defence industries in the field of ship defence. Whilst Israel pioneered the field of anti-ship missiles, it was also the first country to lose a warship to an anti-ship missile when the Israeli destroyer "Eilat" was sunk by the Soviet-made "Styx" missiles in 1967. This compelled Israel to develop a ship defence missile system, the "Barak 1" which is designed to destroy sea skimming anti-ship missiles. The "Barak 1" is currently in service in the Israeli Navy as well as in several foreign navies.

Another significant specialization in the Israel defence industry is the conversion and upgrading of combat and commercial platforms. This was originally driven by Israel's inability to acquire first class weapons due to political constraints. To overcome this, Israel's nascent defence industries converted and modernized obsolete aircraft and armoured vehicles. The experience gained by such conversion and modernization projects served as a springboard for contemporary upgrade programmes both for local use by the IDF and for the export markets. Some disclosed examples are the current generation of the Israel Air Force airborne early warning systems based on commercial Gulfstream G550 business jets (ELW-2085 – CAEW 2017), refuelling jets based on Boeing airliners (Katz 2011), the A-50Ehl airborne early warning system, based on Ilyushin 76 military transports, sold to India as well as modernization kits for the US made M 60 tanks sold to Turkey (SIPRI Arms Transfers Database 2016).

Joining forces with foreign partners for the development of defence products needed by their respective armed forces is an important business practice of Israel's defence industries. The programmes are specified to satisfy the operational requirements of both partners, are jointly funded and the workload is shared between the engineering and production teams of both countries. The best example of such a joint programme is the Barak 8 ship defence system, developed by India and Israel. The Barak 8 has recently completed its acceptance test and is now being supplied to both the Israel and Indian Navies (Note: Barak 8 is an entirely new system, unrelated to Barak 1, except by name) (see India Israels Barak 8 SAM Development Project(s) 2016)

Terror is a weapon that has been used against Israel's population almost constantly since its establishment in 1948. It has prompted significant homeland security measures and anti-terrorist R&D programmes not only in the core Israeli defence industries but also in numerous start-ups that have been established by former IDF members. As a result, a broad spectrum of innovative technologies and products has been supplied to Israel's police and Special Forces, as well as to friendly nations.

The present: Israel defence business at a glance

At the time of writing, the major product lines of Israel's defence industries include, among others (Corporate Overview 2016, Homepage – IAI 2016, Homepage – IMI 2016, Homepage – Rafael 2016)

- Land Warfare: Main Battle Tanks, armoured personnel carriers, vehicle passive and active defence systems, mobile artillery and mortar systems, infantry weapons (assault rifles and squad LMG), minefield clearance systems, ammunition of all relevant calibres, pin-point precision surface-launched short-range missiles (both ballistic and non-line-of-sight [NLOS]).
- Surface to air weapons: Ground- and ship-based missile defence systems, ground- and ship-based air defence systems.
- Air Warfare: Air-to-air missiles (both IR and radar), air-to-ground precision-guided munitions, ground-launched GBAD suppression systems.
- Naval Warfare: fast patrol boats, unmanned sea vehicles, ship protections systems against ant-ship missiles.
- ISR (Intelligence surveillance and reconnaissance): Air surveillance systems (Medium Altitude Long Endurance [MALE] UAV's and modified executive jets), space based surveillance systems (satellites and space launch vehicles [SLV's], and ground-based radar surveillance systems.
- Homeland security: anti-terrorist close-quarter surveillance and combat systems.

Table 1 provides a summary of Israel's defence industries' sales in 2014. Table 2 lists the total value of new export contracts signed each year since 2010.

The Israel Ministry of Defense registry of defence contractors lists approximately 1000 defence contractors, of which 680 have export licences. It is estimated that the total number of employees in defence-related businesses is about 150,000 (Sadeh 2014)

US military aid and its effects

Israel has been a recipient of sizable US military aid since the conclusion of the Peace Accord with Egypt in 1979. This aid is given mainly as funds usable only in the US for the purchase of US made weapons and military supplies,[9] and does not provide for technology cooperation or transfers. All sales to Israel are governed by US legislation, particularly the Defence Export Act, which includes controls and restrictions on US weapons transfers to foreign governments.

Table 1. Israel's defence industry sales in 2014.

Company	No. of employees	Sales (Deliveries, $bn)
IAI	16,500	3.83
RAFAEL	6000	1.96
ELBIT SYSTEMS	10,000	2.96
IMI	3500	0.44
Total	36,000	9.19

Notes: This comprises the four main system houses, but excludes smaller defence contractors and high tech start-ups that sell their own products locally and abroad, with an estimated business volume of about 0.3–0.5 B$ and a total of 500–1000 employees. The total number of employees in the four main system houses constitutes about 1% of Israel's work force, but generates about 3% of the GDP and about 11% of the export earnings. (Bank of Israel – Data & Statistics 2017) https://www.boi.org.il/en/DataAndStatistics/Pages/Default.aspx

Sources: Elbit Systems Reports Fourth Quarter and Full Year 2014 Results (2015), IAI Publishes its Financial Statements for 2014 (2015), Rafael Finished 2014 with Record Orders Totalling $3b (2015) and Management Presentation – IMI Company Overview (2016.).

Table 2. Total value of new export contracts signed since 2010.

Year	Sales (New Contracts, $bn)
2010	5.7
2011	5.6
2012	6.5
2013	7.3
2014	5.6
2015	5.7

Notes: It is estimated that this represent about 70–80% of the total volume of new orders Israel ranks between the 5th and 7th largest arms exporters worldwide.

Sources: Ben-David (2013) and Cohen (2015).

On the whole, the US military aid tends to constrict Israel's military industries, since it offers the Israel Defense Forces competitive armaments at no cost to the defence budget. The demise of the Lavi programme was a case in point where the US-made F-16 fighters had been preferred to an in indigenous one on a cost basis. Another adverse side effect (from the Israeli industry's perspective) is the migration of some industrial capacity to the US in order to draw on US aid. Thus, subsidiaries of Israel's major arm makers are manufacturing Israeli designed systems and components in the US allowing the Israeli military to buy them with US aid dollars.

There have been a few important exceptions, the most notable one in the field of missile defence where the US – out of regional security considerations – provided Israel with convertible funds that could be used to partially finance its own indigenous programmes (the rest of the financing has been coming from Israel's own defence budget).

Ownership and structure[10]

As noted above, all major defence industries in Israel started as government ventures, and (except in the case of Elbit), started their existence as departments in the Israel Ministry of Defense (IMOD). Economic and management realities compelled the MOD to divest itself of them, since the capability of any regulatory bureaucracy to run industrial enterprises efficiently and profitably are generally severely limited. However, this divestment process took some time and was done piecemeal.

The most straightforward divestment case was that of IAI. IAI originated from a US aircraft overhaul business owned by Al Shwimmer, an American entrepreneur who helped supply the newborn Israel Air Force with transport aircraft during the 1948 war. Schwimmer transplanted his US business to Israel under the name of Bedek (Hebrew for "Overhaul") Aviation. With his American business background, Schwimmer lost no time in separating his business from its original bureaucratic affiliation with the Israeli Government and incorporated it as a wholly government-owned LLC, complete with a board of directors and corporate management (in which Schwimmer served as the CEO for 24 years). IAI is still a government-owned LLC today.

The divestment of two other organizations – IMI and Rafael – has been more convoluted and is still not completed. IMI is the successor entity to the pre-state clandestine armament industry. In the early 1950s, the disparate underground workshops were consolidated into a unified industrial entity that operated as a government arsenal. In 1990, IMI was transformed into a government-owned LLC. The transformation exacerbated the financial problems of the new company and was accompanied by massive layoffs. In 2005, the Government of Israel (GOI) decided to privatize IMI, a process which encountered significant difficulties and which has not yet been completed. To prepare it for sale, IMI has been split into two separate entities of which one – the core rocket division – will remain fully government-owned, and the other which comprises all the rest of the company will be sold to private investors. It is currently expected that the privatized segment of IMI will be purchased by Elbit Systems.

Rafael originated from the Scientific Corps, organized in 1948 as part of the Israel Defense Forces and staffed with civilian scientists. In effect, it was an Army arsenal. In 1952, the arsenal was transferred to the control of the MOD and became its R&D division. A further change occurred in 1958 when the organization was separated from the MOD to become the Weapon Development Authority (Hebrew acronym RAFAEL). The growth in business volume and sophistication required a further reorganization into a fully government-owned LLC in 2002. The lessons from the less than successful reorganization of IMI were implemented, and in the case of Rafael Ltd (the name was retained) the transition from authority to company was successful, allowing the company to expand and enhance its portfolio with cutting edge systems and technologies.

We have already described above the origins of Elbit System, a privately owned company which has grown to become the second largest defence contractor in Israel. From its humble origins as a small contractor it grew into what is in Israeli terms a giant corporation by judicious selections of its core business, expanding into new areas in military technologies and through a series of acquisitions of smaller defence contractors – among them Silver Wings (UAVs), El Op (military electro optical systems), SOLTAM (artillery), Elisra (military electronics) and Tadiran Systems (command and control). Its shares are traded in the Tel Aviv and New York stock markets and it is currently the most profitable Israeli defence contractor.

Israel's defence export handbook lists more than 200 contractors, but most defence exports come from a small number of them. Still, several of the smaller contractors have grown into nearly first rank exporters. For example, Plasan Ltd, a Kibbutz-owned company specializing in vehicle armour, had sold nearly $2B worth of armoured vehicles to the US Army. Another example is Aeronautics Defense Systems Ltd, a company specializing in UAVs, which has reached an annual sales volume of more than a hundred million dollars.

Human resources

Whilst the history of Israel defence industry has had its ups and downs as described above, the companies that compose it are today both a mainstay of Israel's defence and a major source of export revenues. On the whole, this industry is vigorous and profitable. Becoming one of the world's leading defence exporters is a remarkable achievement for the industry of one of the smallest countries in the world. Few would argue that the historical evolution of Israel's defence industries is a success story.

This success comes first and foremost from the quality and culture of its human resources. Israel has compulsive military service, where the more technically oriented services are breeding grounds for technologically sophisticated young people who are the driving force behind Israel's high tech industry. Israel's defence industries, focused as they are on advanced technologies, are essentially part of this high-tech industrial complex, which benefits from this outflow of talent from the armed forces (Becker 2014) The second important factor determining this success is cultural: Israelis in general tend to be contentions, individualistic, disobedient yet resourceful. This results in a culture of "creative chaos" which is conducive to innovative, out of the box thinking both in business and in technology (Mitzner 2015)

Government legislation and defence export controls[11]

Israel defence exports are regulated by the Israel Defense Export Act (IDEA), December 2007. The IDEA endows the Israel Ministry of Defense full power to control defence export licencing, in consultation with the Israel Ministry of Foreign Affairs. To that effect, the MOD established the Defense Export Control Agency (DECA), whose head is authorized, together with the IMOD director general, to issue or deny specific licences. DECA's stated objectives are first, to realize the policy and advance the interests of the State of Israel in preventing proliferation of defence technologies, information and goods, and second, to offer the defence exporter efficient licensing and training services.

The two tier licensing process involves first, a licence to negotiate and second, a licence to sell. The DECA is authorized to fine transgressors by up to 1 million Israeli Shekels (about $260,000) for a single transgression, with no recourse for appeal.

Since 1992, Israel has adhered to the Missile Technology Control Regime. It joined the Wassenaar Arrangement in 2005. Whilst licensing the export of dual use items for defence purposes is the responsibility of the MOD, licencing dual use items that are destined for non-defence purposes is the responsibility of Israel's Ministry of Commerce and Industry. Israel's defence export policy is coordinated with the US, and in general, it refrains from exporting defence items to countries which are proscribed by the US. Defence export to China is subject to US consent by a specific 2005 agreement (Kumaraswamy 2006.) Since then there have been no reports of any Israel defence exports to China.

As a rule, detailed information on specific defence export deals remain classified and is rarely disclosed. Legislative oversight is exercised by the Defense and Foreign Relations Committee of the Knesset (Parliament) behind closed doors. This secrecy is mandated by Israel's complex relations with many defence customers, and by their need to keep their military relations with Israel in low profile. Israel however publishes generic information on the volume of its defence exports, and provides general breakdown into customers' continents. Often some partial information is released, such as the identity of the exporter and the value of the transaction. A few select export deals are made more fully public, apparently from political consideration. Such as, for example, is the partnership with India in developing the Barak 8 ship defence system as well as some of the programmes mentioned above.

Future trends

Given Israel's political-military history, it stands to reason that it's defence industries will shift further away from major weapon platforms, focusing more on battlefield robotics and precision guided munitions in the future. These are widely considered to be "force multipliers" in land, sea, air and anti-terror warfare – the demand for which will increase both internationally and domestically.

From a business perspective, both the government as well as the major defence industries, mainly IAI and Rafael, are striving for privatization and perhaps more consolidation. This however seems a difficult if not impossible prospect, at least in the foreseeable future, on two counts. First, the highly unionized work force is adverse to privatization with its diminished job security and almost inevitable loss of jobs. Second, the large size of these companies now might make them unaffordable to local buyers. Selling them to outside investors, however, is highly problematic due to Israel's vital national security considerations. It is more likely that both IAI and Rafael will continue to be fully owned by the government at least for the next decade or two.

Notes

1. The origins and early history of Israel's defence industry is taken from Evron (1980).
2. For a brief history of Elta Systems see "Jobs at Elta Systsems: IAI," n.d. https://ww.dialog.co.il/tools/hitech-companies-in-Israel/working-for-elta; For a brief description of the current structure of the company see,"Elta," Wikipedia, https://en.wikipedia.org/wiki/Elta.
3. For a detailed history of Rafael, see Munia Mardor "Rafael – in the tracks of R&D for Israel's security" Israel Ministry of Defence Publishing House, 1981 (in Hebrew).
4. Producing the tank at the IDF shops was criticized as overly expensive. It was also argued that it makes the tank less attractive as an export item due to its military provenance (Egozi 2003) https://www.ynet.co.il/articles/0,7340,L-2829919,00.html.
5. Zakheim's book tells the story of US pressure to cancel the Lavi.
6. Rabin's view on the role of Israel's defence industries as described here is based on Rabin's statements during various meetings attended by the present author during the late 1980s, and on the present author's interview with Brig. General (Res.) Hagai Regev, Rabin's ADC (aide-de-camp) from 1984 to 1989. Also see Inbar (1999, pp. 111–112).
7. The destruction of the Syrian GBAD system (Operation Mole Cricket 19) took place in 9 June 1982, see Uri Milstein (2016).
8. For a concise and fairly accurate history of Elbit Systems, see "Elbit Systems" in Wikipedia, https://en.wikipedia.org/wiki/Elbit_Systems.
9. Israel has had the ability to convert 26.3% of annual Foreign Military Financing grants from dollars to shekels for defence production and purchases in Israel. However, according to the terms of the 2019–2028 Memorandum of Understanding (MOU) between Israel and the US, (signed September 14, 2016) Israel's ability to spend FMF funds on military equipment produced in Israel will gradually be phased out between FY2024 and FY2018 (Sharp 2016, p. 6).
10. For later history of Israel's defence industry as well as many useful insights about its evolution see Lifshitz (2011).
11. Information concerning Israel Defence Export Act and DECA is from the DECA website (About DECA 2016) https://www.exportctrl.mod.gov.il/ExportCtrl/ENGLISH/About+DECA/.

Disclosure statement

No potential conflict of interest was reported by the author.

Suggested further reading

For further reading about the history and politics of Israel's defence industrial development, see:

Hoyt, T.D., 2006. *Military industry and regional defence policy: India, Iraq, and Israel*. New York: Routledge.

Katz, Y. and Bohbot, A., 2017. *The weapon wizards: how Israel became a high-tech military superpower*. New York: St. Martin's Press.

Klieman, A.S. and Pedatzur, R., and 1992. *Rearming Israel: defense procurement through the, 1990s*. Jerusalem: Jerusalem Post Westview.

Peres, S., 1971. *David's sling*. New York: Random House.

Reiser, S., 1989. *The Israeli arms industry: foreign policy, arms transfers, and military doctrine of a small state*. 1st ed. New York: Holmes & Meier Pub.

References

About DECA, 2016. *Defense export controls agency* [online]. Available from: https://www.exportctrl.mod.gov.il/ExportCtrl/ENGLISH/About+DECA/ [Accessed 12 August 2016].

A Brief History of the Merkava Tank, 2006. *Defense update – international online defense magazine* [online]. Available from: https://defense-update.com/features/du-2-06/merkava-brief.htm [Accessed 12 August 2016].

Bank of Israel – Data & Statistics, 2017. *Bank of Israel* [online]. Available from: https://www.boi.org.il/en/DataAndStatistics/Pages/Default.aspx [Accessed 8 May 2017].

Becker, M., 2014. Factory and lab: Israel's war business. *Spiegel Online* [online]. Available from: https://www.spiegel.de/international/world/defense-industry-the-business-of-war-in-israel-a-988245.html [Accessed 12 August 2016].

Ben-David, A., 2013. Israeli defense exports increase by 30% in 2012. *Aviation Week Network* [online]. Available from: https://aviationweek.com/defense/israeli-defense-exports-increase-30-2012 [Accessed 12 August 2016].

Cohen, G., 2015. Israeli arms exports down $1 billion in 2014. *Haaretz* [online]. Available from: https://www.haaretz.com.ezproxy.cul.columbia.edu/israel-news/.premium-1.657613 [Accessed 12 August 2016].

Company History at a Glance, 2016. *Israel shipyards* [online]. Available from: https://www.israel-shipyards.com/history.asp [Accessed 12 August 2016].

Corporate Overview, 2016. *Elbit systems* [online]. Available from: https://elbitsystems.com/about-us-introduction/ [Accessed 12 August 2016].

Egozi, A., 2003. אורדן ותע"ש מציעות לרכוש את קו הייצור המרכבה [Ordan and IMI offer to buy the Merkava production line]. *YNET* [online]. Available from: https://www.ynet.co.il/articles/0,7340,L-2829919,00.html [Accessed 8 May 2017].

Eilam, U., 2011. *Eilam's arc: how Israel became a military technology powerhouse*. Brighton: Sussex Academic Press.

Elbit Systems Reports Fourth Quarter and Full Year 2014 Results, 2015. *PR newswire* [online]. Available from: https://www.prnewswire.com/news-releases/elbit-systems-reports-fourth-quarter-and-full-year-2014-results-300048799.html [Accessed 12 August 2016].

ELW-2085 – CAEW, 2017. *Israel aerospace industries* [online]. Available from: https://www.iai.co.il/2013/36666-36643-en/BusinessAreas_ISRSystems.aspx [Accessed 8 May 2017].

Evron, J., 1980. *התעשייה הבטחונית בישראל*. Tel Aviv: משרד הבטחון.

Greenberg, Y., 2002. Economic and security aspects of the decisions to produce an airplane and a tank in Israel. *Iyunim Bitkumat Israel*, 12, 175–194.

Homepage – IAI, 2016. *Israel aerospace industries* [online]. Available from: https://www.iai.co.il/2013/22031-en/homepage.aspx [Accessed 12 August 2016].

Homepage – IMI, 2016. *IMI systems* [online]. Available from: https://www.imi-israel.com/ [Accessed 12 August 2016].

Homepage – Rafael, 2016. *Rafael advanced defense systems Ltd* [online]. Available from: https://www.rafael.co.il/Marketing/203-en/Marketing.aspx [Accessed 12 August 2016].

Huertas, S.M. and Briasco, J.R., 1987. *Argentine air forces in the Falklands conflict*. Poole: Arms and Armour Press.

IAI and the Security of Israel, 2016. *Israel aerospace industries* [online]. Available from: https://www.iai.co.il/2013/12019-en/CompanyInfo-IAIandtheSecurityofIsrael.aspx [Accessed 12 August 2016].

IAI Publishes its Financial Statements for 2014, 2015. *Israel aerospace industries* [online]. Available from: https://www.iai.co.il/2013/32981-46408-en/MediaRoom.aspx [Accessed 12 August 2016].

Inbar, E., 1999. *Rabin and Israel's national security*. Washington, DC: Woodrow Wilson Center Press; Baltimore, MD: Johns Hopkins University.

India Israels Barak-8 SAM Development Project(s), 2016. *Defense industry daily* [online]. Available from: https://www.defenseindustrydaily.com/india-israel-introducing-mr-sam-03461/ [Accessed 12 August 2016].

Katz, Y., 2011. IAF to get midair refueling tanker. *The Jerusalem Post* [online]. Available from: https://www.jpost.com/Defense/IAF-to-get-midair-refueling-tanker [Accessed 8 May 2017].

Kumaraswamy, P.R., 2006. At what cost Israel–China ties? *Middle East Quarterly*, 13 (2), 37–44.

Lifshitz, Y., 2011. *The strategic and economic role of Israel's defense industries*. Ramat Gan: The Begin-Sadat Center for Strategic Studies, Bar-Ilan University.

Management Presentation – IMI Company Overview, 2016. *Ministry of Finance* [online]. Available from: https://www.gca.gov.il/NR/rdonlyres/0371BF50-8EB0-4306-AD26-DC6ECB674171/0/IMICompanyOverview5315.pdf [Accessed 12 August 2016].

Milstein, U., 2016. Operation mole cricket 19: 34 years later, the IAF's most decisive victory remains the standard. *The Jerusalem Post | JPost.com* [online]. Available from: https://www.jpost.com/Magazine/Operation-Mole-Cricket-19-456909 [Accessed 12 August 2016].

Mitzner, D., 2015. 5 reasons behind Israel's startup success. *The Next Web* [online]. Available from: https://thenextweb.com/insider/2015/07/07/5-reasons-behind-israels-startup-success/ [Accessed 12 August 2016].

Rabinovich, A., 1988. *The boats of Cherbourg*. New York: Seaver Books.

Rafael Finished 2014 with Record Orders Totaling $3b, 2015. *Israel defense* [online]. Available from: https://www.israeldefense.co.il/en/content/rafael-finished-2014-record-orders-totaling-3b [Accessed 12 August 2016].

Rubin, U., 2001. Historical background. *In*: B.-Z. Naveh and A. Lorber, eds. *Theater ballistic missile defense*. Reston, VA: American Institute of Aeronautics and Astronautics, 11–31.

Sadeh, S., 2014. How Israel's arms manufacturers won the Gaza war. *Haaretz* [online]. Available from: https://www.haaretz.com.ezproxy.cul.columbia.edu/israel-news/business/.premium-1.610032 [Accessed 12 August 2016].

Sharp, J.M., 2016. *U.S. foreign aid to Israel*. Washington, DC: Congressional Research Service, No. RL33222.

SIPRI Arms Transfers Database, 2016. *Stockholm international peace research institute* [online]. Available from: https://www.sipri.org/databases/armstransfers [Accessed 18 March 2016].

Zakheim, D.S., 1996. *Flight of the Lavi: inside a U.S.-Israeli crisis*. Washington, DC: Brassey's.

Between defence autarky and dependency: the dynamics of Turkish defence industrialization

Çağlar Kurç

ABSTRACT

Turkish defence industries have significantly improved their production capabilities since the 1980s. According to the official documents, Turkey reached 54% local production level in 2011. Encouraged by this impressive defence industrial development, the government of Turkey declared that defence industrial autarky, the country's main goal since the 1980s, would be reached by 2023. This paper evaluates the possibility of Turkey's defence autarky. Contrary to the existing approaches in the literature that assess technological capabilities and cost-effectiveness, this paper argues that Turkey's search for defence autarky is hindered by the interplay of institutional deficiencies, dependency on foreign inputs, and the United States' continuing influence over Turkish politics.

Introduction

The transformation of arms production has created opportunities for many states. Through defence industrial partnerships, recipient states can now exploit foreign component technology and technical knowledge to produce advanced military systems. Thus, a growing number of states, that once bought completed major platforms from major powers, now have acquired more sophisticated defence industrial capabilities.

Yet, the transformation process has mainly benefitted major arms producing companies. Marc DeVore argues that "today's multinationals possess human and financial resources outstripping those of many medium-sized states" (2015, p. 572). Many small and emerging states, therefore, seek the help of developed states and their defence companies to climb the development ladder of defence industrialization. This ladder broadly includes learning how to maintain weapon systems, how to master foreign military technology and know-how through joint and licensed production, finally reaching the level of independent research-and-development (R&D) and production capabilities (Bitzinger 2003, pp. 16–18). However, except for a few cases, such as Sweden and Japan, most defence industries in the developing world have deficiencies in weapons design, engineering, and manufacturing because they "suffer from shortages of skilled personnel and sufficient scientific and technical infrastructures to pursue breakthroughs and applied research in many critical defence technologies" (Bitzinger 2003, pp. 24–38, 2010, p. 216). Under these conditions, defence autarky – self-reliance in arms production – is a problematic pursuit. Consequently, the general expectation among analysts is that most emerging states will abandon their hopes for autarky, and instead integrate themselves into global production chains and focus on niche markets (Hartley and Sandler 2003, Struys 2004, Hartley 2007). Yet, a handful of emerging states continue to pursue defence autarky.

The process of defence industrialisation does not follow a single path in many emerging states. Rather, we observe a variety of industrialization strategies and goals. Richard Bitzinger observes that the so-called "globalization of defence production" varies from one country to another, which, he believes, throws into question the validity of the "globalization" concept itself (Bitzinger 2010, pp. 208–220). For example, several countries including Israel, South Africa, and Brazil, as predicted, have accepted their dependent positions and embraced integration into the global production chains by focusing their limited resources toward niche markets (Bitzinger 2003, pp. 39–62). Still others, such as Turkey, continue to seek defence autarky despite various industrial inefficiencies and the need to make significant investment to improve existing capabilities (Bitzinger 2011, 2013).

Some scholars argue that the differences in financial power, scientific and technical infrastructure, and the overall structure of the economy explain the variation in the defence industrialization process (Bitzinger 2003, 2010, Devore 2015). On the other hand, Goldman and Andres argue that such variation is due to the relationship between technology, and the organization of the particular society and culture (Goldman and Andres 1999, p. 124). Departing from Goldman and Andres' point, this paper shows how institutions, domestic politics and foreign relationships, both in defence industry and security, shape defence industrialization goals and progress through an in-depth look at the Turkish defence industrialization.

The Turkish defence industry is clearly expanding and becoming more capable of producing sophisticated weapons systems. According to the state's Strategic Plan of 2017–2021, Turkey reached 41.6% local production level in 2007 and hit the 54% mark in 2011 (SSM 2017a, p. 43). Parallel with its increased defence industrial capability, Turkey aims to reach an arms export level of 25 billion USD (SSI 2012, 2014) and defence autarky (the holy grail of Turkey's defence industrialization goals since the 1980s) by 2023. During his opening remarks at the 12th International Defence Industry Fair, President Recep Tayyip Erdoğan declared "Our goal is to rid our defense industry of foreign dependency by 2023 completely" (Hogg and Sezer 2015). The year 2023 is the centennial of the foundation of the Turkish Republic, thus it gives Erdogan's declared defense autarky goal a symbolic value. While recent developments in defence production promote the belief that autarky is attainable, such a hopeful view overlooks the structural problems in the Turkish defence industrialization process. First, we contend that institutional deficiencies, which arise from weak planning capacity and the nature of civil–military relations, impede the establishment of a sustainable defence industry and effective procurement policies. Second, we argue that Turkey's active pursuit of international defence industrial cooperation comes at the expense of creating in-house production capabilities. Finally, we contend that Turkey continues to emulate and follow the United States to the detriment of its own military industrial development. Procurement decisions reflect a country's security relationships and Turkey continues to purchase advanced military equipment from the United States, rather than seeking innovative solutions for its specific industrial problems. In the end, we maintain that Turkish defence industrialization will fail to reach self-sufficiency unless the country addresses its own institutional, organizational, and economic contexts, and adjusts its defence industrial policies to reflect its security needs.

Policy-making and Turkey's defence industry: institutional deficiencies

Lack of planning and goals

As Turkey was integrated into the Western political and military structures, thanks to the military assistance provided by the Truman doctrine in 1947 and its NATO membership in 1952, Turkey began to lose its ability to independently plan and implement defence policies both at the strategic and operational levels.

Initially, US military aid was limited to supplying equipment and training Turkish personnel in maintenance and operations. However, the US military missions came to the realization that training on the use and maintenance of American equipment would not be enough to transform the *Türk Silahlı Kuvvetleri* (TSK – Turkish Armed Forces) into an independent fighting force, thus the restructuring of the TSK and *Milli Savunma Bakanlığı* (MSB – Ministry of National Defence) has become the priority in 1948 (Güvenç 2010, pp. 264, 278). For example, it was the United States Air Force Group (USAFG) that restructured and reorganized Turkey's order of battle to conform to that of the United States Air Force. Furthermore, USAFG ordered new aircrafts for Turkey (such as F-84E Thunderjets), transformed the Turkish Air Forces' supply and maintenance systems, and constructed its airfields (Livingston 1994, pp. 796–798, 801–806, 811). In 1966, Denis Allen, the British Ambassador to Turkey, observed that the "Turkish Armed Forces [TSK] follow United States doctrine and procedure almost on entirely tactical, training and organizational, administrative and logistical matters" (Quoted in Göktepe 2005, p. 434). Despite the differences with the United States in shaping the defence policies, TSK and MSB have become dependent on the United States' guidance on many strategic and operational issues such as future military needs, force structures, maintenance schedules, and procurement. A Turkish General summarizes the general situation of TSK as follows:

> Every year we used to submit a list of our needs to the USA. These lists were unnecessarily long, covering everything from helmets to batteries, from ropes to tanks or anti-aircrafts. The rule was to ask for as much as possible. The main reason was that we had no armament policy of our own, nor any national objectives, nor even any idea of what we really needed. The Americans shipped over whatever they thought necessary and, regardless of their use, we were too pleased to be at the receiving end. What's more, everything was donated. (…) For instance, the M-48 tanks that were replaced by the M-60 in the US Army were shipped to Turkey. Two thousand Reo trucks and 10,000 jeeps, even if they dated from World War I, were also welcome. (…) We had so little planning that we had to be reminded by the Americans which part in the warships or aircraft to replace and when. All the details were recorded in their computers which alerted them, for instance, replacements had to be made on the F-100s and the warships. Sometimes we would get huge boxes, and we wouldn't know what to do with them until the replacement instructions arrived. (Unnamed General at TSK, quoted from Birand 1991, p. 194)

Inadvertently, the pursuit and reliance on the US military aid resulted in the weakening of the institutional capability for constructing and pursuing coherent military and defence industrial policies. Institutional weaknesses came to light as Turkey struggled to follow a coherent industrialization process in support of procurement policies and military needs during the early years of defence industrialization.

On paper, Turkey follows a coherent defence and industrial policy-making. Officially, *10 Yıllık Tedarik Programı* (OYTEP – 10 Year Procurement Program) determines the procurement priorities and shapes the process in a 10-year framework, which is designed according to the Strategic Goal Plan of *Genelkurmay* (the Chief of General Staff) and defence industry development priorities (SSM 2007a). Furthermore, as the defence industrialisation progressed, civilian defence industrial and procurement planning began to emerge in the 1990s. "The Principles of Defence Industry Policy and Strategy," published on 20 July 1998 in the *Official Gazette*, sets out the principles of Turkish defence industrialization. The core principle of the defence industry policy was to increase domestic production through developing national weapon systems and technologies. The industry would be supported through investments and export incentives, although foreign partners were welcomed (*Türk Savunma Sanayii Politikası ve Stratejisi Esasları* 1998).

Policy papers that have been produced since 2007 share similar core principles with the *Official Gazette* document. In 2007, the *Savunma Sanayii Müsteşarlığı* (Undersecretariat for Defence Industries – SSM) published its first strategic plan (2007–2011 Strategic Plan) for the management of defence procurement and defence industries, followed by the Strategic Plan 2012–2016 and the Strategic Plan 2017–2021. In 2009, the Defence Industry Sectoral Strategy Document for 2009–2016 was published. Two other papers, namely: the UAV Road Map 2011–2030 and Technology Management Strategy 2011–2016, also provide detailed road maps for technology acquisition and industrial management. One of the core principles in these documents is to increase the share of domestic products in weapons systems and to move toward indigenous designs. In the 2007–2011 Strategic Plan, one specific clause sets the bar for meeting TSK needs at 50% of local production (SSM 2007b) – a goal that had been reached in 2011.

While the following strategy documents continue to itemize increased production capabilities (development, production, and supporting the major weapon systems with local components and subsystems),[1] they do not mention any specific goal for the local production level (SSM 2012, p. 12, 2017a, pp. 11–14). Although neither OYTEP nor the *Genelkurmay*'s Strategic Goal Plan is publicly accessible, the official statements and the SSM's strategy documents argue that Turkey has become increasingly more efficient in industrial development management through setting concrete goals and principles, while upholding the core principles of the 1990s. However, the reality appears to be different than what it is expressed in the official documents. Investigations into the establishment of an aerospace company in the 1970s, an attack helicopter tender (1995–2007), and a main battle tank tender (1997–2007) disclose delays and a lack of coherent policy implementation despite the official statements regarding the improvements in defence planning.

The early defence industrialization efforts in the 1970s show how institutional weaknesses, specifically the lack of policy guidance from decision-makers, created a disconnect and lack of harmonization between the military and the civilian elites as well as among the civilian elites themselves.

As early as 1970, these institutional weaknesses were evident. The defence industrialization process began with the "Build Your Own Airplane" initiative of the *Hava Kuvvetleri Komutanlığı* (HvKK – Turkish Air Force Command) in 1970. The initiative aimed to encourage the establishment of an indigenous aerospace industry under the auspices of *Hava Kuvvetleri*

Güçlendirme Vakfı (HKGV – Air Force Support Foundation). The foundation had two priorities: (1) to direct procurement of advanced fighter aircrafts and (2) to establish a national defence industry by collecting subscriptions from the public, which would finance the state-owned defence corporations. Three years after HvKK called for action, a ministerial bill was finally submitted and approved (Batur 1985, p. 464). The foundation established a jet accessories and a spare parts shop within a military factory in Central Anatolia in 1972 as the first step toward producing an indigenous airplane (İnöntepe 1972). The bill for the establishment of *Türk Uçak Sanayii Anonim Ortaklığı* (TUSAS – Turkish Aeroplane Industry) was also approved in 1973. However, the MSB was dissatisfied with the fact that TUSAS was under *Sanayi ve Teknoloji Bakanlığı* (Ministry of Industry and Technology). The MSB refused to appoint members for the board of directors, thus rendering the company non-functional (Mevlütoğlu 2016). The government did not allocate the necessary resources for airplane production until the fiscal year of 1974 (Batur 1974), mainly due to disagreements between the coalition parties regarding the benefits and end goals of a national aircraft industry.

The initial purpose of TUSAS was to build fighter planes. This was later changed to a jet trainer, only to be canceled later. The possible production of a fighter jet attracted some interest from US companies. McDonnell-Douglas proposed a complete production facility for F-4, while both Lockheed (Lancer) and Northrop (F-5 and YF-17) discussed the possibility of establishing an aircraft factory in Turkey (Cumhuriyet 1975a, 1975b). Meanwhile, Turkey expressed interest in the F-16 and wanted to take part in a coproduction project (Cumhuriyet 1975c). Later, Turkey decided that production of a jet trainer was a better choice since Turkish pilots faced restrictions and limitations during their training in other countries. Thus, it was argued that a jet trainer would better suit Turkey's needs. The production of a jet trainer was also thought to be more economically and technically feasible. In 1976, TUSAS opened an international tender for a jet trainer production in Turkey. Four competitors – F-5F (USA), Alpha Jet (Germany), Hawk (UK), and Macchi MB-339 (Italian) – submitted serious proposals, in which they agreed to produce a jet trainer in Turkey as a first step toward the eventual production of a fighter aircraft (Yıldız 1977a). During the tender process, the MSB was invited to send a representative to the tender commission. The MSB refused and requested that TUSAS submit the tender result to *Genelkurmay* and MSB for approval (Mevlütoğlu 2016). TUSAS selected the MB-339 in 1977; however, MSB opposed TUSAS's decision and recommended the procurement of the British Hawk (Yıldız 1977b). In order to obstruct the TUSAS decision, MSB sent a letter to the then-Prime Minister Süleyman Demirel, arguing that the MB-339 decision had been taken hastily and there had not been any coordination between the ministry and TUSAS (Mevlütoğlu 2016). Without attempting to resolve the issue and reach a compromise, then-Prime Minister Demirel canceled the procurement of the MB-339 on the grounds that TUSAS had behaved hastily. He argued that the decision should have to come from the government instead (Yıldız 1977c). Thus, the conflict between civilian and military decision-makers halted the aircraft's production and resulted in an idle aerospace company. TUSAS finally began production in 1980 with the selection of the F-16 which later became the backbone of the Turkish aerospace industry. The lack of institutional harmonization, however, continued even after Turkey started to produce policy papers and strategy documents on defence industrialization policy.

The attack and reconnaissance helicopter project (ATAK) is another example. The ATAK project was initiated in 1995 to meet the capability gap of TSK. It took 12 years to reach a conclusion. When the ATAK tender was introduced, the plan was to conclude the procurement process by 2000 and start deliveries in 2003. Turkey received bids from American Bell AH-1Z King Cobra and Boeing AH-64D Longbow, British-Italian AgustaWestland A-129 International, French-German Eurocopter Tiger, and Russian-Israeli Kamov/IAI Ka-50-2 Erdogan. Bell AH-1Z King Cobra was selected as the preferred bidder in 2000, while Kamov/IAI was declared the reserve choice. Negotiations began with Bell but ran into difficulty when the United States insisted on retaining its own mission computer in the King Cobra as opposed to replacing it with Turkey's indigenous device, as requested by Turkey. In 2002, the two sides tried to resolve the dispute with an agreement to coproduce the US equipment. However, the Turkish authorities declared their intention to reevaluate the Kamov/IAI offer, rather than finalizing with Bell (IHS Jane's 2006). In 2003, then Undersecretary of Defense Industries Prof. Dr. Ali Ercan recommended the procurement of Kamov/IAI Erdogan on the grounds that it was less expensive ($38 million/unit for Kamov vs. $45 million/unit for Bell (Jane's Defence Weekly's 2002a)). Moreover, the Russian offer included "an offset agreement under which Turkey could coproduce the Ka-115 light utility helicopter, with 100% technology transfer and permission to conduct third-party sales of the aircraft" (Jane's Defence Weekly's 2002a). However, TSK resisted the SSM's recommendation. It remained strongly in favor of procuring the AH-1Z King Cobra due to its performance, commonality with the existing inventory of AH-1P Cobra and AH-1 W Super Cobra helicopters as well as some other unclear, undefined criteria (Military Technology 2005, p. 69). In 2004, however, when Murad Bayar became the new Undersecretary of Defence Industries, Turkey leaned toward canceling the tender. Undersecretary Bayar argued that the Bell option did not fulfill Turkey's need to acquire an avionics integration capability and mission computers, while the Kamov/IAI option did not have a functioning helicopter (Jane's Defence Weekly's 2004a). A third option was later adopted, and the ATAK-1 tender was canceled. It was followed by a new tender, ATAK-2. The final decision for ATAK-2 was made in 2007, which AgustaWestland won. After 12 years, Turkey managed to reach a final agreement on the attack and reconnaissance helicopter project (ATAK).

In a similar fashion, the Main Battle Tank project was initiated in 1997 with two procurement options: either off-the-shelf purchase of foreign tanks with updated new technology or the development of a design jointly with a foreign partner to be coproduced in Turkey under license (Jane's Defence Weekly's 1997a). The initial tank procurement plan called for a foreign contractor and a local contractor to coproduce the new tank. Initially, the competing tanks were Giat Leclerc (France), KMW Leopard 2A5 (Germany), Vickers Defence Systems Desert Challenger (UK), and General Land Systems M1A2 Abrams (Jane's Defence Weekly's 1997b). In 1999, the procurement plan changed. Turkey now required, in the tender, the participation of one main local contractor and five local subcontractors, forcing foreign companies to form partnerships with Turkish companies (Jane's Defence Weekly's 1999, 2000). In 2003, South Korea offered Turkey participation in the joint development and production of a new battle tank (Jane's Defence Weekly's 2003). This was followed, in 2004, by Pakistan's offer to coproduce the Pakistani Al-Khalid MBT (Jane's Defence Weekly's 2004b). When Turkey began tank feasibility studies to reach a final decision in the tender process, it turned its attention to Asian countries, which as then-Undersecretary for Defence Industries argued "... we could meet the needs of the militaries of the countries involved in the production while creating opportunities for the sale to the third countries" (Jane's Defence Weekly's 2004c). In May 2004, Turkey announced that it had canceled the MBT procurement tender with the statement "New requests for proposals with an emphasis on new procurement models based on higher local industrialisation will be issued" (Jane's Defence Weekly's 2004d). As the tank feasibility studies for local production continued, Turkey shifted its attention to the procurement of ex-German Army Leopard 2A4 in 2004 (Jane's Defence Weekly's 2004e) and began the procurement of second-hand Leopard 2A4s in 2005 (*SIPRI Arms Transfers Database* 2016), which derailed the new tender process. The derailed process was restored in 2007, when Turkey decided to build the Altay indigenous tank with design help from the Republic of Korea. Turkey's indecisiveness with the aforementioned regarding its procurement policy as well as its shifting priorities illustrates Turkey's inability to follow a coherent defence industry policy that guides tenders and upholds Turkey's stated defence industrialization principles.

As the above examples show, the dissonance between Turkey's declared goals for its defence industry and the steps it has taken to achieve those goals have negatively affected Turkey's defence industrialisation process. Despite the declared strategic plans and 10-year procurement program, major procurement decisions have taken a very long time due to constant shifts in the procurement models and expected defence industry outcomes. The absence of agreed goals and the lack of coordination between the institutions show that Turkish defence industrialization is precarious. Despite the recent improvements in defence industrial capabilities, consistency in defence industry plans and procurement is still lacking. As we argue below, part of the problem is Turkey's inability to construct an effective organizational structure that clarifies the roles and responsibilities of the military and civilian elites and puts an end to the continuing, destructive civilian–military rivalry.

Civil–military rivalry: who is in charge?

Defence industrial and procurement practices are not immune to the ongoing civil-–military rivalry in Turkey. Civil–Military relations in Turkey have fluctuated between the "liberal-democratic model," where the military is subordinate to civilian power and remains outside of politics, and the "the praetorian model," where the military is directly involved in the political process (Heper and Guney 1996, p. 620). Since the *Adalet and Kalkınma Partisi* (AKP – Justice and Development Party) came to power in 2002, civil–military relations in Turkey have moved closer to the "liberal-democratic model" in conjunction with the push from the European Union accession process (Karaosmanoğlu 2011, pp. 253, 257). The government's ability to rally popular support to curb the military's influence over politics has also been an important factor. (Cilliler 2016). While TSK's intervention in politics has been largely curbed through reforms, problems persist when it comes to building effective defence policy, i.e. developing viable structures (Yıldız 2014, pp. 392–393) and management strategies. The problem is evident in a number of policy issues: including a clear division of responsibilities, agreement on the appropriate structure of the defence industry, the ownership of the companies that belong to the *Türk Silahlı Kuvvetleri Güçlendirme Vakfı* (TSKGV – Turkish Armed Forces Foundation),[2] and the role of military factories and shipyards in defence production.

Consequently, Turkey's defence industrialization reflects the struggle between the civilian and military elites for dominance in decision-making and control of the production, which negatively affects Turkey's ability to meet its military's needs in a timely manner.

The TSK has enjoyed a significant influence over the defence procurement decisions. In 1983, a civilian agency, *Savunma Donatım İşletmeleri Genel Müdürlüğü* (SDIGV – Defense Equipment Directorate), was founded. This new directorate, which was a state corporation, aimed to control every aspect of defence industrialization and procurement. It had the responsibility for the production and procurement of almost every need of the TSK, ranging from ammunition to weapon systems to medicine (*KHK/101* 1983). Its executive board was comprised entirely of civilian bureaucrats nominated by the Ministry of Defence (3) and the Ministry of Finance (1). The decision-making authority was given to the Prime Minister, the Minister of Finance, and the Minister of Defence. Furthermore, the executive order establishing the SDIGV also required the transfer of other TSK-controlled companies to the control of SDIGV. These were major efforts away from military to civilian control over defence production and procurement. In 1985, the government decided that military foundations were to be disbanded and foundation-owned defence companies (including TUSAS, Aselsan, and Havelsan) were to be transferred to SDIGV (Milliyet 1985). This decision, however, was never implemented. Rather than the transfer defence companies to civilian control, SDIGV was disbanded since it threatened the control of the military over defence industries.

A weaker civilian institution, *Savunma Sanayii Geliştirme ve Destekleme İdaresi* (SaGeB – Administration for Improvement and Support of Defence Industries), was founded in its place by law 3238 on 7 November 1985. It had limited executive and oversight responsibilities on defence industrialization and procurement practices (*3238 Sayılı Kanun* 1985), and the decision-making power was given to two committees, one of which provided representation for the military elites. The first committee, *Savunma Sanayi Yüksek Koordinasyon Kurulu* (The Supreme Board of Coordination for the Defence Industries), consisted of 13 members, which included the Chief of General Staff, Force commanders, and the Gendarmerie commander. The Supreme Board convened twice a year under the chairmanship of the Prime Minister, and carried out planning and coordination activities. The second committee, *Savunma Sanayii Icra Kurulu* (The Defence Industry Executive Committee), consisted of the Prime Minister, the Minister of Defence, and the Chief of General Staff. It was responsible for making decisions on the procurement of arms and other equipment, and gave directives to SaGeB on the oversight of procurement decision. While this institutional setting provided civilians some influence over defence industry and procurement policies, the organizational structure provided the military an overwhelming influence over defence industrial issues. In 1989, SaGeB became *Savunma Sanayii Müsteşarlığı* (SSM – Undersecretariat for Defence Industries), without any change in the institutional setting and responsibilities.

As an example of the continuing civil–military rivalry, in 1997, MSB, under the influence of TSK, made a bid to replace SSM with a new institution to further increase the control of the military over defence industrial policy. The new institution, *Milli Silahlanma Direktörlüğü* (MSD – National Armaments Directorate), would be under the control of TSK. The case was made on the grounds that the SSM failed to provide local input required to establish a more self-sufficient defence industry and SSM's budget, which was supported by the extra budgetary income from the Defence Industry Support Fund, was increasing. TSK argued that the new MSD would have a new strategy that aimed at opening up to international markets and making more cost-efficient decisions. In the end, MSB and TSK decided not to go through with their plan without a public explanation (Sarıibrahimoğlu 1997a, 1997b, Jane's Defence Weekly's 1998). The SSM kept its autonomy from the military, but the rivalry did not end there.

TSK may have backed away from the struggle to control the new procurement agency, but it kept control of its own procurements well into the 2000s. The SSM was given the responsibility for the oversight, planning, and coordination of modernization programs in accordance with the general strategy that was approved by the government in accordance with Strategic Goal Plan and OYTEP. However, TSK continued to have separate procurement agencies and resisted transfer of major weapons system procurement responsibilities to SSM. In effect, a dual procurement system existed. TSK mostly favored direct procurement on the grounds that TSK had immediate and unique needs in its fight against *the Partiya Karkeren Kurdistan* (PKK – the Kurdistan Workers Party), the SSM, on the other hand, sought for joint projects for the development of national defence industries (Sarıibrahimoğlu 1997c). Although MSD failed to replace the SSM, it continued to control various procurement projects in 1998. The division of responsibilities between MSD and SSM was unclear during this period. For example, MSD controlled programs such as F-4 modernization, heavy lift helicopter project, tactical area communication system (TASMUS) project, 1400-tonne submarine project, and frigate construction project, whereas SSM controlled armored combat vehicle, modern tank, attack helicopter, SAR [Search and Rescue], CSAR [Combat Search and Rescue] and general purpose helicopter, UAV [Unmanned Aerial Vehicle] and Early Warning and Control Aircraft (Kuloğlu 1998, p. 42). Even though many projects failed to be completed during the 1990s, such as the modern tank, heavy lift helicopter, and attack helicopter, SSM was able to establish its primacy on defence industry and procurement decisions.

Because of the dramatic shift in political dynamics in Turkey in the 2000s, the influence of the TSK was diminished, causing MSD to became defunct. The European Union candidacy in 1999 brought an onslaught of reforms between 1999 and 2005, including the civilianization of the state. This meant that the TSK had to transform, yield its political power, and accept civilian control (Balancar and Elmas 2010, p. 157).

As TSK's political power decreased, civilian control over procurement increased and TSK became more willing to yield decision-making to the SSM. This is reflected in a number of procurement projects for which the SSM is responsible. Whereas the annual number of projects had remained below 50 between 1985 and 2003, they had increased to 62 in 2004 and to 288 in 2011 (SSM 2012, p. 16). Although the civilian elites came out victorious from the rivalry over the control of the procurement agency, the tensions between civilian and military elites continue over the control of production in the defence industry.

In Turkey, today, TSK has noteworthy control over the Turkish defence industry through the military factories, maintenance facilities, and TSKGV-owned and partnered defence firms. While the industry is organized around state-owned and private defence firms, TSKGV has a peculiar place in the system. It can hold shares in both state and private defence firms, thus cutting across the public–private division. TSKGV owns shares in major state-owned defence companies such as TAI (%54.49), Aselsan (%84.58), Roketsan (%35.86), Havelsan (%98), Isbir (%99.76), and Aspilsan (%97.7). These companies hold 33% of the revenues in the country's defence market (Yazgan 2008, p. 3). TSKGV also has shares in private defence firms, including Netas (%15), TEI (%3.02), and Mercedes-Benz Türk (%5). Moreover, TSKGV has indirect subsidiaries in Havelsan EHSIM Airborne Electronic Warfare Systems Engineering and Havelsan Technology Radar.

TSKGV's grasp of the defence sector goes beyond the market share of its companies. Some companies are monopolies in their sectors, such as Aselsan in electronics, TAI in airframe production, and Roketsan in missiles and rockets. Therefore, other defence companies must cooperate and buy from these companies. As a result, TSKGV companies have become too big to fail. These companies acquire critical know-how either by acting as subcontractors to foreign prime contractors or by assuming a prime contractor role that conducts research and development projects. Consequently, TSKGV acquires work share from nearly every indigenously produced system. This increases its bargaining power against other Turkish defence companies as well as the civilian authorities. Over time, these dynamics strengthen the TSK's hand in the Turkish defence sector and in defence industrial decision-making. The Armed Forces serve as both the customers and the suppliers.

The AKP government continues to develop organizational methods to diminish TSK's control over defence production. In 2006, SSM wanted to unite four TSKGV-owned companies, Aselsan, TAI, Havelsan, and Roketsan, under one holding company called the *Savunma Teknolojileri Holding* (Defense Technologies Holding) (Hürriyet 2006, Uras 2006), which would have a civilian general manager (Jane's Defence Weekly's 2006). The private defence companies opposed this proposal even though it would ultimately expand their market power at the expense of the TSK. Instead, the companies argued that the proposal was against free-market principles. They claimed that the *Holding* would dominate the market (Jane's Defence Industry's 2006, Jane's Defence Weekly's 2006). Unable to resolve the conflict, the government initiated a different strategy in 2013 by appointing civilian members to the board of the TSKGV-owned companies and planned to decrease the shares of TSKGV by opening up its shares to public trading (Sarıibrahimoğlu 2013a). The AKP's policies included "the increasing input of the civilian bureaucracy in weapons procurement, supplies and services for the TSK, and moves to break up the monopoly of defense companies managed by retired generals" (Gürcan 2016). While the outcomes of these policies remain to be seen, the government seems to have backed away from breaking up the ownership of TSKGV, which still holds significant shares in these four TSKGV-owned companies.

Another strategy to decrease the TSK's influence in production is the transfer of production know-how from military facilities to the private sector. This strategy is best observed in the MilGem (National Ship) Corvette project. *Deniz Kuvvetleri Komutanlığı* (DzKK – Naval Forces Command) initiated the MilGem project in 1994 (Sariibrahimoglu 1999), yet the project remained limited to developing requirement documents until 1998 (Örnek 2016, p. 85).

When it was revived in 1998, the civil–military rivalry between the SSM and DzKK resulted in a series of changes in Turkey's procurement models. The constant changes in the procurement model, which continued well into 2005, caused significant delays (Örnek 2016, pp. 87–91, 93, 115, 163). For the SSM, the separation between the end user (DzKK), the procurement agency (SSM), and the main contractor (a private company) was necessary in the MilGem Project. The SSM wanted the transfer of technology and know-how from naval shipyards to private companies since the beginning of the MilGem project in 1998. However, little happened until 2004 when the SSM became more assertive. According to Özden Örnek, the Commander of the Turkish Naval Forces between 2003 and 2005, the SSM argued that DzKK should be in the role of end user but should not get involved in the procurement, design, and building (Örnek 2016, p. 127). Since naval shipyards were responsible for the building of the ships, according to the SSM, there was no separation between the end user and the contractor (Örnek 2016, pp. 126, 156). On the contrary, the DzKK maintained that the offered model, a private company assuming the role of main contractor, was only suitable for the procurement of the existing ship design, and neither local nor foreign companies would like to invest in an untested ship design (Örnek 2016, pp. 128, 157). Therefore, it was argued that DzKK should be responsible for the design and production of the ships.

In 2005, an agreement was reached. STM, the state-owned defence company, and the SSM assumed the responsibility of procurement of the equipment, while DzKK was responsible for the design and building of the initial ships (Örnek 2016, p. 160). Istanbul Naval Shipyard, a military-owned facility, was responsible for the development and production of two MilGem corvettes because of its prior warship building experience and in-house know-how. The follow-on manufacturing would be completed by private shipyards. Although RMK Marine, a subsidiary of Koç Holding, won the production of the follow-on ships in 2011, the tender was canceled when Sedef Shipbuilding company, which did not officially take part in the tender process, issued a complaint on the tender process two years after it was concluded (Tringham 2013). Due to cancelation of the tender, Istanbul Naval Shipyard continued to construct follow-on ships.

The Turkish Government argues that this system allows for the diffusion of production capabilities and technical know-how from the military facilities to private industries, thus increasing the overall production capabilities of the industry (Jane's Navy International's 2011). It was claimed that this system will eventually lead to the withdrawal of military facilities from defence production since the limited Turkish defence budget could not support the multitude of defence companies operating within the same sector. The 2009–2016 Defence Industry Sector Strategy Document supports this claim. The SSM envisions limiting the number of potential bidders for the classes of "auxiliary ships" and "corvettes and frigates" to four private shipyards from current seven. The document does not mention naval shipyards in these areas, yet only recognizes Gölcük Naval Shipyard for submarine production (SSM 2009, pp. 20–21).

In sum, the civil–military rivalry resulted in redundancies and inefficiencies in the defence production practices. TSK still enjoys a critical role in the Turkish defence industry and acquires considerable shares from the market. However, the rivalry over market control gives little sign of abating.

The blessing and the curse: foreign partnerships and sustainability of defence production

Foreign defence companies have been an integral part of Turkey's defence industry development since the 1980s. They are critical for acquiring the much needed military technology and know-how, facilitating the development of local production capabilities. Despite the significant increases in production capability and range of weapons systems, industrialization is sustainable only if Turkey finds foreign partners that are willing to cooperate and share technology. The contemporary structure of global arms production seems to be providing willing partners.

At the initial stages, the direct investment and joint ventures are critical to Turkish defence industrialization. Many major defence companies in Turkey have been established through direct investment and joint ventures and some still continue to operate with their foreign partners. Most notable examples are: in the aerospace sector – TUSAS-*Türk Havacılık ve Uzay Sanayii A.Ş.* (TAI – Turkish Aerospace Industries Inc.),[3] *TUSAS Motor Sanayi A.Ş.* (TEI – TUSAS Engine Industry Inc.),[4] and Alp Havacılık; in land systems – FNSS (FMC-Nurol Savunma Sanayii A.S.),[5] MTU-TR; in the electronics and software sector – AYESAS, SELEX, NETAS, SIEMENS, ESDAS, and YALTES; and in the rocket and munitions sector – STOEGER. As production capabilities increased, the preference for direct investment in the Turkish defence industry began to wane but never ended.

Inter-firm partnerships have become the main driver for the increased capabilities of Turkish defence industries. They enable the production of a variety of indigenous weapon systems via cooperative relationships ranging from subcontracting and co-development to coproduction and technical advice. Cooperation between Turkish and foreign defence companies not only aligns their economic interests but also creates a mutual dependency. As Turkish defence companies rely on critical foreign technologies to produce many of the indigenous weapons systems (see Table 1), foreign firms enjoy the benefit of providing technology and critical components for indigenous weapon systems without engaging in direct investment.

Turkey also seeks military–technical and defence industry cooperation agreements with several foreign countries. The goal is to diversify sources of military technology, know-how, and necessary components for defence products. Another goal is to create new export markets. The government, therefore, actively seeks work shares in multinational projects. It also encourages local defence firms to and make direct investments in the defence companies of possible customer countries (SSM 2017b). For example, the Republic of Korea and Turkey have also signed agreements to improve trade relations, to enhance collaboration in defence science and technology, and to ultimately coproduce South Korean-made materiel (Grevatt 2012). As similar initiatives enable Turkey's defence industry to integrate with the global producers, they contradict the country's stated goal of achieving autarky.

While cooperation with various states and companies has improved Turkey's defence industrial capabilities, the relative ease of finding partners has resulted in weak investment in indigenous research and development (R&D). There is nothing extraordinary for defence companies to cooperate with each other to produce weapon systems and this does not necessarily prevent a state's search for defence autarky. The problem arises when there is dissonance between the goals and the investments, especially in R&D. Although the number of indigenous weapon systems has increased, Turkish defence R&D spending, which has

Table 1. Examples of Turkish and foreign company relationships on critical military technology.

Recipient	Supplier	Type of relationship	Technology/know-how	Product
BMC	Hatehof (Carmor) (ISR)	Technical Assistance	System Design	"Kirpi" MRAP & "Vuran" MPAV
FNSS	General Purpose Vehicle (USA)	Co-Development	System Design	Pars 8x8 AFV
FNSS	Deutz (DEU)	Direct Procurement	Engine	Pars AFV
MIKES	BAE Systems (GBR)	Subcontracting	Electronic Warfare Systems	AN/ALQ-178(V)5+
Otokar	Hyundai Rotem (ROK)	Technical Assistance	Land System Design	Altay MBT
Otokar	AM General (USA)	Direct Procurement	Automotive Components and Suspension	Cobra APC
Otokar	Mercedes-Benz (DEU)	Direct Procurement	U-500 UNIMOG Chassis	Kaya MPV
Otokar	Mercedes-Benz (DEU)	Direct Procurement	FGA 14.5 Torsionally flexible Chassis	Kaya 2 MPV
Otokar	MTU (DEU)	Direct Procurement	MTU-883 Common Rail Diesel Engine	Altay MBT
Otokar	General Motors (USA)	Direct Procurement	V8 Diesel	Cobra APC
Roketsan	CPMIEC (CHN)	License	WH-1 302 mm Self-Propelled MRL	T-300
Roketsan	CPMIEC (CHN)	License	B-611 Surface-to-Surface Missile	J-600T
Roketsan	SAAB (SWE)	Co-Development	Short/Medium Anti-Tank Missile	/
Roketsan	MBDA (EU)	Technical Assistance	70 mm Laser Guided Weapon System	/
TAI	The Light Helicopter Turbine Engine Company (USA)	Direct Procurement	CTS-800 Turboshaft	T-129 ATAK
TAI	Agusta-Westland (ITA/GBR)	Co-Development	System Design	T-129 ATAK

Sources: (IHS Jane's 2004, 2014, Grevatt 2012, Mevlütoğlu 2013, Brown 2014, Smith 2014, *SIPRI Arms Transfers Database* 2016).

fluctuated between USD 579 million (constant 2005) and 1515 million (constant 2005) since 2008, has remained significantly lower than some of its major defence industrial partners including the United States, the Republic of Korea, the United Kingdom, Germany, and France[6] (OECD 2016). Furthermore, as Selin Arslanhan Memiş observes, the problem of weak R&D investment extends well beyond the defence industry. Turkey is trying to develop and indigenize many different civilian and military technologies, such as an indigenous fighter jet, a car, and medicine, with a very low overall R&D budget (0.94% GDP in 2013) when compared to other G-20 countries such as South Korea (4.15% GDP), China (2.01% GDP), and Brazil (1.15% GDP) (Arslanhan Memiş 2016). Although Turkey is attempting to develop its production capabilities through investments in human skill base and R&D, the devoted resources are well below those allocated by other states. Because of weak investment in its defence sector, Turkey inadvertently perpetuates dependency on technology transfer and international cooperation. Because foreign partners maintain high R&D budgets, they will retain their technological edge. Although Turkey is able to indigenize a number of existing technologies, without greater investment in R&D, it will be unable to close the technological gap and will fail to innovate in the defence sector. Under these circumstances, Turkey will be forced to direct its resources to technologically catching-up and making modest improvements on existing military technologies.

Furthermore, Turkey does not have control over what it receives from the international partnerships. The division of labor between partners potentially forces Turkey into a relatively lower level of technology production, while inhibiting its access to state-of-the-art technology. For example, Turkey wanted to join the System Development and Demonstration phase of the F-35 program as a Level 2 partner, but it was only permitted to join as a Level 3 partner (Güvenç and Yanık 2012, p. 120). This meant that Turkey had lower level of access to the design and development process of the F-35 program than it sought (Di Domenico 2006, p. 7).

This work sharing agreement means that certain parts of the F-35 are not produced in Turkey and other companies control the transfer of those parts. The question here is how critical are those parts to Turkey? In the F-35 program, Turkey was able to secure $4.2 billion worth of local work share. TAI will manufacture the center fuselage for 400 of the F-35 and so it acquired the bulk of the work share. Turkey, however, failed to gain access to source codes, despite its repeated requests (Güvenç and Yanık 2012, pp. 124–125). The critical technology, the source codes in this case, were withheld from Turkey. Overall, foreign partnerships have worked well for Turkey by increasing its production capabilities in certain technologies, but in the end, Turkey has not been able to break its dependency on foreign technologies and know-how.

Continuing dependency on the United States by other means

The pursuit of defence autarky has its roots in Turkey's desire to pursue an independent foreign policy. In 1964, when Turkey tried to act independently to protect its interests in Cyprus, the US threatened abandonment and an arms embargo. In 1975, Turkey was put under the embargo, when it intervened in Cyprus. As a result, Turkey began to question the reliability of the United States as a security partner (Altunışık 2013, p. 161). The arms embargo in 1975 reinforced Turkey's "awareness of the need to become self-sufficient in arms production, to avoid the restrictions attached to military aid … since the reliance on imports entails the risk of an embargo or a severe scarcity of foreign exchange" (Günlük-Şenesen 1993, p. 255). Since then, the aim of Turkey's defence industrialization has been to break its dependency on foreign suppliers, especially on the United States. However, the United States and Turkey have a deep cooperation relationship in both defence industry and security.

Even during the cold war, a close defence industrial relationship existed between two states, although Turkey relied heavily on the US for military aid. For example, the United States, for security rather than commercial reasons, helped establish *Türk Willys Anonim Ortaklığı* (Turkish Willys Joint Stock Company or Tuzla Jeep) in 1954 to produce jeeps in Turkey for both military and civilian use. Between 1954 and 1971, Tuzla Jeep galvanized the development of Turkish automotive sector and related sectors (Güvenç 2014, pp. 544, 547). It established the base upon which the modern Turkish automotive sector is built. In the same period, Turkish naval shipyards started to improve their production capabilities. Initially, the shipyards undertook the overhaul activities of submarines and destroyers, which were previously done in the US. This was followed, in the second half of the 1960s, by the construction of escort destroyers in Turkey. In the early 1970s, the shipyards began to cooperate with international shipyards for the building of modern warships in Turkey (Naval Forces 2004, pp. 42–43). When Turkey initiated its defense industrialization plan in the 1980s, it sought the help of the United States – the very state Turkey wanted to be less dependent on.

The close military cooperation with the United States that was established during the cold war also continued even after the defence industrialization began in the 1980s. Turkey looked to the US to help it increase its planning capabilities. In parallel to establishing civilian agencies for defence industries and procurement, Turkey also sought to increase its capacity for military planning by opening new military training and doctrine centers. In 1985, TSK established *Kara Kuvvetleri Eğitim Komutanlığı* (Land Forces Training Command) to increase its military training capacity (KKK Tarihçesi 2013). In 1994, it was restructured to become *Kara Kuvvetleri Eğitim ve Doktrin Komutanlığı* (EDOK – the Land Forces Training and Doctrine Command), which was modeled after the US Army Training and Doctrine Command. The primary responsibility of the EDOK, where several US officers worked as advisors, was to develop a new doctrine for TSK suitable for the information war of the twenty-first century (Foss *et al.* 1997). Consequently, it should not be surprising that Turkey adopted the Network Centric Warfare doctrine, rather than the European version of Network Enabled Capabilities, as the guidance for its force planning, and defence industry and procurement planning (SSM 2009).

Furthermore, the United States initiated a bilateral missile defence study, which was "designed to identify Turkey's defence needs and the system(s) [Patriot PAC-3, MEADS, THAAD and Arrow-2] that best could meet them" (Jane's Defence Weekly's 2002b). While Turkey wanted to become more independent in its military doctrines and defence planning, it nevertheless continued to seek and receive US assistance and guidance. The deep relationship between the two countries in both defence industrial affairs and military–technical cooperation created an affinity for US weapon systems. As Turkey learned, force planning, doctrines, and training are based on the capabilities of the US weapon systems.

Turkey's dependence on US weapons systems and its desire to acquire them through favorable US technology transfers is evident in Turkey's procurement behavior. Between 2000 to 2016, the United States' share of arms exports to Turkey was 40.3%, while the share of other states was much less, the European states: Germany 18.5%, the United Kingdom

4.7%, France 4.3%, Italy 5.5%, Spain 3.4%, and the Netherlands 2.2%. South Korea had a share of 10.7% and Israel had 6.6% (*SIPRI Arms Transfers Database* 2016). The Russian Federation had a share of only 0.2%, while China had 2.2% during this time frame. Furthermore, the United States had the received the largest share (30%) of Turkish defence exports, mostly through offset agreements, while Europe combined had 17% (SASAD 2016). The proportional arms transfer shares clearly show close defence cooperation between the United States and Turkey but indicate an indirect avenue for the United States to exercise influence over Turkey's defence policies. When the United States fails to satisfy Turkish demands for technology transfer, Turkey seeks to cooperate with other countries, which, at times, is used as leverage against the United States; the most recent example is the T-LORAMIDS (Turkish Long Range Air and Missile Defence System) tender.

Turkey first expressed its interest in acquiring the Patriot system following the deployment of Patriots during the Gulf War to protect Incirlik Air Base. But plans to acquire the Patriots were later abandoned (Sarıibrahimoğlu 1999a). In 1999, Turkey's interest in the system was revived, but quickly dissipated following the deployment of Patriots by NATO to Turkey because deployment was seen as the short-term solution to the air and missile defence capability gap problem (Sarıibrahimoğlu 1999b).

Again in 2007, Turkey revived its interest in acquiring a long-range air and missile defence system with the declaration of the T-LORAMIDS project. Turkey's initial plan, which was shaped after the talks with then Secretary of Defense Roberts Gates in 2008, was the direct procurement of a missile defence system to protect its borders, which would be followed by coproduction of a second missile defence system with significant local industry contribution. When NATO deployed Patriots to counter the threat posed by Syria, Turkey decided to cancel off-the-shelf procurement and move toward coproduction of the system (Sarıibrahimoğlu 2013b). In 2013, Turkey declared China Precision Machinery Export-Import Corporation (CPMIEC) FD-2000 (export version of HQ-9) as the winner of the tender because, as then Undersecretary of Defence Industries Murad Bayar argued, "it was better than rival bids in terms of 'price, technology, local work share, technology transfer and credit financing terms ... The Chinese bid is perfectly in compliance with our terms and conditions.'" (Bekdil 2013). For two years, Turkey conducted parallel negotiations with the United States and China. It is possible that Turkey was leveraging China's competition to draw the US and European prices down or to convince Raytheon to share its technological know-how. However, finally, Turkey was forced to cancel the tender on November 2015. When Turkey declared China as the winner of missile defence system, the United States threatened Turkey with canceling ongoing and forthcoming defence industry contracts, including TAI's participation in the F-35 consortium and coproduction of S-70 Black Hawk (Erkuş 2013). The scrapping of the tender did not necessarily bring an end to Turkey's quest for air defence system, but suggests the extent of US influence over Turkey's procurement choices.

Following the cancelation of the tender, Turkey first declared that it will seek to build an indigenous long-range air defence system (Bekdil 2015a), but later decided to procure off-the-shelf (Bekdil 2015b). In February 2017, the American–German–Italian consortium offered the Medium Extended Air Defense System to Turkey, which, as the consortium argued, could allow Turkey to improve its capabilities. According to the Defence News, Turkey was considering the procurement of the system (Bekdil 2017). On the other hand, Turkey also declared, in 2017, that it had begun talks with the Russian Federation for the S-400 system (Işık 2017). This was against a background of mounting disagreements with the United States over the

Kurds in Syria and the fight against ISIS. Some analysts believe that the negotiations with Russia is another reflection of Turkey's desire for military–technological independence from the US, Turkey's dissatisfaction with the lack of technology transfer from NATO countries, and the tense relations between Turkey and its NATO allies (Kasapoglu 2017, Majumdar 2017). On the other hand, some believe that Turkey might be again leveraging against its allies, as it did with Chinese system, but will not purchase the Russian system (Majumdar 2017, Taştekin 2017). First, as of 30 May 2017, the final agreement with Russia had not been announced despite the expectation that it would be declared following Erdoğan–Putin meeting on 3 May 2017 (Daily Sabah 2017). Second, it has been reported that Turkey wants to procure optical lenses and spare parts, which are not manufactured in Turkey but required for the production of advanced UAVs, from the United States (Gürcan 2017). This may be an indication of Turkey's continued dependence upon and need to cooperate with the US for advanced components and suggests Turkey's caution in the procurement of the Russian weapon system.

In the end, the outcome of the first tender shows that the United States continues to have important leverage over Turkey's procurement decisions, derived from its defence industrial relations with Turkey. If the factors that shaped the outcome of the Chinese system play out the same way, it is likely that the procurement of S-400 will not be realized.

Finally, Turkey's quest for autonomy in foreign policy does not diminish the value of its security relationship with the United States. During and after the cold war, both states had their fair share of disagreements and crises. Yet, the relationship between the United States and Turkey has shown its resilience. As Ian Lesser argues, "Turkish–American relations since the 1960s have been characterized by recurring tension. Yet the relationship has endured because of shared interest in larger strategic 'projects'" (Quoted in Altunışık 2013, p. 171). These shared interests can be observed in Turkey's participation in US-led coalitions in the 1990s. According to a 2003 RAND study, Turkey participated in 7 of 14 U.N. and 16 of 26 Non-U.N. operations, thus becoming the third most frequent NATO coalition partner after the United Kingdom (29 of 40) and France (28 of 40) (Larson *et al.* 2003, pp. 6–8). Despite the disagreements on the Middle East policies, such as the Turkish-Brazilian-brokered Iran nuclear deal (Önis 2011, pp. 52–53) and initial disagreements on the no-fly zone in Libya (Park 2015, p. 587), Turkey and the United States managed to sustain their security relationship. As Kibaroğlu and Sazak argue, Turkey is willing to make bold and unconventional moves when its allies resist Turkey's desire to upgrade itself from a "junior partner to a 'regional power'" (Kibaroğlu and Sazak 2015, p. 108), but this does not mean that Turkey is moving away from the Western alliance. As long as the United States and Turkey continue to share a close defence relationship, however, it is likely that the United States will keep its primacy and influence over the Turkish defence and security decision-making. In the end, Turkey will have to accept limited autonomy when it comes to foreign policy decision-making, the type of weapon systems it can procure, and the defence industrial relationships it can establish.

Conclusion

Without doubt, defence industrialisation has enhanced the military capabilities of Turkey. It has not only provided Turkey with a certain level of control over its arms production and procurement that the country did not have before, but Turkey has also able to build various high-technology weapon systems, such as the T-129 Attack Helicopter, MilGem Corvette,

Altay Main Battle Tank, and Baykar TB-2 Tactical UAV and ANKA S Armed UAV. Turkey seeks to increase its industrial capabilities via production of the Landing Platform Dock, Indigenous Light Utility Helicopter, and TF-2000 Air Defence Frigate. Furthermore, defence industrialisation has provided Turkey with some protection from arms embargoes and some ability to shift between the suppliers and partners, especially since the 2000s. Turkey's military operations and production will not be affected as long as Turkey is able to find collaborators in the areas where its production capability is weak. Its increased defence production capabilities, however, will not necessarily lead to defence autarky.

While Turkey's declared goal is defence autarky, the structure of the Turkish defence industry is unlikely to deliver this outcome. Turkey's defence industry remains inefficient because weak institutions and civil–military rivalry continue to override long-term procurement planning. Although foreign partnerships accelerated the development of Turkish defence companies, these companies suffer from weak investments in R&D. This inadvertently has resulted in continued dependence on foreign firms for technology and know-how transfers for state-of-the-art military technologies. Finally, the United States is still Turkey's most important partner in the defence sector, despite the political rough patches between the two. We have shown that while Turkey has been able to decrease its dependence on the US particularly since the cold war, the *nature* of its dependency has also changed considerably. Although there are now more opportunities for the defence industry to diversify at the international level, the United States (alongside its European counterparts) continues to be a major partner for Turkey. Unless and until Turkey addresses these three key issue areas – civil–military rivalry, weak investment in R&D, and technological reliance on its Western allies – defence autarky will continue to be a distant possibility.

Note on the sources

The newspapers and trade journals used in this paper are mainstream sources and generally considered as reliable. The author refrained from using any speculative comments and cross-checked the data from multiple sources.

Notes

1. The strategic plans also envision increasing the local testing capabilities. However, information about the capabilities of testing facilities and the level of dependency on raw materials is not mentioned in the official documents.
2. TSKGV was born from the unison of Army, Navy, and Air Force Support Foundations in 1987 to facilitate establishment of national defence.
3. TAI was founded in 1984 as a joint company of Turkish (TUSAS – HKGV) and US partners (General Dynamics, later Lockheed). TAI is nationalized in 2005.
4. TEI was founded in 1985 with TAI and General Electric.
5. FNSS is a joint venture of Nurol Construction and Trade (%49) and FMC (%51). BAE Systems bought FMC shares.
6. Turkey only outspent Germany and France in 2008.

Disclosure statement

No potential conflict of interest was reported by the author.

ORCID

Çağlar Kurç http://orcid.org/0000-0001-6191-1834

References

Altunışık, M.B., 2013. The middle east in Turkey–USA relations: managing the alliance. *Journal of Balkan and near eastern studies*, 15 (2), 157–173.

Arslanhan Memiş, S., 2016. Milli uçak mı, milli otomobil mi, milli ilaç mı yoksa hepsi mi? [National plane, national car, national medicine or all of it?] [online]. *TEPAV*. Available from: https://www.tepav.org.tr/tr/blog/s/5466/Milli+ucak+mi_+milli+otomobil+mi_+milli+ilac+mi+yoksa+hepsi+mi_ [Accessed 2 Dec 2016].

Balancar, F. and Elmas, E., 2010. Military interference in politics and the politicization of the Army. *In*: A. Bayramoğlu and A. İnsel, eds. *Almanac Turkey 2006–2008: security sector and democratic oversight*. Istanbul: TESEV, 157–171.

Batur, M., 1974. Uçak Sanayi Kurmak mı, Uçak Almak mı? [Constructing aerospace industry or buying planes?] *Milliyet*, 31 Oct, p. 2.

Batur, M., 1985. *Anılar ve Görüşler: Üç Dönemin Perde Arkası* [Memoirs and opinions: behind the scenes of three periods]. 2nd ed. Istanbul: Milliyet Yayınları.

Bekdil, B.E., 2013. Controversy deepens over chinese air defenses for Turkey [online]. *Defense News*. Available from: https://www.defensenews.com/article/20131003/DEFREG01/310030021/Controversy-Deepens-Over-Chinese-Air-Defenses-Turkey [Accessed 3 Oct 2013].

Bekdil, B.E., 2015a. Turkey leans toward local air defense system [online]. *Defense News*. Available from: https://www.defensenews.com/story/defense/policy-budget/industry/2015/11/28/turkey-leans-toward-local-air-defense-system/76284788/ [Accessed 20 May 2017].

Bekdil, B.E., 2015b. Turkey mulls stopgap air defense acquisition [online]. *Defense News*. Available from: https://www.defensenews.com/story/defense/air-space/2015/12/12/turkey-mulls-stopgap-air-defense-acquisition/76976836/ [Accessed 20 May 2017].

Bekdil, B.E., 2017. New terms offered for a Turkish MEADS missile-defense system [online]. *Defense News*. Available from: https://www.defensenews.com/articles/new-terms-offered-for-a-turkish-meads-missile-defense-system [Accessed 21 May 2017].

Birand, M.A., 1991. *Shirts of steel: an anatomy of the Turkish armed forces*. London: I.B. Tauris.

Bitzinger, R.A., 2003. *Towards a brave new arms industry*. New York: Routledge.

Bitzinger, R.A., 2010. Globalization revisited: internationalizing armaments production. *In*: A.T.H. Tan, ed. *The global arms trade: a handbook*. London: Routledge, 208–220.

Bitzinger, R.A., 2011. China's defense technology and industrial base in a regional context: arms manufacturing in Asia. *Journal of strategic studies*, 34 (3), 425–450.

Bitzinger, R.A., 2013. Revisiting armaments production in southeast Asia: new dreams, same challenges. *Contemporary South Asia*, 35 (3), 369–394.

Brown, N., 2014. Eurosatory 2014: Roketsan and Saab extend ATGW collaboration. *Jane's Defence Weekly*, 51 (30).

Cilliler, Y., 2016. Popular determinant on civil-military relations in Turkey. *Arab studies quarterly*, 38 (2), 500–522.

Cumhuriyet, 1975a. ABD Askeri Yardımının Kesilmesinde Savaş Uçağı Yapımcılarının Katkısı Bulunduğu Öne Sürülüyor [Aerospace firms are accused to be supportive of cessation of US military aid]. *Cumhuriyet*, 3 Oct.

Cumhuriyet, 1975b. Fransa Mirage, Ingiltere Jaguar Satmak İstiyor [France wants to sell mirage, while England offers jaguar]. *Cumhuriyet*, 25 Aug, p. 1.

Cumhuriyet, 1975c. 'Türkiye'nin YF-16 Savas Uçaklarıyla İlgili Ortak Projeye de Katılmak İstediği Belirtiliyor' [Statements on Turkey's desire to join multilateral YF-16 fighter plane project]. *Cumhuriyet*, 18 Nov, p. 1.

Daily Sabah, 2017. S-400 missile deal likely to be finalized at Erdoğan-Putin meeting [online]. *Daily Sabah*. Available from: https://www.dailysabah.com/diplomacy/2017/05/01/s-400-missile-deal-likely-to-be-finalized-at-erdogan-putin-meeting [Accessed 30 May 2017].

Devore, M.R., 2015. Defying convergence: globalisation and varieties of defence-industrial capitalism. *New political economy*, 20 (4), 569–593.

Di Domenico, S.G., 2006. *International armament cooperative programs: benefits, liabilities, and self-inflicted wounds – The JSF as a case study*. Maxwell Air Force Base, AL: Center for Strategy and Technology, Air University.

Erkuş, S., 2013. US, NATO clarify Chinese missile system not interoperable [online]. *Hurriyet Daily News*. Available from: https://www.hurriyetdailynews.com/us-nato-clarify-chinese-missile-system-not-interoper.aspx?PageID=238&NID=57309&NewsCatID=344 [Accessed 31 Jan 2014].

Foss, C.F., Kemp, I., and Sarıibrahimoğlu, L., 1997. Turbulent times for forces in transition. *Jane's Defence Weekly*, p. 39.

Göktepe, C., 2005. The Cyprus crisis of 1967 and its effects on Turkey's foreign relations. *Middle eastern studies*, 41 (3), 431–444.

Goldman, E.O. and Andres, R.B., 1999. Systemic effects of military innovation and diffusion. *Security studies*, 8 (4), 79–125.

Grevatt, J., 2012. South Korea signs defence collaboration agreements with India, Turkey and Thailand. *Jane's Defence Weekly*, 49 (16).

Günlük-Şenesen, G., 1993. Turkey: the arms industry modernization programme. *In*: H. Wulf, ed. *Arms industry limited*. Oxford: Oxford University Press, 251–267.

Gürcan, M., 2016. Turkey's latest 'civilian coup' [online]. *Al-Monitor*. Available from: https://www.al-monitor.com/pulse/originals/2016/05/turkey-civilian-coup-military-owned-enterprise-oyak.html [Accessed 3 Jan 2017].

Gürcan, M., 2017. Did Erdogan leave Trump meeting empty-handed? [online]. *Al-Monitor*. Available from: https://www.al-monitor.com/pulse/originals/2017/05/turkey-united-states-trump-erdogan-summit.html [Accessed 21 May 2017].

Güvenç, S., 2010. ABD Askeri Yardımı ve Türk Ordusunun Dönüşümü: 1942–1960 [US Military Aid and Transformation of Turkish Military: 1942-1960]. *In*: İ. Akça and E.B. Paker, eds. *Türkiye'de Ordu, Devlet ve Güvenlik Siyaseti [Military, State and Security Policy in Turkey]*. İstanbul: İstanbul Bilgi Üniversitesi Yayınları, 255–284.

Güvenç, S., 2014. The cold war origins of the Turkish motor vehicle industry: the Tuzla jeep, 1954–1971. *Turkish studies*, 15 (3), 536–555.

Güvenç, S. and Yanık, L.K., 2012. Turkey's involvement in the F-35 program: one step forward, two steps backward? *International journal*, 68 (1), 111–129.

Hartley, K., 2007. Arms industry, procurement and industrial policies. *In*: T. Sandler and K. Hartley, eds. *Handbook of defense economics*. Amsterdam: Elsevier, 1140–1176.

Hartley, K. and Sandler, T., 2003. The future of the defence firm. *Kyklos*, 56 (3), 361–380.

Heper, M. and Guney, A., 1996. The military and democracy in the third Turkish republic. *Armed forces & society*, 22 (4), 619–642.

Hogg, J. and Sezer, C., 2015. Erdogan aims to turn Turkey into major defense industry power [online]. *Reuters*. Available from: https://www.reuters.com/article/us-turkey-election-defence-idUSKBN0OC0FT20150527 [Accessed 16 May 2017].

Hürriyet, 2006. Savunma Teknolojileri Holdingi TSK'ya çalışacak [Defense technologies holding will work for TSK] [online]. *Hürriyet*. Available from: https://www.hurriyet.com.tr/savunma-teknolojileri-holdingi-tsk-ya-calisacak-4225309 [Accessed 20 Jun 2017].

IHS Jane's, 2004. AN/ALQ-178(V) [online]. *C4ISR & Mission Systems: Air*. Available from: https://janes-ihs-com.ezproxy.cul.columbia.edu/Janes/Display/1525537# [Accessed 18 May 2017].

IHS Jane's, 2006. TAI (Bell) AH-1Z King Cobra [online]. *Jane's All the World's Aircraft*. Available from: https://janes.ihs.com/Janes/Display/1343814 [Accessed 19 Jan 2016].

IHS Jane's, 2014. FNSS Savunma Sistemleri Pars armoured fighting vehicle [online]. *Land Warfare Platforms: Armoured Fighting Vehicles*. Available from: https://janes.ihs.com/Janes/Display/1501246 [Accessed 16 Oct 2015].

İnöntepe, H., 1972. Jet Aksesuar Atelyesi Hizmete Giriyor. [Jet parts manufacturing site enters service.] *Cumhuriyet*, 8 Jul, p. 1.

Işık, E., 2017. Ankara, Moscow continue negotiations over S-400 defense systems, gov't sources say [online]. *Daily Sabah*. Available from: https://www.dailysabah.com/diplomacy/2017/01/25/ankara-moscow-continue-negotiations-over-s-400-defense-systems-govt-sources-say [Accessed 20 May 2017].

Jane's Defence Industry, 2006. Turkey approves foundation of defense industry holding company [online]. *Jane's Defence Industry*. Available from: https://janes-ihs-com.ezproxy.cul.columbia.edu/Janes/Display/1135345 [Accessed 5 Nov 2015].

Jane's Defence Weekly, 1997a. Turkey wants share in new design MBT [online]. *ProQuest Advanced Technologies & Aerospace Collection*. Available from: https://search.proquest.com/docview/198540580?accountid=12492 [Accessed 7 Nov 2013].

Jane's Defence Weekly, 1997b. Bidders line up for Turkish tank contest [online]. *ProQuest Advanced Technologies & Aerospace Collection*. Available from: https://search.proquest.com/docview/198509808?accountid=12492 [Accessed 7 Nov 2013].

Jane's Defence Weekly, 1998. Turkish military backs off from SSM takeover plan [online]. *ProQuest Advanced Technologies & Aerospace Collection*. Available from: https://search.proquest.com/docview/198526545?accountid=12492 [Accessed 11 Jul 2013].

Jane's Defence Weekly, 1999. Turkey's MBT project shifts gear [online]. *Jane's Defence Weekly*. Available from: https://janes.ihs.com/Janes/Display/1672261 [Accessed 19 Jan 2016].

Jane's Defence Weekly, 2000. Turkey reconsiders MBT strategy as trials begin [online]. *Jane's Defence Weekly*. Available from: https://janes.ihs.com/Janes/Display/1639027 [Accessed 19 Jan 2016].

Jane's Defence Weekly, 2002a. Turkey re-opens attack helicopter talks [online]. *Jane's Defence Weekly*. Available from: https://janes.ihs.com/Janes/Display/1165225 [Accessed 19 Jan 2016].

Jane's Defence Weekly, 2002b. Turkey adopts aerospace and missile defence concept [online]. *Jane's Defence Weekly*. Available from: https://janes-ihs-com.ezproxy.cul.columbia.edu/Janes/Display/1163495 [Accessed 27 Jan 2016].

Jane's Defence Weekly, 2003. Turkey examines tank offer from South Korea [online]. *Jane's Defence Weekly*. Available from: https://janes.ihs.com/Janes/Display/1167983 [Accessed 19 Jan 2016].

Jane's Defence Weekly, 2004a. Turkey's King Cobra purchase in doubt again [online]. *Jane's Defence Weekly*. Available from: https://janes-ihs-com.ezproxy.cul.columbia.edu/Janes/Display/1170089 [Accessed 5 Feb 2015].

Jane's Defence Weekly, 2004b. Pakistan and Turkey to discuss tank co-operation [online]. *Jane's Defence Weekly*. Available from: https://janes.ihs.com/Janes/Display/1169623 [Accessed 19 Jan 2016].

Jane's Defence Weekly, 2004c. Turkey begins tank feasibility study [online]. *Jane's Defence Weekly*. Available from: https://janes.ihs.com/Janes/Display/1171188 [Accessed 19 Jan 2016].

Jane's Defence Weekly, 2004d. Turkey cancels attack helicopter, tank and drone projects [online]. *Jane's Defence Weekly*. Available from: https://janes.ihs.com/Janes/Display/1170501 [Accessed 19 Jan 2016].

Jane's Defence Weekly, 2004e. Turkey's Leopard plan puts local tank project in jeopardy [online]. *Jane's Defence Weekly*. Available from: https://janes.ihs.com/Janes/Display/1171946 [Accessed 19 Jan 2016].

Jane's Defence Weekly, 2006. Turkey to set up military-owned holding company [online]. *Jane's Defence Weekly*. Available from: https://janes-ihs-com.ezproxy.cul.columbia.edu/Janes/Display/1153244 [Accessed 5 Nov 2015].

Jane's Navy International, 2011. MILGEM charts a course for Turkey's naval sector plan [online]. *Jane's Navy International*. Available from: https://janes.ihs.com/Janes/Display/1208743 [Accessed 13 Dec 2016].

Karaosmanoğlu, A.L., 2011. Transformation of Turkey's civil-military relations culture and international environment. *Turkish studies*, 12 (2), 253–264.

Kasapoglu, C., 2017. Why Turkey might buy Russia's S-400 defence system [online]. *Al Jazeera*. Available from: https://www.aljazeera.com/indepth/opinion/2017/03/turkey-buy-russia-s400-missile-defence-system-170323131537509.html [Accessed 10 May 2017].

Kibaroğlu, M. and Sazak, S.C., 2015. Business as usual: the U.S.-Turkey security partnership. *Middle east policy*, 22 (4), 98–112.

Kuloğlu, A., 1998. The activities of Turkey's national armament directorate. *NATO's sixteen nations & partners for peace*, (Special Supplement), 39–42.

Larson, E., *et al.*, 2003. *Interoperability of U.S. and NATO allied Air Forces: supporting data and case studies*. No. MR-1603. Santa Monica, CA: RAND.

Livingston, C., 1994. 'One thousand wings': the United States Air Force group and the American mission for aid to Turkey, 1947–50. *Middle eastern studies*, 30 (4), 778–825.

Majumdar, D., 2017. Would Russia really sell the deadly S-400 to Turkey? [online]. *The National Interest*. Available from: https://nationalinterest.org/blog/the-buzz/would-russia-really-sell-the-deadly-s-400-turkey-19543 [Accessed 20 May 2017].

Mevlütoğlu, A., 2013. Siyah Gri Beyaz: Yüksek İrtifa, Uzun Menzil, Karışık Kafalar – II [Black Gray White: high altitude, long range, confusion – II] [online]. Available from: https://www.siyahgribeyaz.com/2013/10/yuksek-irtifa-uzun-menzil-karsk-kafalar.html [Accessed 17 Oct 2013].

Mevlütoğlu, A., 2016. Türkiye'nin Son Anda İptal Edilen Eğitim – Taarruz Uçağı Projesi. [Turkey's last minute cancelled training – attack aircraft project.] *Siyah, Gri, Beyaz*. [online] Available from: http://www.siyahgribeyaz.com/2016/02/turkiyenin-son-anda-iptal-edilen-egitim.html [Accessed 24 May 2017].

Military Technology, 2005. Turkey's 'Year of the Helicopter'. *Military technology*, 29 (4), 68–70.

Milliyet, 1985. Silahlı Kuvvetler Vakıfları Kalkıyor. [Armed forces foundation is being abolished.] *Milliyet*, 20 Aug, p. 12.

Naval Forces, 2004. Naval industrial base. *Naval forces*, (Special Issue), 42–47.

OECD, 2016. Research and development statistics: government budget appropriations or outlays for RD [online]. *OECD Science, Technology and R&D Statistics (database)*. Available from: https://doi.org/10.1787/data-00194-en [Accessed 29 Jul 2016].

Önis, Z., 2011. Multiple faces of the 'New' Turkish foreign policy: underlying dynamics and a critique. *Insight Turkey*, 13 (1), 47–65.

Örnek, Ö., 2016. *Milgem'in Öyküsü* [The story of Milgem]. İstanbul: Kırmızı Kedi Yayınevi.

Park, B., 2015. Turkey's isolated stance: an ally no more, or just the usual turbulence? *International affairs*, 91 (3), 581–600.

Sariibrahimoglu, L., 1999. One year on. *Jane's Defence Weekly*, 32 (12), 1.

Sarıibrahimoğlu, L., 1997a. Military bid for Turkish agency. *Jane's Defence Weekly*, 22 Oct, p. 10.

Sarıibrahimoğlu, L., 1997b. Turkish agency 'should remain autonomous'. *Jane's Defence Weekly*, 3 Dec, p. 12.

Sarıibrahimoğlu, L., 1997c. Savunmada Yetki Tartışması. [Authority debate on defence.] *Cumhuriyet*, 8 Oct, p. 3.

Sarıibrahimoğlu, L., 1999a. Turkey approaches USA for patriot system. *Jane's Defence Weekly*, 31 (23), 1.

Sarıibrahimoğlu, L., 1999b. The Janes interview. *Jane's Defence Weekly*, 31 (15), 1.

Sarıibrahimoğlu, L., 2013a. Turkey acts to reform its defense sector. *Jane's Defence Industry*, 30 (8).

Sarıibrahimoğlu, L., 2013b. Turkish T-Loramids programme derailed by NATO Patriot deployment. *Jane's Defence Weekly*, 50 (5).

SASAD, 2016. *Savunma ve Havacılık Sanayii Performans Raporu 2015* [Defence and aerospace performance report]. Ankara: SASAD.

Savunma Donatım İşletmleri Genel Müdürlüğü Kuruluşu Hakkında Kanun Hükmünde Kararname [Executive Order on Establishment of the Defense Equipment Directorate], 1983. KHK/101

Savunma Sanayii Geliştirme ve Destekleme İdaresi Başkanlığının Kurulması ve 11 Temmuz 1939 Tarih ve 3670 Sayılı Milli Piyango Teşkiline Dair Kanunun iki Maddesi ile 25 Ekim 1984 Tarih ve 3065 Sayılı Katma Değer Vergisi Kanununun Bir Maddesinde Değişiklik Yapılması Hakkında Kanun [The Law on Establishment of Administration for Improvement and Support of Defense Industries, and Changes to the two articles of Establishment of National Lottery of 11 July 1939 and Law Number 3670, and changes to one article of Value Added Tax Code of 25 October 1984 and Law Number 3065], 1985. 3238

SIPRI Arms Transfers Database, 2016. Stockholm International Peace Research Institute. [online] Available from: https://www.sipri.org/databases/armstransfers [Accessed 18 Mar 2016].

Smith, M., 2014. MBDA teams up with Roketsan for laser-guided rockets. *Jane's Defence Weekly*, 51(27).

SSI, 2012. Turkish defence and aerospace industry exports are on the attack. Target: 2 billion-dollar exports [online]. *Turkish Defence and Aerospace Industry Exporters Association (SSI)*. Available from: https://www.turksavunmasanayi.gov.tr/events/Event/25 [Accessed 18 May 2017].

SSI, 2014. Savunma Sanayi, Devletten Daha Fazla 'Yerli Ürün' Kullanımı İstiyor [Defense industry want more 'Indigenous System' use from the State] [online]. *Turkish Defence and Aerospace Industry Exporters Association (SSI)*. Available from: https://www.turksavunmasanayi.gov.tr/tr/Etkinlik/25 [Accessed 18 May 2017].

SSM, 2007a. 2007-2011 Stratejik Plan [2007–2011 strategic plan] [online]. *Savunma Sanayii Müsteşarlığı*. Available from: https://www.ssm.gov.tr/anasayfa/kurumsal/Documents/SP/sto.html [Accessed 28 May 2017].

SSM, 2007b. *Stratejik Plan 2007-2011 (VER 1.2) Güncellenen Hedefler* [Strategic plan 2007–2011 (VER 1.2) updated goals]. Ankara: SSM.

SSM, 2009. *2009–2016 Savunma Sanayii Sektörel Strateji Dokümanı* [2009–2016 defence industry sector strategy document]. Ankara: SSM.

SSM, 2012. *2012–2016 Stratejik Planı* [2012–2016 strategic plan]. Ankara: SSM.

SSM, 2017a. *Stratejik Plan 2017–2021* [Strategic plan 2017–2021]. Ankara: SSM.

SSM, 2017b. *2017–2021 Uluslarası İşbirliği İhracat Stratejik Plan* [2017–2021 international cooperation export strategic plan]. Ankara: SSM.

Struys, W., 2004. The future of the defence firm in small and medium countries. *Defence and peace economics*, 15 (6), 551–564.

Taştekin, F., 2017. Turkey determined to test NATO [online]. *Al-Monitor*. Available from: https://www.al-monitor.com/pulse/originals/2017/03/turkey-russia-ankara-tests-nato.html [Accessed 20 Jun 2017].

Tringham, K., 2013. Turkey resets MILGEM procurement plan [online]. *Jane's Defence Weekly*. Available from: https://janes.ihs.com/Janes/Display/1587988 [Accessed 13 Dec 2016].

Türk Kara Kuvvetleri Tarihçesi [History of Turkish Army] [online], 2013. *Kara Kuvverleri Komutanligi*. Available from: https://www.kkk.tsk.tr/GenelKonular/Tarihce/icerik.asp [Accessed 5 Aug 2013].

Türk Savunma Sanayii Politikası ve Stratejisi Esasları [The principles of Turkish defence industry policy and strategy], 1998. 98/11173.

Uras, G., 2006. Savunma teknolojileri holding kuruluyor [Defence technologies holding is being established] [online]. *Milliyet*. Available from: https://www.milliyet.com.tr/savunma-teknolojileri-holding-kuruluyor/gungor-uras/ekonomi/yazardetayarsiv/17.04.2006/153764/default.htm [Accessed 21 Jun 2017].

Yazgan, M.K., 2008. *2007'de Sayılarla Savunma Sanayiimiz* [Defense industry statistics in 2007]. Ankara: SASAD.

Yıldız, A., 1977a. TUSAS, Yabancı 10 Büyük Firmadan Teklif İstedi [TUSAS requested proposals from 10 major companies]. *Milliyet*, 13 Dec, p. 5.

Yıldız, A., 1977b. TUSAS, İtalyanlara 'Evet' Diyor [TUSAS says 'Yes' to Italians]. *Milliyet*, 14 Dec, p. 5.

Yıldız, A., 1977c. Yerli Uçak Sanayiinin Kurulması Şimdilik Donduruldu [The establishment of local aerospace industry is frozen for now]. *Milliyet*, 15 Dec, p. 5.

Yıldız, U.B., 2014. Rethinking civil-military relations in Turkey: the problems of the democratic governance of the defense and security sectors. *Turkish studies*, 15 (3), 386–401.

Turkish defense industry facing major challenges

Arda Mevlutoglu

ABSTRACT
The reform process of Turkish defense industry as launched in the last quarter of the twentieth century has seen several achievements, as well as downfalls, and passed through major milestones. The resultant industrial structure is unique, compared to the other sectors in the country. Dominated by the TSKGV (Turkish Armed Forces Foundation), the major goal of the sector has always been involved in attaining self-sufficiency, indicative of an import substitution-oriented industry policy. This strategy is evident in decision-making and execution processes of virtually all defense procurement programs. However, lack of an efficient mechanism for science and technology policy-making mechanism, is observed as a major obstacle toward sustainable development of the sector. Although benefited from the overall economic take-off during the 2000s, today the Turkish defense industry faces to the challenge of sustainability, which is heavily dependent on export performance. The forthcoming period will test the sector, revealing the necessary coordination and communication by and between the military and civilian bureaucracies.

Introduction

The development of Turkish defense industry in the last two decades deserves a comprehensive analysis by an interdisciplinary perspective. The sector has its foundations laid during the early Republican period from 1923, but the current state of the sector is a result of an approximate period of 50 years. Several factors, both internal and external, impacted the course of Turkish defense industry, which is a wealthy source for case studies on science and technology policy-making in developing countries.

Turkish defense sector has achieved significant developments in the last 15 years. This leap, supported by a focus on indigenous development programs, resulted in the increase in the number of firms and employees operating in the sector. One major driver of this strategy has been to increase the percentage of local solutions to meet the requirements of Turkish Armed Forces' (TAF), while export sales considered secondary.

The "localization" process formed the defense sector based on a mutual relationship between the end-user, i.e. TAF, and the procurement agency, i.e. the Undersecretariat for Defense Industries (SSM: Savunma Sanayii Mustesarligi). As an indirect result the requirements of the end-user, occasionally missing the current trends that prevail in the global market and technology, directly controlled the research & development, innovation and technology management capacity of the defense & aerospace sector in Turkey: a sectorial mindset suited to a form of import substitution.

The first efforts toward national defense industry started shortly before the foundation of the Republic. Establishment of weapons and ammunition production lines was one of the main topics during the İzmir Congress of Economics held between 17 February and 4 March 1923. The period between 1923 and early 1940s saw a number of military factories founded in Ankara as well as Golcuk and Taskizak naval shipyards (Savunma Sanayii Mustesarligi 2016a).

In the aviation sector, Tayyare ve Motor Türk AŞ (TamTAŞ) started operation in 1926, producing a total of 112 aircraft of German and US origin. There were also private enterprises in the aviation sector at the time: Nuri Demirag founded an aircraft company in Istanbul, designing and manufacturing several sports and passenger aircraft between 1936 and 1943 (Savunma Sanayii Mustesarligi 2016b).

These activities in defense and aviation industry came to an abrupt end shortly after Turkey entered NATO in 1952. Large quantities of military aid made available to Turkey resulted in a prioritization of foreign supplied materiel over local products at the cost of undermining the development of an indigenous defense industry. Consequently, Turkey joined the other allies that provided their equipping its armed forces almost exclusively with US supplied equipment (Güvenç 2010).

The Johnson Letter Incident is arguably the first milestone in the birth and expansion of the Turkish defense industry. In 1964, Turkey decided to intervene in Cyprus, where violence against the Turkish population by EOKA, a Greek Cypriot terrorist group rapidly escalated. The US President Lyndon Johnson sent a letter to his Turkish counterpart, Ismet Inonu, on 5 June 1964, subsequent to a notification by the Turkish Government of its intention to launch a military intervention to the island based on her right as guarantor state. The letter was blunt and harsh far beyond diplomatic standards and conveyed the message to Turkish Government that the US might never allow such an operation on the grounds of preventing a possible Turkish – Greek stand-off. Furthermore, the letter stated that NATO might not choose to defend Turkey in the event of a possible Soviet attack on Turkish soil. Referring to the 1947 Turkish – American agreement on American aid to Turkey, the letter warned that using US-supplied military equipment in an intervention to Cyprus would mean direct violation of the terms of the agreement (Güvenç 2010).

The letter had significant effects on Turkish public as well as political circles. The Turkish public perception of United States changed and the alliance had begun to be questioned. The notion of self-sufficiency in foreign policy became more popular and a quest for self-sufficiency in military capability commenced as a reflection of that trend.

The US arms embargo following the Cyprus Operation in 1974 was a major milestone in the quest for domestic defense industry. The embargo inflicted heavy blow to TAFs, especially the Air Force, since this service was more dependent upon provision of US-supplied equipment, parts, and supplies compared to the army or navy. Turk Silahli Kuvvetleri'ni Guclendirme Vakfi (TSKGV; Turkish Armed Forces Foundation) and several defense and aerospace companies including Askeri Elektronik Sanayii Anonim Sirketi (ASELSAN) and Turk Ucak Sanayii (TUSAS) were established in that period with the exclusive aim of achieving self-sufficiency in military capacity, especially in terms of operation. In other words, Turkey or arguably the

TAFs began to seek import substitution policy in defense industry. Lack of technology, industrial infrastructure, and qualified human resources were main challenges. License production method was adopted to develop the necessary technology base, human resources, and expertise. In that period F-16 fighter jets, AIFV armored vehicles, and radio systems were manufactured under license.

It should be noted that, starting from the early 1980s, the number of joint ventures in the defense sector grew rapidly. Most of these joint ventures were formed by local contractors mainly from construction sector and their international partners, including FMC Nurol Savunma Sanayii (FNSS), TUSAS Aircraft Industries (TAI), and MIKES. This trend of import substitution through private initiatives as personally promoted by the then prime minister Turgut Ozal, continued for at least a decade. Starting from the late-1990s, the wind changed again with the dominance of TSKGV affiliated companies designated as prime contractors, leading the course of the sector.

From a wider perspective, the short history of the Turkish defense sector can be considered a typical example of starting with good plans and consistently failing to follow them, as Kurc (forthcoming) points out. One of the main reasons for this problem can be claimed as the lack of coordination and communication between the civilian and military bureaucracy at almost all levels of national security and defense industry policies. Lack of a robust and long-term industrial policy has also been manifest in the form of increased dependency on foreign suppliers as regards critical subsystems and technologies being used in indigenous platform and system development programs. This vicious cycle has produced certain setbacks such as re-importation and exposure to political, commercial, and industrial risks. Kurc precisely identifies this major complication by stating that the external competency has not decreased, but changed its characteristics. He claims that the Turkish Government as well as the sector itself pursues a strategy that deepens international cooperation and collaboration to increase mutual dependency, rather than promoting self-sufficiency. This debate, joined with the indicator of the percentage of domestically manufactured products in the TAF inventory is still ongoing within the sector in Turkey.

Defense strategy and procurement planning system in Turkey

After joining NATO, Turkey fully integrated its national security and defense mechanism to the alliance. The primary threat was the Soviet Union and the Warsaw Pact and therefore the military posture was entirely built upon to meet this threat, with the doctrine, planning, training, procurement, and sustainment procedures heavily depending on NATO and particularly the United States.

The Turkish Army, Navy, and Air Force inventories composed almost exclusively of surplus US hardware and platforms. As an example, Turkish Air Force (TurAF) has never operated any combat aircraft designed by a country other than the United States. Even the training and transport aircraft came from United States with one single exception of German C-160 Transalls in 1971.

Sayan (2009) underlines in his thesis that, the Law 1324 of 1970 provided the very basis of the current defense planning and procurement system. The Law prescribed the responsibilities of Turkish General Staff (TGS) in defense planning and procurement management. Similarly, the Law 1325 of 1971 set the responsibilities of Ministry of National Defense (MoND) for coordination and cooperation with TGS in the procurement processes. Law 1325 clearly states that MoND is responsible of procuring the required hardware, products, and services as well as managing national arms industry activities.

The legal framework that provided TGS with the responsibility of defining, planning, and conducting policy-making activities as regards requirements includes sub-procedures (Sayan 2009).

The first phase of the aforementioned activities is the TUMAS (Turkiye'nin Milli Askeri Stratejisi – National Military Strategy of Turkey) document, which sets the general framework for the military strategic planning and threat analysis of Turkey. While TUMAS is considered the basis for the military's capability building requirements and forecasts. The Concept-Based Requirements System (CBRS) defines requirements accordingly.

The CBRS is developed to meet the requirements of US Training and Doctrine Command (TRADOC) for requirements management. CBRS is implemented as a backbone, connecting Doctrine, Organization, Training, Leadership, Materiel and Soldiers (DOTLMS) level requirements. The core of this system is a forecast of concepts of warfighting in the foreseeable future. According to Weber (2007), CBRS is an ideal system for known threats and a symmetrical threat environment, such as the cold war period.

The following planning phase is the preparation of Strategic Targets Plan (SHP) document, based on the TUMAS document and Operational Requirements Plan (ORP). SHP is the principal guideline to the OYTEP (On Yillik Tedarik Plani – the Ten-Year Procurement Plan). Preparation, prioritization, and budgeting of programs are carried out as per the OYTEP. This process is concluded by the preparation of Project Definition Documents (PDD). A PDD defines what type of product or service is going to be procured, as well as the general requirements, timeframe, and expectations.

The release of PDD effectively starts the procurement project, through two main channels: MoND and Savunma Sanayii Mustesarligi (SSM; Undersecretariat for Defense Industries). The project is mostly administered by SSM in case the procurement program involves in the contribution of local industry in terms of research and development (R&D) or envisaged as a production under license or joint development. Direct procurement programs are usually handled by MoND, upon authorization by the Council of Ministers. The Savunma Sanayii Icra Komitesi (SSIK; Defense Industry Executive Committee) authorizes SSM to commence the programs (Savunma Sanayii Mustesarligi 2015).

The above process in its entirety has *top secret* level security clearance and the main product of it, the PDD is a classified document. Military bureaucracy undertakes preparation of all documents and plans from TUMAS to PDD. At least in theory, government oversight is required at each step, although there is lack of a feedback mechanism or communication and coordination mechanisms in preparation of these plans and strategic documents. In line with the basic principles of CBRS approach, the main aim of the defense procurement planning cycle is to meet mainly symmetric, conventional threats. Furthermore, according to Romero (1988), the CBRS system is notorious for its inability to adapt to rapidly changing threat environment.

A closer look at this mechanism reveals several challenges and setbacks, when compared to the threat and security environment prevailing in the post-cold war era:

(i) For defense hardware, the time period from the start of requirement definition phase to acquisition usually exceeds 10 years. Adding the service and retirement phases, the overall time interval for most of the programs is around 20 years or more. Such a policy-making cycle may meet the requirements of armed forces facing a symmetrical, static threats. However, Renz and Smith (2016) claim that this cycle fails to adapt to rapidly changing geopolitical environment, asymmetrical threats and new generation warfare concepts such as low intensity conflicts or "Hybrid Warfare."

The Baris Kartali (Peace Eagle) project is an illustrative program at point, to have gone over the critical 20-year milestone. Started in 1996, the project called for direct procurement of eight airborne early warning and command & control (AEW&C) aircraft for the TurAF. SSM issued a Request for Proposal (RfP) in June 1998. Boeing, Northrop Grumman, Lockheed Martin and Raytheon – IAI submitted their bids in December the same year. SSIK selected Boeing's proposal as winner in November 2000 and the $1.5 billion contract for four AEW&C aircraft was signed in June 2002 (Sünnetçi 2013). The project saw significant delays due to problems in the development and integration of the main sensor system of the aircraft. The first aircraft, designated as E-7T, made its maiden flight in September 2007 and entered into service with the TurAF in January 2014. It was only May 2016 that the fleet reached full operational capability (FOC), marking an end to a 20-year saga (kokpit.aero 2016).

(ii) The military bureaucracy executes the national defense policy cycle and procurement planning activities. It is questionable whether the economic, commercial, cultural, sociological, etc. aspects of national defense and security are taken into comprehensive consideration and included in the analyses throughout the planning and program preparation phase.

The Long-Range Air and Missile Defense System (LORAMIDS) program is a typical case where defense planning and procurement mechanism in Turkey simply failed to adopt an interdisciplinary approach to utilize broad field of view.

Accordingly, the First Gulf War of 1991 made the requirement for a long-range high-altitude missile defense system evident, when Iraq used its arsenal of Scud ballistic missiles against targets in Israel and Saudi Arabia. Turkey's existing strategic air defense system was designed to counter Soviet strategic bomber fleets in the event of a conflict between the two blocs. Therefore, the backbone of the air defense structure was composed of interceptor aircraft and Nike Hercules air defense missiles supplied by US and NATO.

The on and off procurement attempts throughout the 1990s and 2000s did not produce any tacit results. Finally, SSIK launched a direct procurement tender in June 2006. The RfP called for four batteries plus four more options with a minimum range of 120 km. The TurAF had an extensive requirement list of performance criteria and specifications. Raytheon – Lockheed Martin partnership from United States (PATRIOT PAC2 and PAC3), Rosoboronexport from Russia (Antei 2500), CPMIEC from China (FT-2000), and Franco-Italian EuroSAM (SAMP-T) submitted their bids.

The lengthy evaluation period concluded with the SSIK meeting in September 2013 (Savunma Sanayii Mustesarligi 2013). The selection of the Chinese system was a surprise for many observers. The subsequent period saw heated discussions and exchange of messages between Turkey and her NATO allies. The reaction of NATO and especially United States was strong. Main arguments of the criticism for the decision were focused on the integration with the rest of NATO's air defense structure, information and operation security, and Turkey's standing as an ally.

Additionally, the selection decision alone caused a serious backlash for the Turkish defense industry. A number of major Turkish Defense R&D programs reportedly began suffering delays due to delays in export licenses and export authorization of critical subsystems and equipment. The main reason for this was reportedly to prevent access to critical technologies and know-how by China, after the start of a possible cooperation between the two countries.

Contract negotiations with the Chinese company lasted for two years and finally SSIK canceled the project in November 2015, to be followed by a new project to develop similar systems locally.

Undersecretary of SSM, Ismail Demir soon revealed that the selection of the Chinese system was completely based on technical grounds, i.e. by comparing the performance of the system against TurAF technical requirements. Demir, speaking at a panel on strategic air defense roadmap in Ankara shortly before the SSIK decision, admitted that political, industrial and strategic parameters were not incorporated into the evaluation process (Mevlütoğlu 2015).

(iii) There is a gap or lack of healthy communication and coordination between the civilian and military bureaucracy. One typical example to this gap is the existence of an R&D department in the ranks of both MoND and SSM (Ministry of National Defense 2015). Both departments prepare, manage, and coordinate defense-related R&D activities. Furthermore, the said institutions do not participate in each other's R&D planning and project management panels, further complicating the issue of coordinating the defense-related R&D in Turkey. TGS has openly criticized delays and budget overruns in projects managed by SSM. Ismail Demir, Undersecretary for Defense Industries on the other hand, replied with the argument that TGS has been placing too much emphasis on direct procurement, which creates the risk of negatively effecting the development of defense industry (Dunya 2016).

The mistrust and lack of coordination between the armed forces and civilian policy-makers has marked the course of Turkish defense industry from the very early stages. One interesting example is the trainer and light attack aircraft project for the TurAF in early 1970s. As Kurc mentions, the project involved competition by American Northrop (F-5F), Italian Aermacchi (MB339), British Hawker Siddeley (Hawk), and German Dornier (Alpha Jet) (Kurc, forthcoming). The TurAF, which preferred Hawk aircraft based on purely performance characteristics, exploited rivalries and disagreements among the partner parties of the coalition government and applied pressure on the MoND to prevent TUSAS from signing contract with Aermacchi, which was preferred on technical and commercial grounds (Mevlütoğlu, 2016). The program has subsequently been canceled altogether.

(iv) The defense sector in Turkey follows a strict import substitution-oriented industrial policy. Doing so, a "top-down" approach, a platform-based technology policy is adopted for procurement through local development.

Embodied in the motto "Kendi Uçağını Kendin Yap" ("Make your own airplane"), Turkish defense industry is structured to meet virtually all requirements of the TAF from domestic sources. As an armed forces organization, TAF's requirements vary from combat aircraft to communication systems, from warships to rockets, etc. This means that the Turkish defense & aerospace industry had to be established to provide all types of products and services that a large armed force like TAF would need. This motivation is apparent in the number and types of current projects undertaken by the SSM: the range of projects that local companies are prime contractors varies from helicopters to unmanned aerial vehicles (UAV), from land vehicles to the full range of C4ISR systems (Savunma Sanayii Mustesarligi 2016a).

(v) The process of requirements definition is designed for the needs of the cold war era. This process is unidirectional and is almost completely closed to feedback from the defense sector or research community. Furthermore, it is executed around a tactics-based perspective. Technological, social, economic, or cultural aspects of force building, modernization, and procurement are broadly neglected, where operational doctrine is the decisive factor for setting the qualities and quantity of systems regarding the requirements definition. A typical requirements definition process takes three to five years to deliver an input for the procurement process. Such an inflexible and slow decision-making cycle is not capable of adapting to rapidly changing, dynamic nature of today's security environment.

Another aspect of this issue is the problem known as the "requirements creep." Also known as "scope creep," it is defined as loss of controlled changes and modifications to requirements in a project, mostly in a continuous manner (Lewis 2002). The point where requirements are frozen and where the design, development phase begins is lost. This is the case in virtually all programs in Turkish defense industry, especially when the main contractor is a local company. The end-user constantly applies modifications to requirements, even after certain program management milestones such as Critical Design Review (CDR) where all requirement definition activities are expected to have been finalized and frozen. This is a major factor for budget and schedule overruns in local development and production programs such as T129 ATAK attack helicopter and Anka unmanned aerial vehicle (UAV).

In the case of Anka UAV program, TUSAS signed a contract for development of medium altitude long endurance (MALE) class UAV in December 2004 (Sünnetçi 2015). The contract covered development and testing of one UAV system together with ground support equipment. The first prototype, designated Anka Block A made its maiden flight in December 2010. Anka A carried an electro optical payload. Anka Block B, a version carrying a synthetic aperture radar (SAR) in addition to electro optical camera made its first flight in 2015 (Kahvecioglu and Oktal 2014).

Meanwhile, TUSAS signed a contract with SSM in 2013 for serial production of 10 Anka UAV's, designated Anka S for the Turkish Air Force. Anka S is a completely different design than Anka Block A and Block B, featuring satellite communications (SATCOM) system, a new electro optical payload by ASELSAN, communications relay systems, and advanced ground control system (Kahvecioglu and Oktal 2014). The program saw considerable delays due to failure in freezing technical requirements and design process. The first prototype made its maiden flight in September 2016 and tests are still underway (Bekdil 2016).

(vi) The procurement planning and execution process is implemented without proper priorization among requirements. This defect manifests itself, especially in budget estimation and allocation. There are three main symptoms of this defect:

First of all, budget estimations are prepared almost exclusively by the military, without healthy communication or feedback from civilian bureaucracy. The result of this approach is usually unrealistic cost estimates of procurement programs. Procurement decisions reflect short-term tactical requirements, based almost entirely on quantitative analysis, lacking interdisciplinary perspective. Without adequate input from government and academy, the resultant procurement plan is prone to many revisions in due course.

Second, the 10-year procurement plan, the OYTEP, is usually prepared as a "wish list," rather than an objective, realistic guideline. This handling of the plan results with spreading the already limited financial resources over a large number of ambitious projects (Mevlütoğlu 2016).

Third, because the overall procurement cycle lacks interdisciplinary perspective to assess the threat environment and strategic foresight, it usually fails to meet urgent operational requirements. In other words, the system is not capable of establishing balance between long-term local development programs and urgent requirements (Kurc, forthcoming).

Technology management and industrial policy

Bruton (1998) states that government planning and strategy capacity is especially important in import substitution policies. He says that the governments of developing countries are staffed by mostly incompetent people, which resulted in inadequate or false policies and market failures. Such government mechanisms are themselves incapable of making protective or corrective decisions. In such an environment, the imports, foreign technology licenses, and investment permits become more advantageous for those who could afford.

Bruton also underlines the relationship between import substitution and learning process and knowledge accumulation. Industrial development requires a force multiplier in the form of technology, which is only possible through an increase in the local stock of knowledge. Import substitution implementation may be detrimental to this capacity, providing an easy life for local industry (Bruton 1998). This is especially the case with the aerospace sector.

The share of exports in the total revenues generated by the Turkish defense & aerospace industry shows the focus on import substitution, exports, though rising, have little weight. The sector is dependent on the demands of local customers, which is primarily the TAF followed by other government agencies. With nearly 60% coming from offset obligations, the exports constitute around 25–27% of the total revenues (SASAD 2013).

Technology management policies of the defense& aerospace sector is coordinated by SSM, through Defense Industry Technology Management Strategy (Teknoloji Yönetim Stratejisi) document, the latest version of which covers the period of 2011 and 2016. The strategic targets outlined in this document are as follows (Savunma Sanayii Mustesarligi 2011):

(1) Establishment of necessary technological infrastructure to meet the requirements of the TAFs
(2) Establishment of an effective university – industry cooperation mechanism
(3) Application of Technology Acquisition Obligation (Teknoloji Kazanım Yükümlülüğü) policies at every defense procurement programs.
(4) Coordination of technology development activities at the sectorial level.
(5) Coordination of and participation to international technology development and R&D activities.
(6) Design of incentive programs to support defense-related R&D.

As seen, import substitution-based policies are clearly evident in the technology management strategy, with export-related activities are of secondary importance.

This framework is developed based on the operational and systems/platform level requirements of the TAFs. In other words, the primary output of this procurement framework is a platform, neither a solution nor a capability. This may be considered as the primary reason behind the platform-centric development course of Turkish defense industry.

Gaining momentum in the late 1990s, the local defense industry base produced many important platforms such as Anka unmanned aerial vehicle system, ATAK T129 attack helicopter, MilGem warship, and Altay main battle tank. Those are all major combat platforms with significant local design and technology output, yet they are dependent on foreign technology, systems and know – how on many critical items such as the engine, transmission, satellite communications, sensors, and electronics hardware (Star, 2013). This pattern is reminiscent of a "top – down" approach, i.e. producing the platform first and indigenization of critical subsystems and units later.

The advantage of this technology management paradigm is associated with a relatively short development phase and the opportunity of adopting a proven foreign-originated design/solution and modifying it to local requirements. On the other hand, the product will be dependent on constant flow of foreign critical subsystems for manufacturing, operation, and exports, until "true" self-sufficiency can be achieved. From this perspective, the Turkey's roadmap for achieving defense self-sufficiency may function contrary to its goal: the industry has begun producing indigenous products; nevertheless it became even more dependent on foreign inputs to sustain the local capacity to manufacture them.

One recent example for this dilemma is the engine issue with the Firtina self-propelled howitzer system. The Firtina was selected by Azerbaijan to equip its artillery units. However, this export sale opportunity was shelved because Germany denied permission for export license of the engine (İsmailov 2015). Industrialization and achieving self-sufficiency in subsystem and critical technologies require robust, long-term technology management strategies, which may turn out to be more difficult especially in the developing countries.

According to SASAD (2013) data, there are more than 33,000 employees working in the Turkish defense sector. Thirty six percent of this workforce is engineers and 12% is academicians. Therefore, around 15,000 personnel are working in research & development (R&D) and manufacture projects. The total revenue of the sector for the same year is $5.076 billion (SASAD 2013). This means the total revenue per employee is around $153,000.

For comparison, Swedish defense sector employed around 15,000 personnel in 2012 with a revenue of around $4.3 billion (Swedish Security and Defence Industry Association 2013). The total revenue per employee is around $287,000, almost double of the same indicator for Turkey.

One of the two Turkish companies in the DefenseNews Top 100 list, ASELSAN employs around 5,000 people, which can be considered as quite low compared with other entries in the list (Mevlütoğlu 2016). Total revenue per employee for 2015 is around $190,000, which is significantly low compared to other companies with the same revenue range or active in the same solution areas.

The above data underlines several issues in the human resources aspect of Turkish defense industry:

(i) *Effectivity*: Heavy focus on import substitution has created a negative effect on the competitive power of the sector, especially on the major contractors. The entire sector is dependent on local market, which is TAFs and security agencies, on revenues. SASAD as the main industrial association for example, repeatedly underlines the necessity of growth of domestic market for sustainability of the defense industry (Mevlütoğlu 2015). The sector gives the priority to meeting domestic customer's requirements, R&D or innovation are handled as means of developing solutions for the local market. There is inadequate motivation in place for increasing effectiveness, competitiveness, or innovation within this supply – demand balance. Furthermore, with the exception of naval shipbuilding and land vehicle sectors, competition among companies is almost nonexistent: most of the program contracts are awarded to designated contractors which are TSKGV companies. This exclusive position inherently erodes stimulation for innovation, which eventually affects the workforce employed in these companies.

(ii) *Quantity*: Turkish defense industry today shoulders a plethora of programs, from intelligence satellites to warships, precision guided munitions to helicopters, and unmanned aerial vehicles. Such a wide range of complex systems and products require vertical and horizontal expansion of know-how, technology, and experience background supported by a strong academic infrastructure. The sector employs between 33,000 and 35,000 personnel, almost half of which are engineers and R&D people. Compared with the number and content of the large number of development and production projects, most of which are controlled by SSM, this number is critically low.

To overcome this challenge, SSM runs a program called "Program to Develop Researchers for Defence Industry" (SAYP; Savunma Sanayii Araştırmacı Yetistirme Programi), which is a protocol between universities and defense companies to fund joint research projects and train graduate level researchers for the industry. Several protocols between different universities and companies have been signed (Savunma Sanayii Mustesarligi 2016a).

(iii) *Lack of focus and vertical expertise*: As mentioned above, the Turkish defense industry is engaged in a vast range of programs covering all spectrum of armed forces' requirements. Combined with the limited number of R&D personnel and experienced researchers, the sector is overwhelmed by significant technological barriers. The number of projects and programs per researcher as well as officers within the procurement mechanism is high, resulting in a lack of focus and deficiency for developing expertise. Additionally, the above-mentioned "top-down" approach results in considerable delays in programs, especially in the projects incorporating several subsystems opted for indigenous development for entailing critical technologies.

Conclusion

Having achieved remarkable breakthrough in the last 15 years, the Turkish defense sector seems to have reached to crossroads: current export figures and the rate of increase do not promise a significant growth in the near future. There are several reasons behind this situation: first, the major projects such as Anka UAV, T129 attack helicopter or Altay main battle tank have not matured, i.e. development phases have not been completed and the platforms did not enter service, at least with full operational capabilities. The sector, thus, could not provide a matured platform to the export markets.

Another critical issue besides the lack of completed platform, is the dependence on foreign suppliers in terms of subsystems, equipment, and technologies. This very posture of the industry poses a critical vulnerability, where successful execution of serial production and export of any platform depends on foreign companies and their respective governments. This brings bilateral relations and inter-governmental politics into the equation. To make things more complicated, Turkey's position as a rising defense & aerospace exporter might not be welcome by developed countries with well-established customer bases. These countries may use export licenses as a tool to disrupt the momentum of Turkish defense and aerospace industry. Not surprisingly, Turkish contractors have very strong technological and trade relations with companies from these countries.

R&D and innovation capacity of the sector relies mainly on the requirements of the local market. Combined with import substitution policies in the sector, this can be considered as a weakness in terms of competitiveness in the global market. Local market's demands may not always be consistent with the trends and conditions of the global market and local companies may find it difficult to penetrate in emerging markets. On the other hand, focusing solely on export has the risk of not producing sufficient results, since it is almost impossible to successfully market an aerospace product to international customers when that product has not seen service with the local end-user.

Lack of coordination and communication between military and civilian bureaucracy is a major impediment for successful planning and policy-making. Additionally, the linear policy-making and planning procedure lacks efficient and interdisciplinary feedback mechanisms, i.e. policy design phases are not fed by input from various academic disciplines. In the dynamic and unpredictable threat environment of the twenty-first century, national security and defense posture planning should include inputs from various perspectives such as economy, science & technology management, and sociology. Current system of defense planning is based on quantitative analyses and comparisons on an almost arithmetic base. Such a system has very low response time to changing threats and requirements, thus failing to manage successful procurement programs and supervise local industry.

In conclusion, the potential of the Turkish defense industry has its fate tied to the development of a long-term and robust industrial policy and technology management strategy. The sector is in a trend of steady growth, both in terms of local market and export sales, but further increasing the rate of those would only be possible through more emphasis on R&D, innovation, and sound business development strategies. Achieving successful export figures and developing competitive power are not purely technical issues, but require strong skills in social, economic, and techno-political aspects of the field. Turkish defense sector seemingly started to learn this very fundamental lesson.

Disclosure statement

In accordance with Taylor & Francis policy and my ethical obligation as a researcher, I am reporting that I have no ties to a company that may be affected by the research reported in the enclosed paper.

ORCID

Arda Mevlutoglu http://orcid.org/0000-0001-7443-7836

References

Bekdil, B.E., 2016. *Turkey rushes armed drones after increased ISIS threat* [Online]. Available from: https://www.defensenews.com/story/defense/air-space/2016/05/05/turks-rush-armed-drones-after-increased-isis-threat/83960442/ [Accessed 14 Aug 2016].

Bruton, H., 1998. A reconsideration of import substitution. *Journal of economic literature*, 36 (2), 903–936.

Dunya, 2016. SSM Müsteşarı Demir: *'Acil alım fırtınası ile karşı karşıyayız* [Online]. Available from: https://www.dunya.com/ekonomi/ekonomi-diger/ssm-mustesari-demir-acil-alim-firtinasi-ile-karsi-karsiyayiz-300306 h.htm [Accessed 12 Aug 2016].

Güvenç, S., 2010. ABD Askeri Yardımı Ve Türk Ordusunun Dönüşümü: 1942–1960. *In*: İ. Akça and E. B. Paker, eds. *Türkiye'de Ordu, Devlet Ve Güvenlik Siyaseti*. İstanbul: İstanbul Bilgi Üniversitesi Yayınları, 255–284.

İsmailov, E., 2015. *Güney Kafkasya'da Silahlanma Yarışı* [Armament Race in the South Caucasus]. BilgeSAM Analiz, Issue 1179.

Kahvecioglu, S. and Oktal, H., 2014. Turkish UAV capabilities as a new competitor in the market. *International journal of intelligent unmanned systems*, 2 (3), 183–191.

kokpit.aero, 2016. *HİK uçakları 'tam harekât yeteneğine' kavuştu* [Online]. Available from: https://www.kokpit.aero/hik-ucaklari-operasyonel?filter_name=bar%C4%B1%C5%9F%20kartal%C4%B1 [Accessed 6 Aug 2016].

Kurc, C., Forthcoming. *Between defense autarky and dependency: the dynamics of turkish defense industrialization*. Defense Studies (Special Edition).

Lewis, J., 2002. *Fundamentals of project management*. New York, NY: AMACOM.

Mevlütoğlu, A., 2015. *Yüksek İrtifa, Uzun Menzil, Karışık Kafalar – III: Türkiye Nike Hercules'ü Seçti* [Online]. Available from: https://www.siyahgribeyaz.com/2015/11/yuksek-irtifa-uzun-menzil-karsk-kafalar.html [Accessed 6 Aug 2016].

Mevlütoğlu, A., 2016. *Türkiye'nin Son Anda İptal Edilen Eğitim – Taarruz Uçağı Projesi* [Online]. Available from: https://www.siyahgribeyaz.com/2016/02/turkiyenin-son-anda-iptal-edilen-egitim.html [Accessed 16 Aug 2016].

Ministry of National Defense, 2015. MoND Department of R&D [Online]. Available from: https://www.msb.gov.tr/Arge/icerik/mill-savunma-arge-faaliyetleri [Accessed 14 Aug 2016].

Renz, B. and Smith, H., 2016. *Russia and hybrid warfare – going beyond the label* [Online]. Available from: https://www.helsinki.fi/aleksanteri/english/publications/presentations/papers/ap_1_2016.pdf [Accessed 16 Aug 2016].

Romero, P., 1988. *Developing and assessing concepts for future U.S. army warfighting: a progress report*. Santa Monica: RAND.

SASAD, 2013. *Savunma ve Havacılık Sanayii Performans Raporu 2013* [Online]. Available from: https://www.sasad.org.tr/uploaded//SASAD-PERFORMANS-RAPORU-2013-_4_4-son.pdf [Accessed 14 Aug 2016].

Savunma Sanayii Mustesarligi, 2011. *SSM Teknoloji Yönetim Stratejisi Dokümanı 2011–2016*. Ankara: SSM.

Savunma Sanayii Mustesarligi, 2013. SSIK press statement [Online]. Available from: https://www.ssm.gov.tr/anasayfa/hizli/duyurular/PressReleases/arsiv/2013/Sayfalar/20130926_SSIK.aspx [Accessed 8 Aug 2016].

Savunma Sanayii Mustesarligi, 2015. *Tedarik Yönetimi*[Online]. Available from: https://sanayilesme.ssm.gov.tr/SSM/Documents/SP/sto.html [Accessed 5 Aug 2016].

Savunma Sanayii Mustesarligi, 2016a. *SAYP* [Online]. Available from: https://www.ssm.gov.tr/anasayfa/savunmaSanayiimiz/Sayfalar/SAYP.aspx, [Accessed 8 Aug 2016].

Savunma Sanayii Mustesarligi. 2016b. *Turkish defense industry – historical development* [Online]. Available from: https://www.ssm.gov.tr/home/tdi/Sayfalar/historical.aspx [Accessed 29 May 2017].

Sayan, Z., 2009. *The position of contracting officership in US armed forces' acquisition activities and organizational alteration recommend on adaptation of Turkish Armed Forces acquisition system*. Thesis (Masters). Ankara.

Star, 2013. *Şimdi sıra 'milli motor'da* [Online]. Available from: https://haber.star.com.tr/guncel/simdi-sira-milli-motorda/haber-799227 [Accessed 8 Jun 2015].

Sünnetçi, İ., 2013. *Türkiye'nin Savunmasında Gerçek Bir Güç Çarpanı: HİK Uçağı*. Savunma ve Havacılık, p. 32.

Sünnetçi, İ., 2015. *Türkiye'de Hizmetteki İHA Sistemlerine Bir Bakış*. Savunma ve Havacılık, Issue 169, p. 133.

Swedish Security and Defence Industry Association, 2013. *Facts 2012–2013*. Stockholm: SOFF.

Weber, J., 2007. *Handbook of military administration*. Boca Raton, FL: CRC Press.

The Arab Gulf defense pivot: Defense industrial policy in a changing geostrategic context

Heiko Borchert

ABSTRACT

Arab Gulf countries have been trying to set up a local defense industrial base for decades. Recently, these efforts have become much more serious due to a changing geostrategic context, local transformation, and the striving for a more active foreign policy role beyond the region. Today's Arab Gulf defense pivot rests on four pillars: broadening the traditional defense-supplier base; establishing indigenous defense industries; setting up a defense-industrial network within and beyond the region; enlarging foreign policy clout by way of defense exports, defense-material donations, and third-country defense funding. Despite progress, challenges regarding strategic and financial stability and local skill sets remain.

Introduction

Bahrain, Kuwait, Oman, Qatar, Saudi Arabia, and the United Arab Emirates (UAE)—the six nations that together constitute the Gulf Cooperation Council (GCC)—are important defense markets. From 1990 to 2016, nations globally spent around US$676 billion on arms imports, with the GCC nations accounting for roughly 11 percent.[1] The purchasing power of the GCC nations is only half the story, however. As this article argues, the GCC nations have embarked on ambitious policies to establish local defense industries that are about to compete with established defense suppliers for access to GCC markets and foreign export markets.

Ambitious GCC actors like Qatar, Saudi Arabia, and the UAE believe in hard power as an instrument to drive an increasingly assertive foreign policy, establish strategic relationships with extra-regional partners, and advance the local technology base. Setting up an indigenous defense industry is the means to achieve all of these goals. In addition, the Qatar crisis underlined the vulnerability of smaller GCC nations and the need for robust defense. As a consequence, the momentum to establish local defense industries is growing stronger. Overall, defense industries serve the political goal to deepen and advance techno-industrial relations with partners that ambitious GCC nations will try to leverage to their benefit.

Although legitimate given the very complex security environment that surrounds the GCC nations, the defense-industrial boost creates different problems. First, an increasing zero-sum mentality among key leaders heats up competition. This is likely to deepen differences among the GCC nations that operate at different levels of defense industrial maturity and could produce potentially destabilizing effects, such as the procurement of weapon systems that could be used against neighbors, the export of local conflicts to other regions, and attempts to create mutually exclusive defense partnerships. In addition, ambitious GCC defense actors are increasingly willing to adopt "reverse divide and conquer" policies to offset defense suppliers against each other, which entails the risk of turning Arab Gulf foreign relations sour.

Second, Qatar, Saudi Arabia, and the UAE follow remarkably similar approaches, as they use the same policy instruments, cooperate with the same partners, and focus on similar market segments and technologies. Irrespective of the amount of money these countries are willing to spend on defense, this raises the question of whether their strategies are sustainable for maintaining local defense industries as attractive partners for others. This is all the more important, as the narrative about the role of local defense industries in economic transformation and diversification is Janus-faced. The costs of transferring technologies and skills from foreign partners to local entities are hardly addressed. Defense companies create local economic value and generate jobs, but at a limited scale. At the same time, the need to integrate commercial technologies in the defense environment is growing rapidly. This requires local integration skills that have yet to emerge. Thus, there is a serious risk that current endeavors could backfire, thereby undermining regional stability and the credibility of local rulers that support the local defense industry.

This article develops these arguments in six steps. First, it provides an overview of the main drivers that shape local defense industrial ambitions. Second, the article briefly discusses the challenging search for partners that provide ambitious GCC nations with political clout and are ready to share skills and technologies. The third section looks at key defense industrial policy instruments, such as technology transfer, strategic investments, and investment funds, as well as defense exports, material donations, and third-country funding. Section four argues that diversification of defense material is challenging but can also open up new opportunities for GCC defense industries if they are able to master systems integration. Section five speculates on the likely impact of Arab Gulf defense-industrial ambitions on foreign relations. The conclusion focuses on four aspects that Arab Gulf industrial leaders should address to make their ambitions more sustainable.

Drivers to set up an Arab Gulf defense industry

The drivers that fuel Arab Gulf defense-industrial ambitions are multifold. As Figure 1 shows, the key impulse for robust indigenous defense industrial capacities stems from the conviction of the region's most ambitious players that a more active foreign policy is needed to solve problems in the region and beyond. A neorealist understanding of politics, in which a zero-sum logic of international relations prevails, characterizes the worldview of key leaders such as Mohammed bin Zayed Al-Nahyan (MbZ), crown prince and deputy supreme commander of the UAE armed forces, and Mohammed bin Salman (MbS), crown prince, first deputy prime minister and minister of defense of Saudi Arabia.[2] This translates into an assertive foreign policy underwritten by military power. The defense industry is considered to be a strategic asset that helps advance military capabilities and promote foreign policy ambitions.

An active and powerful foreign policy responds to the challenging regional security environment. Five aspects define the regional conflict picture: first, there is the unresolved question as to which extra-regional partner is best suited to help stabilize the region, as Washington's policy vis-à-vis the GCC is fuzzy. Second, the Qatar crisis, which emerged in summer 2017 over Qatar's alleged proximity to Iran and its sponsorship of international terrorism, underlined the vulnerability of some of the GCC members and has effectively brought GCC-wide cooperation to a halt. This is of particular relevance for military cooperation, which had gained steam until then and showed promising sings of delivering tangible results on long-held plans like the Peninsula Shield Force and the establishment of new maritime components. Third, the Qatar crisis is the tip of a proxy conflict between Saudi Arabia and Iran over regional hegemony that is supplemented by legacy problems that create bilateral rifts among all GCC members. Fourth, domestic conflicts emanate from the rise of anti-establishment opposition forces that demand broader political participation. Demographic challenges that will significantly increase the financial burden of all GCC

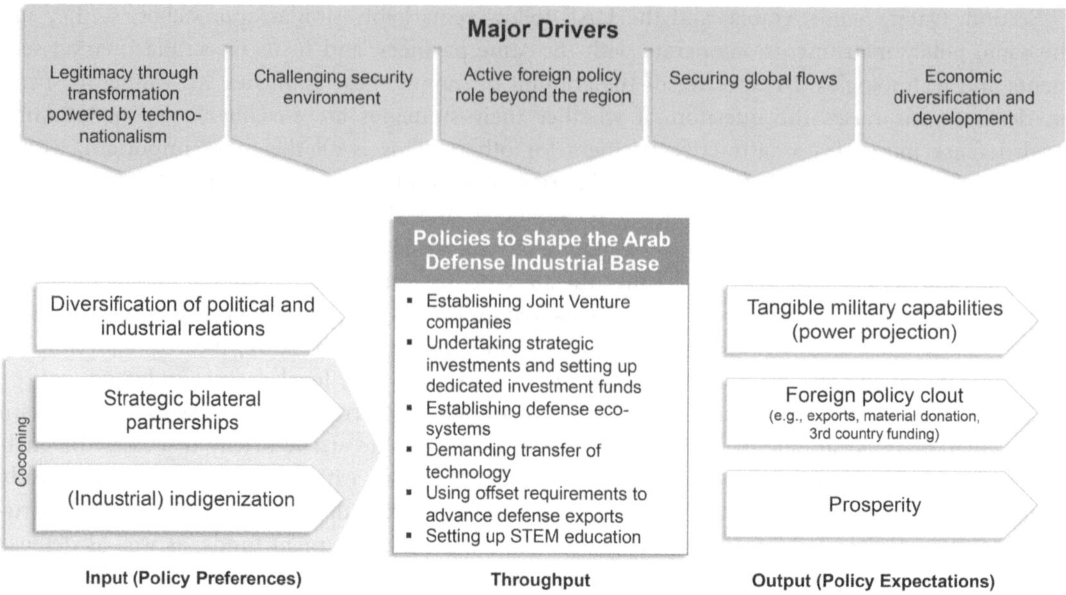

Figure 1. Arab Gulf defense industrial model.

nations reinforce domestic challenges. Finally, various threats such as piracy, smuggling, illegal money laundering, and cyber attacks create additional strain.[3]

Risks that affect the GCC nations' proper integration into the global economy are becoming more important, as the six are increasingly aware that global connectivity is a key currency in the twenty-first century. Thus, they strive to integrate local economies into global supply chains. Already today, the Asia-Pacific region plays the most important role as the GCC's pivotal energy partner. GCC nations learn that investments in the security of global flows of goods, capital, services, and information are important to ensure connectivity, which in turn spurs local and regional prosperity through trade and foreign direct investment. This also underlines the importance of economic diversification and development in light of global energy markets that are transforming due to the gradual shift from fossil to renewable energy. Changes in energy consumption patterns—with lower long-term energy demand in Europe but growing energy consumption in the Middle East and in the Asia-Pacific region—reinforce the GCC's political and economic pivot to the East. This comes with increasing demands for military power projection into areas of strategic interest beyond the Arabian Peninsula, such as Northern Africa and Eastern Africa, which are essential for providing food security for Arab Gulf nations. Trade and energy relations with partners in the Asia-Pacific region increase the relevance of blue-water naval capabilities to secure the sea lanes of communication.[4]

Spurred by the need to develop new economic models for long-term societal sustainability, GCC ruling elites engage in identity, nation, and citizen building. Innovation in general plays a key role, as it underlines the nations' readiness to embark on societal transformation. Command of cutting-edge technology is of particular importance, as it bestows legitimacy on the ruling elites who portray themselves as smart stewards that are able to steer the respective nations into the twenty-first century, where high technology exemplifies economic diversification and promises alternative sources of economic growth. Establishing an indigenous defense industrial base therefore serves different purposes: Local defense industries epitomize societal transformation from the age of "oil for security" to the dawn of a new era in which the local defense industrial base is considered to be an element of national pride and identity that furthers the GCC nations' international esteem.[5] The fact that the defense industry is central to the leading rulers' worldview and to societal transformation explains why a lot of political attention is devoted to this policy area. But it also makes clear that failure to deliver tangible results will backfire—not only on the industry but also on the elite that supports it.

Who wants to partner for independence?

The core rationale for an indigenous defense industrial base is straightforward: If you want to conduct active foreign policy with a military footprint, you must be able to use the respective defense systems whenever and wherever needed. Traditionally, defense systems provided by foreign partners come with strings attached that limit their use and encroach upon the recipient's foreign policy leeway. The ultimate goal, therefore, is to overcome these limitations by establishing an indigenous defense technological and industrial base that is largely self-sufficient.

Against this background, reducing dependence on foreign suppliers by diversifying sources of supply and ramping up indigenous defense-industrial capacities is key to designing future relationships with foreign defense partners. GCC nations like the UAE, Saudi Arabia, and Qatar have set up a two-pronged approach. First, they step up demands for the transfer and localization of skills and technology that partners must meet in order to establish the foundation of an indigenous defense technological and industrial base. Saudi King Salman left no doubt in April 2017 that any future strategic arms deal with Saudi Arabia would be contingent upon localizing advanced technology in the kingdom. The localization ratio should reach 50 percent for deals in excess of US$500 million. This goes hand in hand with the ambitious Vision 2030 to localize 50 percent of all military spending by 2030.[6] Second, the UAE and Saudi Arabia in particular start manufacturing their own defense goods, thereby striving to advance cooperation among themselves in order to further reduce dependence on outside partners, as will be discussed later.

The challenge, however, is twofold. Reference to defense-industrial independence is ubiquitous, but the concept remains opaque. Ultimately, conceptual and technological independence in the defense sector is hard to achieve. Some authors even argue that true independence is detrimental to producing cutting-edge defense material that depends on closely integrated supply chains involving partners from many different countries.[7] This argument notwithstanding, design and concepts, research and development, production and integration, maintenance, repair, and overhaul, as well as distribution, would all have to be mastered indigenously to achieve full defense-industrial independence. Until today, however, it remains unclear which levels of self-sufficiency the leading Arab Gulf defense industry players have achieved in each of these areas of work.

In addition, not all partners are ready to share skills and technology, because their own competitive advantages depend on them. Thus, the search for partners that are ready to share will broaden the supplier base and change client-supplier relationships.[8] This fits into the overall foreign policy drive of Saudi Arabia, Qatar, and the UAE. But the question is if those countries that are ready to share skills and technology are suitable to provide enough foreign policy leverage for ambitious GCC nations to shape the international agenda. Doubts are justified:

- Ukraine, Belarus, Serbia, and Bulgaria are important partners to modernize former Soviet equipment in use with GCC countries and co-develop and supply unmanned aerial vehicles (UAV), electronic warfare systems, and transport planes. These countries also provide investment opportunities and contribute to GCC food security, but their ability to advance GCC foreign policy clout is limited.
- Turkey is different, as the country has become a strategic partner for Saudi Arabia, Qatar, and the UAE in segments like land systems, naval systems, missiles, UAV, and defense electronics. Ankara also engages in defense research and provides advice on armed-forces modernization. But despite the fact that Saudi Arabia and the UAE have invested heavily in the Turkish

defense industry, Turkey's support for Qatar is affecting its role in the region, as will be discussed below.

- Asia-Pacific nations are on the rise as potential defense partners. For example, prior to visiting Tokyo in September 2016, MbS, who was then Saudi deputy crown prince, had expressed increasing interest in naval shipbuilding cooperation with Japan. Since then, reports indicate Saudi Arabia's growing interest in exploring possibilities to localize Japanese technology in the fields of aerospace, communications, and sensors technologies.[9] But Japan's lack of substantial international defense cooperation due to decades of self-restraint questions the plausibility of this idea. China's position is similar. Although there can be no doubt that China's strategic relevance on the Arabian Peninsula is growing—not least because of the One Belt, One Road program that is to connect Arab Gulf harbors with China's maritime silk road—it is far from sure that China would be willing to provide the security guarantees that the United States, France, and the UK had granted in the past. So far, China "perceives the Middle East as a 'market.' Its military force has therefore kept a low profile … to safeguard its geo-economic profile."[10]
- Russia, by contrast, has put herself back on a high-profile track in the region.[11] Moscow is again in high esteem as an energy and defense industrial partner. So far, Russia has agreed to transfer specific technologies (Table 1), but Moscow is far from willing to share everything, as current negotiations for the S-400 air defense system illustrate.[12] As Moscow and Teheran grow closer,[13] the Saudi and Emirati attempt to reach out to Moscow in order to balance Washington is most delicate. Russia is aware that, for example, Abu Dhabi's interest in the Su-35 fighter jets could just be used as leverage in negotiations to purchase U.S.-built F-35 Joint Strike Fighters.[14]

Arab Gulf defense-industrial policy: Key instruments

Talking about defense-industrial policy in the GCC is a bit of a misnomer, as none of the nations has a full-fledged policy in the proper sense. Truly thought-through priorities in terms of long-term capability requirements and the respective defense-industrial capacities needed for local research and development, production, and maintenance have yet to emerge. Instead, defense-industrial policy results from a combination of different instruments that evolve around significant procurement projects underpinned by broad ideas about long-term defense-industrial ambitions.

Six priority instruments can be identified. First, the transfer of technology from foreign partners to local entities is indispensable to build up a local defense-industrial base. Second, technology transfer most often comes via joint ventures with local partners that help advance knowledge and skill diffusion. Together these two elements help design defense-related ecosystems involving industry, research, and education partners as the third instrument. Fourth, advancing local skills requires increased investment in STEM[15] education, which is provided by local universities and in cooperation with international defense-industrial partners that engage in setting up tailored training and education programs. Fifth, these programs are part of broader offset requirements that come with additional demands for local economic return, for example via investments in defense-industrial capacities or other industry sectors. Sixth, strategic investments in defense-industrial capacities abroad and dedicated funds can be leveraged to advance the local defense-industrial portfolio.

The following analysis will focus on the transfer of technology and strategic investments as the primary defense-industrial policy instruments. In line with political ambitions, Saudi Arabia, Qatar, and the UAE increasingly understand defense-industrial policy as a means to advance foreign policy goals. This trend is important to understand, as it furthers preferential political relations among countries and will be discussed as well.

Table 1. Illustrative examples of demands for defense-related transfer of technology and localization in Saudi Arabia since 2017.

Segment	Transfer of Technology (ToT) or Technology Acquisition Demand	Localization and (Joint) Industrialization Demand
Aircraft	• Lockheed Martin agreed on technology and skills transfer related to Black Hawk purchase	• Local production of unspecified components of Eurofighter components under discussion • TAQNIA-Rockwell Collings joint venture for maintenance, repair and overhaul • Saudi-Boeing joint venture for sustainment services
UAV		• Local Wing Loong UCAV production • Saqr 1 indigenous UAV program by KACST
Satellites		• Cooperation with NASA on localizing satellite-related technology
Vehicles	• Discussions with Russia on ToT related to possible purchase of T-90M main battle tanks • Interest in localizing technologies for military engineering vehicles	• SAMI interest in licensed production of US vehicles • Local production of Bradley Infantry Fighting Vehicles under discussion • General Dynamics agreed to localize vehicles-related design, engineering, manufacturing, and support skills
Vessels	• Demand for ToT related to spare parts and electronics for FREMM frigate • Interest in localizing technologies for survey ships	• Local joint venture with SAMI and Navantia for the Avante 2200 corvette with a focus, among other things, on combat system integration, system engineering, system architecture, and electronics
Missiles and bombs	• Russia agreed on ToT for anti-tank guided missiles and multiple launch rocket systems • Raytheon agreed on missile-related ToT	• Demands for localization of bunker-busting bombs and air-to-ground missiles
Missile defense	• Negotiation on ToT for S-400 air defense system • Discussion with U.S. companies in transferring laser technologies for ballistic missile defense	
Sensors and electronics	• Demands for intelligence surveillance, and reconnaissance technology, command and control, and battle management systems technology • Demands for sensor and (night) vision systems technology in particular from U.S. partners	• Aselsan-TAQNIA joint venture for radar systems, electro-optical technology, and electronic warfare systems • Common electronics industrialization with Portugal under discussion
Cyber		• Localization of unspecified cyber technologies from suppliers in France, the United Kingdom, and the United States under discussion

Source: author's compilation based on various open sources.

Localization and transfer of technology

The UAE has established a very sophisticated approach to skills and technology localization. Traditionally, defense-industrial partnerships to advance technology transfer had been channeled through Tawazun Holding and Mubadala as the main government-led investment entities and Emirates Advanced Investment Groups and International Golden Group as private investment holdings.[16] This led to a much diversified defense-industrial landscape that was hard to control. In response, in 2014 MbZ decided to streamline the structure by bringing most of the established entities under the umbrella of the new Emirates Defence Industries Company (EDIC), which created thorny questions relating to the transfer of assets to EDIC. At the same time, the transition ignited a power game between incumbent players and the new actor with regard to evaluating if and to what extent partners had fulfilled requirements to share technology and advance local capacities.[17]

Localization and transfer of technology helped establish local Emirati defense outfits such as NIMR Automotive, Abu Dhabi Shipbuilding (ADSB), arms producer Caracal, and UAV manufacturers Abu Dhabi Autonomous Systems Investments (ADASI) and ADCOM Systems. But up to today, the degree of indigenous work in relation to foreign contributions is unclear. In this regard, the recent development of the B-250 counter-guerilla aircraft is illuminating. According to *Intelligence Online,* local manufacturer Calidus worked together with Novaer of Brazil on the design. Rockwell Collins and L-3 Technologies (United States) and LIG Nex1 (South Korea) provided components such as optronic pods. In addition, Brazilian and South African engineers and experts at a European subsidiary of Israel's Elbit Systems have been hired to do the integration work.[18]

Saudi Arabia shares the UAE's defense-industrial ambition but lags behind in terms of local expertise. Saudi Arabia's Economic Offset Program was launched in the mid-1980s. The program produced several defense joint ventures that did not yield tangible industrial benefits.[19] Since 2015, things have been poised to change. The institutional setup has been trimmed with the new company Saudi Arabian Military Industries (SAMI), which is to act like EDIC in the UAE. In addition, the General Authority for Military Industries is the government body for the industry sector that will, among other things, propose relevant policies and strategies and handle acquisitions for the Ministry of Defense and the Ministry of the Interior.[20]

Within this context, Saudi Arabia is embarking on an aggressive transfer of technology agenda. As Table 1 shows, Saudi Arabia seems to be targeting almost every relevant defense industry segment at the same time. Tangible outcomes will very much depend on a long-term technology development road map that remains to be announced and the formation of local expertise to absorb technology. Regarding the latter, Saudi Arabia has been setting up TAQNIA and the King Abdulaziz City for Science and Technology (KACST).[21] Both are key to the Saudi defense-industrial ecosystem, as they engage in transferring technology from international partners to Saudi Arabia and in diffusing technology and skills among local Saudi partners. KACST, for example, is developing the Saqr UAV program,[22] and TAQNIA has set up different specialized companies in the fields of robotics, cyber, and satellite manufacturing.[23] Together, both companies work with Ukraine's Antonov on the AN-132 light multipurpose aircraft, for which KACST owns 50 percent of the intellectual property.[24]

Strategic investments and investment funds

Strategic investments mainly outside GCC nations and dedicated investment funds to promote the local defense industry complement the transfer and localization of technology and skills. Strategic investments abroad can be seen as door openers that help establish relationships with foreign partners that can be leveraged for technology transfer. This is the way that the UAE has used Mubadala, the state investment and development fund.[25] Mubadala maintains a diversified portfolio, but its engagement with Italian aerospace manufacturer Piaggio Aero is exemplary. Mubadala had been a shareholder in the Italian company starting in 2006 and became the sole owner in 2015.[26] Piaggio Aero manufactures the P.180 Avanti executive transport aircraft, which was the basis for the P.1HH Hammerhead UAV. Emiratis partnered with Piaggio Aero in 2010 to develop this UAV. Italy and the UAE have both committed to purchase the platform. Thanks to this program, the UAE indirectly partners in the European DESIRE II program, which is looking at the use of satellite-based communication to integrate UAV into civilian aerospace. Most tellingly, intellectual property for the platform has reportedly been filed in the UAE. As the Emirates are not part of the Missile Technology Control Regime that provides the regulatory framework for UAV exports, the UAE has great leeway for potential future exports of the system.[27]

The UAE approach to strategic defense investments has set the example that other GCC nations emulate:

- Saudi Arabia takes a dual-pronged approach to strategic investments. One strand runs through Saudi investment vehicles. Here the Public Investment Fund (PIF) plays the key role, as it is essential to implement Vision 2030. Estimates assume that by 2030 the fund could control up to $2 trillion. The fund will be engaged in many different sectors, but the signing of a series of mega deals with the United States in mid-2017 made it clear that it will play a heavy hand in defense through SAMI, its subsidiary. The PIF is said to be the brainchild of MbS, who also uses the Prince Mohammed bin Salman Foundation (MiSK) to engage with international partners. For example, MiSK and Lockheed Martin are cofinancing a graduate business school in Riyadh. In parallel, Saudi Arabia uses foreign investment partners to shore up support for technology development that has a defense and security impact. PIF and Japan's Softbank are playing in a league of their own with their joint tech fund. Worth around US$93 billion, it is to invest in artificial intelligence and robotics and counts Mubadala, Apple, Foxconn Technology, and Sharp as investors.[28]
- Qatar is following in the footsteps of the UAE and Saudi Arabia. The Barzan Holdings was established to build local defense systems. In March 2018, Barzan Holdings signed several partnership agreements with companies like Aselsan, BMC, Fincantieri, Kongsberg, Qinetiq, Raytheon, and Rheinmetall to set up joint venture companies and explore opportunities for cooperation and transfer of technology. In 2014, the Qatar Armed Forces Industry Committee took over a 49 percent stake in Turkish automotive manufacturer BMC, which also produces armor-protected vehicles. BMC, in turn, is part of the RBSS joint venture with Rheinmetall (Germany) and Etika Strategi (Malaysia), which is reportedly in talks with Qatar to deliver up to 1,000 vehicles.[29]
- In 2016, Oman's State General Reserve Fund took a 32.2 percent stake in Mecanizados Exribano, a Spanish manufacturer of precision components for aerospace and defense and other sectors. This investment fits Oman's defense-industrial expertise in land systems.[30]

Defense exports, material donations, and third-country funding

Arab Gulf defense-industrial ambitions have a strong outbound dimension. This is supposed to underline the proficiency of the local defense-industrial base and further the countries' foreign policy clout. Defense exports, material donations, and third-country funding are the instruments of choice.

UAE defense exports mirror current defense-industrial capacities. ADCOM has used its know-how to develop the Yabhon Aldura UAV together with a partner in Malaysia. The Yabhon system has reportedly also caught Algeria's and Russia's interest, but purchase confirmations are lacking up to now. In contrast, reports suggest that Nigeria procured the Yabhon Flash-20 UAV. In 2012, NIMR Automotive sealed a license-produced export contract for vehicles in Algeria. Five years later, the company bagged the first export contract from Turkmenistan. NIMR also agreed on a marketing and distribution partnership with partners in Malaysia and Thailand and with VOP CZ (Czech Republic) to target Central and Eastern European and Baltic markets. In addition, ADSB has been awarded a contract by the Ministry of Defense in Kuwait to build eight different vessels.[31]

Material donations are effective means to dispose of surplus equipment. For example, Libya received armored personnel carriers and Mirage 2000 jets from the UAE, which also provided Air Tractor 802U aircraft to Yemen and Jordan. More recently, the UAE provided five light aircraft to Yemen and trained 15 Yemeni pilots. Qatar has provided Sudan, Eritrea, and Somalia with 4 x 4 wheeled vehicles and anti-tank rockets. In addition, Doha has also invested in developing 400 4 x 4 M-ATV and M1117 vehicles by Oskhosh and Textron Systems, respectively. These vehicles are to be kept in U.S. Army depots until sold or donated by Qatar. From a strategic perspective, donations can open up distribution channels for one supplier while crowding out others. This is what could happen if Qatar were to view the 400 U.S. vehicles as an instrument to block access for Emirati suppliers in export markets.[32]

Finally, third-party funding gives the financial sponsor a say in partners' weapons procurement. The UAE has funded vessels and vehicles procurement for Yemen, wheeled and tracked vehicles for Libya, and UAV and fighter jets for Egypt. Egypt also receives substantial financial support from Saudi Arabia, which helped fund the acquisition of Mistral helicopter landing decks and German submarines. Saudi Arabia's financial support for Pakistan is of equal strategic importance, in particular regarding Pakistan's nuclear program. Furthermore, Riyadh is the main sponsor of Bahrain's weapons acquisition program. Saudi funds opened the door to China, which has sold two CH-4 Rainbow UAV to Manama. Saudi Arabia has also joined forces with the UAE in funding an intelligence, surveillance, and reconnaissance program for Morocco with U.S. and Israeli equipment. Qatar is following on the heels of the UAE and Saudi Arabia and reportedly seems prepared to fund defense industrialization projects with Pakistan if Islamabad keeps neutral in the ongoing Qatar crisis.[33]

Risks and opportunities of a diversified military portfolio

Despite the fact that ongoing military missions have led to a stronger focus on urgent operational requirements, the tendency to shore up loyalty with arms procurement is still alive. The 2017 arms deal between Saudi Arabia and the United States worth around US$110 billion and Qatar's purchase of 96 fighter jets worth US$20 billion since June 2017 are testimonies of this all too familiar tendency. But things are about to change.

Defense capabilities emerge from the interplay of four different elements: doctrine and concepts of operations, which embody the intellectual basis of why and how to conduct military operations; defense institutions made up of structures and processes to organize military power; training, which shapes the habits and routines needed to transfer doctrine and concepts of operations into action; and technology. This interplay is very much influenced by practical operational experiences of Arab Gulf armed forces, and this is where the most distinct differences emerge:

- For around 15 years, the UAE have been stepping up efforts to improve military preparedness. Since the UAE's first deployment, to Afghanistan in 2003, the UAE leadership has carefully chosen ever more demanding military tasks while at the same time investing in equipment, ramping up educational efforts, and investing in capabilities for independent military operational planning. These efforts culminated in the 2014 UAE Air Force combat operations in Iraq and Libya and the landing of amphibious forces in Yemen in August 2015. Not surprisingly, the UAE has also invested in power-projection capabilities through establishing an air base in Libya and air and naval bases in Eritrea and Somaliland. But the UAE also suffered losses. The country lost 45 soldiers when a camp was attacked in 2015 in Yemen. In 2016, a UAE naval vessel was hit off the coast of Yemen. Setbacks prompted the UAE leadership to focus on urgent operational requirements stemming from operations in Yemen. Among other things, reports suggest that locally manufactured armored vehicles have not fully lived up to expectations, which might explain the comeback of Finnish vehicle producer Patria and new inroads for Polish vehicle producer Rosomak.[34]
- Saudi Arabia, in contrast, picked a fight with Houthi rebels in Yemen, believing that its prestigious weapons arsenal would lead to a quick win. A fast and decisive outcome was what MbS,

who was then deputy crown prince and defense minister, wanted, as he had been in a fierce battle with Prince Mohammed bin Naif, the former Saudi minister of the interior, over the succession to King Salman. Open questions regarding the succession have been clarified since then but fighting in Yemen goes on. The challenging mountain terrain and the skills of Yemeni fighters matter. But overall, this case illustrates that Saudi Arabia's armed forces were not yet ready to accomplish what they had been expected to do—despite significant investments in weapon systems, training, and the intelligence and material support provided by the United States, France, and the United Kingdom.[35]

Arab Gulf preferences for defense systems from different suppliers are reinforcing the operational challenges discussed above, because they render maintenance, repair, overhaul, and logistics more cumbersome and increase life-cycle costs. As a rule of thumb, it can be argued that diversity of foreign weapon systems in Arab Gulf nations is strongest where defense systems are less complex; in contrast, supplier homogeneity reigns when defense systems are more complex. For example, GCC nations use 16 variants of armored personnel carriers from 12 countries and 53 patrol boat models from nine countries.[36] By contrast, only four nations provide main battle tanks to the region. When it comes to fighter jets, all six GCC nations fly either U.S. or European platforms. And for ballistic missile defense, the United States has so far enjoyed a near monopoly.[37] However, this segment seems likely to be more contested in the future, as Bahrain, Saudi Arabia, and Qatar are negotiating with Russia on the purchase of the S-400 air defense system and the Emirates are reportedly showing interest in this system.[38]

Overall, interoperability demands grow hand in hand with the complexity of the weapons systems and the military operations conducted. Thus "homogeneity in diversity" helps keep the challenge under control. In addition, the UAE is about to turn the ability to handle a diversified weapons portfolio into an asset. Emirates' Tawazun is reportedly assisting Egypt to integrate communication, observation, and target localization systems onto the Wing Loong UAV, which Abu Dhabi financed for Egypt. At the same time, Tawazun is said to supply and integrate Al Tariq missiles, co-developed with South Africa's Denel, onto Mirage fighters of Egypt's Air Force, thereby outrivaling Dassault and MBDA.[39] In addition, the Emirates and Saudi Arabia are showing increasing interest in C4ISR,[40] which is key to integrating all military assets into a joint federation that provides seamless interaction between sensors and shooters. Given growing indications that both nations could join forces in establishing joint defense companies, the prospect of a Saudi-Emirati C4ISR company would illustrate that these nations are serious about addressing one of the most challenging interoperability areas and ready to compete with traditional (Western) suppliers that have dominated this segment up to now.

Arab Gulf defense ambitions and foreign policy: It's difficult

In the past 15 years, Arab Gulf states have achieved remarkable economic progress. With the UAE, Qatar, and Saudi Arabia, three GCC members are among the world's 30 most-competitive nations according to the 2017 World Economic Forum ranking, but they are losing ground.[41] This is where the current regional instability kicks in.

Arab Gulf defense ambitions are likely to change the region's foreign relations because they serve as a catalyst. As argued above, key Arab Gulf leaders today follow a neorealist, zero-sum logic of international relations. In addition, the Qatar crisis has made it all too obvious that today's rulers no longer adhere to the consensus-oriented leadership style of their predecessors.[42] Instead, they are ready to take risks to make their point. The neorealist worldview attaches great importance to hard power, and this in turn shapes the way that leading Arab Gulf nations choose their defense partners. As Saudi Arabia, Qatar, and the UAE want to grow their local defense-industrial base, they are looking for partners that are ready to buy into their worldview and agree on localizing and sharing technology. In the long run, this is likely to lead to a convergence of policy attitudes or will at least help to reduce differences that are detrimental to local defense-industrial ambitions.

Limiting the outside-in impact

Traditionally, arms exporters argue that long-term defense-industrial relations provide opportunities to engage with partners, which can positively influence the way these partners act. However, the long-term ambition of any policy aimed at defense-industrial independence is to limit—if not stop—outside influence. This is exactly what is going to happen in the Arab Gulf region.

First of all, Saudi, Qatari, and Emirati rulers are fully aware that big military spenders are attractive to defense suppliers. All three nations are attempting to leverage their role in favor of policy concessions by partners. Saudi Arabia's MbS seems to have adopted the most assertive agenda, as he is reportedly demanding, in particular, that Western defense suppliers lower barriers for defense exports to Saudi Arabia in return for trade relations with the country.[43] In addition, he is also willing to completely overhaul defense-industrial relations with partners if they do not fit his ambition. For example, after two years of strong resistance from MbS and the Saudi Ministry of Defense, the French defense export agency ODAS is no longer in charge of handling any French-Saudi arms contract. When MbS visited Paris in April 2018, the French president and the French minister of defense agreed that all future arms-related contacts with Saudi Arabia will be handled directly by MbS.[44]

Second, relationship diversification reinforces the momentum gained through leveraging economic attractiveness. Ambitious GCC nations play a "reverse divide and conquer" game, as diversifying the portfolio of suppliers effectively limits the influence of every single partner. Defense export nations' individual interests in maintaining their own defense industrial base suggests that export nations will hardly agree on aligning export preferences with competitors, which plays into the hands of ambitious GCC rulers.

Third, extra-regional powers have diverging views on almost all policy issues relevant for the long-term stability of the Arab Gulf region. Iran is the best example. Whereas Washington and Jerusalem tend to agree on the hard line adopted by Riyadh and Abu Dhabi, European nations are more forward-leaning toward Iran. This provides leading Arab Gulf nations with the opportunity to set extra-regional powers against each other.

Finally, Saudi Arabia and the UAE increasingly engage in defense industrial cocooning—that is, they are forming an ever-closer strategic partnership that could effectively shield them against outside interference and at the same time promote independence. MbS and MbZ are said to be mulling the idea of establishing a joint military company and discussing the option of replacing—and possibly dissolving—the GCC Peninsula Shield Force with a new joint military force also including Bahrain.[45] If this were to mature, the regional impact would be significant.

Expanding the inside-out impact

If leading Arab Gulf nations sustain defense-industrial ambitions at current levels, their foreign policy impact on other actors is likely to grow. First of all, the Qatar crisis is turning Arab Gulf foreign relations sour, and defense-industrial preferences are reinforcing the trend. MbS is said to be taking an increasingly firm line against nations that support Qatar. He has reportedly pressured Washington to stop sales to Qatar, and the United States also seems to exert pressure on France and the UK to do likewise.[46] Qatar, on the other hand, reaches out to exactly the same nations, promising more defense deals in reward for continued support.[47] These intra-GCC differences are about to be exported to other regions that benefit from defense-material donations and defense funding. Growing polarization at the Horn of Africa and Sudan is a case in point. Somaliland has taken sides with Saudi Arabia and the UAE, whereas Somalia remains loyal to

Qatar and Turkey, which is supporting Doha, too. Sudan, which benefits from Riyadh and Doha, is struggling to keep a balanced position.[48]

Second, the increasingly assertive military action of Saudi Arabia and the UAE abroad is causing increasing domestic problems for traditional Western defense partners. The war in Yemen has prompted more and more demands in the United States, the United Kingdom, France, Germany, Canada, and Scandinavian countries to stop defense sales. Whether the respective governments give in depends on their overall political calculation and the strategic relevance attached to defense relations and defense sales. Here, the UK is of particular interest, as BAE Systems is supplying Eurofighter Typhoon fighter jets to Saudi Arabia, Oman, and Qatar.[49] Brexit reinforces London's readiness to leverage defense relations as a foreign policy tool, which gives defense-industrial considerations a strong voice in resisting calls to stop defense exports, as illustrated by the March 2018 UK-Saudi Memorandum of Intent to "finalize discussions for the purchase of 48 Typhoon."[50] Germany, in contrast, might be more willing to put defense relations with the region on the back burner, as Berlin never really felt at ease with the idea of arms sales as a foreign policy instrument.

Yet, defense-industrial partners like Turkey or Pakistan could increasingly feel the pressure to take sides. Turkey's future role will be indicative. Like the rulers in ambitious GCC nations, Turkish President Erdogan sees defense relations as a key foreign policy instrument and a source of domestic legitimization.[51] As argued above, Turkey has carved out a special role for itself. So far, Ankara has fared relatively well in the Gulf storm, despite taking sides with Doha. However, unease with Ankara is growing in Riyadh. MbS is reportedly considering signing no arms deals with Turkey in the near future and has identified Turkey, Iran, and hardline Islamist groups as forming a "triangle of evil."[52] Thus, Turkey's fate will be a test for both sides: for Turkey in view of withstanding pressure from the outside, and for Saudi Arabia and the UAE in view of their willingness to pull through demands for loyalty vis-à-vis a partner that shares much-needed technology.

All of this suggests that the combination of raising domestic opposition in some supplier countries coupled with broad defense-industrial diversification will open up opportunities for other nations. The Saudi-Chinese deal on localizing the manufacturing of Wing Loong UCAV in the kingdom[53] and Qatar's purchase of China's SY400 missile system with reach against neighboring countries[54] might be a harbinger of things to come that also illustrates the potentially destabilizing consequences for Arab Gulf stability.

Conclusion

Saudi Arabia, Qatar, and the UAE have embarked on an ambitious journey to establish a local defense-industrial base. This drive is motivated mainly by the will to reduce dependence on traditional outside defense suppliers and the ambition to play a more active foreign policy role underwritten by hard power. This approach will affect well-established client-supplier relations and influence Arab Gulf foreign relations.

Despite remarkable progress, several challenges lie ahead for the emerging Arab Gulf defense players. First and foremost, everything depends on sustained levels of funding. Although ambitious Arab Gulf nations have carefully established an image of big spenders on defense, recent figures from the International Institute for Strategic Studies show that defense spending among the GCC is flattening or gradually falling.[55] Saudi Arabia will undergo a challenging societal transformation in the near future that will absorb funds. Aging, which hardly hits the news headlines, is probably the single most important financial challenge across the region. Projections suggest that Saudi Arabia needs to increase age-related spending from around 6 percent of the national gross domestic product (GDP) right now to close to 14 percent by 2050.[56] Thus, the need to prioritize policy areas will grow even among the richest GCC nations.

Second, the narrative of the defense industry as an engine for economic prosperity is Janus-faced. Saudi Arabia's SAMI wants to contribute around SAR14 billion (US$3.7 billion) to the GDP by 2030 and create approximately 40,000 jobs. Today, however, the country's GDP stands at around US$656 billion, and Saudi Arabia's workforce counts more than 12 million. Economic contributions by the defense industry are important but limited in scale. In addition, costs of technology and skill transfer from foreign partners to regional companies will need to be weighed against the economic gains through local production and exports, but so far, no one has conducted the respective analysis. Thus, instead of pushing for broad economic diversification and prosperity fueled by defense indigenization, the narrative of smart economic specialization might be more appropriate. Here, systems integration is pivotal. As more and more defense technologies are of commercial origin, pulling over commercial expertise into the defense domain is critical. Emphasizing smart economic specialization by way of mastering systems integration would position ambitious Arab Gulf nations in both worlds—the commercial-technology and the defense-technology camps.

This is related to the third aspect, the unresolved question as to the unique selling proposition (USP) of the local defense industry. Reengineering what is already available on the defense market is justified to establish local skills, but it is difficult to carve out a niche in international markets with the respective products. The UAE, Saudi Arabia, and Qatar will face the challenge of focusing their defense-industrial efforts in terms of market segments, technologies to be mastered, and local production development plans. Today's portfolios are too diversified to be sustained by national governments only—and current defense products are not yet ripe to compete with big-ticket systems provided by Western, Russian, or Chinese suppliers. Advanced regional manufacturers such as the UAE-based aerospace company Strata have recognized the challenge. In an interview with *The National*, a local newspaper, the company's CEO Ismail Abdullah said that Strata was in talks with TAQNIA to "outsource work on aerostructures production to (Saudi Arabia) in two years and *avoid duplicating efforts* of the neighbouring countries' aerospace sectors."[57]

Finally, discussions about the local defense industrial USP cannot be separated from the local skill set. Up to now, this has been the Achilles' heel. Hiring foreign designers and engineers can only work as an interim solution, because it prolongs dependence on outside contributions. Thus, local defense-industrial ambitions need to be translated into human-resources plans. For example, not every local company needs to educate and employ all types of skills. Should systems integration be chosen as a strategic focal point, a cross-sector systems-integration company could be established that would retain critical mass and at the same time support all other national companies. As long as these companies do not compete with each other, everyone would benefit from this approach to pooling critical human expertise.

ORCID

Heiko Borchert http://orcid.org/0000-0003-0065-9684

Notes

1. Figures from http://armstrade.sipri.org/armstrade/html/export_toplist.php (accessed May 10, 2018.
2. Eldar Mamedov, "Arab Neoconservatives and Peace in the Persian Gulf," *Lobe Log*, February 5, 2018, http://lobelog.com/arab-neoconservatives-and-peace-in-the-persian-gulf/; Kristian Coates Ulrichsen, "Can the Gulf Cooperation Council Survive the Current Crisis?" *Arab Center*, Washington, DC, September 7, 2017, http://arabcenterdc.org/policy_analyses/can-the-gulf-cooperation-council-survive-the-current-crisis/ (accessed May 10, 2018).
3. For more on this, see in particular: Andreas Krieg, "Gulf Security Policy after the Arab Spring: Considering Changing Security Dynamics," in *The Small Gulf States. Foreign and Security Policies Before*

and After the Arab Spring, edited by Khalid S. Almezaini and Jean-Marc Rickli (Abingdon: Routledge, 2017), 47–63; Victor Gervais, "The Changing Security Dynamic in the Middle East and Its Impact on Smaller Gulf Cooperation Council States' Alliance Choices and Policies," in *The Small Gulf States,* edited by Almezaini and Rickli, 31–46; Kristian Coates Ulrichsen, "Links Between Domestic and Regional Security," in *The Changing Security Dynamics of the Persian Gulf,* edited by Kristian Coates Ulrichsen (London: C. Hurst & Co.), 23–43.

4. Theodore Karasik and Jeremy Vaughan. 2017. *Middle East Maritime Security: The Growing Role of Regional and Extraregional Navies* (Washington, DC: The Washington Institute for Near East Policy, 2017), www.washingtoninstitute.org/uploads/Documents/pubs/PolicyNote41-KarasikVaughan.pdf (accessed May 10, 2018).
5. Calvert W. Jones, *Bedouins into Bourgeois: Remaking Citizenship for Globalization* (Cambridge: Cambridge University Press, 2017); Emma Soubier, "Mirages of Power: From Sparkly Appearances to Empowered Apparatus, Evolving Trends and Implications of Arms Trade in Qatar and the UAE," in *The Arms Trade, Military Services and the Security Market in the Gulf States: Trends and Implications,* edited by David B. Des Roches and Dania Thafer (Berlin: Gerlach Press, 2016), 135–151; Florence Gaub and Zoe Stanley-Lockman, *Defence Industries in Arab States: Players and Strategies* (Paris: EU Institute for Security Studies, 2017), https://www.iss.europa.eu/sites/default/files/EUISSFiles/CP_141_Arab_Defence.pdf (accessed March 15, 2018), 9–10; Richard A. Bitzinger, "Defense Industries in Asia and the Technonationalist Impulse," *Contemporary Security Policy* 36, no. 3 (2016), 453–472. doi:10.1080/13523260.2015.1111649.
6. *Vision 2030* (Riyadh: Kingdom of Saudi Arabia, 2016), 48, http://vision2030.gov.sa/sites/default/files/report/Saudi_Vision2030_EN_2017.pdf (accessed May 10, 2018); "KSA: Localization of Military Industries, " *Tactical Report Weekly,* April 7, 2017, 3.
7. Stephen G. Brooks, *Producing Security: Multinational Corporations, Globalization, and the Changing Calculus of Conflict* (Princeton: Princeton University Press, 2005).
8. *UAE Security Forum 2017: Defense Industry and Economic Diversification* (Washington, DC: The Arab Gulf States Institute in Washington), 7, www.agsiw.org/wp-content/uploads/2018/02/UAESF-2017_ONLINE.pdf (accessed May 10, 2018).
9. "KSA: Naval Cooperation with Japan", *Tactical Report Weekly,* September 2, 2016, 3; "KSA: Military Cooperation with Japan," *Tactical Report Weekly,* April 17, 2017, 3.
10. Degang Sun, "China's Military Relations with the Middle East," in *The Red Star & the Crescent: China and the Middle East,* edited by James Reardon-Anderson (London: C. Hurst & Co.), 83.
11. For more on this see in particular Theodore Karasik, "Russia's Financial Tactics in the Middle East," The Jamestown Foundation, December 20, 2017, https://jamestown.org/program/russias-financial-tactics-middle-east/; Anna Borshchevskaya, "The Tactical Side of Russia's Arms Sales to the Middle East." The Jamestown Foundation, December 20, 2017, https://jamestown.org/program/tactical-side-russias-arms-sales-middle-east/ (accessed May 10, 2018).
12. Jeremy Binnie, "Saudi S-400 Talks Complicated by Tech Transfer," *Jane's Defence Weekly,* February 8, 2018, www.janes.com/article/77731/saudi-s-400-talks-complicated-by-tech-transfer (accessed May 10, 2018).
13. Robin Wright, "Russia and Iran Deepen Ties to Challenge Trump and the United States." *The New Yorker,* 2 March 2018, www.newyorker.com/news/news-desk/russia-and-iran-deepen-ties-to-challenge-trump-and-the-united-states (accessed May 10, 2018).
14. Reuben F. Johnson, "Dubai Airshow 2017: Russian Officials Remain Cautious over Possible UAE Su-35 Buy," *Jane's Defence Weekly,* November 16, 2017, www.janes.com/article/75735/dubai-airshow-2017-russian-officials-remain-cautious-over-possible-uae-su-35-buy (accessed May 10, 2018).
15. Science, technology, engineering, and mathematics.
16. Gaub and Stanley-Lockmann, *Defence Industries in Arab States,* 47–52.
17. Author's interviews, Abu Dhabi, March 6, 2016, and August 26, 2016.
18. "Calidus Behind Abu Dhabi's Mystery Counter-Guerilla Planes," *Intelligence Online,* January 17, 2018, 8.
19. Bilal Y. Saab, *The Gulf Rising: Defense Industrialization in Saudi Arabia and the UAE* (Washington, DC: Atlantic Council, 2014), 29–31, www.atlanticcouncil.org/images/publications/The_Gulf_Rising.pdf.
20. "11 Targets for General Authority of Military Industries," *Saudi Press Agency,* August 15, 2017, www.spa.gov.sa/viewfullstory.php?lang=en&newsid=1656691 (accessed May 10, 2018); "GAMI, SAMI: The New Defence Procurement Decision-Makers," *Intelligence Online,* April 11, 2018, 5.
21. KACST also holds Saudi Arabia's scientific government institutions and as such supports the government in advancing the country's overall scientific research base. For more on this, see www.kacst.edu.sa/eng/about/Pages/About.aspx (accessed May 10, 2018).
22. KACST, www.kacst.edu.sa/eng/about/news/Pages/news535.aspx (accessed May 10, 2018).
23. TAQNIA, www.taqnia.com/en/portfolio/ (accessed May 10, 2018).

24. KACST, www.kacst.edu.sa/eng/rd/pages/content.aspx?dID=97 (accessed May 10, 2018).
25. Mubadala, www.mubadala.com/ (accessed May 10, 2018).
26. Mubadala is in the process of selling the company's business-jet unit to the Chinese-backed consortium PAC Investments. See "Mubadala to Go Ahead with Sale of Piaggio Aerospace Unit—Source," *Arabian Business,* February 1, 2018, www.arabianbusiness.com/transport/388885-mubadala-to-go-ahead-with-sale-of-piaggio-aerospace-unit-source (accessed May 10, 2018).
27. "Mubadala Completes 100% Takeover of Piaggio," *Arabian Aeropsace,* September 18, 2015, www.arabianaerospace.aero/mubadala-completes-100-takeover-of-piaggio.html; "EDA and ESA Launch DESIRE II Demonstration Project," *European Defence Agency,* May 18, 2015, www.eda.europa.eu/info-hub/press-centre/latest-news/2015/05/18/eda-and-esa-launch-desire-ii-demonstration-project; "Discreet Race for Drones," *Intelligence Online,* November 20, 2013, 1; Tom Kington, "Italian AF First to Buy Hammerhead UAV," *Defense News,* February 26, 2015, www.defensenews.com/home/2015/02/26/italian-af-first-to-buy-hammerhead-uav/; Tom Kington, "UAE to Buy 8 Italian-Made Drones for €316M," *Defense News,* March 8, 2016, www.defensenews.com/air/2016/03/09/uae-to-buy-8-italian-made-drones/ (accessed May 10, 2018).
28. Sarah Algethami, "How Saudi Arabia is Building its $2 Trillion Fund," *Bloomberg,* October 22, 2017, www.bloomberg.com/news/articles/2017-10-22/how-saudi-arabia-is-building-its-2-trillion-fund-quicktake-q-a (accessed March 15, 2018); "Washington and Riyadh Proceed with Plans to Make Morocco an ISR Heavyweight," *Intelligence Online,* January 17, 2018, 8; Andrew Torchia "Softbank-Saudi Tech Fund Comes World's Biggest with $93 Billion of Capital," *Reuters,* May 20, 2017, www.reuters.com/article/us-softbank-visionfund-launch/softbank-saudi-tech-fund-becomes-worlds-biggest-with-93-billion-of-capital-idUSKCN18G0NP (accessed May 10, 2018).
29. Burak Ege Bekdil, "Turkish Amor Makers in Talks to Produce 1,000 Vehicles for Qatar." *Defense News,* December 29, 2016, www.defensenews.com/land/2016/12/29/turkish-armor-makers-in-talks-to-produce-1000-vehicles-for-qatar/; "Enthemm Sancak," *Intelligence Online,* June 18, 2014, 1; "Barzan Holdings, Doha's Mystery Defense Project, Gets Off the Ground," *Intelligence Online,* January 31, 2018, 5; "Barzan Holdings Sings Multiple Agreements to Meet Qatar's Long-Term Defence and Security Needs," *Qatar Is Booming,* March 13, 2018, www.qatarisbooming.com/article/barzan-holdings-signs-multiple-agreements-meet-qatar%E2%80%99s-long-term-defence-and-security-needs; "Fincantieri will cooperate with Barzan Holdings," *Fincantieri Press Release,* March 14, 2018, www.fincantieri.com/en/media/press-releases/2018/fincantieri-will-cooperate-with-barzan-holdings/ (accessed May 10, 2018).
30. "Oman Sovereign Wealth Fund Buys into Spanish Manufacturer Escribano," *Reuters,* October 2016, www.reuters.com/article/oman-spain-ma/oman-sovereign-wealth-fund-buys-into-spanish-manufacturer-escribano-idUSL8N1D12WY (accessed May 10, 2018).
31. "ADSB to Build 8 Vessels for the Kuwait Ministry of Defense," *ADSB Press Release,* undated, www.adsb.ae/news/adsb-to-build-8-vessels-for-the-kuwait-ministry-of-defense/; "NIMR Automotive Expanding into Southeast Asia," *Al Defaiya,* November 10, 2017, www.defaiya.com/news/Regional%20News/UAE/2017/11/10/nimr-automotive-expanding-into-southeast-asia; "Russia Mulls United Yabhon 40 UAV Purchase from UAE," *Air Force Technology,* July 18, 2013, www.airforce-technology.com/news/newsrussia-mulls-united-yabhon-40-uav-purchase-from-uae/; "UAE's NIMR to Supply Turkmenistan with Military Vehicles," *Arabian Business,* November 6, 2017, www.arabianbusiness.com/industries/transport/382878-uaes-nimr-to-supply-turkmenistan-with-military-vehicles; James Bingham, "NIMR to Demo Ajban 440A to Baltic Forces," *Jane's Defence Weekly,* September 14, 2017 www.janes.com/article/74006/nimr-to-demo-ajban-440a-to-baltic-forces; "Algeria and UAE to Jointly Produce Armored Vehicles in Algeria," *DefenceWeb,* July 24, 2012, www.defenceweb.co.za/index.php?option=com_content&view=article&id=26936:algeria-and-uae-to-jointly-produce-armoured-vehicles-in-algeria&catid=50:Land&Itemid=105; "Nigeria Air Force Arms Third Alpha Jet; Acquiring Yabhon Flash-20 UAVs," *Defence Web,* August 23, 2016, www.defenceweb.co.za/index.php?option=com_content&task=view&id=44783&catid=35&Itemid=107; Guy Martin, "Asian Region UAV Capability on the Rise," *Defence Review Asia,* December 20, 2012, www.defencereviewasia.com/articles/195/Asian-region-UAV-capability-on-the-rise; "Algeria: Reinforcing Aerial Defense," *The North African Post,* November 19, 2013, http://northafricapost.com/4577-algeria-reinforcing-aerial-defense.html; "The Agreement with NIMR," VOP Press Release, February 20, 2017, www.vop.cz/en/clanek/29-the-agreement-with-nimr.aspx (accessed May 10, 2018).
32. Heiko Borchert and Cyril Widdershoven, "The Dawn of a New Arab Defense Industrial Network." *Arab Defense Industry Papers* 1, July 3, 2017, www.arabdefenseindustry.com/cmsfiles/publications/ADIP_01-16_3.pdf (accessed March 15, 2018); "Yemen: Air Support Aircraft from the UAE," *Tactical Report Weekly,* 9 February 2018, 2; "Qatar: Used US Military Vehicles," *Tactical Report Weekly,* March 3, 2017, 2.
33. Borchert and Widdershoven, "The Dawn of a New Arab Defense Industrial Network," 17–18; "Washington and Riyadh Proceed with Plans to Make Morocco an ISR Heavyweight," *Intelligence Online,*

January 17, 2018, 4; "Qatar: Military Cooperation with Pakistan," *Tactical Report Weekly*, February 16, 2018, 2.

34. Hussein Ibish, The UAE's Evolving National Security Strategy (Washington, DC: The Arab Gulf States Institute in Washington, 2017), 17–22; Heiko Borchert and Shehab al Makahleh, "Sharpening the Falcon's Claws," *European Security and Defense* 1 (February 2017), 26–26, David B. Roberts, "The Gulf Monarchies' Armed Forces at the Crossroads," *Focus Stratégique 80* (Paris: IFRI, 2018), 26, www.ifri.org/en/publications/etudes-de-lifri/focus-strategique/gulf-monarchies-armed-forces-crossroads (accessed May 10, 2018).
35. Glen Carey, "Saudi Cash Can't Buy Military Clout," *Bloomberg*, January 11, 2017, www.bloomberg.com/news/articles/2017-01-11/saudi-cash-can-t-buy-mideast-clout-as-foreign-policy-misfires (accessed March 15, 2018). Saudi Arabia spent around US$267 million on foreign military sales in fiscal years 2016 and 2017 for military training in the United Sates. See *Foreign Military Training Report: Fiscal Years 2016 and 2017. Joint Report to Congress Volume 1* (Washington, DC: Department of Defense/Department of State, 2017), Section III, 6, www.state.gov/documents/organization/275295.pdf (accessed May 10, 2018).
36. *The Emerging GCC Defence Market: The $30 Billion Opportunity* (Dubai: Strategy&, 2017), 8–10, www.strategyand.pwc.com/media/file/The-emerging-GCC-defence-market.pdf (accessed May 10, 2018).
37. Based on SIPRI trade registers, http://armstrade.sipri.org/armstrade/page/trade_register.php (accessed May 10, 2018).
38. Interest in the S-400 air defense systems grows because of failures witnessed with Raytheon's Patriot air defense system. See Roberts, "The Gulf Monarchies' Armed Forces at the Crossroads," 16. Growing interest in Russian systems also illustrates the strive for diversity, but it is fair to assume that some of the challenges that have hindered Washington's attempt to establish an integrated missile defense shield on the Arabian Peninsula are likely to haunt Moscow, too. This is particularly true for the lack of trust among the GCC nations that has prevented truly collaborative solutions on data sharing for early warning and consensus about who would have the power to shoot down incoming missiles over neighboring territories.
39. "Abu Dhabi Exports Counter-Guerilla Material," *Intelligence Online*, September 20, 2017, 1.
40. Command, Control, Computers, Communications, Intelligence, Surveillance, Reconnaissance.
41. *The Global Competitiveness Report 2017-2018* (Geneva: WEF, 2018), ix www3.weforum.org/docs/GCR2017-2018/05FullReport/TheGlobalCompetitivenessReport2017%E2%80%932018.pdf (accessed May 10, 2018).
42. Kristian Coates Ulrichsen, "Can the Gulf Cooperation Council Survive the Current Crisis?"
43. "KSA: Rules of Reciprocity with Arms Exports," *Tactical Report Weekly*, May 13, 2016, 4.
44. "ODAS Goes for Broke in Riyadh," *Intelligence Online*, June June2016, 5; "MBS en France: les contrats d'armement au service de Vision 2030," *Middle East Strategic Perspectives*, April 9, 2018, www.mesp.me/2018/04/09/mbs-en-france-les-contrats-darmement-au-service-de-vision-2030/ (accessed May 10, 2018); "KSA: Armament Relations with France," *Tactical Report Weekly*, April 13, 2018, 4.
45. "KSA-UAE: GCC Affairs and Military Industry," *Tactical Report Weekly*, December 8, 2017, 1; "KSA: A joint Military Task Force with the UAE," *Tactical Report Weekly*, October 27, 2017, 1.
46. "KSA: Qatar and Arms Deals," *Tactical Report Weekly*, June 30, 2017, 1; "Qatar: Washington and Arms Deals," *Tactical Report Weekly*, November 24, 2017, 1.
47. Ali Bakeer, "Making Sense of Qatar's Military Buildup," *Gulf International Forum*, March 8, 2018, https://gulfif.com/making-sense-of-qatars-military-buildup/ (accessed May 10, 2018).
48. "The Qatar Crisis Hits the African Continent," *The New Arab*, October 12, 2017, www.alaraby.co.uk/english/indepth/2017/10/12/the-qatar-crisis-hits-the-african-continent (accessed May 10, 2018).
49. For 2017, BAE Systems has posted turnover of roughly £19.6 billion. The sale of 24 Eurofighter Typhoon fighters signed by Qatar in December 2017 is valued at around $5 billion. See *Preliminary Accouchement 2017* (London: BAE Systems, 2018), 1, https://investors.baesystems.com/~/media/Files/B/Bae-Systems-Investor-Relations-V3/PDFs/results-and-reports/results/2017/2017-preliminary-announcement.pdf (accessed March 15, 2018).
50. "Memorandum of Intent between the Kingdom of Saudi Arabia and the UK Government," BAE Systems Press Release, March 9, 2018, www.londonstockexchange.com/exchange/news/market-news/market-news-detail/BA./13562011.html (accessed May 10, 2018).
51. Hüseiyn Bagci and Caglar Kurc, "Turkey's Strategic Choice: Buy or Make Weapons," *Defence Studies* 17, no. 1 (2016): 38–62. doi:10.1080/14702436.2016.1262742.
52. "KSA: Arms Deals with Turkey Put on Hold?" *Tactical Report Weekly*, September 15, 2017, 3; "Saudi Prince Says Turkey Part of 'Triangle of Evil': Egyptian Media," *Reuters*, March 7, 2018, www.reuters.com/article/us-saudi-turkey/saudi-prince-says-turkey-part-of-triangle-of-evil-egyptian-media-idUSKCN1GJ1WW (accessed March 15, 2018).

53. Ian Armstrong, "What's Behind China's Big New Drone Deal?" *The Diplomat,* April 20, 2017, https://thediplomat.com/2017/04/whats-behind-chinas-big-new-drone-deal/ (accessed March 15, 2018).
54. Awad Mustafa, "Why is Qatar Showing Off Its New Short-Range Chinese Ballistic Missile?" *Al Arabiya,* December 20, 2017, http://english.alarabiya.net/en/News/gulf/2017/12/20/Qatar-showcases-offensive-ballistic-missiles-targeting-neighbors.html (accessed March 15, 2018).
55. *The Military Balance 2018* (Abingdon: Routledge, 2018), 327, 345, 354, 357, 358, 367.
56. Marko Mrsnik, Global Aging 2016: 58 Shades of Gray (New York: Standard & Poor's Ratings Direct, 2016), http://media.spglobal.com/documents/SPGlobal_Ratings_Article_28-April-2016_Global+Aging_58+Shades+of+Gray1.pdf (accessed May 10, 2018).
57. Deena Kamel, "Exclusive: Strata Eyes Saudi Arabia, Far East to build Global Supply Chain." *The National,* May 2, 2018, emphasis added, www.thenational.ae/business/aviation/exclusive-strata-eyes-saudi-arabia-far-east-to-build-global-supply-chain-1.726424 (accessed May 2018).

Egypt's defense industry: Dependency, civilian production, and attempts at autonomy

Zeinab Abul-Magd

ABSTRACT
Egypt's defense industry is the oldest and largest in the Arab world. However, most of its military factories have converted into manufacturing consumer goods to the civilian market for profit. Meanwhile, they continue to produce traditional weapon systems that mostly do not respond to urgent needs to combat terrorism in asymmetric warfare. In addition, Egypt is largely dependent on U.S. firms for procurement and co-production. After a political crisis in 2013, the Ministry of Military Production (MoMP) has attempted to revive defense production through new co-production initiatives with international arms firms. The country also attempts to reduce its dependence on the U.S. by seeking procurement from other states such as France, Russia, and Germany. Such efforts remain noticeably limited, because the Egyptian military still focuses on its civilian business enterprises.

1. Introduction

Egypt's defense industry has a long history for the past six decades that renders it the oldest and largest among the Arab states. It started to expand in the 1950s–1960s and reached its peak in collaboration with Western manufacturers in the 1980s. However, it has suffered from a problem of dependency on Western technology, especially the U.S., and has limited R&D. This problem, and other economic reasons, led to substantial conversion of the military industrial base into civilian production for profit in the 1990s–2000s. For the past three decades, military factories have been mostly converted into manufacturing consumer or capital goods for the civilian market. Meanwhile, they have continued to produce traditional weapons systems that do not particularly respond to recent needs to combat terrorism and asymmetric warfare with scattered fundamentalist cells on the country's eastern and western borders. The last few years have witnessed a degree of change towards reviving arms production, especially after 2013 when a severe crisis with U.S. supply took place and a war on terrorist groups erupted. In today's Egypt, there are efforts to diversify sources of supply outside U.S. firms. In addition, there are ongoing attempts to achieve autonomy through co-production with international manufacturers. However, the outcomes of such efforts remain limited, as most of the Egyptian military's attention still focuses on its civilian business enterprises that target the domestic consumer market for profit.

This article investigates the historical roots and current realities of the Egyptian defense industry. It begins by presenting a historical background of the industry, emphasizing issues of dependency on Soviet and Western technology from the 1950s to the 1980s. This period was marked by generous government spending on developing the industry. The article then moves to the problematic period of massive defense conversion to civilian production in the 1990s–2000s, which took place due to the country's economic reform and liberalization scheme that entailed cuts in the military's budget. Such conversion came about in a global context in which many other states adopting neoliberal policies reduced military budgets and allowed their armies to engage in civilian business to compensate them for their financial losses. Finally, the paper looks at the past five years in the developments taking place in Egypt's defense industry under the current military President Abdel Fattah al-Sisi. It, therefore, examines the regime's attempts at reducing dependency on the U.S. through seeking procurement from European suppliers while also concluding co-production agreements with European firms. While investigating these three periods between the past and the present, the article highlights domestic, regional, and global conditions that made the Egyptian state and its defense industry opt for certain decisions regarding procurement and partnership.

The article concludes with policy recommendations about advancing Egypt's defense industry as an emerging state in a globalized market. If Egypt seeks to join other emerging countries in arms manufacturing, its military factories that currently focus on production for the civilian consumer market should divest themselves of civilian business enterprises and re-focus on partnership efforts with international firms.

2. Historical Dependency: From the Soviets to the U.S. (1950s–1980s)

In the 1950s–1960s, Egypt's defense industry started to develop within a socialist state and in a Cold-War context, when Egypt was aligned with the Soviet Union. The first military regime that ruled the country after the end of British colonialism, led by then young colonel Gamal Abd al-Nasser, sought to establish military power for the recently independent republic because of a combination of domestic, regional, and international factors. Egypt was a state with a national desire to build a strong army to defend itself against potential aggression from European imperial powers or Israel, similar to the Suez Crisis of 1956. The regime also had regional ambitions to expand its Arab nationalist and later socialist ideology against conservative Arab monarchies, such as Saudi Arabia, and their Western backers, which was reflected by their support for movements of national independence and socialist endeavors in other countries in the region.[1]

During this period, Egypt found itself caught between the two camps of the Cold War, and opted for the Soviet Union's side after the U.S. repeatedly declined Nasser's requests for arms deals and economic aid. Nasser turned Egypt into a socialist state in the early 1960s, and he followed an Import Substitution Industrialization (ISI) model to foster overall economic development. Thus, the regime invested in a nascent defense industry with an import-substitution plan, but primarily with Soviet technology. Nasser, for example, erected factories to manufacture Soviet automatic assault rifles and short-range ballistic missiles. With West Germany's support, it built a supersonic jet fighter. During this period, military factories enjoyed exceptional financial support from the underdeveloped state's budget.[2]

However, the USSR noticeably granted Egypt limited access to technology transfer, and equipment manufactured by Soviet designs had to be shipped to Russia for maintenance. Moreover, after being defeated by Israel in 1967, and falling subsequently into an economic crisis, Egypt's defense industry severely suffered. The war economy's budget constraints and public austerity drastically affected spending on the arms factories. As a result, most

Western manufacturers, such as West Germany, left the country and technology transfer attempts were aborted. As Florence Gaub and Zoe Stanley-Lockman indicate, "[t]wo years after the war, several programs had to be shut down and three quarters of military industrial capacity diverted to civilian production, and the Ministry of Defence Production was abolished."[3] This situation continued through the 1973 war and for the rest of the 1970s, as the Egyptian economy was exhausted by two wars and unable to substantially invest in a largely halted defense industry.

In the 1980s, the Egyptian defense industry recovered with significant expansion, taking advantage of new shifts in international and regional conditions. Although Egypt's wars with Israel had ended in 1973 and a peace treaty was signed in 1979, the military remained the most powerful state institution. Under Field Marshal Abdel-Halim Abu Ghazala, Minister of Defense, and Military Production from 1981 till 1989, the defense industry expanded tremendously by relying on Western technology. Abu Ghazala craftily re-positioned the Egyptian military and its arms production within fluid international and regional contexts and took advantage of them. Two ex-military Presidents that Abu Ghazala served, Sadat (r. 1970–1981) and Hosni Mubarak (r. 1981–2011), had already switched Egypt's Cold-War alliances from the Soviet camp to the U.S., and this helped Abu Ghazala with concluding co-production deals with American firms. With many ambitious initiatives in existing or newly opened military factories, Abu Ghazala exported Egypt's increasing production of heavy and small armaments to neighboring countries—such as Iraq, which was engaged in a prolonged war with Iran. He also succeeded in concluding a co-production agreement of the M1A1 tank with the U.S.[4]

Abu Ghazala reactivated the Egyptian military's role within a global context of the Cold War as it was approaching its end. Because Egypt at this point was already on the U.S. side in this war, the Ronald Regan Administration annually granted $1.3 billion in military aid. As part of this aid package, Abu Ghazala successfully pressed the U.S. to sign an agreement of co-production for the M1A1 tank in 1987. Abu Ghazala convinced the U.S. assistant secretary of defense for international security affairs, who was then attending the annual meeting of the U.S.-Egyptian Cooperation Committee in Cairo, to go ahead with the project, and even identified a location for manufacturing the tank in a factory under construction in Abu Za'bal, north of Cairo. The U.S. sent a team to Egypt to inspect military production facilities that could be expanded and improved for new activities.[5] Prestigiously for Abu Ghazala, Egypt was the first country to build this tank outside the U.S., and he hoped to produce 1000–1500 pieces. Nonetheless, he needed U.S. permission for intended exportation, and the Americans retained the right to veto any undesired re-sales. According to the *Washington Post*, Abu Ghazala "lobbied Washington for more than a year to get approval for the M1 … and has overcome U.S. Army opposition in Defense Department Deliberations." However, the newspaper cited controversy in the capital about transferring sensitive military technology to Egypt, and critiques of Egypt's ambition to become a military power—a threat to Israel.[6]

In return for large aid and such military advantages, the U.S. had specific—albeit unwritten—regional expectations from Egypt. The long list included assisting in Persian Gulf security or the protection of the oil-producing Arab states; containing the radical Palestinian front and persuading the Palestinian Liberation Organization (PLO) to sit at the negotiating table towards long-term Israeli security; targeting Libya, as it was led by radical Mu'ammar al-Qadhafi, a close Soviet ally; watching Syria, as led by Hafez al-Assad, a recipient of heavy Soviet military aid who regularly intervened in Lebanon; targeting the new Islamic republic in Iran, a prominent enemy of the U.S. since the 1980 hostage crisis; and reducing communist influence in the Sudan by maintaining good and militarily cooperative relations with them and countering neighboring Qadhafi's intervention in the country. Throughout the 1980s, Egypt fulfilled its duty against Iran when it provided Iraq with weapons during its prolonged war against Iran's newly born Islamic republic under Ayatollah Khomeini, and militarily threatened Libya and was a few times on the brink of war with Qadhafi.[7]

General Dynamics collaborated with Egypt's Military Factory 200 in Abu Za'bal to modify this facility to adapt to producing M1A1 Abrams on a large scale. Egypt was to make 40 percent of the tank, and the rest was to be manufactured in the U.S. and assembled in Factory 200—which also repaired M60 tanks and produced light armored vehicles. It was the "best tank in the world," as U.S. Defense Secretary then asserted after signing the deal with Abu Ghazala at the end of 1988, authorizing him to produce only 524 tanks.[8] The factory opened for business in 1991. However, when the U.S. General Accounting Office (GAO) assessed the project a few years later, it concluded that the U.S. should not have responded to Egypt's pressure to engage in this expensive partnership. It was a $3.2 billion project, where the U.S. carried $2.491 billion and Egypt $663 million of the cost. A GAO report asserted that selling Egypt the complete tanks was a much cheaper choice, with a cost of only $1.9 billion.[9] Moreover, the same report revealed that Egypt would not reach her hopes of technology transfer and self-sufficiency in tank production through this project. "Six increments of production were initially planned, with Egypt progressively completing more of the tank. However, the plans for Egypt completing more of the tank in each increment have been reduced, limiting the production technologies transferred to Egypt…"[10] The report affirmed that the Egyptian goal from the project conflicted with those of the U.S. It stated, "from the program's inception Egyptian self-sufficiency was limited because, for security reasons, the United States retained control of key technology items needed to produce the tank,"[11] and added that financial constraints made technology transfer minimal.

Aside from this complicated project, Abu Ghazala considerably expanded arms manufacturing after obtaining technology from various advanced sources, including Britain, France, and China. When Abu Ghazala assumed his position in 1981, two main state bodies were already engaged in arms production. The first was the Ministry of Military Production (MoMP), with 15 factories, 70,000 employees, and $240 million value of production. The second was the Arab Organization for Industrialization (AOI), with 7 factories, 18,000 employees, and $100 million value of production. The latter was founded in 1975 in collaboration with three Gulf countries, Saudi Arabia, UAE, and Qatar, providing capital to build a strong Arab defense industry as it signed co-production agreements with European firms. When Sadat signed the peace treaty with Israel, the three Gulf countries withdrew from the project and demanded their money back, while European partners were hesitant to continue. But Abu Ghazala carried on.[12] His expanded military plans reached 30 factories with about 100,000 employees and an average of $400 million value of production. His exports jumped from $30 million in 1981 to $550 million in 1988.[13] These plants assembled French jets, Chinese fighters, Brazilian trainers, British helicopters, British missiles, aircraft engines, guns and ammunitions, and much more. These systems attracted orders from oil-producing Arabian Gulf states and Egypt's African neighbors.[14] Interestingly, the U.S. granted Egypt the right to export arms to the American market, but experts opined that this agreement—signed between Abu Ghazala and U.S. Defense Secretary—was mainly symbolic.[15]

During this promising time, Egypt made considerable profits from arms sales, especially those to Iraq to use in its long war against Iran as well as to the Afghan *mujahidin*, who were backed by the U.S. against the Soviets.[16] However, Egypt suffered from technological difficulties and a noticeable problem with sustainability. Philip Stoddard, of the Defense Intelligence College, stated,

> [m]ilitary sales in 1982 reached $1 billion, making weapons Egypt's second largest source of export revenue after oil. Much of this trade was with Iraq, financed by subsidies from the Gulf states … Whether Egypt will be able to maintain sales at these levels is open to question … much of Egypt's arms industry is in the developing stage….[17]

Likewise, LTC Stephen H. Gotowicki, of the U.S. Army, argued that Egypt's engagement in assembling advanced weaponry with Western producers did not render it technologically capable. "The Egyptians receive kits for assembly, but the technology involved is closely maintained by the Western partner."[18] Regarding U.S. technology in particular, Ralph Sanders, Professor at the National Defense University, asserted that buyers of American arms generally enjoyed trivial access to the technology to help to independently manufacturing them.[19]

By the end of the 1980s, Egypt reduced spending on military industries once more because of budget constraints. The industry needed around $4–6 billion to properly develop. For example, a report by the EU's Institute for Security Studies states,

> The development of the Sakr-80 missile for instance cost $100 million in R&D. As a result of these resource constraints, Egypt was not able to provide seed money or investment capital for new ventures. It also had to limit its projects of production under license, thereby hindering its acquisition of skills and know-how. Lastly, lack of funds stood not only in the way of the development of a national arms industry. It also affected existing projects as they were either cancelled (such as the Lynx helicopter programme) or delayed.[20]

Therefore, by the early 1990s, lack of technology and budgetary problems led to a state decision to convert considerable parts of the arms production lines into civilian manufacturing. The Egyptian defense industry witnessed a period of drastic decline in the following three decades, but the military institution managed to generate immense profit through creating a business empire of civilian enterprises functioning within, or rather above, the domestic market.

3. Defense Conversion and Continuous Dependency (1990s–2000s)

By the end of the 1980s, experts predicted that Egypt's arms production was highly promising and most likely would increase.[21] Unfortunately things went in the opposite direction over the following decade. In the early 1990s, the growing Egyptian arms industry faced an economic crisis, as domestic, regional, and international factors once more pushed it toward defense conversion to the production of civilian goods. It embarked on a process of massively transforming much of its military production lines to serve the civilian market and generate profits locally. Meanwhile, Egypt continued to be almost fully dependent on the U.S. for procurement, through the annual military aid package. Egypt's only significant co-production project remained to be that of General Dynamics' M1A1.

In fact, the army's business activities in the civilian market had already started in the 1980s under Abu Ghazala. Upon signing the peace treaty with Israel in 1979, the Egyptian military created an economic entity called the National Service Projects Organization (NSPO) to establish business enterprises and assimilate the efforts of officers and conscripts alike into them. The NSPO continued to rapidly expand its profitable economic endeavors through the 1990s, but it was no longer the only military body doing so. Military factories that had formerly produced ordnance such as ammunitions, missiles, aircrafts, rockets, explosives, pistols, and armors were now heavily utilizing their facilities and labors to produce consumer goods such as washing machines, refrigerators, TVs, kitchenware, fertilizers, and more.[22]

In 1991 in particular, defense conversion was inevitable in Egypt. This year marked the eruption of the Gulf War in the immediate aftermath of the Cold War, which negatively affected the country's arms sales and consequently its manufacturing programs. At the regional level, Egypt's defense industry lost its existing and future market in Iraq as well as the U.S.-backed Arab Gulf states, and its arms sales in this area plummeted. This market was not only closed because of the end of the Iraq-Iran war in 1988,[23] but also due to the sanctions imposed on Saddam Hussein during the 1990s after his invasion of Kuwait and defeat by the U.S.-led operation to liberate this small oil-producing country. The end of another long-standing Cold-War dispute, the Afghan war, similarly closed a considerable market for Egyptian arms sales to the jihadists.[24] Furthermore, oil-producing Arab Gulf states that had been current or prospective customers of Egyptian arms sales now switched directly to the most advanced producer, the U.S., which had militarily saved them during the crisis of Iraq's invasion of Kuwait. The U.S. sold its regional clients an ever-increasing amount of ordnance over the following two decades.

More important, right after the end of the Gulf War, the George H.W. Bush Administration took serious steps to restrict weapons production in the Middle East, by introducing an "arms control initiative" restraining technology transfer of non-conventional and conventional weapons to the region. A report published by the Congressional Research Service (CRS) in May 1991, titled "Middle East Arms Control and Related Issues," highlighted the expansion of Egypt's defense industry. It states that

> Egypt has a rapidly growing military industrial sector. It has cooperative ventures with several countries ... Egypt produces jet trainers of French design and Brazilian design and helicopters designed by French, British, and Italian firms. Small arms, machine-guns, motors, recoilless weapons, rocket launchers, artillery and electronic equipment produced by Egypt were designed in the Soviet Union, Sweden, Czechoslovakia, and Italy. Argentina and Italy cooperated on the development of the Condor II surface-to-surface missile until the project was terminated under U.S. pressure.[25]

At the end of the same month that this report appeared, President Bush issued the "White House Fact Sheet on the Middle East Arms Control Initiative" seeking "to restrain destabilizing conventional arms build-ups in the region ... The initiative calls on the five major suppliers of conventional arms to meet at senior levels in the near future..."[26] The U.S. later even considered breaking its already existing agreements of co-production of M1A1 with Egypt.[27]

Now that Egypt's old ambitions to build a large military industry targeting global markets were no longer feasible, mass defense conversion began. At this point of the early 1990s, Egypt had at least 25 publicly known military factories: 16 functioned under MoMP and nine under AOI. They were mostly built between the 1950s and 1970s, and were geographically concentrated in limited areas—especially in Helwan in the south of Cairo, Abu Za'bal in the north of Cairo, and on the Cairo-Suez road. By 2010, 40 percent of the MoMP's production turned civilian, and the remaining 60 percent still military.[28] The situation was more drastic at the AOI. By 2009, 70 percent of the AOI's outcome became civilian, with only 30 percent still military.[29]

For example, the MoMP's Helwan Company for Engineering Industries, also known as Factory 99, was one of the large plants that went through this conversion process. For more than three decades since it was built in 1958, Factory 99 specialized in manufacturing casings for various sorts of ammunition, including anti-armor warheads, runaway bombs, and artillery rockets. It switched to producing completely different consumer and non-consumer goods: stainless steel tableware and kitchenware, fire extinguishers, gas regulators, and auto parts such engines and bumpers. Also, for more than three decades since it was built in 1954, the MoMP's Shubra for Engineering Industries Company, known as Factory 27, produced small arms ammunition. It shifted to manufacturing electric engines to use in assembling consumer goods such as electric fans and washing machines. The Helwan Metal Devices Company, or Factory 360, built in 1964, began by producing sheet metal used in the construction of trenches and making mines sapper charges. It switched to manufacturing washing machines and other home appliances, such as refrigerators, freezers, air conditioners, water heaters, and gas ovens. Furthermore, the Heliopolis Chemical Industries Company, Factory 81, once manufactured ammunition for anti-aircraft guns and developed long-range bombardment rockets. It transitioned into non-military goods such as paints and raw rubber for car tires.[30]

At the AOI, the Arab British Dynamics Company used to produce guided missiles with an English partner—British Aerospace Dynamics. In 1998, the company faced a crisis with the withdrawal of the British co-producer, leaving it with no sources of advanced technology. It reduced its activities to only installing missile launchers on jeeps. In addition, it shifted to manufacturing tobacco-producing machines, auto parts, gas stopcocks, medical equipment, industrial burners for bakeries, and furnaces. Another instance at the AOI is the Sakr Factory, which originally produced artillery rockets, light guided missiles, and grenades. It switched to manufacturing water storage plants, large electronic monitors for stadiums and advertisement boards, loaders, minibuses, agricultural and irrigation machines, and different sorts of trucks for sewer cleaning, water carrying, and postal services. The AOI's Aircraft Factory originally assembled and produced aircrafts, and had to diversify to produce ambulances, garbage recycling machines, and treatment plants for sewage, potable water, and industrial drainage. It also produced furnished trucks transporting vaccines and medical waste. The Electronics Factory that originally specialized in avionics, such as producing aircraft communications systems and radar, now shifted to producing TVs, personal computers, digital satellite receivers, telephone switching systems, photocopiers, and printers.[31]

The hasty conversion process suffered from a noticeable lack of institutional planning, so various corps duplicated the production of the exact same goods without taking into consideration the prospect of competing with each other over the same local market. Several of the factories of the MoMP and AOI copied each other's work, and they both copied NSPO's products. The most striking example is the number of factories that manufactured water and sewage sanitation plants. Military Factories 10 and 270, the AOI's Engine Factory, and the Aircraft Factory all assembled similar systems mainly to sell to government projects. Another example is in the chemicals sector. While the NSPO had a large chemicals complex geared for civilian production, the MoMP had three chemicals plants (Factories 18, 81, and 270) engaged in overlapping activities. Moreover, the Chemical Warfare Department produced pesticides, drugs, detergents, and vinegar—copying the goods of the NSPO's chemicals complex. The Supply Authority also produced drugs—duplicating the work of the latter two. In addition, many converted industries produced vehicles and trucks of various forms, including Factory 200, the Sakr Factory, and the Aircraft Factory. Both Banha for Electronic Industries, or Factory 144, and the AOI's Electronics Factory produced TVs, personal computers, and satellite receivers. Many enterprises overlapped in manufacturing kitchenware, home appliances, furniture, irrigation equipment, sports equipment, and garbage recycling systems. The Department of Weapons and Ammunition produced sports equipment, which military Factories 54 and 999 already produced. Outside factories in the field of commercial agriculture, the NSPO's large commercial farms yielded processed food, and so did the Third Army's farms.[32]

Switching from military to civilian production took place within a pervasive milieu of transforming Egypt into a market economy. Upon the collapse of the Soviet Union, Egypt among other previously socialist regimes faced U.S. pressure to transform into a free-market economy—neoliberalism. In 1991, Egypt concluded U.S.-backed agreements with the IMF and the World Bank to apply an economic reform and structural adjustment program. One of the cornerstones of this program was the reduction of fiscal deficit through significant cuts in public spending.[33] Amidst swiftly applying these market measures, the Egyptian defense industry was hurt in some areas, but benefited in many others. Mending the budget deficit entailed cuts in military expenditure as a considerable part of public spending. The Military budget drastically dropped in the early 1990s.[34] Nevertheless, the regime compensated the military for these budget losses by allowing it to expand its civilian production activities, initially by converting large parts of the defense industry and later by creating new business ventures. Not only military factories weathered all waves of privatization and maintained their subsidies and privileges intact, but they also expanded further. By the end of the 1990s, military industries employed about 200,000 workers.[35]

While Egypt undertook these transformations, i.e., neoliberal transition moving hand in hand with defense conversion, there was an ongoing global wave of similar changes in many other states that once aligned with the Soviets. The end of the Cold War rendered the American economic system a global model for all former socialist and post-communist states to follow. Economic liberalization measures that regimes transitioning into the market economy applied required substantial cuts in public spending, including in military budgets. Many of these regimes allowed their military institutions to create business enterprises that compensated for their financial losses, most especially in order to avoid officers' mutinies or potential coups d'état. The phenomenon of military business, or "Milbus" as Jörn Brömmelhörster and Wolf-Christian Paes refer to it, emerged when the IMF and the World Bank pushed governments transforming to neoliberalism to adopt more conservative fiscal policies. In order to coup-proof their regimes, these governments hid military expenditures in "a complex web of budgetary and off-budgetary transactions, often incorporating elements of military business."[36] This generated the global phenomenon of "Milbus" in many places, including Russia, China, Indonesia, and Pakistan all the way to Argentina, Guatemala, Costa Rica, and Panama.[37]

Evidently, undertaking defense conversion in a neoliberal milieu led to failure in achieving its manifest goal: making armies help with national economic development. On the contrary, the experiences of many states show that conversion while transitioning to the market economy made armies a burden on the economy rather than a fair competitor in and contributor to it. This is due to the extensive privileges they receive from their regimes at the expense of public and private businesses. According to free-market theoretical assumptions, defense conversion should take place smoothly and efficiently with little state intervention: the market should fix any problems that might occur during the process. Nevertheless, many theorists debunk this assumption and insist that centralized planning is essentially needed, at least because of the very nature of military business that resents abiding by the rules of a free market and superiorly acts beyond them.[38] Probably Russia presents the most conspicuous example of defense conversion that went wrong because it took place while applying economic reform, whereas China presents an opposite case where the process succeeded because it occurred under heavy government planning.

Unfortunately, the 1990s Egyptian experience was closer to the Russian model, and thus came out inefficient.[39]

During the 2000s, the Egyptian military business embarked on a new stage of substantial expansion in its economic activities. This was when the ambitious elder son of President Mubarak, Gamal, delved into the political and economic scene with an apparent scheme to inherent his father's presidential seat. Gamal Mubarak accelerated the rate of transitioning to the market—which came at great benefit of the military entrepreneurs. He took over the ruling party by forming the "Politics Committee," whose membership was composed of his close patronage circle of business tycoons and neoliberal minds in the country. From this very circle, a cabinet dominated by private business figures took form in 2004, and remained in office until the 2011 uprisings. This cabinet rapidly privatized more public-sector enterprises, eliminated subsidies, liberalized the agricultural land rents, and reduced spending on public services, among other things. Similarly, the elected parliaments of 2005 and 2010 were dominated by Gamal's business cronies and issued laws that contributed to the hastened market transformations. In order to appease the military institution that watchfully witnessed a young civilian approaching the presidential seat—which had been occupied by only officers ever since 1952—Mubarak allowed the army to extensively expand their civilian enterprises.[40]

Within this domestic milieu, the military seized many public-sector enterprises that were up for sale and transferred their ownership to the various military entities. Because advanced technology was indispensable in old and new ventures, the officers partnered with American, German, Chinese, French, Eastern European, Japanese, and more firms now entering the open market. With them, the military invested in new heavy industries, such as railway wagons, luxury cars, ships, steel, cement, etc. Military business continued to enjoy various forms of tax and customs breaks. When the country's stock market was reactivated and both private and public enterprises became listed, none of the military companies registered themselves—the officers maintained full lack of transparency about their capital and annual revenue, and sought to avoid having stockholders to share their firms with.[41]

For example, the AOI seized the only state-owned manufacturing plant of railway wagons in the country when it was privatized in 2004, and thus established a monopoly over this sector. With a long career and good connections with global technology, SEMAF was founded as a public-sector company in 1955. In 1986, SEMAF entered into a joint venture with a French rail group to introduce the first fleet of underground metro cars to the long waiting inhabitants of crowded Cairo.[42] Taking advantage of the extended wave of privatization, the AOI "annexed" SEMAF—located in Helwan near many other factories of the AOI—with its more than 1400 workers. The plant carried on with manufacturing train and underground wagons for its new military owner, which made deals worth billions of Egyptian pounds and presented overhauling services to the government.[43]

In another incident of the military seizing vital state-owned enterprises that were supposed to be privatized, the military appropriated several maritime and river transport companies. In 2003, the MoD created a new organization called the Maritime Industries and Services Organization (MISO), as a corporation enjoying its own legal entity. MISO immediately took over three gigantic public sector firms: the Egyptian Company for Ship Repairs and Building, the Alexandria Shipyard, and the Nile Company for River Transport—in 2003, 2007, and 2008, respectively. Moreover, MISO created another new venture, Triumph for Maritime Transport, in 2009. Needless to say, ex-navy officers head the organization and its subsidiaries. The property rights of the Alexandria Shipyard were "transferred" from the state to MISO.[44] When the organization appropriated the Nile Company for River Transport from its mother state-owned holding company, the head of the latter was another former navy officer.[45] MISO fostered good ties with Chinese, Eastern European, French, and local firms.[46]

Moreover, the military ventured into the manufacturing of a crucially resource: steel making.[47] In 2005, the MoMP finished the construction of a large steel rolling plant as part of military Factory 100.[48] Also known as the Abu Za'bal Company for Engineering Industries, Factory 100 was established in 1974 and originally produced ordnance such as anti-aircraft, tube artillery, and tank guns.[49] The attached gigantic steel plant needed large capital in order to acquire Western technology and expertise, which the regime made available to the military. The MoMP invested LE1.5 billion in this mill, in collaboration with a German company, SMS Siemag, and other global steelmakers.[50] As usual, this new venture enjoyed advantageous tax breaks: the minister of military production insured that his projects in steel and other sectors were exempt from customs or pay very little duties.[51] Another NSPO company benefited from the venture by feeding the mill with needed iron scrap, particularly the NSOP's Queen Service company which was active in scrap trading.[52]

In another sector of production of strategic goods, the NSPO invested in a large cement plant. It created Arish Cement Factory in North Sinai in 2010.[53] The brand-new facility was erected on an appropriated piece of state land, around 210 acres, in addition to seizing hundreds of other acres of surrounding quarries to feed it with raw material, and more land to construct roads connecting the plant to those quarries. This time, the military chose to collaborate with a non-Western partner to obtain technology and construct the facility: a Chinese state-owned company, and the MoD footed a bill of $370 million in total cost. According to a company statement, Sinoma Group was the first incident of a Chinese contractor working in Egypt's construction sector. The plant has about 800 workers—all civilians except for the top managers who are generals; many of them traveled to China to receive professional training.[54]

These are only a few examples from the civilian business empire that the Egyptian military expanded before the 2011 uprisings. One of the most frequently asked questions about the military business empire in Egypt is its exact size: how many enterprises developed, and how much profit they generate annually, and their proportion of the national economy. Because military enterprises are untaxed and unaudited by either the parliament or public accountability agencies, and they are not even listed in the stock market with publicly open company profiles, it is almost impossible to estimate their precise number and gain access to their annual profit. Robert Springborg estimates their size from anywhere between 5 and 40 percent of the country's economy and asserts that they make billions of dollars.[55] Economist Ahmed al-El-Naggar calculated them at only 1.8 percent in 2013. The ex-minister of defense and current military President, Abdel Fattah Al-Sisi, also presented an estimate, asserting that they made up only 2 percent of the national economy in 2014.[56] Whereas high estimates take into consideration the military formal and informal control over state land and other public construction and service sectors, the lower estimates mostly depend on materially counting the visible commercial facilities they own.

After a new military president took back full power in 2014, this empire was conspicuously further extended into old and new sectors of manufacturing and services. In the meantime, the new military regime faced a crisis that pressured it to give attention back to its long-neglected defense industry.

4. Attempts at Autonomy: Diversification and Co-Production (2013–2018)

In 2013, a crisis with U.S. military aid forced Egypt to make serious attempts to diversify its sources of procurement and increase recent co-production initiatives. In the summer of that year, then minister of defense, al-Sisi, relied on widespread mass protests to overthrow the Islamist president and subsequently formed an interim government. In summer 2014, al-Sisi swept the presidential election and assumed full power. As a result, the Obama Administration informally perceived the events as a military coup and suspended U.S. arms shipments due to Egypt as part of its aid package for two years, until 2015. Such an act placed pressure on the Egyptian military to limit its dependency on U.S. arms by diversifying and seeking new co-production agreements with non-American firms, namely European companies in states that were willing to collaborate with the ex-general. In addition, a war on terrorist groups that proliferated in the country upon deposing the Islamist president, especially the Islamic State in Iraq and the Levant (known as ISIL or ISIS) in the Sinai Peninsula, and their repeated attacks across the country further pressured the military to diversify and co-produce new weapon systems. Regional actors in support of Islamists that posed a military threat to the Egyptian regime, especially Turkey and Qatar, contributed to such pressure. Meanwhile, other regional actors, especially the UAE and Saudi Arabia, financially backed al-Sisi's military endeavors towards reduced dependency on the U.S.

For around a decade before this crisis and under President Mubarak, Egypt had already ventured into new initiatives towards co-production away from the U.S. According to Shana Marshall, Egyptian military industries sought partnership with "second- and third-tier" international defense manufacturers, but at a limited scale in comparison to the large number of licenses that were successfully acquired in the1980s. Marshall argues that the Egyptian defense producers, hoping for reduced reliance on U.S. firms, attempted to form ties with lesser-ranked or smaller manufacturers and engage in small-scale projects with them with a goal of technology transfer.[57]

Marshall indicates that Egypt's new co-production partners then were subsidiaries or small independent suppliers that benefitted from sales contracts with a country in desperate need for access to technology. Such efforts were largely concentrated in the "Mubarak Complex for the Defense Industry," constructed primarily to provide new facilities to old military factories in the outskirts of the densely populated Cairo. According to Marshall, contracts concluded with foreign firms included, for example, the production of,

> [A] waterjet-powered fire-fighting vessel (with 4X4 vehicle deployment ramp) built in 2004 ... based on design technology and materials provided by Teknicraft Design (of New Zealand) and the local Egyptian agent of Hamiltonjet (also of New Zealand) ... The website of an Egyptian consulting firm revealed that it had worked on another product development plan, this one encompassing the military-owned firms Arab International Optronics and Benha Electronics Factory, along with Motorola and the French defense firms Thales (which owns half of Arab International Optronics) and Thomson CSF.[58]

Meanwhile, the Egyptian military was far from terminating its dependency on the U.S. The MoMP continued to co-produce M1A1 with General Dynamics, and aimed at increasing its share in manufacturing the tank from 80 to 90 percent. Other projects with American firms that were closely tied to this tank's production with other major manufacturers needed to continue. Marshall indicates that they included "a 2005 agreement with United Technologies to co-produce M88A2 tank recovery vehicles, and a twenty million US dollar contract signed with Oshkosh Defense in 2009 to co-produce the M1070 tank transport and refueling vehicle."[59]

More importantly, Egypt continued to receive U.S. military aid, at the considerable annual amount of around $1.3 billion. This was in the form of financing arms sales from U.S. firms to Egypt. For the previous three decades, Egypt traditionally used this grant to purchase "large-scale conventional military equipment" from major American defense manufacturers. On the eve of the 2013 crisis, the list of U.S. companies that supplied Egypt included Lockheed Martin, Boeing, DRS Technologies, L3 Communications, Raytheon, AgustaWestland, US Motor Works, Goodrich, and Columbia Group.[60] According to a CRS report, the Obama Administration shifted this tradition by announcing that "grants may only be used to purchase equipment specifically for 'counterterrorism, border security, Sinai security, and maritime security' (and for sustainment of weapons systems already in Egypt's arsenal)."[61]

Up until 2013, most of Egypt's procurement came primarily from U.S. firms except for a small portion from European manufacturers. These purchases included vehicles from AM General, Apache AH-64D from Boeing, CS gas allegedly used in Tahrir from Combined Company, M1A1from General Dynamics, F-16C/D from Lockheed Martin, and Black Hawk aircraft from Sikorsky (UTC). Aside from this, Egypt received sales from the British multinational BAE Systems of aircraft KF-16C/D, airbuses from the joint German-French company EADS, and a joint Turkish-British BAE System project of tracked and wheeled armored combat vehicles.[62]

Three weeks after the al-Sisi-led coalition overthrew the Islamist president, the Pentagon suspended a shipment of 12 Lockheed Martin's F-16 fighter jets to Egypt, probably for the first time since Egypt started to receive an annually fixed military aid package three decades earlier after signing the peace treaty with Israel. This was followed by freezing the shipment of 20 Boeing Harpoon missiles and around 125 M1A1 Abrams tank kits. Furthermore, the "Bright Star" routine mutual exercise between the Egyptian and U.S. armies was canceled. However, the U.S. decided in 2014 to deliver ten Apache helicopters "to help combat terrorism, particularly in the Sinai."[63] Suspended supplies were only released about two years later, after al-Sisi was elected president and spent many months in office.[64] During this period, al-Sisi sought procurement elsewhere, especially in Russia. Before he was elected president and in his capacity as minister of defense, Field Marshal al-Sisi visited Vladimir Putin near Moscow to negotiate a $2 billion arms deal. On the same visit, Putin supported al-Sisi's candidacy in the presidential election.[65] The Obama Administration resumed military aid in March 2015, after a visit by U.S. Secretary of State John Kerry to Cairo, during which he attended an international economic conference to support the military regime's economic development plan.[66]

The UK and the EU as a whole similarly suspended arms sales to Egypt after the events of the summer of 2013. The UK revoked arms deals for components of military combat vehicles with Egypt. Like the U.S., the UK resumed those sales in 2015.[67] As for the EU, according to a report published by the Campaign against Arms Trade (CAAT), it suspended a large number of licenses on the grounds of their potential use in domestic oppression of civilian opposition, but it later allowed some of them to resume provisions. In August of 2013, the EU "suspended 49 existing licenses as well as new license applications for the Egyptian Army, Air Force and Internal Security Forces or Ministry of the Interior until further notice."[68] In October of the same year, the EU completed assessing the situation and declared that,

> 24 licenses would have the suspension lifted as it did not judge the goods might be used for internal repression, seven would be revoked as there was a clear risk that the goods might be used for internal repression, and the remaining 16 would remain suspended because the goods might be used for internal repression.[69]

Therefore, the 2013 crisis stirred the military regime to intensify efforts to diversify suppliers and pursue new co-production contracts. As a result, the last few years, under al-Sisi and with his minister of military production ex-general Mohamed al-Assar, have witnessed renewed and increased attention on the domestic arms industry. Although most of al-Assar's activities continue to focus on civilian production, he has initiated some attempts at military co-production with international firms.[70]

In 2017 al-Assar claimed that military manufacturing increased by 230 percent in 2015/2016. Nevertheless, he did not provide specific details about the items produced or the volume of output, insisting that such information constitutes a national security secret and should be kept hidden from the public. He stated that his ministry manages 20 companies, which include 17 factories that engage in military and civilian production, a construction company, and a research center. They employ around 34,500 workers.[71] He affirmed that his ministry plans to focus on efforts of military co-production with international firms instead of importing, and he specified Russian firms in this regard and named UAE as an Arab partner. He also reached out to France, Portugal, Belarus, Croatia, Serbia, and Pakistan to discuss collaboration. Al-Assar asserted that Egypt hoped to rely on manufacturing partnerships with other countries for arms supply as an alternative to imports.[72] However, the results of such numerous talks were not announced, nor manifested in actual projects launched on the ground.

There are currently only two publicly known co-production initiatives that Egypt is engaged in—apart from the continuity of the M1A1 tank project with the U.S. The first was contracted in 2014, with the French shipbuilder Naval Group (formerly DCNS) to make the Gowind 2500 corvette, which is considered the most advanced naval technology in France. In 2014, Egypt concluded a contract with the French state-owned firm to purchase four ships, three of which were to be constructed in the Egyptian military-owned Alexandria Shipyard. Technology transfer was included in the procurement agreement, and it was to take place in the military shipyard. In 2016, Egypt received the first ship and gave it the name of "ENS El Fateh." In 2018, Egypt completed the building of the second ship and gave it the name of "ENS Port Said." In mid-2019, it completed and launched another one and called it "al-Moez (981)." In order to provide "in-service support," the Naval Group created an Egyptian subsidiary, Alexandria Naval, to take charge of such tasks.[73]

The second co-production initiative was also contracted in 2014, but with an American partner which meant that it didn't count for attempts at diversifying. It was between the Egyptian Navy and the Louisiana-based firm Swiftships, and the firm indicated that its project does include technology transfer. The transaction, according to the company's webpage, was for:

> [B]uilding up to thirty Patrol Craft in a period of seven years. The shipyard in Egypt was replicated to Swiftships' ISO standards by the company's own Subject Matter Experts (SMEs) specializing in shipbuilding and ship repair. The work was performed by local labor under direct Swiftships-trained Egyptian supervisors and SMEs. The Co-production program allows the EN to train their craftsmen at the Swiftships Academy in Morgan City, Louisiana, to gain in-depth knowledge of the capabilities and quality of the product, while enforcing product quality and management.[74]

However, Egypt continues to heavily rely on arms imports much more than its own production. It purchased items from European states that were willing to deal with the new military president for mutual interests—based on counterterrorism efforts and for benefiting their national manufacturers. It concluded especially large deals with France and Russia, with Germany coming in third. According to the Stockholm International Peace Research Institute's (SIPRI) 2016 report of "Trends in International Arms Transfers," Egypt was the 11th largest importer of major weapons globally between 2012 and 2016. The World

Bank's aggregates indicate that these imports tripled after the 2013 wave of terrorism and the need to contain ISIL in Sinai. They increased from $630,000,000 in 2011, $675,000,000 in 2013, to $1,483,000,000 in 2016. This marked a 69 percent increase in recent years. France alone was the source of 40 percent of the country's imports—an equal parentage to that of the U.S. at the time. Egypt is currently the largest client of France with deals worth billions of Euros for fighter jets and warships. It has also signed many large arms deals with Russia, including contracts for 50 combat aircraft and 46 combat helicopters. Germany "quintupled" its arms sales to Egypt and Saudi Arabia—a main regional backer of al-Sisi—with deals worth hundreds of millions of Euros.[75] The UK resumed much smaller arms deals worth around only £48.8 million in 2015. It was anticipated that China might become one of Egypt's suppliers away from the U.S., but it did not because Egypt continued to prefer Western suppliers. China tried to compete with Germany and offered two cheaper submarines in 2015, but the deal didn't work out. Egypt purchased the German submarines instead.[76]

Egyptian imports tremendously increased again in the following year. According to SIPRI's latest report "Trends in International Arms Transfer" of 2017, Egypt jumped into the ranking of the third largest importer of weapons globally during the last five years. Egyptian imports increased by 4.5 percent, and it came third after India (12 percent) and Saudi Arabia (10 percent). France replaced the U.S. as the largest exporter of weapons to Egypt. Between 2008 and 2012, the U.S. was the main supplier with around 45 percent of Egyptian imports. Between 2013 and 2017, France took this place by providing Egypt with 37 percent of its procurement.[77]

Thus, since 2013 France has been by far the largest supplier to Egypt, after the sale of the 24 Rafale aircraft manufactured by Dassault Aviation, followed by the Mistral warship manufactured by Naval Group (these are in addition to the abovementioned four corvettes Gowind for co-production). The French government lent Egypt a loan of 3.2 billion Euros to conclude the Rafale contract in 2015, and oil-producing Gulf states that are close allies of al-Sisi helped fund the deal.[78] Al-Sisi visited Paris in late 2017 and was received by the newly elected President, Emanuel Macron. As journalist Jenna Le Bras explained in a report published at the Cairo-based *Mada Masr*,

> The relationship between the two countries in recent years has centered on military and security cooperation and counterterrorism, while France has turned a blind eye to Egypt's worrying human rights record. Macron defended this position during Sisi's visit, saying it is not his place to 'lecture' Egypt on civil liberties."[79] The agreement of the Mistral helicopter carrier, manufactured by French shipbuilder DCNS, cost Egypt about $1 billion.[80] By the end of 2017, France expressed an interest to sell Egypt "A400M air-lifters and 36 NH90 helicopters, of which 24 would be land-use Tactical Troop Transports (TTH) and 12 NATO Frigate Helicopter (NFH) for maritime operations.[81]

Oil-producing Arab Gulf states supported other Egyptian deals, besides the abovementioned French Rafale. Saudi Arabia and the UAE are the two main backers of Egypt in this realm. The Gulf Cooperation Council (GCC) announced in 2015 that it was establishing "an armed-forces commission" to provide financial and military aid to counterterrorism activities in Egypt and other Arab countries.[82]

While Egypt intensified its arms importation or co-production activities, it has been entangled in domestic and regional conflicts under al-Sisi. The Egyptian army is engaged in Sinai with ISIL; in Yemen together with Saudi Arabia and the UAE to a limited degree; and on its borders with Libya by aiding its Eastern military ruler. Such engagements pressured the regime to obtain more weapons. According to the 2016 *Military Balance* report, repeated armed attacks of ISIL and other jihadist groups in Sinai and elsewhere in the country resulted in,

> [S]ubstantive troop deployments and military operations, whilst insurgent activity on Egypt's borders has led to closer security cooperation with other North African states. State breakdown in Libya and Syria, and arms smuggling activities across the border, has become of particular concern. In 2015, Egypt was part of the Saudi-led coalition in Yemen, supplying 800 troops, and warships to enforce a maritime blockade in the Bab el-Mandeb.[83]

Moreover, in the Saudi-led "Operation Restoring Hope" in Yemen, Egypt contributed 6 F-16C Fighting Falcons.[84]

It is important to note that the MoMP still gives increasing and noticeable attention to its civilian business enterprises aside from the arms industry. Since he assumed his position in September 2015, al-Assar added numerous civilian projects aiming at lucrative profit for his ministry. This included a pharmaceuticals plant and another one for baby formula in collaboration with the ministry of health, and other initiatives to manufacture electricity meters for the ministry of power, water sanitation plants for the ministry of housing, engines of washing machines, farming machinery, and heavy trucks: that is in addition to public construction projects to build schools for the ministry of education, large sports facilities, and public roads and bridges, and in addition to land reclamation projects for commercial farming ventures. In fact, the vast majority of published news on the MoMP are about its civilian production and services activities, and most of al-Assar statements are about the ministry's contribution to the national economy rather than arms manufacturing.[85]

In addition, under President Sisi the number of ex-generals appointed to key positions in the government has tremendously increased along with the ever-increasing privileges for military civilian businesses. In 2015, to name only a few instances, ex-generals headed the public authorities of industrial development, agricultural development, import and export control, maritime transport, railways, sea and Nile ports, and the Suez Canal. The crucial positions of the minister of transportation, the chairman of the national Telecommunication Holding Company, and the chairman of the Maritime and Land Transport Holding Company were all occupied by other ex-generals. Meanwhile, military contractors continue to function as gigantic parastatal entities that have taken charge of, among other things, executing public construction projects of bridges, roads, hospitals, schools, affordable housing, and sporting clubs.

5. Conclusion

The Egyptian defense industry witnessed a period of rapid growth in the 1950s and 1960s, when Egypt's first military regime received technical and financial support from the Soviet Union during the Cold War. An economic crisis and two large wars with Israel, in 1967 and 1973, deeply affected such growth and placed the industry on hold. In the 1980s, Egyptian arms manufacturing witnessed another period of wide expansion based on primarily Western technology, and enjoyed a lucrative regional market. However, the industry deteriorated again in the 1990s. For the past three decades, Egyptian arms factories have stagnated as a result of shifting domestic, regional, and international conditions. Lack of capital, technology transfer, and potential market pressured the Egyptian military factories to massively convert into producing civilian goods. This was followed by the military institution investing in establishing its own business enterprises in manufacturing strategic and consumer goods while providing services to the civilian domestic market. Military enterprises enjoyed extensive state privileges that allow them a monopolistic status in several sectors, and they function above the supposedly free market in the country. Since Egypt transitioned into neoliberalism in the 1990s, the military lost part of its allocated state budget but compensated for this by creating an extensively profitable and multi-sectoral business empire.

Thus, for the past three decades, Egyptian arms production has declined and the country has been widely dependent on arms imports from the U.S. and other Western suppliers. Egypt faced a serious crisis with the continuity of such imports from the U.S. and Europe in 2013, and had to attempt to diversify and seek new co-production agreements to reduce its dependency—especially on the U.S. These attempts do not seem to have yielded considerable outcomes on the ground. Most of the production of the Egyptian military factories is still dedicated to civilian goods for the domestic market. Meanwhile, Egyptian imports of arms from Western suppliers have increased, and new arms co-production programs are noticeably limited.

If Egypt seeks to join emerging countries in arms manufacturing, its military factories that at present largely produce for the civilian market should divest themselves of civilian business and re-focus on partnership efforts with international firms. With necessary and large-scale divestiture, military factories need to rationalize their management by reducing their over-bloated size and re-training their labor force. Moreover, they should re-orient their activities of co-production and redesign their facilities to manufacture non-conventional weapon systems that would match with recent needs of asymmetric warfare of counterterrorism. Egypt already owns the needed infrastructure and cheap labor to attract Foreign Direct Investment (FDI) and technology for partnership, but it needs to manage these resources efficiently through reviewing its manufacturing policies and restructuring the facilities of arms production accordingly.

Notes

1. See Zeinab Abul-Magd, *Militarizing the Nation: The Army, Business, and Revolution in Egypt* (New York: Columbia University Press, 2017), 35–77.
2. Abul-Magd, *Militarizing the Nation*, 35–7; Joe Stork, "Arms Industries of the Middle East" (MERIP Report 144, January–February 1987), 12–6.
3. Florence Gaub and Zoe Stanley-Lockman, "Defence Industries in the Arab States: Players and Strategies," (European Union Institute for Security Studies, Chaillot Papers, March 2017): 18.
4. See Abul-Magd, *Militarizing the Nation*, 78–111.
5. *Foreign Assistance Legislation for Fiscal Year 1988–89 (Part 3): Hearings and Markup before the Subcommittee on Europe and the Middle East of the Committee on Foreign Affairs, House of Representatives, One Hundredth Congress, First Session, February 3, 10, 23, 25; March 3, 11, And 19, 1987*, 100th Cong. 140–41 (1987) (statement of Robert Pelletreau, Deputy Assistant Secretary for Near Eastern and South Asian Affairs, Department of Defense); Tony Walker, "US Sweeten the Pot for Defense Projects in Egypt," *Financial Times*, May 7, 1987.
6. Patrick E. Tyler, "Pentagon Agrees to Let Egypt Produce M1 Tank; Move Expected to Draw Fire in Washington," *Washington Post*, June 29, 1987. Also see Michael Gordon, "U.S. May Allow Egyptians to Buy and Assemble M-1 Tanks," *New York Times*, June 30, 1987; Barbara Slavin, "A Tankful of Trouble for Egypt? Critics Say Co-producing M-1 Tanks is Misguided Show of Friendship," *St. Petersburg Times*, January 23, 1988.
7. *Supplemental 1979 Middle East Aid Package for Israel and Egypt: Hearings and Makeup before the Committee on Foreign Affairs and its Subcommittee on International Security and Scientific Affairs and on Europe and the Middle East, House of Representatives, Ninety-Sixth Congress, First Session April 26; May 1, 2, 8, and 9, 1979*, 96th Cong. 152 (1979); *Foreign Assistance Legislation for Fiscal Year*

1983 (Part 3): Hearings and Markup before the Subcommittee on Europe and the Middle East of the Committee on Foreign Affairs, House of Representatives, Ninety-Seventh Congress, Second Session, March 15, 23, 30; April 1 and 27, 1982, 97th Cong. 14–15 (1982) (statement of Morris Draper, Deputy Assistant Secretary, Bureau of Near Eastern and South Asian Affairs, Department of State). Also see *Foreign Assistance Legislation for Fiscal Year 1988–89 (Part 3): Hearings and Markup before the Subcommittee on Europe and the Middle East of the Committee on Foreign Affairs, House of Representatives, One Hundredth Congress, First Session, February 3, 10, 23, 25; March 3, 11, And 19, 1987,* 100th Cong. Washington, DC: U.S. Government Printing Office, 1987.

8. "Export Briefs … Egypt, US Sign Pact," *Journal of Commerce*, November 4, 1988. Also see "Egypt and U.S. Agree on a Joint Tank Plan," *New York Times*, November 2, 1988.
9. United States General Accounting Office (GAO), *Military Aid to Egypt: Tank Production Raised Costs and May not Meet Many Program Goals*, GAO/NSIAD-93-203 (Washington, DC: U.S. Government Accountability Office, 1993), 2.
10. United States General Accounting Office (GAO), *Military Aid to Egypt*, 1–2.
11. United States General Accounting Office (GAO), *Military Aid to Egypt*, 15.
12. Jim Paul, "The Egyptian Arms Industry" (MERIP Reports 112, February 1983), 26–8.
13. LTC Stephen H. Gotowicki (U.S. Army), "The Role of the Egyptian Military in Domestic Society," Published at DoD's Foreign Military Studies Office (FMSO), National Defense University, 1997, accessed 29 August 2011, http://fmso.leavenworth.army.mil/documents/egypt/egypt.htm.
14. Stork, "Arms Industries of the Middle East," 12–6.
15. "Egypt Wins Right to Export Arms to the U.S.," *New York Times*, March 24, 1988.
16. See Joe Stork and James Paul, "Arms Sales and Militarizing the Middle East," MERIP 112 February 1983), 5–15.
17. Philip H. Stoddard, "Egypt and the Iran–Iraq War," in *Gulf Security and the Iran–Iraq War*, edited by Thomas Naff (Washington, DC: National Defense University Press, 1985), 36–7.
18. Gotowicki, "The Role of the Egyptian Military in Domestic Society".
19. Ralph Sanders, "Arms Industries: New Supplies and Regional Security [National Security Implications]," *The DISAM Journal* 13 (Winter 1990/1991): 105.
20. Florence Gaub and Zoe Stanley-Lockman, "Defence Industries in the Arab States: Players and Strategies," (European Union Institute for Security Studies, Chaillot Papers, March 2017), 16.
21. See Yezid Sayigh, *Arab Military Industry: Capability, Performance, and Impact* (London: Brassey's: Putnam Aeronautical 1992), 45.
22. See Abul-Magd, *Militarizing the Nation*, 78–111.
23. Business Monitor International Ltd, "Egypt Defence and Security Report," *Quarter* 4, Issue 4 (2011): 59.
24. Stark, "Arms Industries of the Middle East," 14.
25. *Middle East Arms Control and Related Issues*, Foreign Affairs and National Defense Division, CRS Report No: 91-384F (Washington, DC: Congressional Research Service, May 1, 1991), 14.
26. "White House Fact Sheet on the Middle East Arms Control Initiative," May 29, 1991, accessed April 24, 2016, http://www.presidency.ucsb.edu/ws/?pid=19637, 579–80.
27. United States General Accounting Office (GAO), *Military Aid to Egypt: Tank Coproduction Raised Costs and May Not Meet Many Program Goals*, GAO/NSIAD-93-203 (Washington, DC, July 27, 1993), 3.
28. Ibtisam Ta'lab, "Dr. Sayyid Mash'al Wazir al-Intaj al-Harbi li-l-Masry al-Yuom (2-2)," *al-Masry al-Youm*, September 15, 2010.
29. Ahmad Abd al-'Azim, "al-Fariq Hamdi Wahiba- Ra'is al-Hay'a al-'Arabiyya li-l-Tasni'- fi Hiwar ma'a Ruz al-Yusuf," *Ruz al-Yusuf*, November 3, 2009.
30. Sayigh, *Arab Military Industry*, 55–7. The official website of MoMP, accessed January 15, 2014, http://www.momp.gov.eg/Ar/Facts.aspx.
31. Sayigh, *Arab Military Industry*, 57–60; Website of AOI, accessed January 15, 2014, http://www.aoi.com.eg/aoiarab/factories/abdinfo.html; http://www.aoi.com.eg/aoiarab/factories/acfinfo.html; http://www.aoi.com.eg/aoiarab/factories/sakrinfo.html.
32. See Abul-Magd, *Militarizing the Nation*, 112–51.
33. See Karima Korayem, *Egypt's Economic Reform and Structural Adjustment* (Cairo: Egyptian Center for Economic Studies, 1997); Dieter Weiss and Ulrich Wurzel, *The Economics and Politics of Transition to an Open Market Economy: Egypt* (Paris: OECD, 1998), 44–51.
34. See Abul-Magd, *Militarizing the Nation*, 112–51; Tables, 251–52.

35. Jamal Mazlum, *al-Quwwat al-Musallaha wa-l-Tanmiya al-Iqtisadiyya* (Cairo: Markaz Dirasat wa-Buhuth al-Duwal al-Namiya, 1999), 106.
36. Jorn Brommelhorster and Wolf-Christian Paes, eds., *The Military as an Economic Actor: Soldiers in Business* (Basingstoke: Palgrave Macmillan, 2003), 9.
37. For Milbus cases in the Middle East, in states such as Turkey, Pakistan, Iran, Syria, Yemen, and the Sudan, see Zeinab Abul-Magd and Elke Grawert, *Businessmen in Arms: How the Military and Other Armed Groups Profit in the MENA Region* (New York: Rowman & Littlefield, April 2016).
38. Seymour Melman and Lloyd Dumas, "Planning for Economic Conversion," *The Nation*, April 16, 1990. Also see Seymour Melman, *The Demilitarized Society: Disarmament and Conversion* (Montreal: Harvest House, 1990).
39. For the Russian case, see Julian Cooper, "Soviet Military Has a Finger in Every Pie," *The Bulletin of Atomic Scientists* 46 (1990): 22–2. For the Chinese case, see Dongmin Lee, "Swords to Ploughshares: China's Defence Conversion Policy," *Defence Studies* 11 (March 2011): 1–4 and 20.
40. See Holger Albrecht, "Does Coup-Proofing Work? Political-Military Relations in Authoritarian Regimes Amid the Arab Uprisings," *Mediterranean Politics* 20 (2015), 39; Abul-Magd, *Militarizing the Nation*, 112–51.
41 See Abul-Magd, *Militarizing the Nation*, 112–51.
42. Paul Betts, "French Rail Group Awarded Cairo Order," *Financial Times*, January 7, 1986.
43. See the factory's official website, accessed January 15, 2014, http://www.aoi.com.eg/aoiarab/aoi/semaf/pages/AboutA.html; Abd al-Fattah Ibrahim, "800 'Arabat Qitar Jadida bi-'Istithmarat 1.5 Milyar Junayh," *al-Ahram*, May 26, 2004.
44. Muhammad Amin, "al-Liwa' Bahari Ibrahim Jabir al-Dusuqi: Hadafuna Tatwir wa-Raf' Kafa'at Tirsanat al-Iskandariyya," *Uktubar*, January 23, 2011.
45. "Bay' Sharikat al-Nil li-l-Naql al-Nahri ila Jihaz al-Sina'at al-Bahriyya," *al-Ahram*, October 3, 2008; "Wazarat al-Difa' wa-l-Intaj al-Harbi. Qarar Raqam 3 li-Sanat 2010 bi-Sha'n Insha' Sharikat al-Nil lil-Naql al-Nahri," *al-Waqa'i' al-Rasmiyya* 66, year 182, March 21, 2010.
46. Du'a' Najib and Ahmad al-Dimirdash, "al-Intiha' min Tatwir Tirsanat al-Iskandariyya," *Amwal al-Ghadd*, March 18, 2013; Alexandria Shipyard's website, accessed April 15, 2014, http://www.alexyard.com.eg/ar%20first%20stage.html; Mamduh Sha'ban and Jamal al-Khuli, "Tirsanat al-Iskandariyya Tahtafil bi-Tadshin 'al-Huriyya 3'," *al-Ahram*, December 28, 2010; Rubban Muhammad Bahyy al-Dina Mandur, "Takhalluf Sina'at Bina' Sufun A'ali al-Bihar fi Misr," *International* (London) n. d., accessed April 15, 2014, http://www.international-mag.com/index.php?option=com_content&view=article&id=651:2011-12-11-12-50-20&catid=37:getaways&Itemid=532; Website of Chinese company, indicating sources of technology, accessed April 15, 2014, http://www.cstc.com.cn; Muhammad Amin, "al-Liwa' Bahari Ibrahim Jabir al-Dusuqi: Hadafuna Tatwir wa-Raf' Kafa'at Tirsanat al-Iskandariyya, " *Masress*, January 23, 2011, accessed 15 April 2014, http://www.masress.com/october/110405.

    The name of the French company is Bureau Veritas. "Alexandria Shipyard, Acquired Earlier by the Military Production Sector, Delivering Two Large Sized Barges, part of a L.E. Billion Order for 16 Barges Issued by Citadel Group's Affiliate Handling Land River Transport Investments at Home," *AmCham Egypt Project News*, August 10, 2010.
47 See official website of this company, accessed April 15, 2014, http://www.ezzsteel.com/main.asp?pageid=119.
48. 'Usama 'Abd al-'Aziz and Mukhtar Shu'ayb, "al-Ra'is Yaftatih Masna' Darfalat al-Sulb al-Makhsus al-Tabi' li-Wazart al-'Intaj al-Harbi bi-Abu Za'bal," *al-Ahram*, December 7, 2005.
49. Saygh, *Arab Military Industry*, 54.
50. "Mash'al: Mashru' 'Imlaq li-'Intaj wa-Darfalat al-Sulb," *al-Ahram*, March 16, 2004; Mamduh Sha'ban, "Ba'd Najah 'Intaj 'Awwal Lawh min al-Sulb bi-l-Darfala, Mash'al: al-'Intaj al-Harbi Yusahim fi Tatwir al-Sina'at al-Thaqila," *al-Ahram*, September 23, 2005; 'Abd al-'Aziz and Shu'ayb, "al-Ra'is Yaftatih Masna' Darfalat al-Sulb al-Makhsus".
51. Minister Ali Sbri stated this in an interview in March 2012. Zeinab Abul-Magd, "Siyadat al-Liwa' Sayuqatil al-Sha'b," *al-Masry al-Youm*, April 3, 2012.
52. See the company's website, accessed April 13, 2014, http://queenservicealex.blogspot.com.
53. *Al-Waqa'i' al-Misriyya*, no. 160, year 183, July 12, 2010.
54. Dalia 'Uthman, "al-Mushir Yaftatih Masna' 'Asmant al-'Arish," *al-Masry al-Youm*, May 1, 2012; Amira Ibrahim, "al-Mushir Yaftatih 'Awwal Masna' Asmant 'Asakari bi-Taqat 3.2 Tann Sanawiyyan bi-Taklufa 174 Milyun Yuru," *al-Dostor al-Asly*, April 30, 2012; Sinoma, "Kiln inlet steel tower of GOE

Project Line 1 in Egypt contracted by TCDRI installed," accessed April 13, 2014, http://en.sinoma.cn/news/ShowArticle.asp?ArticleID=989. The Chinese company's name is TCDRI, part off state-owned Sinoma Group, and its website, accessed April 13, 2014, http://www.tcdri.com.cn/english/intro.asp.

55. Alex Blumberg, "Why Egypt's Military Cares about Home Appliances," *NPR*, February 4, 2011.
56. "Nass Muqabalat Reuters ma'a al-Sisi," *Reuters*, May 15, 2014.
57. Shana Marshall, "Egypt's Other Revolution: Modernizing the Military-Industrial Complex," *Pambazuka News*, February 16, 2012. https://www.pambazuka.org/governance/egypts-other-revolution-modernizing-military-industrial-complex.
58. Marshall, "Egypt's Other Revolution".
59. Marshall, "Egypt's Other Revolution".
60. "10 U.S. Companies Profiting Most from U.S. Military Aid to Egypt," *Huffington Post*, August 22, 2013.
61. Jeremy M. Sharp, *Egypt: Background and U.S. Relations*, CRS Report No: RL33003 (Washington, DC: Congressional Research Service, March 24, 2017), 22.
62. See Campaign against Arms Trade (CAAT) page on arms supplies companies to Egypt, pages created August 20, 2013, accessed August 1, 2019, https://www.caat.org.uk/resources/countries/egypt/arms-supplying-companies.
63. "Midde East and North Africa," *The Military Balance* 115 (2015): 323.
64. See Zeinab Abul-Magd, "U.S. Military Aid to Egypt Lost Value," *Jadaliyya*, July 25, 2013; Robert Rampton and Arshad Mohammed, "Obama Ends Freeze on U.S. Military Aid to Egypt," *Reuters*, March 31, 2015.
65. "Egypt's Sissi Negotiates Arms Deal in Russia," *Times of Israel*, February 13, 2014; "KSA, UAE to Finance Russian Arms Deal with Egypt," *Egypt Independent*, February 7, 2014; "Putin Backs Sisi 'Bid for Egypt Presidency'," *BBC*, February 13, 2014.
66. U.S. Department of State, "Remarks at the Opening Plenary of the Egypt Economic Development Conference. John Kerry, Secretary of State, Sharm el-Sheikh, Egypt, 13 March 2015," accessed October 10, 2015, http://www.state.gov/secretary/remarks/2015/03/238872.htm; Kevin Liptak, "Obama Lifts Freeze, Ships Arms to Egypt," *CNN*, March 31, 2015.
67. "Britain Quietly Resumes Multi-million Pound Arms Deals with Egypt," *Newsweek*, July 31, 2015.
68. Campaign against Arms Trade (CAAT), "Egypt," November 11, 2013, accessed June 10, 2018, https://www.caat.org.uk/resources/countries/egypt.
69. Campaign against Arms Trade (CAAT), "Egypt".
70. See the website of the Ministry of Military Production and its news, accessed June 10, 2018, http://www.momp.gov.eg/Ar/Default.aspx.
71. Muhammad Hasan and Maha Salim, "Intilaqa Jadidia fi Intaj al-Masani' al-Harbiayya," *al-Ahram*, May 20, 2017; Mahmud al-Badawi, "Wazir al-Intaj al-Harbi: Mustamirrun fi Tasni' al-Asliha…wa-la Nu'lin 'Anha," *al-Watan*, January 24, 2017.
72. "Wazir al-Intaj al-Harbi al-Misri: al-Tasni' al-Mushtarak Badilan 'An Istirad al-Asliha," *Sputniknews*, December 11, 2017.
73. "Middle East and North Africa," *The Military Balance* 117 (2017): 361; "Egypt receives first Gowind 2500 Corvette from France," https://www.egypttoday.com/Article/1/24042/Egypt-receives-first-Gowind-2500-Corvette-from-France, accessed July 17, 2019; "Egypt Launches First Locally Built Gowind Corvette," https://www.egyptdefenceexpo.com/news/egypt-launches-first-locally-built-gowind-corvette, accessed July 17, 2019.
74. "Swiftships offers its international clients the opportunity to build its own vessels under the Co-Production Program," http://swiftships.com/services/co-production/, accessed June 10, 2018.
75. World Bank, "Arms Importers (SIPRI trend indicator value)." https://data.worldbank.org/indicator/MS.MIL.MPRT.KD?end=2016&start=2011&year_high_desc=true, accessed June 10, 2018; Aude Fleurant, Pieter D. Wezman, Siemon T. Wezeman, and Nan Tian, "Trends in International Arms Transfers, 2016," (Stockholm International Peace Research Institute (SIPRI), Sweden, February, 2017), 6 and 11; Ben Knight, "Germany quintuples arms sales to Saudi Arabia and Egypt," *Deutsche Welle*, November 14, 2017.
76. See Campaign Against Arms Trade (CAAT), "Egypt in the News," accessed June 10, 2018, https://www.caat.org.uk/resources/countries/egypt/news; Emir Nader, "UK Arms Deals with Egypt Soar Amid Warming Diplomatic Ties," *Daily News Egypt*, August 1, 2015; Siva Govindasamy and Ahmed

Mohamed Hassan, "China Tries Trying to Undercut Germany on Submarine Offer to Egypt," *Reuters*, September 15, 2015.
77. Pieter D. Wezeman, Aude Fleurant, Alexandra Kuimova, Nan Tian and Siemon T. Wezeman, "Trends in International Arms Transfers, 2017," (Stockholm International Peace Research Institute (SIPRI), Sweden, March 2018); "Ma'had Stockholm li-l-Salam: Misr Thalith Akbar Muswarid Silah fi al-'Aalam bi Ziyada %225 Khilal Khams Sanawat," *Mada Masr*, March 14, 2018.
78. "3.2 Billion Euros of Egypt-French Arms Deal Financed by Loan from Paris: Sisi," *Reuters*, March 1, 2015; Michel Cabirol, "Egypte: douze Rafale cloués au sol par Bercy," *La Tribune*, October 23, 2017; "Middle East and North Africa," *The Military Balance* 116 (2016): 316.
79. Jenna Le Bras, "France and Egypt: Allies of Convenience," *Mada Masr*, October 28, 2017.
80. "Egypt Takes Delivery of Second French Mistral Warship," *Reuters*, September 16, 2016.
81. "Egypt Reportedly Mulling Optional Rafale and Gowind 2500 Purchases," *Quwa: Defense News & Analysis Group*, October 22, 2017, accessed June 10, 2018, https://quwa.org/2017/10/22/egypt-reportedly-mulling-optional-rafale-gowind-2500-purchases/.
82. "Middle East and North Africa" (2016): 316.
83. "Middle East and North Africa," (2016): 316.
84. "Middle East and North Africa," (2017): 412.
85. Hasan and Salim, "Intilaqa Jadidia fi Intaj al-Masani' al-Harbiayy," *al-Ahram*, May 20, 2017.

Bibliography

Abd al-'Azim, Ahmad. "al-Fariq Hamdi Wahiba- Ra'is al-Hay'a al-'Arabiyya li-l-Tasni'- fi Hiwar ma'a Ruz al-Yusuf." *Ruz al-Yusuf*, November 3, 2009.

Abul-Magd, Zeinab. *Militarizing the Nation: The Army, Business, and Revolution in Egypt*. New York: Columbia University Press, 2017.

———. "Siyadat al-Liwa' Sayuqatil al-Sha'b." *al-Masry al-Youm*, April 3, 2012.

———. "U.S. Military Aid to Egypt Lost Value." *Jadaliyya*, July 25, 2013.

Abul-Magd, Zeinab, and Elke Grawert. *Businessmen in Arms: How the Military and Other Armed Groups Profit in the MENA Region*. New York: Rowman & Littlefield, April 2016.

Albrecht, Holger. "Does Coup-Proofing Work? Political-Military Relations in Authoritarian Regimes Amid the Arab Uprisings." *Mediterranean Politics* 20 (2015): 36–54.

Amin, Muhammad. "al-Liwa' Bahari Ibrahim Jabir al-Dusuqi: Hadafuna Tatwir wa-Raf' Kafa'at Tirsanat al-Iskandariyya." *Uktubar*, January 23, 2011.

———. "al-Liwa' Bahari Ibrahim Jabir al-Dusuqi: Hadafuna Tatwir wa-Raf' Kafa'at Tirsanat al-Iskandariyya." *Masress*, January 23, 2011. Accessed April 15, 2014. http://www.masress.com/october/110405.

al-Badawi, Mahmud. "Wazir al-Intaj al-Harbi: Mustamirrun fi Tasni' al-Asliha…wa-la Nu'lin 'Anha." *al-Watan*, January 24, 2017.

Betts, Paul. "French Rail Group Awarded Cairo Order." *Financial Times*, January 7, 1986.

Blumberg, Alex. "Why Egypt's Military Cares about Home Appliances." *NPR*, February 4, 2011.

Brommelhorster, Jorn, and Wolf-Christian Paes, eds. *The Military as an Economic Actor: Soldiers in Business*. Basingstoke: Palgrave Macmillan, 2003.

Cabirol, Michel. "Egypte: douze Rafale cloués au sol par Bercy." *La Tribune*, October 23, 2017.

Congressional Research Service. *Middle East Arms Control and Related Issues*. Foreign Affairs and Nation Defense Division, CRS Report no: 91–384F. Washington, D.C: Congressional Research Service, May 1, 1991.

Cooper, Julian. "Soviet Military Has a Finger in Every Pie." *The Bulletin of Atomic Scientists* 46 (1990): 22–5.

Fleurant, Aude, Pieter D. Wezman, Siemon T. Wezeman, and Nan Tian. "Trends in International Arms Transfers, 2016." *Stockholm International Peace Research Institute (SIPRI)*, Sweden, February 2017.

Gaub, Florence, and Zoe Stanley-Lockman. "Defence Industries in the Arab States: Players and Strategies." *European Union Institute for Security Studies*, Chaillot Papers, March 2017.

Gordon, Michael. "U.S. May Allow Egyptians to Buy and Assemble M-1 Tanks." *New York Times*, June 30, 1987.

Gotowicki, LTC Stephen H. (U.S. Army). "The Role of the Egyptian Military in Domestic Society." *DoD's Foreign Military Studies Office (FMSO), National Defense University*, 1997. Accessed August 29, 2011. http://fmso.leavenworth.army.mil/documents/egypt/egypt.htm.

Govindasamy, Siva, and Ahmed Mohamed Hassan. "China Tries Trying to Undercut Germany on Submarine Offer to Egypt." *Reuters*, September 15, 2015.

Hasan, Muhammad, and Maha Salim. "Intilaqa Jadidia fi Intaj al-Masani' al-Harbiayya." *al-Ahram*, May 20, 2017.

Ibrahim, Abd al-Fattah. "800 'Arabat Qitar Jadida bi-'Istithmarat 1.5 Milyar Junayh" *al-Ahram*, May 26, 2004.

Ibrahim, Amira. "al-Mushir Yaftatih 'Awwal Masna' Asmant 'Asakari bi-Taqat 3.2 Tann Sanawiyyan bi-Taklufa 174 Milyun Yuru." *al-Dostor al-Asly*, April 30, 2012.

Knight, Ben. "Germany quintuples arms sales to Saudi Arabia and Egypt." *Deutsche Welle*, November 14, 2017.

Korayem, Karima. *Egypt's Economic Reform and Structural Adjustment*. Cairo: Egyptian Center for Economic Studies, 1997.

Le Bras, Jenna. "France and Egypt: Allies of Convenience." *Mada Masr*, October 28, 2017.

Lee, Dongmin. "Swords to Ploughshares: China's Defence Conversion Policy." *Defence Studies* 11 (March 2011): 1–23.

Liptak, Kevin. "Obama Lifts Freeze, Ships Arms to Egypt." *CNN*, March 31, 2015.

Mandur, Muhammad Bahyy al-Din. "Takhalluf Sina'at Bina' Sufun A'ali al-Bihar fi Misr." *International* (London). n.d. Accessed April 15, 2014. http://www.international-mag.com/index.php?option=com_content&view=article&id=651:2011-12-11-12-50-20&catid=37:getaways&Itemid=532.

Marshall, Shana. "Egypt's Other Revolution: Modernizing the Military-Industrial Complex." *Pambazuka News*, February 16, 2012. Accessed July 15, 2016. https://www.pambazuka.org/governance/egypts-other-revolution-modernizing-military-industrial-complex.

Mazlum, Jamal. *al-Quwwat al-Musallaha wa-l-Tanmiya al-Iqtisadiyya*. Cairo: Markaz Dirasat wa-Buhuth al-Duwal al-Namiya, 1999.

Melman, Seymour. *The Demilitarized Society: Disarmament and Conversion*. Montreal: Harvest House, 1990.

Melman, Seymour, and Lloyd Dumas. "Planning for Economic Conversion." *The Nation*, April 16, 1990.

Nader, Emir. "UK Arms Deals with Egypt Soar Amid Warming Diplomatic Ties." *Daily News Egypt*, August 1, 2015.

Najib, Du'a', and Ahmad al-Dimirdash. "al-Intiha' min Tatwir Tirsanat al-Iskandariyya." *Amwal al-Ghadd*, March 18, 2013.

Paul, Jim. "The Egyptian Arms Industry." *MERIP Reports* 112 (February 1983): 26–8.

Rampton, Robert, and Arshad Mohammed. "Obama Ends Freeze on U.S. Military Aid to Egypt." *Reuters*, March 31, 2015.

Sanders, Ralph. "Arms Industries: New Supplies and Regional Security [National Security Implications]." *The DISAM Journal* 13 (Winter 1990/1991): 97–108.

Sayigh, Yezid. *Arab Military Industry: Capability, Performance, and Impact*. London: Brassey's: Putnam Aeronautical 1992.

Sha'ban, Mamduh, and Jamal al-Khuli. "Tirsanat al-Iskandariyya Tahtafil bi-Tadshin 'al-Huriyya 3'." *al-Ahram*, December 28, 2010.

Sha'ban, Mamduh. "Ba'd Najah 'Intaj 'Awwal Lawh min al-Sulb bi-l-Darfala, Mash'al: al-'Intaj al-Harbi Yusahim fi Tatwir al-Sina'at al-Thaqila." *al-Ahram*, September 23, 2005.

Sharp, Jeremy M. *Egypt: Background and U.S. Relations*. CRS Report No: RL33003. Washington, DC: Congressional Research Service, March 24, 2017.

Slavin, Barbara. "A Tankful of Trouble for Egypt? Critics Say Co-producing M-1 Tanks is Misguided Show of Friendship." *St. Petersburg Times*, January 23, 1988.

Stoddard, Philip H. "Egypt and the Iran-Iraq War." In *Gulf Security and the Iran-Iraq War*, edited by Thomas Naff, 25–58. Washington, DC: National Defense University Press, 1985.

Stork, Joe. "Arms Industries of the Middle East," *MERIP* Report 144 (January–February 1987): 12–6.
Stork, Joe, and James Paul. "Arms Sales and Militarizing the Middle East." MERIP 112 (February 1983): 5–15.
Ta'lab, Ibtisam. "Dr. Sayyid Mash'al Wazir al-Intaj al-Harbi li-l-Masry al-Yuom (2-2)." *al-Masry al-Youm*, September 15, 2010.
Tyler, Patrick E. "Pentagon Agrees to Let Egypt Produce M1 Tank; Move Expected to Draw Fire in Washington." *Washington Post*, June 29, 1987.
United States General Accounting Office (GAO). *Military Aid to Egypt: Tank Coproduction Raised Costs and May Not Meet Many Program Goals*. GAO/NSIAD-93-203. Washington, DC: U.S. Government Accountability Office, 1993.
U.S. Department of State. "Remarks at the Opening Plenary of the Egypt Economic Development Conference. John Kerry, Secretary of State, Sharm el-Sheikh, Egypt, 13 March 2015." Accessed October 10, 2015. http://www.state.gov/secretary/remarks/2015/03/238872.htm.
'Uthman, Dalia. "al-Mushir Yaftatih Masna' 'Asmant al-'Arish." *al-Masry al-Youm*, May 1, 2012.
Walker, Tony. "US Sweeten the Pot for Defense Projects in Egypt." *Financial Times*, May 7, 1987.
Weiss, Dieter, and Ulrich Wurzel. *The Economics and Politics of Transition to an Open Market Economy: Egypt*. Paris: OECD, 1998.
Wezeman, Pieter D., Aude Fleurant, Alexandra Kuimova, Nan Tian and Siemon T. Wezeman. "Trends in International Arms Transfers, 2017." *Stockholm International Peace Research Institute (SIPRI)*, Sweden, March 2018.

Asian arms industries and impact on military capabilities

Richard A. Bitzinger

ABSTRACT
Asia is a leading consumer of arms, and some of the most modern and most advanced armaments are finding their way into the inventories of Asian militaries. As a result, many Asian-Pacific militaries have experienced a significant, if not unprecedented, build-up over past several years, both in terms of quantity and quality. In addition to this trend, however, Asia has become an increasingly significant producer of armaments. Many nations in the region, if they can, have sought to supplant, or at least supplement, foreign arms suppliers with indigenous producers of needed weapons systems. However, for most Asian-Pacific militaries (the possible exception being China) indigenously produced weapons add only partial value to military capabilities. Consequently, imports of advanced weaponry remain a critical dependency for most of Asian-Pacific nations.

Introduction

Asia is a leading consumer of arms. For the past several years, it has constituted the second largest defence market in the world, and sometimes even the single largest, surpassing even the Middle East. Some of the most modern and most advanced armaments are finding their way into the inventories of Asian militaries. As a result, many Asian-Pacific militaries have experienced a significant, if not unprecedented, build-up over past several years, both in terms of quantity and quality (Theohary 2016, pp. 13, 51).

In addition to this trend, however, Asia has become an increasingly significant producer of armaments. Many nations in the region, if they can, have sought to supplant, or at least supplement, foreign arms suppliers with indigenous producers of needed weapons systems. As a result, nearly country in Asia manufactures some kind of arms. In most cases, however, the types, quantity and quality of weaponry produced are relatively inconsequential, i.e. "low-tech," items such as small arms (e.g. assault rifles, mortars), ammunition, armoured cars, small patrol boats, and the like. Moreover, much of this manufacturing is based on the assembly of foreign weapons systems (Bitzinger 2013, pp. 383–386).

Nevertheless, the ongoing process of regional military modernization has been, and increasingly will be, marked by a growing preference for homegrown weaponry. Consequently, many nations in the Asia-Pacific have invested considerable resources in building up their domestic arms industries. This process has generally entailed a series of gradual and progressive steps in the design, development, and manufacturing of weapon systems, moving from the production relatively simple kinds of weaponry to greater and greater complexity and sophistication, and hence greater and greater self-sufficiency in supply. Some countries – such as China and, to a lesser extent, India and South Korea – have experienced considerable success moving down this path – others, such as Indonesia, much less so (Ross 1989, pp. 1–31, Willett 1997, pp. 107–134).

Despite the considerable barriers to success in advanced armaments production, many Asian-Pacific nations continue to pursue defence industrialization and greater self-sufficiency in armaments as a critical national policy objective. In turn, this process has had a significant impact on many of these countries' military potency. The most critical questions to answer, then, might be: how much military power do these countries gain through this effort, and is it worth it?

Why do countries choose to manufacture their own arms?

Countries have several reasons for developing and producing their own arms. One the strongest of these is the security-driven imperative for self-reliance in arms acquisition. In what is basically an anarchic international security system, nation-states are naturally impelled to seek an independent defence capability. Consequently, autarky, or self-sufficiency in arms acquisition, can be a critical national security objective. This requirement is particularly felt in regions where security challenges are close or many. The Asia-Pacific can especially be regarded as a zone of relative insecurity and potential instability. It contains some of the world's most significant flashpoints: such as the Korean peninsula and the Taiwan Strait – where tensions between nations could escalate to the point of conflict or even a major war. It is replete with a number of unresolved border issues, particularly the overlapping maritime claims in the South and East China Seas, which are as much about national pride as they are about actual or potential natural resources (oil, gas, fisheries). Finally, the region is increasingly a theatre for great-power competition, between the United States (the established hegemon), and a rising challenger, China, and between China and India. In particular, China's increasingly assertive, even belligerent, behaviour in the South China Sea has turned what was once a low-burning territorial dispute into a new potential hot spot for conflict.

In this regard, relying too heavily on arms imports means exposing oneself to embargoes, sanctions, or other supplier-based restrictions that would undermine a nation's ability to acquire the weapons it deems essential to its national defence. Consequently, national security cannot be truly guaranteed unless a nation possesses a secure, indigenous source for armaments. At the same time, a lowered reliance on foreign armaments bolsters national political independence, by reducing the chances that a foreign supplier might use an arms embargo (or the threat of such an embargo) as a coercive mechanism to extract certain kinds of behaviour on the part of the buyer. Overall, therefore, "security of supply" is an important, if not key, driver, behind indigenous defence industrialization policies and programmes.

In addition to fulfilling perceived requirements for self-sufficiency, arms production has often also been seen as an important mechanism for driving a country's overall economic development and industrialization. Defence industrialization had potential backward linkages spurring the expansion and modernization of other sectors of the national economy, such as steel, machine tools, and shipbuilding (Willett 1997, p. 114, Huxley and Willett 1999,

p. 51). Industrialization and technological advancement was seen as feeding into the development of domestic arms-manufacturing capabilities, such as building up general skills and know-how, and in providing lead-in support or equipment for arms production. The construction of warships, for example, stimulated the establishment of indigenous shipbuilding industries, for example, while production of military vehicles required steel mills and automotive factories to provide critical parts and components, such as armour plating, chassis, and engines, and skilled labour to assemble these vehicles.

As a result, in many countries (including some in Asia), armaments production had come to be viewed as a critical component in the national economy. Arms manufacturing is often viewed as an engine for economic development, by driving technological innovation and spurring the growth of new industries, particularly in the area of aerospace, electronics and information technologies sectors (Cheng and Chinworth 1996, pp. 245, 246, Elliot and Bonsignore 1998, p. 31). Military aerospace programmes, for example, have often constituted the basis for civil aircraft and aviation production in nearly all of latecomer arms-producing states. In addition, defence industrialization is both an important import-substitution strategy (i.e. limiting the outward flow of capital, due to arms imports, while also creating jobs), and a potential source of export-led growth, if a country is able to successfully sell its domestically produced armaments overseas.

The converse is equally accurate: commercial industrialization and technological advancement have frequently driven the development of domestic arms-manufacturing capabilities, such as building up general skills and know-how, and in providing lead-in support or equipment for arms production. The establishment of the South Korean commercial shipbuilding industry, for example, facilitated the construction of warships, while the creation of a domestic steel industry and, later, a domestic automobile industry, provided the parts and materiel (such as armor plating, chassis and engines), as well as the skilled labour necessary for the production of military vehicles (Nolan 1987, pp. 218, 219).

Finally, one cannot discount the effects of nationalism, status and prestige on defence industrialization, particularly in the case of states that aspire to regional or even global great power status (Green 1995, pp. 11–13). Possessing an independent defence industrial capability feeds directly into their concepts of national power – not only by creating military power but also by demonstrating the country's industrial and technological prowess, and thereby confirming its status as a great power in the broadest sense. Consequently, many aspiring great powers – such as Japan during the nineteenth century and the Soviet Union during the twentieth century – have often devoted considerable resources to building up their capacities for indigenous arms production – what some have dubbed the "technonationalist impulse" (Bitzinger 2015a, p. 454). Technonationalism is not only a driver of defence industrialization but a model for development, one that generally (and perhaps paradoxically) entails dependencies on foreign armaments and military technologies – at least, at the initial stages of development – but with the long-range goal of using these crutches as a means by which to ultimately achieve autarky. Technonationalism, therefore, can be seen in the defence industrialization programmes of would-be great powers such as China and India, have invested large quantities of time, money and manpower in domestic arms-manufacturing. At the same time, such impulses can also be found in lesser but equally aspiring regional Asian powers, particularly South Korea and Indonesia.

Obviously other economic and technological factors come into play when it comes to decisions to undertake the arduous task of indigenous armaments production. The technonationalist impulse is, of course, not limited to just armaments production, and many other industrial sectors in the region have benefitted from such industrial-technological strategies, such as iron and steel, automobiles, electronics, shipbuilding, and the like. Japan and Korea, for example, have invested billions in building up domestic aircraft industries.

Armaments production in key Asian-Pacific states

Japan was the first country in Asia to industrialize and to modernize, beginning in the late nineteenth century; during this initial phase, technology imports and licensing were commonly used to short-cut the process of development. Imperial Japan, after the Meiji restoration, was also the first Asian state to pursue indigenous defence production in a major fashion. After its defeat in 1945, Japan was essentially demilitarized and disarmed, and much of its defence industry was converted to civilian production, such as motor scooters and railway carriages. With the outbreak of the Korean War (1950–1953) and spread of the Cold War to Asia, however, US occupying forces permitted Japan to restart armaments production. The post-war period of Japanese defence production has generally been characterized as the pursuit of *kokusanka*, or self-reliance, in arms manufacturing (Chinworth 1992, Samuels 1994, Green 1995, Hughes 2011, pp. 451–477). In reconstituting its postwar defence industrial base, Japan pursued a classic incrementalist and globalist approach, of moving from highly import-dependent types of armaments production to greater and greater autarky. The earliest-produced armaments during this period were US weapons systems, built under license and often including, initially at least, critical subsystems and components purchased directly from the United States. For example, Japan's first jet fighter, the F-86F *Sabre*, was licensed assembled by Mitsubishi Heavy Industries (MHI), with the engine and armaments, particularly the AIM-9B Sidewinder air-to-air missiles (AAM), acquired off-the-shelf from their US suppliers. This was followed by the full licensed-production of the F-104 J, F-4EJ, and F-15 J combat aircraft, including their jet engines and radar (Alexander 1993, pp. 38–42). Other US weapons systems subsequently licensed produced in Japan included the AIM-7F and AIM-9L AAMs, CH-47 and UH-60/SH-60 helicopters, and the P-3 maritime patrol aircraft.

By the late 1950s, however, Japan was already attempting to replace or supplement the licensed-production of foreign-designed systems with indigenous products. The country designed and flew its first indigenous jet aircraft, the T-1 trainer, in 1958; altogether, 66 aircraft in this series were produced, and the last 20 were even powered by a domestically developed turbojet engine. The T-1 was followed by the T-2/F-1 supersonic trainer/close-support attack aircraft, of which a total of 167 were built in the early 1970s. The F-1 was a relatively simply ground attack and maritime interdiction aircraft, and 42 % of its parts were produced under license, including its engine; nevertheless, it constituted Japan's first independently developed combat jet (Gunston and Spick 1988, pp. 136,137, Alexander 1993, p. 39). Similar indigenous development and production programmes were undertaken in the missile sectors, e.g. the AAM-1, AAM-4, and AAM-5 air-to-air missiles; the Type-03 and Type-91 surface-to-air missiles; and the ASM-1 and ASM-3 antiship cruise missiles.

Japan's aircraft industry entered its next phase with the F-2 combat aircraft programme, initiated in the 1980s as the FSX (Fighter Strike Experimental) project (Lorell 1996). Originally, it was conceived as a true "Rising Sun" fighter, totally indigenous from stem to stern, optimized for air defence and maritime strike. It was supposed to incorporate the latest technology found in Japan's highly advanced industrial base, including the heavy use of non-metal composites and a then-revolutionary active electronically scanned array (AESA) radar. However, US political pressure, together with Tokyo's growing realization that designing and developing a totally indigenous fighter would likely be extremely challenging (and likely prohibitively expensive), eventually forced Japan to abandoned this idea in favour of a much more modest co-development project with the United States. Consequently, in 1987, Tokyo and Washington signed a memorandum of understanding to co-develop the F-2, based on the already existing US F-16 Fighting Falcon. The F-2 bore a superficial resemblance to the F-16, but differed in many important aspects, including: (1) a 25 % larger wing area; (2) the use of composites (such carbon-fibre materials), to reduce the aircraft's weight and radar signature; (3) a larger tailplane and air intake; (4) a new canopy; and (5) a larger nose in order to accommodate the AESA radar (Lu 2012, pp. 58–60).

Japanese efforts at *kokusanka* have perhaps been the most pronounced in the ordnance and shipbuilding sectors. Nearly every major weapon system in the Ground Self-Defense Force (GSDF) is of Japanese origin, from small arms to main battle tanks. Japan has been building its own tanks since the early 1960s. Its current main battle tank, the Type-10, is equipped with an indigenously developed 120 mm smoothbore gun and modular ceramic composite armour. In addition, Japan has long produced its own destroyers, submarines and amphibious ships. This includes the novel *Izumo*-class "helicopter destroyer," which is really a large helicopter-based amphibious assault vessel; the 19,000-ton *Izumo* features a through-deck design and below-deck hangars, and it closely resembles a small aircraft carrier, prompting speculation that it could be used as the basis for Japanese fixed-wing carrier, launching short-take and vertical landing (STOVL) combat aircraft like the F-35B Joint Strike Fighter (JSF). Japan also constructs its own submarines, the latest of which is the *Soryu*-class. Armed with *Harpoon* antiship missiles and equipped with the Stirling engine for air-independent propulsion (which provides for longer periods of submerged sailing), the *Soryu* is one of the most advanced conventionally powered submarines in the world.

All in all, Tokyo has put considerable resources into building up and maintaining a technologically advanced domestic arms industry, and the "indigenization" of defence production has long been national policy. On the surface, this practice has been highly successful: Japan is capable of building its own locally designed tanks, armoured vehicles, warships, submarines and various missile systems. Consequently, the Japan Self-Defense Force (SDF) is almost entirely self-sufficient in military equipment. Where it has been forced to import, often because the cost of indigenous development was too high, Tokyo has secured licences to manufacture these weapons in Japan; even then, the long-term goal has always been to eventually replace licensed-production with domestically developed systems.

China, too, has long pursued a fiercely ambitious self-reliance strategy when it comes to indigenous arms production. Gill and Kim observed that the Chinese quest for autarky in armaments goes back to the 19th Century, noting that modernizers during that time knew that China could "not simply import complete weapons systems but also [had to] learn from foreign production techniques in order to establish a self-sufficiency in arms production" (Gill and Kim 1996, p. 11, Frankenstein 1999). This became the basis for the so-called *tiyong* concept of the Qing dynasty: *zhongxue weiti, xixue weiyong* ("Chinese learning for substance, Western learning for use"); inherent in this concept is the idea that China should exploit foreign technology as much as it can in order to wean itself eventually off of it (Gill and Kim 1996, p. 2).

The idea of being autonomous in the development and manufacture of arms has been no less critical under the present-day People's Republic of China (PRC) (Crane *et al.* 2005, Medeiros *et al.* 2005, Cheung 2009a, 2009b, 2011). Self-reliance (*zili gengsheng*) remains even more so an "indispensible component … of national security" (Park and Park 1988, p. 119), and, as such, the PRC's defence industry has always been "geared toward the objective of autonomy" (Boutin 2009, p. 213). Even though the PRC in its early years (1949–1961) had to rely heavily upon the Soviet Union for military technology (both weapons systems and production capacities), it was always China's long-term goal to "return to the first path" of self-reliance (Crane *et al.* 2005, p. 137). If anything, China's unhappy experiences with foreign military-technical assistance – i.e. the abrupt cut-off of Soviet military aid in the early 1960s and the Western arms embargo following the 1989 Tiananmen Square crackdown – only reinforced its natural impulses to become eventually self-reliant in arms production (Gill and Kim 1996, pp. 8–47). By the early 1970s, therefore, the Chinese were actively engaged in the development of a number of indigenously designed weapon systems, including fighter aircraft, ballistic and antiship cruise missiles, tanks, surface combatants and submarines (and, of course, nuclear weapons).

The current phrase to express this desire for autarky in defence production and acquisition is, according to Tai Ming Cheung, *zizhu chuangxin*, or "innovation with Chinese characteristics" (also sometimes translated as "indigenous innovation," "autonomous innovation," and "self-reliant innovation") (Cheung 2011, p. 326). According to Cheung, *zizhu chuangxin* is a "core aspiration" of China's political, military, and defence-industrial leadership, and, in particular, it has been formalized in the 2006–2020 Medium- and Long-Term Defense Science and Technology Development Plan (Cheung 2011, pp. 326,327). It basically entails four broad approaches towards technological innovation and development: (1) introduce, (2) digest, (3) assimilate, and (4) re-innovate (what Cheung dubs the IDAR strategy). Interestingly, China's IDAR strategy very closely resembles the same model that Samuels uses to describe the Japanese technonationalist guidelines of indigenization-diffusion-nurturing (Cheung 2014, pp. 2, 3).

By the second decade of the twenty-first century, China has nearly self-sufficient in armaments. It has, built more than a dozen new destroyers of three different types between 2000 and 2015, including one class (the Type-052C/D) outfitted with an *Aegis*-type air-defence radar and fire-control system; these vessels are equipped with indigenous anti-ship cruise missiles (ASCMs), as well as Chinese-built surface-to-air missiles (SAM), housed in vertical launch systems (VLS), for local air defence. The PLAN has also acquired at least a 18 new frigates of the Type-054A class, which features a stealthy design and is armed with ASCMs and VLS-deployed SAMs. Other new Chinese warships include the new-generation Type-022 *Houbei*-class catamaran-hulled missile fast attack craft, of which at least 60 have been built.

China has also greatly expanded its submarine fleet over the past 15 years. Since the late 1990s, the PLAN has acquired at least 26 Type-039 *Song*-class and Type-41 *Yuan*-class diesel-electric submarines. These boats are the first Chinese-built submarines to feature a modern "Albacore" (or teardrop-shaped) hull and a skewed propeller (for improved quieting), and to carry an encapsulated ASCM capable of being fired while submerged (through a regular torpedo tube), as well as antisubmarine rockets. Additionally, there is speculation that the Yuan-class may be outfitted for air-independent propulsion (AIP). Furthermore, the PLAN has begun replacing its small and ageing fleet of nuclear-powered submarines, i.e. five *Han*-class nuclear-powered attack boats (SSN) and one *Xia*-class nuclear-powered ballistic missile-carrying submarine (SSBN). The first in a new class of SSNs, the Type-093 *Shang*-class, was launched in 2002 and commissioned in 2006; at least five Type-093 boats have entered service, and some sources estimate that up to eight boats in this class could be built. The PLAN has also launched four new SSBNs of the Type-094 *Jin*-class (more are planned), each carrying 12 JL-2 submarine-launched ballistic missiles (SLBMs) with a range of 7000 km (three times greater than that of the JL-1 SLBM carried by the *Xia*).

China is also currently in full-scale production of its first indigenous fourth-generation-plus combat aircraft, the J-10. The J-10 is an agile fighter jet in roughly the same class as the F-16C, and it features fly-by-wire flight controls and a glass cockpit (but nevertheless equipped with the Russian AL-31 engine, underscoring China's continuing difficulties with developing a usable jet engine). While the J-10 had a rather rocky start, the programme took on new momentum around the turn of the century, and perhaps 300 to 400 J-10s have been delivered so far to the PLAAF, with production continuing at a rate of about 30 aircraft a year (Baddeley 2012).

In addition, China has two "fifth-generation" combat aircraft programmes – the J-20 and the J-31 – currently in the works. Each aircraft is the product of China's two leading fighter jet enterprises: the J-20 is being developed by the Chengdu Aircraft Industry Group, while the Shenyang Aircraft Corporation is in charge of the J-31 program. The J-20 first flew in January 2011, and the J-31 followed suit in October 2012. Both planes nominally resemble currently flying fifth-generation combat aircraft (that is, the US F-22 and F-35 Joint Strike Fighter).

Self-reliance has long been a fundamental goal of indigenous armaments production in *India* (Mohanty 2004, 2009, Cohen and Dasgupta 2013). Such an objective had military, political, and economic salience. As Ajay Singh put it:

> After independence, and the adoption of a policy of non-alignment, it was ... obvious that foreign policy would need to be reinforced by a policy of self-reliance in defense ... Prime Minister Jawaharlal Nehru believed that no country was truly independent, unless it was independent in matters of armaments. (Singh 2000, pp. 126, 127)

Quite early on, a distinction was made between "self-sufficiency" and "self-reliance." Singh has defined the former as requiring that "all stages in defense production (starting from design to manufacture, including raw materials) ... be carried out within the country." He added that, "To be self-sufficient, a country must not only have the material resources required for defense production, but also the technical expertise to undertake design and development without external assistance." Self-reliance, on the other hand, was much more modest, as while it entailed the indigenous production of armaments, it allowed for the importation of foreign designs, technologies, systems and manufacturing know-how (Singh 2000, p. 127).

While self-sufficiency was the preferred approach, self-reliance has long been the practice when it comes to Indian armaments production. As such, New Delhi has long conceded the need to import considerable amounts of foreign military technology – mostly from the Soviet Union/Russia but also from France and the United Kingdom – in order to establish and expand its indigenous military-industrial complex. Thus, from the early 1960s to the late 1980s, India undertook the licensed-production of several foreign weapons systems, including MiG-21 and MiG-27 fighter jets, *Jaguar* strike aircraft, *Alouette* III helicopters, T-55 and T-72 tanks, *Milan* antitank weapons, and *Tarantul* corvettes (Baskaran 2004, pp. 211–213, 221–226).

At the same time, however, it was always New Delhi's intention to gradually and incrementally replace licensed-production with indigenously developed and designed weaponry. Consequently, starting as far back as the 1950s, the manufacture of foreign-sourced military systems was complemented with local products (Pardesi and Matthews 2007, pp. 421–429, Matthews and Lozano 2013). India began development of its first indigenous fighter jet, the HF-24 *Marut*, in 1956, with first flight occurring in 1961. Truly indigenous armaments development and production, however, did not really take off until the 1980s, with the inauguration of several ambitious home-grown projects, such as the Light Combat Aircraft (LCA, renamed the *Tejas* in 2005), the Advanced Light Helicopter, the Arjun tank, and, especially, the Integrated Guided Missile Development Program (IGMDP), which involved the development of a number of tactical missile systems. While many of these "indigenous" programmes still incorporated considerable amounts of foreign technology or subsystems, the objective has always been to reduce this dependency along the lines of the evolutionary "ladder-of-production" model, and eventually achieve true "self-sufficiency" (Bitzinger 2003, pp. 16–18). This intent was underscored, for example, in 1995 when New Delhi announced that within 10 years it would increase its "local content" of weapons systems in the Indian armed forces from 30 to 70% (Singh 2000, p. 151).

Self-sufficiency is also evident in the *Republic of Korea's* (ROK) historical approach to indigenous armaments production (Bitzinger 1995, Cheng and Chinworth 1996, Bitzinger and Kim 2005). The ROK is committed to a strategy of "cooperative self-reliant defense" (Noh 2005, p. 5) includes the goal of "acquiring the ability to independently develop primary weapon systems for core force capability" (ROK Ministry of National Defense 1999, p. 145). Moreover, the South Korean Government sees an advanced domestic defence industry as an important symbol of the country's "coming of age," both as a high-technology powerhouse and as a regional power. Consequently, Seoul places a strong emphasis on a "domestic weapons first" policy, a course of action that goes back to the early 1970s and the implementation of the Yulgok Project, an ambitious programme of defence industrialization that was intended to lay down "a basic foundation for a self-defence capability for the 21st century" (Choi 1998, p. 183).

South Korea arms manufacturing began in the early 1970s, with the assembly of M-16 assault rifles under licence from the United States. Local armaments production expanded greatly after the promulgation of the Nixon Doctrine, which reduced US defence commitments to Asia but at the same time liberalized the export of advanced military technologies to Asian allies. Consequently, Seoul invested billions of dollars into the domestic development and production of fixed wing and rotary aircraft, missile systems, tanks and armoured vehicles, artillery systems, large surface warships, and submarines. As a result, whereas in 1985 only 59 % of South Korea's arms were procured domestically, by 1995 this amount has risen to nearly 80 % (Choi 1998, p. 185).

The ROK has particularly promoted its aerospace sector as a key strategic industry. It has poured billions of dollars into indigenous combat aircraft programmes, starting with the licensed-production of F-5 and later F-16 fighters, and the MD-500 light helicopter. The ROK aerospace industry's first indigenous product was the KT-1 *Woongbi*, a turboprop basic trainer/light-attack aircraft, developed under the auspices of Daewoo Aerospace. Initiated in the late 1980s, the KT-1 had its maiden flight in November 1991, and production started in 1999. Eventually, 105 *Woongbis* were built for the ROK Air Force (ROKAF). The KT-1 was followed by the T-50 *Golden Eagle*, an even more ambitious programme to design and manufacture a supersonic advanced trainer/light attack jet. The T-50 is Korea's first indigenous jet aircraft, intended to replace T-38, A-37, and F-5 fighters in the ROKAF, as well as export sales. Launched in the mid-1990s, the plane was originally a joint venture between Samsung Aerospace and Lockheed Martin, with the US company supplying critical technologies relating the aircraft's wing, computerized flight-control system, and avionics suite. The T-50 first flew in August 2002 and the aircraft entered service with the ROKAF in 2005. Later versions include the TA-50, a lead-in fighter/trainer/attack plane, and the FA-50, a dedicated fighter aircraft outfitted with more advanced avionics and capable of employing a broader suite of weapons. More recently, the ROK has begun work on an advanced fighter jet, the so-called KF-X programme, which is intended to enter service with the ROKAF sometime during the 2020s. These projects, along with other military and commercial programmes (including a planned 90-seat passenger plane), are part of a long-term strategy to propel the South Korean aircraft industry into the world's top 15 global aerospace producers by 2020.

Seoul also expects to greatly expand its defence exports, an area where it has traditionally been a minor player. South Korea has, for example, sold tanks and artillery systems to Turkey and infantry fighting vehicles to Malaysia. It has also enjoyed some success marketing its military aircraft; it has sold KT-1 trainer planes to Indonesia, Turkey and Peru, and T-50 jets to Indonesia, Iraq and Philippines.

Indonesia undertook armaments production in earnest in the mid-1970s, with the establishment of several state-owned "strategic enterprises", the most important of which were PT *Industri Pewsawat Terban Nusantara* or IPTN (aircraft), PT PAL (shipbuilding) and PT Pindad (small arms and munitions) (Singh 1989, p. 251, *IHS Jane's Navigating the Emerging Markets: Indonesia's* 2012, pp. 20–23). Under Suharto, Jakarta viewed armaments production both as a way to overcome the country's backward state of industrial and technological development, and as a means to leapfrog the country into the forefront of regional great powers. Suharto was particularly influenced by his minister for research and technology, B.J. Habibie (who later succeeded Suharto as president of the republic). Habibie, an aerospace engineer by training, explicitly viewed the establishment of an aerospace industry as both an instrument and a model for advancing the country's overall technology and industrial base (Bailey 1992, pp. 51, 52). For him, IPTN in particular was to serve as an indicator of Indonesia's intentions to become a modern industrialized nation and "to prove that a Third World, Muslim-majority country could make a hi-tech leap into global aviation" (Cohen 2000, p. 45). Just as important, a powerful defence industry was intended to make Indonesia into a military power to be reckoned with in South-East Asia. IPTN began by license-assembling helicopters and light transport planes, and later manufacturing components for F-16 fighters and British Hawk trainers being acquired by the Indonesia air force. In the early 1980s, it entered into a joint venture with CASA of Spain to co-develop and manufacture the CN-235 military/commercial transport aircraft (which was subsequently also exported to the United Arab Emirates, Brunei, Malaysia, Pakistan, South Korea and Thailand). In addition, PT PAL built patrol boats for the Indonesian navy, while PT Pindad manufactured assault rifles and pistols, and developed the *Panser*, an indigenous 6×6 wheeled armoured personnel.

Obviously, it would be useful to address defence industries in other Asian-Pacific countries, particularly North Korea, Singapore and Taiwan. However, finding sufficient (and credible) information as to North Korea's conventional armaments production is nearly impossible. Meanwhile, Singapore and Taiwan's arms industries are even more modest than most other countries in the region: Singapore is mostly proficient in only small arms and relatively simple armoured vehicles; and while Taiwan has done some interesting work in tactical missile systems (particularly supersonic cruise missiles and missile defence systems), its defence industry has experienced a serious decline over the past two decades as funding and technology development has dried up.

Impact on regional military capabilities

The arms build-up in the Asia-Pacific over the past 15 years or so is undeniably significant. In the first place, recent acquisitions by regional militaries constitute something more than mere modernization; rather, the new types of armaments being procured and deployed promise to significantly affect regional warfighting capabilities. Local militaries are acquiring greater lethality and accuracy at longer ranges, Stand-off precision-guided weapons – such as land-attack cruise missiles, tactical ballistic missiles, and a variety of smart munitions, some carried by fourth-generation-plus fighter aircraft – have greatly increased these militaries' firepower and effectiveness, making them capable of longer distance and yet more precise attack. Additionally, militaries in the Asia-Pacific are acquiring new or increased capabilities for force projection, operational manoeuvre and speed. Modern submarines and surface combatants, amphibious assault ships, aircraft carriers, air-to-air refuelling abilities and transport aircraft have all extended these militaries' theoretical range of action. Regional militaries are also more survivable, due to the increased use of stealth and active defences, particularly missile defence. Finally, these forces are improving their capabilities for battlefield knowledge, situational awareness and command and control. New platforms for reconnaissance and surveillance, especially in the air and in space, have considerably expanded these militaries' capacities to look out over the horizon and across all five areas of the future battlespace: ground, sea, air, space and cyber.

More importantly, many Asia-Pacific militaries are acquiring the types of military equipment that could fundamentally transform their forces, in some cases, quite radically. Some nations have enthusiastically embraced concepts of cyberwar and network-enabled warfare – known in China as "winning wars under conditions of informationization," and in Singapore as the IKC2 concept – is a potentially historic shift. In particular, regional militaries could be on the cusp of bundling together sensors, computers, communications, command and control systems, munitions, and platforms that would greatly improve the synergy of their fighting effectiveness. Such emerging capabilities, particularly on the part of China, could in turn greatly affect strategy and operations in future military endeavours in the Asia-Pacific.

Certainly, too, most Asia-Pacific militaries in the twenty-first century are a vast improvement over their predecessors of 20 or 25 years ago, given the addition of fourth-generation-plus combat aircraft, new classes of warships and submarines, precision-strike weapons, and so on. In China, for example, the J-10 and Su-30 fighters have replaced MiG-19s and MiG-21s. Likewise F-15s are replacing F-4s in the ROKAF, and the same fighter is replacing F-5s and A-4s in Singapore's air force, while India is supplementing vintage Jaguars, MiG-27s, and Mirage-2000s with Su-30s, the Tejas LCA, and (soon) French *Rafales*. Additionally, beyond-visual-range, active radar-guided air-to-air missiles (AAM), such as the AMRAAM and AA-12, are replacing or supplementing older generation AAMS, such as the short-range AIM-9 Sidewinder or the semi-active AIM-7 Sparrow. Moreover, Japan and South Korea have both signed contracts to acquire the F-35 fifth-generation fighter, and Singapore and perhaps India are also potential customers for the JSF.

In terms of surface combatants, countries such as China, India, Japan and South Korea are acquiring advanced destroyers with sophisticated radars, surface-to-air missiles and combat systems that provide their militaries with long-range air defence at sea – and even missile defence – capabilities that they did not earlier possess. In the past 15 years, countries such as South Korea, Malaysia, Singapore and Vietnam that never possessed much in the way of submarines forces, or, indeed, any submarines at all, are being equipped with modern boats. In the case of Japan, India, the ROK and Singapore, these submarines are outfitted with air-independent propulsion that permits them to remain submerged for much longer periods of time. China and India, for their part, have highly ambitious nuclear-powered submarine (both SSN and SSBN) programmes. Finally, many Asia-Pacific militaries are being equipped for the first time with a variety of stand-off precision-strike weapons, including JDAM (Japan, South Korea, and Singapore), JSOW (Singapore), and the AGM-142 air-to-surface missile (South Korea). Just as importantly, South Korea and Taiwan have developed their own land-attack cruise missiles, while China and India have gained new capabilities for using ballistic missiles as battlefield strike weapons. In addition, these forces are certainly better equipped than in the past with systems for communications, command and control, intelligence, and surveillance. For example, China, India, Japan and Singapore (and soon South Korea) have all acquired airborne early-warning and command aircraft, while UAVs have proliferated throughout the region.

That the Asia-Pacific nations have added considerably to their military arsenals is not in doubt. Nor does the process of military modernization – propelled by regional geopolitical forces, enabled by robust defence spending and a buyer's market in the international arms market, and stirred by the transformative promise of network-centric warfare – seem to show any signs of abating (Fleurant *et al.*, 2017). Moreover, countries in the region are acquiring hardware that, on the surface at least, imbues their militaries with new capacities for warfighting when it comes to mobility, speed, precision strike, firepower, battlespace intelligence and cyber. In short, regional militaries are attaining greater firepower and accuracy at greater ranges, expanded force projection capacities (particularly at the sea), stealth, improved battlefield knowledge and command and control, and increased operational manoeuvre and speed. Consequently, conflict in the region, should it occur, is likely to be more high-tech, that is, faster, more long-distance and yet more precise and more lethal, and, overall, potentially more devastating in its effect.

At the same time, it should be apparent – from looking at the above types of armaments and military equipment that have accrued to these regional militaries over the past two decades or so – that for most Asian-Pacific states, arms imports remain of crucial importance in determining military power. Certainly, local arms industries have experienced some impressive breakthroughs, and many regional militaries can – and do – rely more and more on domestic weapons systems. However, many of the most critical pieces of military equipment – the sharpest edges of the pointiest end of the spear, so to speak – are still comprised of imported equipment. In particular, this includes advanced combat aircraft, submarines, drones and UAVs (beyond the most basic, short-range tactical UAVs), most missile systems (air-to-air, antiship, and air-defence), jet engines, and, above all, highly advanced electronics that are critical for surveillance, communications, intelligence-gathering, fire-control and the like. In these critical regards, most of these nations remain dependent on foreign suppliers to plug the gaps in their defence technological and industrial bases – and probably will remain so for some time to come.

Given these continuing dependencies, it is surprising how little the Asian-Pacific arms producers have globalized their operations – particularly since this region overall comprises the highest concentration of arms-producing nations outside of North America and Europe, and because this region is also a region of considerable growth in arms manufacturing, in terms of value, types of systems, and increasing technological sophistication. Given the enormous economic and technological challenges facing these arms producers, one would have thought that these countries would be prime candidates for embedding themselves in the globalization process (Bitzinger 2003, pp. 6, 7). Armaments production is an immensely capital- and technology-intensive industry, requiring significant investments in R&D, production facilities and skilled personnel. Consequently, small-scale arms manufacturing of the type generally found in countries outside of Europe and America is rarely cost-effective. In fact, by the early 2000s, it was obvious that most of arms-producing states in the Asia-Pacific, excepting perhaps China – a special case, due to the immense resources it has poured into its arms industry since the late 1990s (Bitzinger 2015b) – had failed to gain much in the way of an independent, self-sustaining defence technology and industrial base. Most tended to suffer from shortages of skilled personnel and sufficient scientific and technical infrastructures to pursue breakthroughs and applied research in many critical defence technologies and consequently were often deficient when it came to indigenous capacities for weapons design, engineering, and manufacture (Bitzinger 2003, pp. 24–38). As a result, they still tended to rely heavily upon foreign suppliers when it came to design, R&D, and arcane, sophisticated technologies (such as propulsion, sensors, guidance systems, aerodynamics, information technologies, and microelectronics).

It must be noted as well that when it comes to the global arms business, the barriers to entry remain high. Traditional arms-manufacturing countries – particularly the United States, Russia, and Western Europe – have over time built up a considerable technological lead, and by the time armaments producers in countries with fewer investments in technology innovation have mastered a certain level of technology, the leading producers have already leaped ahead, effectively moving the goalposts. As shown in the Indian, Indonesian, and, to a lesser extent, the Japanese cases, this has been an important factor behind their failure to produce technologically acceptable indigenous weapon systems.

Yet overall there appears to have been little inclination among these arms-producing nations to abandon autarky in exchange for playing a subordinate role in a globalized division of labour (i.e. a "core-periphery" approach to globalized armaments production) (Bitzinger 2003, pp. 69–76). If anything, the commitment of many of these countries to preserving – and in some cases, even expanding – local defence industrial bases has never been stronger. Despite technological hurdles and high entry costs, other factors – particularly perceived national security imperatives, projected technology spin-offs, and even national pride – continue to be very strong impulses acting on most second-tier arms-producing states.

To be sure, some smaller arms-producing states have embraced globalization. In particular, Australia and South Africa have accepted very high degrees of foreign investment and ownership in their national defence industrial bases. Some of Australia's largest arms firms, including ADI Ltd., and Australian Aerospace, are now wholly owned subsidiaries of foreign corporations. South Africa's defence industry is also heavily foreign-owned. BAE Systems, for example, has acquired Land Systems OMC, as well as a 51 % stake in Paradigm System

Technologies and as 20 % of ATE, a local defence electronics firm. Other recent foreign investments in the South African defence industry include the purchase of Denel Airmotive (which makes small aeroengines) by Turbomeca of France, the acquisition of Altech Defense Systems (renamed African Defense Systems) by Thales, and Saab's purchase of Grintek's Avitronics and Communications division, as well as buying 20 % of Denel Aerostructures. In addition, South African arms firms have established a number of joint ventures and strategic alliances with foreign companies. Overall, South Africa's arms industry is struggling to recast itself, both structurally and strategically, as a "natural partner" in future international collaborative arms activities. In general, much of the indigenous defence industry views cooperation and link-ups with leading arms-producing states as critical to its survival, and many local firms see their future in playing an important if niche role as a supplier and systems integrator of subsystems and components to foreign weapon systems.

However, very few Asian-Pacific states have permitted such direct and deep involvement in their domestic arms industries; protectionism continues to dominate industrial policy when it comes to these countries' defence sectors. In South Korea, Samsung has created a joint venture with Thales to produce and market defence electronics systems (later acquired by Hanwha). Singapore Technologies Engineering (STEngg) acquired a large minority percent stake in the Irish company Timoney, which produces suspension systems for armoured vehicles, as well as a controlling interests in Halter Marine, a US shipbuilder; altogether, STEngg has more than 2500 workers – nearly a quarter of its labour force – employed outside Singapore. India recently revised its laws to permit foreign companies to invest in local defence firms, first allowing non-Indian companies to buy shares in domestic enterprises worth up to 26 %, and then in 2015 raising this bar to 49 %. Consequently, Britain's BAE Systems is partnering with the Indian conglomerate Mahindra in order to supply howitzers to the Indian Army (IA), while L&T is collaborating with Airbus and Samsung to produce a track-mounted artillery gun. Tata has partnership with Boeing to produce fuselages for Apache helicopters being delivered to the IA, while Tata Power SED has formed a partnership with Honeywell International to produce navigation systems for military use. In addition, several private companies are currently competing to build the new Futuristic Infantry Combat Vehicle (FICV) for the Indian Army. Tata Motors Ltd has linked up with Bharat Forge and the US-based General Dynamics Land Systems, to bid on the FICV, while other entrants include the Mahindra Group, Larsen and Toubro (L&T), Punj Lloyd Ltd, and the Reliance Group. Finally, Elta of Israel has invested 2.5 billion rupees (US$56 million) in L&T and in Astra Microwave, to develop and build radar and other defence electronics systems.

Even China has said that it will privatize and list some of its assets of its large defence industrial enterprises (admittedly only nonmilitary factories) (Dickie and Mitchell 2009). At the same time, unlike Europe there appears to be no desire or drive to *regionalize* armaments production, particularly within the Asia-Pacific region, as a means of rationalizing production or pooling technological strengths or financial resources.

Some Asian arms-producing countries – particularly Singapore – appear to have adopted a niche production approach to local arms manufacturing, choosing to manufacture and market products where they may find lucrative overseas sales (Singapore, for example, has been a major supplier of small arms to other states in the region, particularly Burma and Indonesia). In addition, Malaysia has tried to position itself to be a preferred subcontractor and critical second-tier supplier in the global production chain (Balakrishnan 2008). These countries may still be reliant upon foreign sources for major weapons systems, but they avoid total dependency by leveraging their core competencies to give them comparative advantages in internationalized production programs.

And yet, all these efforts and initiatives appear to be the exceptions that prove the rule, that autarky is still the singular, prevailing tendency among the leading arms-producing states in the Asia-Pacific. What stands out among nearly all these countries is their continued emphasis on pursuing technonationalist goals of self-sufficiency when it comes to weapons development and manufacturing. Among these nations, there is an almost obsessive preference for self-reliance in arms procurement and production, and hence, they are investing considerable resources into their defence technological and industrial bases. Japan, for example, has never permitted any foreign investment in its defence industry; additionally, it is currently ploughing billions of dollars in two new programmes to develop a maritime patrol aircraft and a cargo plane – and now it is working on a fifth-generation fighter jet. Both China and India have never given any indication that they will ever privatize their huge state-owned defence behemoths; rather, they will continue to protect and nurture these industries as strategic assets (as does Indonesia with its underperforming government-run defence enterprises). This overriding priority on indigenization and self-sufficiency has certainly paid out dividends in terms of adding military power to their defences, but they have also limited that process. In any event, most regional militaries remain highly dependent on foreign suppliers, particularly for many of those most advanced types of military equipment (with the possible exception of China – and even then it suffers from critical shortfalls when it comes propulsion systems, especially jet engines, which it must continue to import from Russia).

Conclusions

As a strategy for increasing military prowess among Asian-Pacific powers, indigenous arms production has been a dubious success. Certainly, many countries in the region have attained a limited level of military-technical self-reliance. In most cases, the process of domestic defence industrialization paid off in a limited fashion, generating at least some autarky and some degree of indigenous military capabilities. In the case of countries like China or Japan, the level of autarky turned out to be both quite high and quite technologically advanced. But it would be too generous to say that this approach to building military capacity was an effective and efficient one. Too often, the resulting weapons were more expensive, and came into service later, than comparable weapons systems that could be found on the international arms market. The autarky model has hardly been a short-cut to more advanced types of arms production; it has rarely aided regional militaries when it comes to filling requirements for cutting-edge weapons systems. Too often, in fact, Asian governments have chosen weapons programmes more for their "doability" (i.e. the likelihood that they will succeed), and for their potential to support and advance local arms industries, rather than for their actual military need. Moreover, this model usually means that considerable amounts of effort and resources are wasted on "reinventing the wheel," i.e. replicating weapons systems (combat aircraft, armoured vehicles, assault rifles, even missile systems) that are widely and more cheaply available on the global arms market. At the same time, governments pay a premium for autarky in armaments acquisition, while also risking losing access to global dynamics of technology diffusion and innovation. Consequently, most domestic defence arms programmes have simply become "self-licking ice cream cones": projects demanding ongoing government support simply to keep arms-producers in business. Overall, autarky has become a high price to pay for, well, further autarky.

Of course, local arms industries *do* provide at least some security and military effectiveness, a modicum of self-reliant military power, as it were. That said, it is arguable whether such results are worth the huge outlays of effort and resources, especially if such capabilities are readily available from foreign suppliers, and especially given the current "buyers' market" for arms (i.e. a worldwide oversupply of desperate arms sellers, aggressively chasing down each potential sale and prepared to deal when it comes to price, offsets, and the like). Overall, however, it is highly unlikely that the Asian-Pacific states will readily abandon their hard-won capabilities for indigenous arms production, despite what comparative value they may accrue from them.

Disclosure statement

No potential conflict of interest was reported by the author.

References

Alexander, A., 1993. *Of tanks and Toyotas: an assessment of Japan's defense industry*. Santa Monica, CA: RAND Corporation, No. RAND/N-3542-AF.

Baddeley, A., 2012. The AMR regional air force directory 2012. *Asian military review*, 20 (1), 21–36.

Bailey, J., 1992. Habibie's grand design. *Flight international*, 51–52.

Balakrishnan, K., 2008. Defence industrialisation in Malaysia: development challenges and the revolution in military affairs. *Security challenges*, 4 (4), 135–155.

Bitzinger, R.A., 1995. South Korea's defense industry at the crossroads. *Korean journal of defense analysis*, 7 (1), 233–249.

Bitzinger, R.A., 2003. *Towards a brave new arms industry*. New York: Routledge.

Bitzinger, R.A., 2013. Revisiting armaments production in Southeast Asia: new dreams, same challenges. *Contemporary Southeast Asia*, 35 (3), 369–394.

Bitzinger, R.A., 2015a. Defense industries in Asia and the technonationalist impulse. *Contemporary security policy*, 36 (3), 453–472.

Bitzinger, R.A., 2015b. Comparing defense industry reforms in China and India. *Asian politics & policy*, 7 (4), 531–553.

Bitzinger, R.A. and Kim, M., 2005. Why do small states produce arms? The case of South Korea. *Korean journal of defense analysis*, 17 (2), 183–205.

Boutin, J.D., 2009. Arms and autonomy: the limits of China's defense-industrial transformation. *In*: R.A. Bitzinger, ed. *The modern defense industry: political, economic, and technological issues*. Santa Barbara, CA: Praeger, 212–226.

Baskaran, A., 2004. The role of offsets in Indian defense procurement policy. *In*: J. Brauer and J.P. Dunne, eds. *Arms trade and economic development: theory, policy, and cases in arms trade offsets*. London: Routledge, 217–232.

Cheng, D. and Chinworth, M.W., 1996. The teeth of the little tigers: offsets, defense production and economic development in South Korea and Taiwan. *In*: S. Martin, ed. *The economics of offsets: defense procurement and countertrade*. London: Harwood, 245–298.

Cheung, T.M., 2009a. *Fortifying China: the struggle to build a modern defence economy*. Ithaca, NY: Cornell University Press.

Cheung, T.M., 2009b. Dragon on the horizon: China's defense industrial renaissance. *Journal of strategic studies*, 32 (1), 29–66.

Cheung, T.M., 2011. The Chinese defense economy's long march from imitation to innovation. *The journal of strategic studies*, 34 (3), 325–354.

Cheung, T.M., 2014. The role of foreign technology transfers in China's defense research, development, and acquisition process. *SITC policy briefs*, 2014 (5).

Chinworth, M.W., 1992. *Inside Japan's defense: technology, economics & strategy.* 1st Printing ed. Washington, DC: Brassey's Inc.

Choi, J.C., 1998. South Korea. *In*: R.P. Sing, ed. *Arms procurement decision making: China, India, Isreal, Japan, South Korea and Thailand*. Oxford: SIPRI/Oxford University Press, 304.

Cohen, M., 2000. New flight plan. *Far eastern economic review*, 163 (9), 45–46.

Cohen, S.P. and Dasgupta, S., 2013. *Arming without aiming: India's military modernization*. Washington, DC: Brookings Institution Press.

Crane, K., Cliff, R., Medeiros, E.S., Mulvenon, J.C., and Overholt, W.H., 2005. *Modernizing China's military: opportunities and constraints*. 2nd ed. Santa Monica, CA: RAND Corporation.

Dickie, M. and Mitchell, T., 2009. Beijing seeks to encourage enterprise in defence arena. *Financial times*, 6 January, 16.

Elliot, J. and Bonsignore, E., 1998. Asia's 'new' aerospace industry: at the turning point? *Military technology*, 22, 24–33.

Fleurant, A., Wezeman, P., Wezeman, S. and Tian, N., 2017. *Trends in international arms transfers, 2016*. Stockholm: Stockholm International Peace Research Institute.

Frankenstein, J., 1999. China's defense industries: a new course? *In*: J.C. Mulvenon and R.H. Yang, eds. *The people's liberation army in the information age*. Santa Monica, CA: RAND Corporation, 187–216.

Gill, B. and Kim, T., 1996. *China's arms acquisitions from abroad: a quest for 'superb and secret weapons'*. 1st ed. Oxford: Stockholm International Peace Research Institute.

Green, M.J., 1995. *Arming Japan: defense production, alliance politics, and the postwar search for autonomy*. New York: Columbia University Press.

Gunston, B. and Spick, M., 1988. *Modern air combat: the aircraft, tactics and weapons employed in aerial warfare today*. 1st ed. New York: Crescent.

Hughes, C.W., 2011. The slow death of Japanese techno-nationalism? Emerging comparative lessons for China's defense production. *Journal of strategic studies*, 34 (3), 451–479.

Huxley, T. and Willett, S., 1999. *Arming East Asia*. Oxford: Oxford University Press for the International Institute for Strategic Studies.

IHS Jane's navigating the emerging markets: Indonesia., 2012. London: IHS Global Ltd.

Lorell, M., 1996. *Troubled partnership: a history of U.S.–Japan collaboration on the FS-X fighter*. New Brunswick, NJ: Transaction Publishers.

Lu, J., 2012. Technology transfer and the F-2 fighter: how the Japanese defense industry defied the odds. *Pointer, journal of the Singapore armed forces*, 38 (4), 55–63.

Matthews, R. and Lozano, A., 2013. India's defence acquisition and offset strategy. *In*: R. Basrur, A.K. Das, and M.S. Pardesi, eds. *India's military modernization: challenges and prospects*. New Delhi: Oxford University Press, 140–168.

Medeiros, E.S., Cliff, R., Crane, K. and Mulvenon, J.C., 2005. *A new direction for China's defense industry*. Santa Monica, CA: RAND Corporation.

Mohanty, D.R., 2004. *Changing times? India's defence industry in the 21st century*. Bonn: Bonn International Center for Conversion, BICC.

Mohanty, D.R., 2009. *Arming the Indian arsenal: challenges and policy options*. New Delhi: Rupa & Company.

Noh, H., 2005. *South Korea's' cooperative self-reliant defense': goals and directions*. Seoul: Korea Institute for Defense Analysis.

Nolan, J.E., 1987. South Korea: ambitious client of the United States. *In*: M. Brzoska and T. Ohlson, eds. *Arms production in the third world 1971–1985*. Oxford: Oxford University Press, 383.

Pardesi, M.S. and Matthews, R., 2007. India's tortuous road to defence-industrial self-reliance. *Defense & security analysis*, 23 (4), 419–438.

Park, H.S. and Park, K.A., 1988. Ideology and security: self-reliance in China and North Korea. *In*: E.E. Azar and C.-I. Moon, eds. *National security in the third world: the management of internal and external threats*. Aldershot: Edward Edgar - University of Maryland, 257–283.

ROK Ministry of National Defense, 1999. *Defense white paper 1999*. Seoul: Korea Institute for Defense Analyses.

Ross A., 1989. Full circle: conventional proliferation, the international arms trade and third world arms exports. *In*: K.-I. Baek, R.D. McLaurin, and C.-I. Moon, eds. *The dilemma of third world defense industries*. Boulder, CO: Westview Press, 278 pp.

Samuels, R.J., 1994. *Rich nation, strong army: national security and the technological transformation of Japan*. Ithaca: Cornell University Press.

Singh, B., 1989. Asean's arms industries: potential and limits. *Comparative strategy*, 8 (2), 249–264.

Singh, A., 2000. Quest for self-reliance. *In*: J. Singh, ed. *India's defence spending: assessing future needs*. New Delhi: Knowledge World, 22–23.

Theohary, C.A., 2016. *Conventional arms transfers to developing nations, 2008–2015*. Washington, DC: Congressional Research Service.

Willett, S., 1997. East Asia's changing defence industry. *Survival*, 39 (3), 107–134.

State vs. *market* in India: How (not) to integrate foreign contractors in the domestic defense-industrial sector

Moritz Weiss

ABSTRACT

India has evolved not only as a rising power in Asia, but as the world's largest arms importer. While facing some international threats, its defense-industrial policy is primarily driven by domestic opportunities and constraints. India's enormous market size enables technology transfers, whereas domestic factors fundamentally exacerbate their effective utilization. Most significantly, attempts to liberalize the defense industries face the challenge of missing institutional prerequisites and political resistance against reforms. To date, the predominance of state institutions has prevailed. This conclusion is derived from combining data on general trends with the exploration of one recent process of fighter-aircraft acquisition.

Introduction

From an international perspective, India is today evolving as a rising power. However, its growth of military strength does not create severe global concerns, as its increasing capabilities are largely regarded as defensive.[1] While India is confronted with security competition in its neighborhood (especially Pakistan, and also China), its environment, nonetheless, provides some room of maneuver to address existing threats. In 1991, the initial founder of the nonalignment movement shifted its foreign policy view toward a *Look East Policy*; and recently to an *Act East* and *Neighbourhood First Policy* under the Narenda Modi government. India's general outlook is continental, rather than maritime.[2] Although naval investments are also rising, the army is still the most powerful military service. Yet, India's strategic culture is mostly characterized as defensive and inward-looking, which is largely driven by its geography, great-power status, and the colonial past.[3] Given that India faces constant, but manageable, international threats, the international system allows the government to act on the global arms market without strong strategic limitations.

From a domestic perspective, however, India's defense sector remains—despite recent attempts of liberalization—constrained. It is predominated by public and thus politically accountable actors and institutions. Foreign defense contractors face a situation of a highly regulated and protected defense sector, which complicates any technology transfers from more advanced defense-industrial nations. The defense bureaucracy has a lot of influence in the Ministry of Defence at the expense of the armed forces, so arms acquisition and technology absorption are dominated by civilian technologists rather than by the military end users. In particular, the Defense Research and Development Organization (DRDO) predominates the innovation of weapons in India, and state-owned industries serve the function of production agencies. Yet, India's goal of self-reliance and uncoordinated activities hinder technology transfer and lead to delays.[4]

Color versions of one or more of the figures in the article can be found online at www.tandfonline.com/ucst.

Against this backdrop, the questions arise of what drives India's defense-industrial policy choices? To what extent do domestic triggers prevail over international factors? This article argues that domestic constraints represent the main challenge for a more effective—and efficient—build-up of India's defense industries. Indeed, the government may choose among a variety of potential suppliers world-wide; yet, it is largely incapable to exploit its enormous domestic market for technology transfers beyond relatively simple manufacturing. While the impact on India's generation of military capabilities is arguably difficult to specify, the available evidence suggests that India's potential, at least, remains underexploited.

This article arrives at this conclusion by proceeding in two interrelated steps. The following section introduces India's defense-industrial sector and, afterwards, addresses India's arms procurement regulations to better understand the opportunities and challenges of the country when it acquires large military platforms, such as combat fighter aircraft. This general trend is—in a second step—illustrated by exploring one particularly prominent procurement process, the recent acquisition of combat fighter aircraft in the so-called Medium-Multi-Role Combat Aircraft (MMRCA) contest.

Opportunities and constraints in India's defense-industrial sector

India's defense industries have decent productions facilities, but not an across-the-board capability for research and development.[5] Historically, India was left into independence *without* a genuine defense-technological sector. With the exception of some ordnance factories, the Indian state was missing a defense-industrial base. Given the combination of this lack with its policy of nonalignment, the state's political objective gradually shifted from self-sufficiency toward the notion of "self-reliance," which "permits technology acquisition from foreign suppliers, but with the intention that this dependency would eventually be reduced through 'indigenisation.'"[6] As a result, the government necessarily needed to collaborate with potent arms suppliers. To date, the sector's structural weakness is, however, illustrated by Figure 1, which contrasts arms imports and exports since the end of the Cold War.

In addition, it seems valuable to dig one step deeper and to give an overview of India's most important arms suppliers (Figure 2). The four major arms suppliers—Russia, the United States, Israel, and the United Kingdom—are jointly responsible for more than 80 percent of all Indian arms imports (and Russia individually for 65 percent).

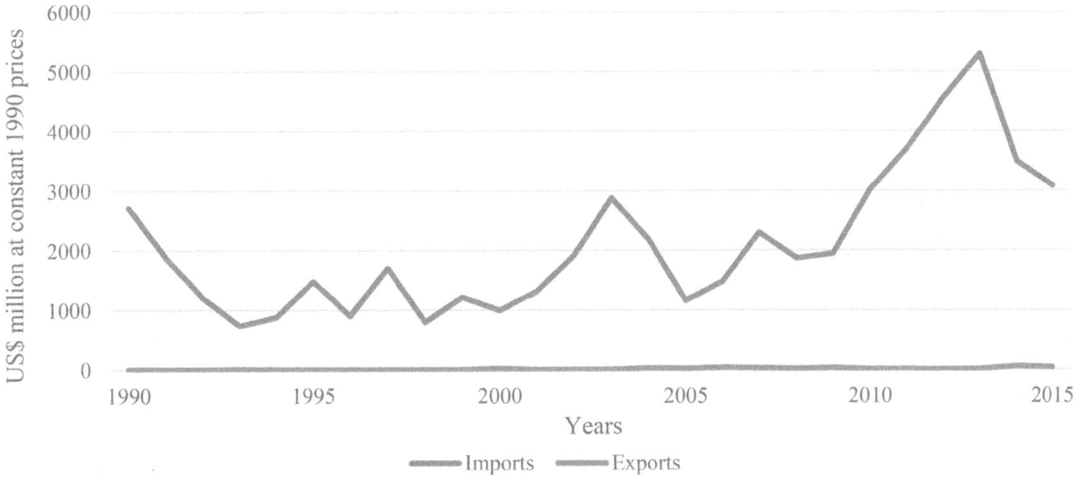

Figure 1. India's arms imports and exports since 1990. Source: Data from SIPRI, 1990–2015 (http://armstrade.sipri.org/armstrade/page/values.php).

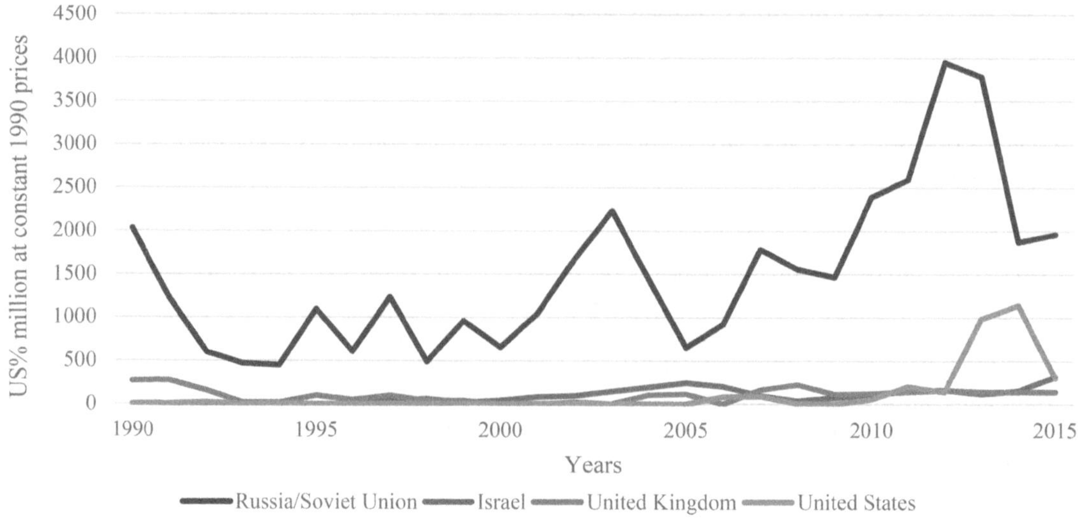

Figure 2. India's arms imports by weapon supplier since 1990. Source: Data from SIPRI, 1990–2015 (http://armstrade.sipri.org/armstrade/page/values.php).

Furthermore, in order to better understand India's defense procurement from foreign sources, we need to focus on its state-owned defense public sector undertakings (DPSUs). In fact, they are highly vertically integrated, so that India has not had a broad base of component suppliers at its disposal.[7] For instance, Hindustan Aeronautics (HAL) possesses end-to-end capabilities. It produces both airframes and engine, which is a constellation completely absent from the West's defense-industrial sector, where these key tasks are always accomplished by separate—and thus, specialized—firms.[8] The government's objective has always been to import selective foreign technologies for modernizing its own economy—yet retaining state control over the structure of national business. This actor constellation and the resulting rents have historically created powerful interest groups within the state-run sector.[9] The "Indian private sector has always been portrayed as being discriminated against with the government favouring state-owned defence industries."[10]

Up to the 1980s, India's license production limited domestic development to a considerable extent. "Although license production has been a stable form of production, it has not made India self-reliant in terms of upper-ends of defence production, especially in the field of design and development."[11] As a consequence, the Indian government increasingly promoted coproduction and—if possible through one of the so far 26 joint ventures—co-development programs (e.g., Sukhoi-HAL; BAe-HAL; Rolls-Royce, and Tata). Within this context, the new defense procurement procedures (DPP) also established opportunities for private Indian companies—after having passed a clearance of the Defense Acquisition Council—to become increasingly involved in the manufacturing of armaments.[12] Moreover, the sources of military equipment have increasingly been diversified. While Russia is still the most important partner, major weapon systems meanwhile stem from Israel, the U.S., the UK, South Africa, France, and others.[13] Through arms collaboration with these different partners, the Indian government ultimately aims to advance technologically by capitalizing on the huge size of its domestic market, which has meanwhile evolved as the largest import market for worldwide (Figure 3).

Yet, not only the sheer size, but tremendous growth makes India a favorable partner for all companies and states. After all, its defense market quadrupled from $3 billion in 2000 to $12.2 billion in 2010.[14] Whereas coproduction has gradually evolved as the norm, co-development is of increasing importance, albeit so far rather the exception.[15] For example, India's aerospace industries may have critical "know-how," yet largely lack the "know-why."[16]

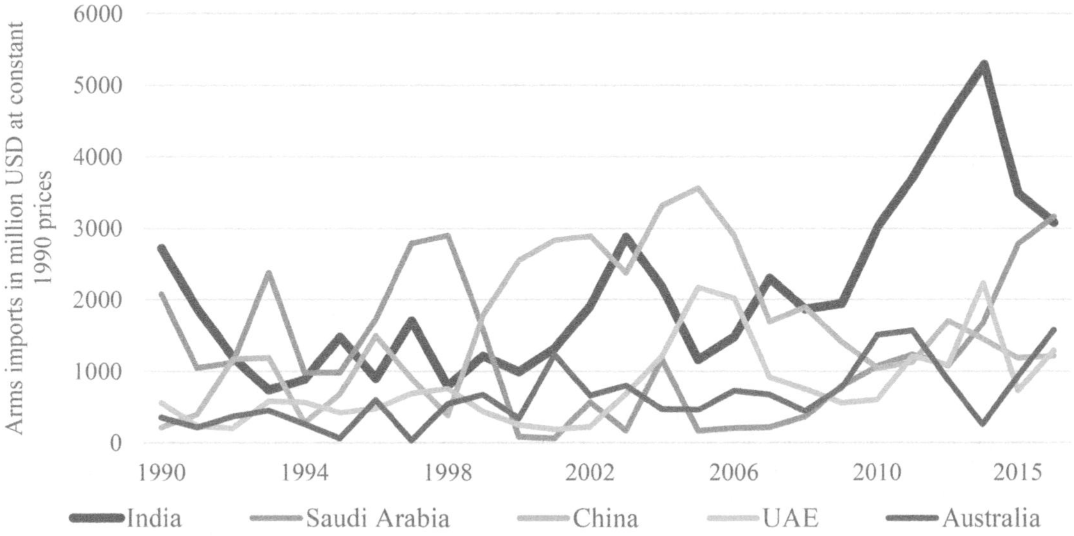

Figure 3. The world's five largest arms importers between 2011 and 2015*. Source: Data from SIPRI, 1990–2015 (http://armstrade.sipri.org/armstrade/page/values.php). *Largest importers during 2011–2015 as specified in SIPRI's "Trends in International Arms Transfers, 2015" (http://www.sipri.org/googlemaps/2016_of_at_top_20_imp_map.html).

To date, India's defense industries have almost exclusively been state-driven. There are ten DPSUs (including about 39 ordnance factories),[17] a defense research and development organization with a network of about 51 laboratories, and a similar amount of science and technology units, which are linked to almost 70 academic institutions. Today, the DPSUs are still the only relevant defense firms in India. Whereas some Western companies have incrementally entered the market, the industry structure remains tilted towards the DPSUs, which has not always been a success story: India "has sufficient political and economic power to demand levels of technology transfer that could conceivably transform its aviation sector. However, the country's underperforming state-run military aircraft manufacturer [i.e., HAL] still requires major reform, while the Indian defence sector as a whole lacks clear strategic direction."[18]

Nevertheless, there are also several indications that liberalizing efforts may be extended toward the defense-industrial sector. For instance, defense management has been under constant reform since the mid-1990s. On the one hand, international collaboration should increasingly follow a value-for-money ratio to reduce development costs and to provide new opportunities for potential Indian exports. On the other hand, there were some moderate privatization efforts, coordinated via an army-industry partnership. It primarily aimed for greater participation of private firms in the arms production process. Yet, their response has been hesitant. Only the large companies, such as Tata's and Larsen & Tubro, have increasingly been involved in the sector, whereas smaller firms merely show an increasing interest in doing defense business in the future.[19]

Historically, the Indian government had restricted both private and foreign investments into its defense-industrial sector. Yet, since 2001, private investors may acquire 26 percent of Indian defense entities and, today, even a 49 percent share is possible on a case-by-case basis.[20] In addition, it removed an earlier provision related to the control of joint ventures, which had required the single-largest resident Indian shareholder to have at least a 51 percent equity share. However, there remains one major obstacle: large multinational companies are highly concerned about the burgeoning bureaucracy and the protection of their intellectual property rights.[21] Thus, the demand for joint ventures or similar involvements are rather modest among private investors. The amount of FDI inflows in the Indian defense sector from April 2000 until December 2015 was only $5,020,000, whereby it contributes less than 1 percent to all of India's FDI during that time span. The defense sector is therefore ranked as sector 61 of 63 when it comes to FDI.[22] The state recently responded to this failure by specifying a "government approval route" of up to 100 percent foreign ownership for instances providing access to modern technology in June 2016.[23] Yet, the prospect for success is not clear.

Defense procurement is predominantly based on (noncompetitive) intergovernmental purchases. More than two-thirds of all acquisitions between 2000 and 2010 were concluded in this mode, whereby they normally include a crucial role for India's state-owned defense companies, the DPSUs, who are licensed to produce the contracted equipment (e.g., Sukhoi Su-30 at Hindustan Aeronautics Limited/HAL).[24] As a result, India's defense procurement is often in a stalemate:

> The complexity of the acquisition procedure itself, the competition between the domestic defense research establishment and the armed forces, the failure of civilian security managers often to understand both national defense requirements and the utility of specific military technologies, and the chokehold exercised by the Ministry of Finance in important matters pertaining to defense have all contributed collectively to the pathologies of defense acquisition in contemporary India.[25]

Since 2002, however, a new DPP is in place. Enforced by several revisions and amendments, the objective is to increase offsets and to apply them as a strategic policy instrument. For instance, a new amendment in 2012 addresses micro-, small, and midsize enterprises and acquisitions of specific technologies by the Defense Research & Development Organization, which should receive a multiplier of offset credits in order to promote the integration of these suppliers into the defense sector. Another amendment in 2013 established a selection process which provides strong incentives for India's private sector to team up with global firms to compete for contracts. As a result, the procurement process is increasingly designed in terms of market prerogatives to capitalize on its own size and to move the defense-industrial sector from coproduction toward co-development projects. Yet, the effects are mixed at best, as the former secretary of defense production admitted in 2010: "Our [defense] industry has been in the habit of taking transfer of technology and building under license until the product dies a technological death. There is no expenditure on R&D and no technology absorption."[26] Whereas the sector's output had been modest, defense management of state authorities is not a persuasive success story: "the ability to build up a set of capabilities that are justified by a national strategy is virtually non-existent in India. The civilian leadership has no clue about defence requirements."[27]

In sum, India's defense industries have largely remained state-dominated. The sector is characterized by coproduction agreements with foreign sellers, implemented by state-owned DPSUs as production agencies, which have not gained strong development skills over time but rather a stable reputation for underperformance. Today, the defense-industrial sector is dramatically growing, whereas foreign direct investment is still negligible. These characteristics are complemented by a complex and state-dominated procurement process. Liberalizing reforms in the previous decade were aiming for more efficiency through competition, but have so far been only reluctantly implemented.

Against the backdrop of these domestic constraints, the next section focuses on the so-called Medium-Multi-Role Combat Aircraft (MMRCA) procurement process from its market-oriented inception toward the renunciation of the competitive procurement procedures in spring 2015. Rather than with technology transfers, India's return to a government-to-government deal with France ultimately provided the country with combat aircraft off-the-shelf only. Hence, the following process analysis will not only illustrate the prevailing impact of domestic factors, but also how defense-industrial relations ultimately constrain India's build-up of technological as well as military capabilities.

The MMRCA: Domestic constraints to liberalizing India's defense sector

As a vital part of the desired transformation toward a more efficient defense sector, the Indian government issued the so-far largest open tender for 126 combat aircrafts—worth up to $20 billion—since 2007. The MMRCA, which was meant to become "the mother of all defence deals,"[28] invited the world's high society of defense contractors to promote their jets and, in turn, to offer significant technology transfers: *F-16* and *F-18* from the United States, *MiG-35* from Russia, *Gripen* from Sweden, *Eurofighter* from various EU countries, and the *Rafale* from France. The latter won the competition and entered government-to-firm negotiations in January 2012. Yet, in April 2015, after more than seven years of applying market mechanisms to the procurement process, the Indian government re-replaced competitive tendering by a simple intergovernmental purchase of a reduced number of fighter jets from France.[29] Modernization through markets, and thus the integration of foreign contractors within India's defense-industrial sector, had arguably failed.

This section seeks to explore the MMRCA process and suggests that domestic constraints were primarily responsible for the failure. It is argued that a defense *market* cannot be established by merely setting strong incentives or following globally accepted standards of governance. Instead, the existence of effective political-economic institutions serves as an important prerequisite of functioning market relationships to evolve. Empirically, the article examines the implementation of India's initial market choice in 2007 up to the ultimate decision for a state-run approach in 2015. It is shown how legal uncertainty and a shortage of private partners led to frictions in the implementation of the market-based MMRCA. Its ultimate failure was triggered by political resistance of the bureaucracy and the state-owned defense industries. The ambiguity of rules and unintended consequences of initial choices empowered these defenders of the status quo so that the government shifted back to a state-run approach. In short, domestic constraints prevailed.

Contradictions between India's defense-industrial sector and a market-based approach

First, several instances of problematic legal protection evolved during the procurement process. These were not unique to the MMRCA, but rather a more widespread characteristic of Indian authorities' negotiations with private arms contractors.[30] Against this backdrop, India's most prominent expert group—the so-called Kelkar Committee—had made eleven recommendations of how to organize defense acquisitions, whereby ten of them aimed to increase transparency and legal certainty.[31]

Most significantly, the lack of legal certainty negatively affected the sensitive nature of technology transfers. Their legal provisions were designed according to historically established intergovernmental purchases "rather than taking the form of minimum government-purpose IPRs [intellectual property rights] in contractually mandated deliverables in terms of design, form, fit and function data and other technical documentation, irrespective of manufacturing by the supplier or by the supplier's sub-contractors."[32] While the government could previously adjust ambivalences concerning property rights according to political considerations, commercial exchanges were becoming highly problematic under the less flexible conditions of arm's-length trade.[33] In other words, the government had chosen a market-based approach; yet, the more specific procedures continuously required political bargaining practices rather than the consistent application of legal provisions.

This sense of legal uncertainty about property rights increasingly came to the fore when India's government entered commercial negotiations with French private contractor Dassault after January 31, 2012.[34] The latter had defeated the competitors on the basis of, first, technical and, second, monetary evaluations. Put simply, these negotiations were about the exchange of property rights between Dassault, on the one hand; and India's government, on the other. Yet, it was not about exchanging material assets in the form of delivering components, but about technology transfers and thus the *process of system integration* invented and owned by Dassault: What makes modern technology 'modern' is not the blueprints or designs, but rather the process. Western technological superiority is not based on designs it is based on process. To acquire these processes, we [India] need to guarantee solid intellectual property protection."[35] Consequently, technology transfers in terms of the coproduction agreement with the DPSU, HAL, evolved not only as the centerpiece of commercial negotiations, but also as the main obstacle to India's build-up of military capabilities.

In particular, accountability under the condition of ambivalent property rights was at stake: who would be responsible for potential delays and cost overruns of 108 coproduced jets by HAL? As HAL had a reputation for inefficiencies in handling complex manufacturing and technology transfers, Dassault proposed to arguably clarify property rights and thus accountability by having separate contracts for the 18 and the 108 aircrafts, respectively. Yet, this contradicted the terms of the market-based approach so that the Indian MoD "completely rejected this suggestion and made it clear to Dassault that it will be solely responsible for the sale and delivery of all 126 aircraft."[36] In contrast to previous weapon acquisitions, India's contract partner was now a private firm highly concerned about its property rights (e.g., process of system integration), rather than a government interested in a wide spectrum of potential gains. While an intergovernmental purchase was largely complementary to a vague protection of property rights, the latter constituted a contradiction between India's institutional setting and the requirements of a market-based approach.[37]

Second, not only some of the legal conditions contradicted arm's-length contracting, but also private firms remained structurally constrained in India's defense-industrial sector. The expansion of private business was exacerbated at both the legislative and the organizational level. While India's defense procurement policy (DPP)—despite several amendments—continuously favored state industries in numerous critical areas,[38] private firms were systematically deprived of access to the Department of Defense. For instance, the "secretary of the Department of Defence Production does not have a dedicated wing under his command to examine issues related to private industries."[39]

Beyond these structural constraints, the bureaucracy continuously endorsed informal coordination through historically evolved channels rather than by formal contracting with private actors.[40] This excluded—or, at least, did not integrate—foreign and private suppliers of defense goods. Yet, putting, for example, offset agreements into practice as part of the MMRCA tender would have necessarily required engaging private actors, because the extent was too large for state industries to absorb.[41] Indeed, the MMRCA should have promoted private entry into the defense sector; yet, property rights were insufficiently protected and state-owned companies should continuously be sheltered from potential competition. The "Indian private sector has always been portrayed as being discriminated against with the government favouring state-owned defense industries."[42] In turn, "*over-lapping* institutional mechanisms" and "non-accountability"[43] could be better compensated by an intergovernmental purchase, where political flexibility trumped transparency and legal certainty.

In sum, the discrepancies between India's existing prerequisites and the requirements of the MMRCA implied that the deep-seated pervasiveness of the state could not be changed from scratch. Instead, it was deeply embedded in its institutional structures and thus shaped serious constraints on India's build-up of military capabilities by a market-based approach.

The political resistance against the market-based approach

Governments can hardly implement reforms unilaterally. Instead, they need to build coalitions among the most relevant stakeholders. Within the context of the MMRCA, the defense bureaucracy primarily organized the procurement process, HAL served as production agency across the supply chain, and the IAF was the end user and thus the technical evaluator. The latter's primary interest was in modern military capabilities from Western states, whereas the choice of a market-based approach vs. an intergovernmental purchase was of less importance.[44]

However, the most powerful coalition of India's defense sector was the informal alliance between civilian bureaucrats (e.g., DRDO, Ministry of Defense, Ministry of Finance, Cabinet Secretariat) and state-owned defense companies (e.g., HAL), both of which largely preferred intergovernmental purchases to extract rents from the existing system. Close and often informal exchanges between policymakers, bureaucrats, and partly the armed forces were the primary coordination mechanism of this coalition.[45] This kind of state prevalence was reinforced by the fact that DPSUs were not only the most powerful actors, who integrated military platforms at the end of the supply chain, but they coproduced themselves large parts of components and subsystems. In fact, a monopolist supplier—rather than the market—had supplied military platforms. The corollary was strong vertical integration in the defense sector, a weak private supplier base, and unfamiliarity in horizontal market exchanges.[46] Existing stakeholders had benefited from this institutional status quo as the defense market was substantially rising since the mid-1990s: "There are too many bureaucrats who have vested interests in keeping these white elephants [i.e., DPSUs, such as HAL] going."[47]

Their exercise of power was pervasive in India's defense-industrial policymaking system as it had remained under-balanced in practice by private actors with a preference for a market-based approach.[48] In contrast to smaller developing states, the sheer size of India's domestic market had provided the government with a strong bargaining position vis-à-vis foreign vendors to achieve at least some technology transfers and lucrative offset deals for its state-owned industries. As a result, neither foreign capital nor private defense firms were required for domestic arms production.[49] Given that the involvement of private firms was historically not necessary, private actors had not sufficiently gained a foothold in India's arms production, resulting in negative feedback processes. There was severe shortage of societal allies, as most actors were predisposed toward *noncompliance* with market exchanges. Hence, the question arises of *how* this coalition could unfold its political influence on the MMRCA.

First, market-based rules were ambiguous to the extent that they opened up a political space for potential reform losers to delegitimize the government's approach. Already the precise formulation of a competitive request for proposals (RfP) had raised serious problems. The consequences of this cumbersome process were two-fold. It harmed not only the reputation of the contracting authorities, but it also inhibited capitalization from offsets by integrating domestic private firms. The demand issued for offsets was initially so large that India's industry could hardly absorb it. Given the insufficient coordination with private defense industries, the government suddenly turned—in the midst of the ongoing process—back from its initial requests. This ambiguity exacerbated compliance and smooth implementation. Long after the competitors had submitted their proposals, the Indian authorities allowed for indirect (i.e., not defense-related) offsets by revising some parts of the DPP in January 2011.[50] Thus, the government could no longer gain security benefits from its market-based approach. This weak performance deprived some of the defense-sector's interest groups from expected benefits and, thus, damaged the reputation of the contracting authorities. Accordingly, criticism of managing the MMRCA often served as the point of departure for them to question the market-based approach itself and to propose the allegedly more efficient intergovernmental purchase.[51]

Second, the initial choice of a market-based approach led to several unintended consequences. For instance, the government's deliberate decision for implementing the procurement by the sophisticated criterion of life-cycle costs, rather than much simpler fly-away costs, affected the commercial negotiations with Dassault in 2015. While the IAF has never promoted this procedure, both the Ministry of Finance and the Cabinet Office stressed its huge opportunities.[52] In contrast, India's defense-finance bureaucracy had always been critical toward reforms, such as life-cycle costing, and exercised its power by repeatedly sabotaging this approach. However, it is important to note that this domestic alliance was equipped by powerful arguments, since the life-cycle costs approach was chosen for long-term economic reasons, whereas the government had neglected the immediate legal repercussions.[53]

This *problematique* became evident after the down-selection of the *Rafale* and the *Eurofighter*, when the new phase of the procurement process targeted a feasible combination of costs and technology transfers. One challenge was, for the first time in India's procurement history, to arrive at an ownership/life-cycle cost of both aircrafts over a 40-year/6.000 hr. run.[54] Yet, the more severe challenge was to establish comprehensible results, possibly standing up in court against the defeated competitor's litigation. In other words, a formal appeal with reference to life-cycle costs was comparably simple given the inherently contested nature of these calculation models. For instance, Dassault had sued Korean authorities for procedural reasons, because it had lost a similar competition in 2002.[55] The precedence was set. Although the opportunity of legal recourse was an unintended consequence of an economically induced choice, it increasingly evolved as a sword of Damocles for the MMRCA as a whole. Air Marshal Matheswaran, who was responsible for the MMRCA process on behalf of the Indian Air Force, admitted that "the procurement got stuck in the intricate cobwebs of the acquisition process that we created."[56]

At the very moment that the Indian government would have signed a final contract with Dassault, the five losers of the competition could have potentially turned to Indian courts and legally attacked the government's decision.[57] This is common practice in more liberal market economies, but would have resulted in further delays and legal uncertainty for both the government and the Indian Air Force. Building on information deliberately provided by opponents of the market-based approach, the potential lawsuit could be either based on the tender poorly drafted, or on noncompliance within, the evaluation process.[58]

Most crucially, the "fear of corruption, or even the allegations thereof, which are usually leveled by the losers or other interested bystanders in a competition has had the stultifying effect of either paralyzing the acquisition process or delaying it interminably, or, on rare occasions, even nullifying procurement decisions already announced or on the cusp of being unveiled."[59] Opponents of liberal reforms could realistically threaten to undermine the successful conclusion of the MMRCA. Against this backdrop, the whole MMRCA process was suspended in April 2015, and a new—or, rather old—procurement procedure was inaugurated: a government-to-government deal with France.[60]

In sum, the available evidence suggests that India's return to an intergovernmental purchase was based on domestic constraints, which prevented not only the implementation of the initially chosen market-based approach, but also the build-up of massive military capabilities.

Conclusion

This article departed from illustrating the general trends of India's state-run defense-industrial sector, which had recently faced several liberal reforms, yet proved relatively resilient. The government's policy choices were subsequently explored in an investigation of one of the most prominent acquisition projects in recent years. I suggested that, first and foremost, domestic constraints made the MMRCA competition fail. More specifically, the contradictions between India's historically evolved defense sector and the prerequisites of markets shaped frictions. Neither sound legal protection was guaranteed beyond doubts; nor was a sufficient number of private partners at the disposal of government reformers. In addition, the politics of implementation revealed how some interest groups increasingly resisted reform efforts by exploiting ambiguous rules and capitalizing from unintended consequences of initial institutional choices like the life-cycle costs criterion.

Therefore, the article suggests that, if the preconditions for markets to function are largely absent, political flexibility—rather than transparency and legal certainty—will evolve as the key currency for resolving coordination problems. As a consequence, state-run practices reproduced a historically grown state-run sector and significantly exacerbated the integration of foreign contractors in India's defense-industrial sector. In short, domestic constraints prevailed over the opportunities provided by international factors and prevented the build-up of India's military capabilities.

Notes

1. Aseema Sinha, "Partial Accommodation without Conflict: India as a Rising Link Power," in *Accommodating Rising Powers: Past, Present, And Future*, edited by T. V. Paul (Cambridge: Cambridge University Press, 2016), 222–46; Sandy Gordon, *India's Rise as an Asian Power. Nation, Neighborhood, and Region* (Washington, DC: Georgetown University Press, 2014).
2. Gordon, *India's Rise as an Asian Power*, 112–13.
3. Chris Ogden, *Indian Foreign Policy* (Cambridge: Polity Press, 2014), 34–35.
4. Kartik Bommakanti, "Innovation in Strategic Technologies: India's Experience in a Conceptual and Historical Context," in *India's Military Modernization: Strategic Technologies and Weapons Systems*, edited by Rajesh Basrur and Bharat Gopalaswamy (Oxford: Oxford University Press, 2015), 18–19, 38–41. This view was also expressed by several Indian interviewees; for instance, by a former undersecretary of the defense accounts department (Ministry of Defense; Frankfurt/New Delhi: February 9, 2018 [phone]).
5. "By the end of the Cold War, India was 100 per cent reliant on Soviet-era material for its ground-air defence, 75 per cent dependent on Soviet equipment for its fighter aircraft defence, 60 per cent for its ground attack aircraft, 100 per cent for its tracked armoured vehicles, 80 per cent for tanks, 100 per cent for its guided missile destroyers, 95 per cent for its conventional submarines, and 70 per cent for its frigates." Manjeet S. Pardesi and Ron Matthews, "India's Tortuous Road to Defence-Industrial Self-Reliance," *Defence & Security Analysis* 23, no. 4 (2007): 426; see also Richard A. Bitzinger, "Prospect for Future Indo-European Defence Industrial Cooperation," Policy Brief (Nanyang Technological University: RSIS, August 2014).
6. Pardesi and Matthews, "India's Tortuous Road," 420; see also Richard A. Bitzinger, "China vs. India: The Great Arms Contest," RSIS Commentary, May 4, 2016.
7. Interview with policy expert from think tank on the MMRCA (Frankfurt/New Delhi: February 9, 2018 [phone]). See also Brajesh Chhibber and Rajat Dhawan, "A Bright Future for India's Defense Industry?" *McKinsey on Government*, Spring 2013, 46.
8. Ashley J. Tellis, *Dogfight! India's Medium Multi-Role Combat Aircraft Decision* (Washington, DC: Carnegie Endowment for International Peace, 2011), 59–60.
9. Laxman K. Behera, "India's Defence Public Sector Undertakings: A Performance Analysis," *Journal of Defence Studies* 3, no. 4 (2009): 118–30; Trefor Moss, "Eastern Fast Air," *Jane's Defence Weekly*, August 17, 2011.
10. Vinod K Mishra, "Remarks on 'Streamlining India's Defence Procurement System,'" Observer Research Foundation (ORF) Seminar Series (New Delhi: ORF, 2012).
11. Deba R. Mohanty, *Changing Times? India's Defence Industry in the 21st Century* (Bonn: Bonn International Center for Conversion [BICC], 2004), 26.
12. Rahul Bedi, "India Struggles to Break Free of Imports," *Jane's Defence Weekly*, July 20, 2011.
13. Pardesi and Matthews, "India's Tortuous Road," 424–29; Jane's Defence Weekly, "Briefing: Indian Air Force Capabilities—High and Mighty," *Jane's Defence Weekly*, February 2, 2011.
14. Chhibber and Dhawan, "A Bright Future?" 45.
15. See also *Jane's Defence Weekly*, "Briefing: Indian Air Force Capabilities."
16. Tellis, *Dogfight! India's Medium Multi-Role Combat Aircraft Decision*, 62.
17. Stephen P. Cohen and Sunil Dasgupta, *Arming without Aiming: India's Military Modernization* (Washington, DC: Brookings Institution Press, 2013); Pardesi and Matthews, "India's Tortuous Road," 432. The DPSUs are: BEML, Bharat Dynamics Limited, Bharat Electronics Limited, Goa Shipyard Limited, GRSE, Hindustan Aeronautics Limited, Hindustan Shipyard Limited, Mazagon Dock Limited, Mishra Dhatu Nigam Limited, and Ordnance Factory Board.
18. Moss, "Eastern Fast Air"; See also Chhibber and Dhawan, "A Bright Future?" 46. A similar conclusion can be drawn from Department of Industrial Policy and Promotion and Department of Defence Production 2017; as well as from www.makeinindiadefence.gov.in/.

19. Pardesi and Matthews, "India's Tortuous Road," 428; Chhibber and Dhawan, "A Bright Future," 51; see also Deba R. Mohanty, "From MIC to NSIC," ORF, October 11, 2011, www.orfonline.org/research/from-mic-to-nsic/.
20. International Institute for Strategic Studies (IISS), *The Military Balance 2015* (London: IISS, 2015), 220–22, 220; Department of Industrial Policy and Promotion, "Foreign Direct Investment," www.makeinindia.com/policy/foreign-direct-investment (accessed March 7, 2016). The revised FDI policy also removed an earlier provision related to the control of joint ventures, which required the single-largest resident Indian share-holder to have at least a 51percent equity share. Under the new regulations, however, this shareholder now has the power to appoint a majority of the directors in a joint venture. IISS, *The Military Balance 2015*, 221.
21. Chhibber and Dhawan, "A Bright Future," 53; Dinakar Peri, "Rafale Deal to Boost Strategic Partnership," *The Hindu*, April 11, 2015.
22. Department of Industrial Policy and Promotion, "Quarterly Factsheet on Foreign Direct Investment," 2015, 10, http://dipp.nic.in/English/Publications/FDI_Statistics/2015/FDI_FactSheet_OctoberNovember December2015.pdf.
23. The Hindu, "It's 100% FDI in Most Sectors, Including Defence," *The Hindu*, June 20, 2016, www.thehindu.com/news/national/Its-100-FDI-in-most-sectors-including-defence/article14434009.ece; P. R. Sanjai, "India Allows 100% FDI in Defence via Govt Approval," June 20, 2016, https://www.livemint.com/Politics/25SUpO8jkE9v9jjAQv72LL/India-allows-100-FDI-in-defence-via-govt-approval.html; see also Department of Industrial Policy and Promotion and Department of Defence Production, "Defence Manufacturing Sector: Achievements Report" (New Delhi, February 13, 2017).
24. Chhibber and Dhawan, "A Bright Future," 45–46.
25. Tellis, *Dogfight! India's Medium Multi-Role Combat Aircraft Decision*, 10.
26. Cited from Bedi, "India Struggles to Break Free of Imports."
27. Cited from Moss, "Eastern Fast Air"; See also Deba R. Mohanty, "Why India's Defence Procurement Is Problematic," ORF, April 10, 2012, www.orfonline.org/research/why-indias-defence-procurement-is-problematic/.
28. Rahul Bedi and Damian Kemp, "Contenders Line up for Indian Fighter Contest," *Jane's Defence Weekly*, February 14, 2007; see also Chhibber and Dhawan, "A Bright Future," 47.
29. Times of India, "Direct Purchase of 36 Fighters Will Alter Original Rafale Deal," *Times of India*, April 11, 2015; Amit Cowshish, "New Twist in the MMRCA Tail," Comment (New Delhi: Institute for Defence Studies and Analyses, April 15, 2015).
30. Comptroller and Auditor General of India (CAG), "Procurement of the SU-30K," Audit (New Delhi: CAG, 2000); Comptroller and Auditor General of India, "CA 18 Air Force and Navy: Coast Guard," Audit (New Delhi: CAG, 2008); Comptroller and Auditor General of India, "Acquisition of Helicopters for VVIPs," Audit (New Delhi: CAG, 2013); See also Bitzinger, "Prospect for Future Indo-European Defence Industrial Cooperation"; Bitzinger, "China vs. India."
31. Ministry of Defence, "Kelkar Committee Submits Report on Defence Acquisition," Press Information Bureau, Government of India, April 5, 2005, http://pib.nic.in/newsite/erelease.aspx?relid=8386.
32. Sandee Verma, "India's Defence Procurement Procedure: Assessing the Case for Review and Reforms," Institute for Defense Studies and Analyses Issue Brief (New Delhi: IDSA, 2014), 6.
33. Peri, "Rafale Deal to Boost Strategic Partnership"; see also IISS, *The Military Balance 2015*, 221.
34. "Rafale Edges Out Eurofighter," *The Hindu*, February 5, 2012; Jay Menon, Robert Wall, and Michael Bruno, "Vive La MMRCA," *Aviation Week & Space Technology*, February 6, 2012.
35. Abhijit Iyer-Mitra, "In Defence of 100 per Cent FDI," Observer Research Foundation Analysis (New Delhi: ORF, 2014).
36. Agence France-Presse, "Report: India-France Rafale Deal Stalled," *Defense News*, April 5, 2013; see also Agence France-Presse, "Indian Negotiator for Giant Rafale Fighter Deal Dies," *Defense News*, October 3, 2013.
37. This legal uncertainty was even enhanced by the corruption *problematique*. While several complaints were raised that "procedural deviations" had enabled the *Rafale* to evolve as the preferred bidder of the MMRCA, the government rejected these specific objections (Rahul Bedi, "MMRCA in Trouble over Evaluation 'Irregularities'" *Jane's Defence Weekly*, March 28, 2012). At the same time, however, the required collaboration with DPSUs (especially technology transfers) introduced coordination on the basis of reciprocity and often informal alliances, both of which could contradict a market-oriented approach. Former Defense Minister Antony admitted that "Efforts to indigenize manufacturing are beset by cumbersome and complex bureaucratic procedures, technological over-reach and limited RandD" (cited from Bedi, "India Struggles to Break Free of Imports"), all of which were hardly compatible with competitive (or, at least, contestable) tendering.

38. Mohanty, "Why India's Defence Procurement Is Problematic"; see also Mishra, "Remarks on 'Streamlining India's Defence Procurement System.'"
39. Deba R. Mohanty, "Military Indianisation: Are We Heading the Right Way?" ORF, June 15, 2011, www.orfonline.org/research/military-indianisation-are-we-heading-the-right-way/.
40. Interviews with former German ambassador to India (Berlin, August 12, 2015) and former German military attaché in Delhi (Munich, October 19, 2015 [phone]). Both interviewees were directly involved in the MMRCA and—independently from each other—stressed this argument.
41. Robert Hewson, "India Looks to Imminent MMRCA Programme RfP," *Jane's Defence Weekly*, July 25, 2007; Bedi, "India Struggles to Break Free of Imports."
42. Mishra, "Remarks on 'Streamlining India's Defence Procurement System'"; see also Iyer-Mitra, "In Defence of 100 per Cent FDI."
43. Mohanty, "Why India's Defence Procurement Is Problematic," emphasis added.
44. Interview with a senior official of the IAF (Frankfurt/New Delhi, January 25, 2018 [phone]); interview with a former German military attaché in Delhi (Munich, October 19, 2015 [phone]).
45. Behera, "India's Defence Public Sector Undertakings"; Verma, "India's Defence Procurement Procedure."
46. Interview with Air Marshal M. Matheswaran of the IAF, responsible for the MMRCA selection process (Frankfurt/Chennai, February 3, 2018 [phone]).
47. Moss, "Eastern Fast Air"; See also Standing Committee on Defence, "Indigenisation of Defense Production—Public-Private Partnership" (New Delhi: Lok Sabha Secretariat, 2008), 19; Cohen and Dasgupta, *Arming without Aiming*.
48. Interview with senior representative of involved prime contractor (Munich, March 2017).
49. Peri, "Rafale Deal to Boost Strategic Partnership"; Pardesi and Matthews, "India's Tortuous Road."
50. Hewson, "India Looks to Imminent MMRCA Programme RfP"; Rahul Bedi, "India Releases Delayed RfP for MRCA Purchase," *Jane's Defence Weekly*, September 5, 2007; Aviation Week & Space Technology, "Diplomacy Will Play a Key Role in Fighter Competition," *Aviation Week & Space Technology*, February 7, 2011.
51. Laxman K. Behera, "India's Interim Defence Budget 2014–2015: An Appraisal," Comment (New Delhi: Institute for Defence Studies and Analyses, February 23, 2014); Cowshish, "New Twist in the MMRCA Tail"; See also Agence France-Presse, "Report: India-France Rafale Deal Stalled"; Agence France-Presse, "Indian Negotiator for Giant Rafale Fighter Deal Dies."
52. Two interviewees who were involved in the implementation process emphasized the importance of life-cycle costing and its unfolding impact on the institutional choice in 2015. Interviews with former German ambassador to India (Berlin, August 12, 2015) and senior official of defense contractor in Delhi (Munich, October 5, 2015 [phone])). See also Standing Committee on Defence, "Indigenisation of Defense Production."
53. Tellis, *Dogfight! India's Medium Multi-Role Combat Aircraft Decision*, 69.
54. Ibid., 66–67; "Dassault, Eurofighter, New Delhi Start Poring Over MMRCA Bids," *Aviation Week & Space Technology*, November 10, 2011; See also, "MMRCA Deal: Europe versus France Contest Begins for World's Biggest Combat Aircrafts," *The Hindu*, November 5, 2011.
55. "Dassault Sues Korea over Fighter Deal," *BBC News*, April 4, 2002.
56. Muthumanikam Matheswaran, "Rafale Deal: Much Needed Infusion for IAF," *South Asia Monitor*, April 13, 2015, http://southasiamonitor.org/detail.php?type=sl&nid=11339.
57. K.V. Prasad, "MMRCA Contract May Be Signed by September, Says Air Chief," *The Hindu*, February 11, 2011.
58. Several interviewees confirmed that defeated competitors had considered filing a lawsuit. Although they deliberately arrived at the conclusion *not* to pursue this strategy (as other corporate activities in India could be damaged), this indicates the importance of this issue. Most crucially, the Indian government could not be 100 percent certain about this possibility, which would have delayed the MMRCA for years.
59. Tellis, *Dogfight! India's Medium Multi-Role Combat Aircraft Decision*, 9; see also Bedi, "MMRCA in Trouble"; "Don't Corrupt Our People, Antony Tells Defence Companies," *The Hindu*, July 13, 2011; Mohanty, "Why India's Defence Procurement Is Problematic."
60. Dinakar Peri, "Deadlock over Rafale Persists," *The Hindu*, February 25, 2015; See also Dinakar Peri, "Rafale Deal Terms Non-Negotiable: Parrikar," *The Hindu*, March 18, 2015; *Times of India*, "Direct Purchase of 36 Fighters Will Alter Original Rafale Deal"; Rahul Bedi and Frédéric Lert, "Modi Announces Rafale Buy," *Jane's Defence Weekly*, April 12, 2015.

Does being part of a semi-regionalized European defense economy change state behavior in armaments policy decision-making?

Jocelyn Mawdsley

ABSTRACT

When states make decisions on armaments policy, it is generally agreed they try to achieve combinations of foreign, security, industrial, economic, and technological policy goals alongside equipping their armed forces as efficiently as possible. It is, however, consistently argued in both the defense-economics and EU-studies literature that for European states things are (or should be) different. This article contributes to this debate by bringing together these disparate literatures to critically examine the proposition that the existence of a semi-regionalized European defense economy fundamentally changes state calculations on armaments policy. It critically examines the two main claims made about behavioral change: that European states accept a liberalized European defense market governed by the EU and make armaments decisions on a value-for-money basis, or that defense interdependence is so advanced that European states no longer need to consider their national interests because these are subsumed in the European interest. The article then considers an alternative perspective, that state behavior has not changed but is restricted by the existence of a European defense market that, intentionally or not, works to protect the interests of the biggest European arms-producing states.

Introduction

Krause suggested that there are three reasons for states to maintain a military industry: the pursuit of victory or survival in war, the pursuit of power and identity, and the pursuit of wealth.[1] If, as realist scholars and many policymakers assume, the international system is innately anarchic, then Krause's considerations could be understood as the underlying drivers of a state's armament strategies. They are likely to be foundational in terms of what armaments relationships are built with other states and foreign defense firms. It is accepted in much of the defense-economics literature that being as self-sufficient as possible in armaments is therefore often a goal for states. Bitzinger noted that emerging arms-producing states also exhibit this policy behavior, observing a tendency to pursue techno-nationalist goals.[2]

What, though, if your regional order features highly institutionalized, cooperative relationships in terms of both economic and security policies? Would this change the calculations states make? If a state no longer fears war with its neighbors; derives its identity and power, at least in part, from its membership in the European Union (EU) or the North Atlantic Treaty Organization (NATO); and is faced with public expenditure needs other than defense, will it act differently? Does the Article V NATO security guarantee mean that states are no longer troubled by security of supply questions? Does the concept of strategic autonomy now only matter at the European rather than national level? Do highly integrated economies and established practices of cooperating on economic policy in the EU mean that defense firms are no longer seen as any different to other firms, and that therefore procurement decisions are made predominantly on a value-for-money basis? It is consistently argued in both the defense-economics and EU-studies literature, that for European states things are (or should be) different and that cooperation on armaments should prevail over national interests. This article contributes to this debate by bringing together these disparate literatures to critically examine the proposition that the existence of a semi-regionalized European defense economy fundamentally changes state calculations on armaments policy.

At least since the 1990s, if not before, Krause's assumptions about how states rationalize their armament policies have been challenged by the pressures of increasing European integration, involvement in NATO, and the internationalization of defense firms.[3] European states have needed to reconcile their national armament strategies with the necessity of cooperating at the bilateral, multilateral, or international organization level, as well as coping with the globalization of technological innovation.[4] Like other states, they try to achieve combinations of foreign, security, industrial, economic, and technological policy goals alongside equipping their armed forces as efficiently as possible, but in an unusual regional environment. One might expect a continent with both a long-established military alliance and highly integrated economies and policymaking machineries to also have a highly integrated defense economy.

However, the European defense market is also frequently criticized for being both fragmented (in terms of both supply and demand) and for remaining protectionist, thus resulting in suboptimal defense capabilities for all European states.[5] After a series of moves toward defense industrial consolidation in the 1990s produced four large prime contractors, BAE Systems, Airbus Group (formerly EADS), Thales, and Finmeccanica, progress slowed. A proposed merger between the then EADS and BAE Systems in 2012 was blocked by Germany, and although the December 2015 completion of the Franco-German merger of military land-industry suppliers, Nexter and KMW, may mark the start of a new wave, the industrial landscape remains surprisingly national, especially in naval industry.[6] Similarly, despite multiple EU and NATO initiatives, programs, and in the EU case, regulation, progress on the demand side has also been minimal. The European Defence Agency (EDA) reported that from 2008 to 2013 collaborative defense procurement spending fell, although the most recent estimated figures (for 2014 and 2015) show some improvement.[7]

What is interesting, however, is that despite the problems, the concepts of a European Defence Equipment Market (EDEM) or a European Defence Technological and Industrial Base (EDTIB) are rarely questioned. This is not the case in other regions of the world, even where defense alliances exist. Moreover, the European region has no credible new entrants challenging its main defense industrial–producing states, although one might have expected some to emerge from the former Warsaw Pact states.[8]

In common with the other articles in this special issue, this article seeks to uncover the main factors impacting decision making on the defense economy within Europe. In proposing that a semi-regional defense economy now exists, the article is not arguing that European states no longer make national defense–economic decisions (they clearly do), but it accepts that they make those decisions in the context of a growing EU regulatory framework, against the backdrop of capability-planning processes in both NATO and the EU, often within specific agencies and bilateral/multilateral agreements for armaments cooperation and with the knowledge of the security guarantees made by both NATO (Article 5) and the EU (Article 42[7] TEU). The article begins by a brief overview of the key themes in the literature on the Europeanization of the armaments sector, from which it will derive hypotheses to test whether the behavior of European states has altered.

Competing claims over behavioral change

The literature and perspectives reviewed in this section are EU-centric and come largely from the field of political science. This reflects the comparative neglect of NATO in recent years by those working on European security issues, but also a longer-term lack of interest in defense economy issues within the alliance, with a few notable exceptions.[9] Nor has there been much interest in the question of how or why NATO might influence behavioral change by states on armaments policy. The interest from defense economists in NATO as an institution has been to see it as a mechanism for correcting market failure or improving market operation, and indeed they view its record on equipment standardization as one of failure.[10] Sandler and Hartley see national governments' choices on whether (or not) to cooperate on armaments within NATO as a cost-benefit analysis, suggesting, in other words, that European cooperation on armaments policy is a matter of rational decision-making—behavioral change should occur if there is a rational case for sacrificing some national goods in return for a collective good.[11] This, however, seems to discount the highly political motivations for armaments policy decision-making—as Fevolden and Tvetbråten argue, economic fallacies may in fact make political sense.[12]

In recent years, there has been significant growth in the EU's role in armaments policy. While the literature rarely directly addresses the extent of state behavioral change due to this new policy environment, and as De Vore has argued does not engage with the existing literature on armaments policymaking, it does, however, offer some propositions about what might motivate behavioral change.[13] From this literature, the article develops two competing perspectives and derives hypotheses to test them. These are complemented with a third perspective that draws explicitly on Krause's work on state behavior, suggesting that structural constraints are a more important driver of state behavior in the European context than positive behavioral change.[14]

The first perspective draws on the role the EU's supranational institutions have played in framing the way defense-economics questions are understood in Europe. Guay, for example, argued that since the 1990s, the European Commission has played a growing role in the shaping of the European defense industry and the European defense-equipment market and that this is further evidence for the neo-functionalist view of the European policy process—i.e., policy action by the European Commission in one area leads in time to a spillover in adjacent policy areas or industry sectors.[15] In this case, European Commission civilian policy actions in the areas of competition policy, science and technology, and public procurement have led to the emergence of defense-industry initiatives. More recently, Blauberger and Weiss have also stressed the role that the European Court of Justice played in setting the limits to defense derogations from the Single Market, and the way the Commission has used these judgements to carve out this regulatory and enforcement role.[16] Other authors have addressed the role of the Commission in trying to frame or organize defense-economic matters in ways that allowed it a regulatory role.[17] While those articles stressed the contested nature of the Commission's attempts, Britz's later work stressed the ultimate success of the market frame.[18] She argues that Europeanization of armaments policy can best be understood as a process of marketization, namely a convergence in national policies around liberal norms like privatization, cost-effective defense procurement (e.g., the UK's Smart Procurement initiative), and open defense markets, that in turn leads them to support Commission liberalization proposals. Strikwerda also finds some evidence of this in her study of the member states' reaction to the Commission proposal for a security and defense-procurement directive.[19]

If this perspective is accurate, then we might expect that European states would accept that the rigors of the market will determine the destiny of "their" defense firms. In other words, this means that one side of Adams's iron triangle, the link between state and defense firm, has now gone.[20] This leads to the following hypotheses:

(1a) national defense procurement decisions would be made on a value-for-money basis to maximize military capabilities, and

(1b) the role of EU supranational institutions to set and enforce the rules for this liberalized market has widespread acceptance.

The second perspective is that European states have now moved from a national to a European-level understanding of defense. As Mérand has argued, as the European security and defense field has been institutionalized, the practices, social representations, and power relations of security and defense actors are fundamentally challenged.[21] Joana and Smith, suggest for instance that negotiations on the A400M transporter aircraft collaborative project were "heavily marked by a change in the social representation of European cooperation in the arms field."[22] What they suggest is that the growing importance of the EU's Common Security and Defence Policy (CSDP) suggests increased solidarity on defense (which applies also to armaments) that might change state behavior. On the defense-industry level, the existence of European, not just national, champions means shifts of loyalties. Member states could be willing to give up national-defense industrial capacity in order to maintain overall capacity in the EU. The economic logic for armaments collaboration would be widely accepted in terms of collaboration on research and procurement, and that agreements on security of supply and reciprocity would give states the confidence to pool and share military capabilities.[23] Giegerich thought that the financial crisis and the defense cuts that it brought might give added momentum to this.[24]

If this perspective is accurate, we might expect that European states have accepted (potentially for purely economic reasons) that the European defense interest subsumes their national interests. It leads to the following hypotheses:

(2a) rising levels of cooperation on research and procurement can be seen, defense-industrial mergers encouraged, and the end of national (but not European level) protectionist measures observed, and,

(2b) increased trust and solidarity mean that defense interdependence through measures like pooling and sharing and specialization is accepted at the European level.

The third perspective comes from the defense-economics literature and suggests that the behavioral changes in European states are best understood by the proposition that since the 1990s, the system has essentially been captured by those states that were at that stage defined as second-tier suppliers, and were intent on maintaining that status. Krause defined the structure of the global arms-transfer system thus:

> First-tier suppliers innovate at the technological frontier, second-tier suppliers produce (via the transfer of capacities) weapons at the technological frontier and adapt them to specific market needs, third-tier suppliers copy and reproduce existing technologies (via transfer of design) but do not capture the underlying process of innovation or adoption.[25]

Krause argued that in Europe, this second tier comprises the UK, France, and Germany, with the possible additions of Italy, Spain, and Sweden.[26] Moves to respond to U.S. defense-industrial consolidation in the 1990s such as the Framework Agreement on defense-industrial restructuring (signed by the six), or the UK, France, Germany, and Italy's agreement to set up OCCAR (the multilateral procurement management agency) set these states apart from other EU and NATO European member states. Arguably, a case can be made that the subsequent EU initiatives merely follow the directions set by this group.[27] Certainly, despite rhetoric to the contrary, both the Commission and the EDA's actions seem largely supportive of these second-tier producers and the large prime contractors that "belong: to them, leaving smaller producers with little choice but to comply with an unfavorable regulatory regime.[28] Meanwhile, these second-tier suppliers tend to ignore directives they find awkward and opt out of real participation in EDA activity.[29] They can do this because the EDEM is so distorted by the presence of a few big players that the large number of small ones are easily kept on the fringes.[30]

If this final perspective is accurate, then we must assume that capture of the system is possible by a few large players, and that others accept (if unhappily) this status quo. From this we can derive the following hypotheses:

(3a) the interests of the second-tier suppliers are so predominant that they comprise the vast majority of the EDEM and EDTIB, and thus system-level capture is possible, and

(3b) the market and regulatory regime distortion is such that smaller states are unable to act in their own interests, and thus are forced to accept the status quo.

The rest of this article investigates the evidence for and against these six hypotheses in turn, starting with those linked to marketization and moving through the three perspectives in the order presented above, before drawing conclusions.

Acceptance of marketization

(1a) national defense procurement decisions would be made on a value-for-money basis to maximize military capabilities, and
(1b) the role of EU supranational institutions to set and enforce the rules for this liberalized market has widespread acceptance.

In the 1990s, the liberalization logic to the EU's Single Market program spread to public procurement, with many European states adopting governance strategies from new-public-management theories. Falling defense budgets after the end of the Cold War raised interest in improving the cost effectiveness of defense procurement. Some predicted that this would bring the end of domestic preference in defense procurement and strengthen the role of the military in Adams's iron triangle, resulting in the opening of domestic markets to foreign suppliers (expected to be mainly American).[31] The establishment of OCCAR was meant to remove protectionism from collaborative procurement and entrench this commercial approach.[32]

Britz has argued that the acceptance of market norms in defense procurement has become widespread, and that this has in turn allowed the European Commission to begin to regulate using a market-driven approach.[33] Work in this vein tends to draw particularly on the Swedish case, where its willingness to accept foreign acquisitions of Swedish defense firms without conditions has been noted.[34] Another example is Belgium, which voluntarily abandoned the use of offsets from 2001–04 to save money, but which led to substantial job losses in Belgian defense firms.[35] However, the Belgian case is interesting in that it did not last. Hoeffler suggests that while evidence of marketization can be seen to varying degrees in many European states, the adoption may well be partial or temporary.[36] Castellacci et al. made a similar point in a comparison of Norway and Sweden.[37] Even the most enthusiastic proponent of marketization in the 1990s, the UK, with its Smart Procurement initiatives, has reverted to more interventionist defense-industrial strategies.[38]

Nor can it be argued that the European market has been substantially opened to foreign suppliers. Kluth has examined the procurement of missiles and defense electronics by the UK, France, Germany, and Italy in the 1980s and then from 2000–2017.[39] He has found evidence of abandonment of domestic suppliers in favor of other European suppliers, although in the missile sector this is largely accounted for by the emergence of MBDA, a European champion and near-monopoly supplier with roots in all four states. What is interesting, though, is Kluth's finding that although the United States supplied a substantial amount of equipment in the 1980s in these sectors, its firms are barely represented from 2000 onward.[40] In part this may reflect negative experiences of both transatlantic collaborative projects (e.g., F-35) and off-the-shelf purchases (e.g., the UK and Chinook helicopters). Kiss also reports that disappointing experiences with offsets in the 1990s have lessened the enthusiasm of Central and East European countries for purchasing from the U.S. to show their pro-NATO foreign policy stances.[41]

The biggest recent European collaborative project, the A400M transport aircraft, despite being explicitly framed as a test for the commercial approach was in fact an example of protectionism, with a European engine consortium led by Rolls Royce being chosen over a better-value product from Pratt-Whitney.[42] According to SIPRI, imports by states in Europe decreased by 36 percent between 2007–11 and 2012–16, with the region accounting for 11 percent of total global imports.[43] The biggest non-European suppliers were the United States and Russia, but both with decreasing overall shares of the European market, suggesting that neither foreign-policy nor value-for-money motivations for defense procurement are currently strong. This suggests that the acceptance of marketization is at best limited to European rather than national purchases, and that hypothesis 1a is therefore not proven.

Turning to the second hypothesis, that there is widespread acceptance of the European Commission setting the rules for and enforcing a liberalized EDEM, again the picture is rather mixed. A series of studies on the adoption of two directives (on procurement and intra-EU arms transfers) that exist thus far have shown that states have accepted regulation even when it arguably went against their initial preferences and interests.[44] However, this picture is perhaps less clear than it might seem at first sight. Fiott, examining the transfers directive, suggests that it has, in practice, had little impact on the EDEM, and that for key players it offered small gains and minimal adoption costs.[45] Strikwerda, looking at the procurement directive, also claimed that big arms-producing states thought it would make little legal difference and that the Commission would be flexible in its enforcement.[46] This suggests that, thus far at least, hypothesis 1b has not fully been tested yet. The regulatory regime has yet to challenge the defense derogations allowed under Article 346 TEU, which apply for defense equipment procurement.[47]

European solidarity

> (2a) rising levels of cooperation on research and procurement can be seen, defense-industrial mergers encouraged, and the end of national (but not European level) protectionist measures observed, and,
>
> (2b) increased trust and solidarity mean that defense interdependence through measures like pooling and sharing and specialization is accepted at the European level.

On the face of it, there is a natural logic to European collaboration on all matters related to the defense economy. Only superpowers can afford to produce technologically advanced major weapons systems alone. However, as Smith points out, it is not always so straightforward:

> In practice, duplication of facilities, differences in requirements, coordination problems, lack of clear control and delays due to different budgetary systems all tend to increase the costs of collaborative projects.[48]

De Vore has questioned whether it is in fact possible for collaborative armaments projects to offer the benefits it is claimed they should offer, given the problems found in their implementation.[49] Certainly, the biggest two recent European projects, the Eurofighter and the A400M transport aircraft, have been dogged by all the problems outlined by Smith.[50]

Here one might expect to see the institutions of the EU and NATO playing a key enabling role. In fact, despite much effort, neither the EU nor NATO have been particularly successful, despite multiple efforts in forging real rather than rhetorical commitment to European armaments cooperation from their member states.[51] Financial crisis and the resulting cuts to defense spending have not brought the cooperation gains that Giegerich predicted.[52] The European Defence Agency reported that from 2008 to 2013, collaborative defense-procurement spending fell, although the most recent estimated figures (for 2014 and 2015) show some improvement.[53] In November 2016, the Commission proposed a Defence Action Plan consisting of three elements: a European Defence Fund, European Investment Bank (EIB) investment coupled with EU co-financing for the modernization of defense supply chains; and strengthening the Single Market for defense.[54] At its 2016 Warsaw Summit, NATO also committed to improving armaments cooperation.[55] It remains to be seen whether these new initiatives are more successful than their predecessors.

So why is there resistance on the part of member states? The article has already shown that the appearance of a regulatory framework within the EU, prohibiting protectionist measures for indigenous defense firms, is somewhat illusory. The argument for European-level rationalization of defense industries has always been underpinned by the belief that existing overcapacity meant that only by rationalization could the defense technological and industrial base be maintained, and that this, even if it came with national losses, was in the long-term interest of the states concerned. A 2015 study for the European Parliament found that European defense firms were heavily reliant on non-European export markets for their survival, but that the markets they have penetrated are often emerging arms producers themselves with hopes of attaining armaments autarky.[56] The existing literature has not systematically investigated recent decisions on mergers and non-mergers to get a clearer picture of state motivations. Briani argued that maintaining highly skilled jobs was a key motivation for blocking mergers.[57] This did appear to be Germany's rationale for blocking the proposed merger between the then EADS (now Airbus) and BAE Systems in 2012, but Germany permitted the land-industry merger between KMW and French firm Nexter in 2015, despite similar issues of national interest being raised by critics.[58] Other mergers seem to collapse due to the firm being deemed vital to the strategic interest of the state. Bellais's evaluation of the naval industry posited that this was a major hindrance to rationalization in this sector.[59] The EU and to a lesser degree NATO have assumed that the strength of their respective alliances is such that security of supply and strategic autonomy concerns at the national level would no longer matter. It is not clear, though, that this is how states understand the matter, which given divergent threat perceptions is understandable. The dividing line between protectionism and legitimate security of supply concern is not clear-cut.

There are some examples where a higher level of trust is evident, but these are predominantly bilateral cooperation deals or small groups of states working together. The Franco-British defense cooperation under the 2010 Lancaster House agreements had a distinct industrial policy rationale from the start. This can be seen most clearly in the missile sector, where a "One Complex Weapons Industry" concept has been established, with the aim of rationalizing the missile sector in Britain and France, hoping to achieve 30 percent savings. The intergovernmental agreement in the field of missiles, which came into force in October 2016, means genuine interdependence in a highly strategic sector, and industrial rationalization between the two countries with the establishment of eight centers of excellence within MBDA.[60] Similar levels of interdependence between France and Britain can be seen in nuclear warhead testing. There is potential for the KMW/Nexter merger to produce a similar interdependence between France and Germany on tank production. Other examples might include NORDDEFCO, the format in which the Nordic states cooperate closely on defense, or the joint Belgian-Dutch naval command, which has led to joint procurement of frigates.

What trends does this analysis suggest? First, if we consider the first hypothesis, that we should be observing rising levels of cooperation on research and procurement and a diminishing role for protectionist measures for national defense firms, the evidence suggests that despite much rhetoric in favor of cooperation, there is comparatively little action. However, this must be caveated by the acceptance of defense interdependence to a greater or lesser extent by smaller groups of like-minded states with similar capacities. It seems that trust and solidarity are more easily found in these settings. In many ways, the armaments-specific decisions detailed here fit well with Valasek's conclusions about the conditions under which pooling and sharing defense resources might succeed.[61] In descending order of importance, he suggested that these are similarity of strategic culture, trust and solidarity, forces of similar size and quality, level playing field for defense companies, clarity of intentions, seriousness of intent, and low corruption, features that he thought the Franco-British agreement, for example, largely met. It would seem that, for the moment at least, European-level trust and solidarity do not exist at the necessary levels. On the balance of the evidence, it appears that neither hypothesis 2a nor 2b really offer an accurate picture.

Domination of large state interests

> (3a) the interests of the second-tier suppliers are so predominant that they comprise the vast majority of the EDEM and EDTIB, and thus system-level capture is possible, and
>
> (3b) the market and regulatory regime distortion is such that smaller states are unable to act in their own interests, and thus are forced to accept the status quo.

The third perspective suggests that rather than making a positive choice to make certain armaments-policy choices, most states are effectively constrained by the system in which they operate. While behavioral change may be observable in the European market due to regulatory and other policy initiatives, in fact what we are seeing is negative rather than positive behavioral changes. Mawdsley argued that regulatory and policy initiatives from both the European Commission and the EDA favored larger arms-producing states and firms, and left little room for smaller states to act in their national interest.[62] This fits with Krause's assertion that European second-tier arms suppliers focused on maintaining their status and thus dominating the European market.[63]

First, it is necessary to recognize that the core of the EDTIB and the EDEM are heavily concentrated in relatively few European states. These are the large arms-producing states, known as the Framework Agreement Group, namely Britain, France, Germany, Italy, Spain, and Sweden, plus to a lesser extent Poland. Béraud-Sudreau et al. calculated that these seven states accounted for 89 percent of European arms industry turnover, 80 percent of defense expenditure, and 90 percent of expenditure on defense procurement and research in 2012.[64] Amongst these states, Britain, France, and Germany vastly outpace the other four on all counts. This concentration is due to historical decisions but has an impact on how the EDEM and EDITB work now.[65] In addition to the sheer importance of relatively few states and firms to the survival of an EDITB, the large firms concentrated in these states, most notably the largest prime contractors, BAE Systems, Airbus, Thales Group, and Leonardo-Finmeccanica have substantial lobbying power. Strikwerda argued that for such large players, even where regulation may seem to level the playing field, in practice, procurement infractions are expected to be largely ignored.[66]

The structural realities of the EDEM have undoubtedly made it hard for challenger arms-producer states to emerge. Military or defense customers and the businesses that supply them operate in a highly unusual environment. Briani and Sartori summarized these conditions as follows: monopsony structure on the demand side; monopoly/oligopoly structures on the supply side; high R&D intensity and long-term production cycles; decreasing production costs; public subsidies in the R&D phase and associated spin-offs. In short, there are considerable barriers to entry for new firms and entry costs are high.[67] Kiss argues that these challenges are increased for any Central or Eastern European state wanting to grow or even sustain indigenous defense industries, because the EDEM is a mature market with established supply chains with known overcapacity, and so offers fewer entry points.[68] In particular, as Mawdsley predicted the classic entry method of using offsets to require technology transfer is made difficult by the EU procurement directive.[69] Similarly, geopolitical changes have made procurement from non-European suppliers less attractive. Moreover, the denseness of the European institutionalization of defense in both the EU and NATO make certain policy decisions less attractive to states. How viable is it to develop a viable twenty-first-century defense industry for states, which are constrained by alliance partnership responsibilities and regulatory restraints, and whose regional market offers few export opportunities because of the activities of existing arms producers? It is questionable whether any EU or NATO state could now achieve any degree of armaments autarky, while meeting their obligations as a member state, if they did not have a thriving DTIB already. While other European states may well share the techno-nationalist ambitions of emerging arms-producing states, their environment inhibits them. The evidence suggests therefore that there is indeed some support for both hypotheses 3a and 3b.

Conclusion

The article started by raising the proposition that being part of a semi-regionalized defense economy might be expected to change the calculations that states make when deciding on their armaments policies. What this article has argued is that, in fact, while behavioral change can be noted, it is not deep-rooted. If European states act differently to other states, it seems to be more about that regulatory environment making certain types of action more viable than others, rather than a conviction that certain goals no longer need to be pursued.

Of the three perspectives considered, neither marketization nor European solidarity seem sufficiently embedded to drive behavioral change, although there is some evidence of greater trust/solidarity between near neighbors. While there is acceptance of the concepts of EDEM and EDITB, and toleration of a degree of regulation, states continue to make economically irrational policy choices, leading to fragmentation.[70] This in turn contributes to the continuing military capability gaps in European states' contributions to both NATO and the EU. Largely, as work on the EDA has shown, European states are better at rhetoric than practice when it comes to armaments cooperation.[71]

But nevertheless, there is some empirical evidence of changing behavior. The tolerance of the European Commission's efforts to begin to regulate the sector, Kiss's account for the failure of any Central or Eastern European state to emerge as a major arms producer, or Kluth's finding of abandonment of domestic suppliers in favor of other European firms suggest that something is different.[72] The article suggests that rather than finding evidence of deep-rooted behavioral change, it is probably more about the constraints placed on the majority of states by the particular concentration of armaments power in very few states. These states and their firms are vital for the survival of an EDEM or EDITB, and therefore their interests dominate the policymaking and regulatory processes. While there is consensus that the current situation is not sustainable in the long term, extra-EU defense export success is allowing the larger arms-producing states to postpone the inevitable.

Other states struggle to maximize their own national interests in this environment, and thus the range of choices they might otherwise have had is restricted by regulation. The question of why smaller arms producers accept these constraints on their domestic armaments decision-making process is interesting. Realist analysis might argue, like Escudé, regarding Argentina and the Condor II missile project, that it is the hierarchical regional system rather than domestic decision-making processes that determine smaller producers' policy options.[73] Is such an argument sustainable in the European context? It remains a question for further research.

This article raises other questions. First, there is a lack of knowledge about variation between states in their behavior on armaments policy decisions. Are certain drivers consistent or not? The recent literature has concentrated on the EU level of decision making, but the national level and NATO remain comparatively neglected. Why does it seem that states feel certain defense-industrial sectors are more sacrosanct than others when it comes to rationalization decisions? If EU and NATO officials wish to encourage greater cooperation, are the strategies presented here (marketization and European solidarity) necessarily the right ones? Might there need to be an open acceptance that the biggest arms-producing states need to be treated differently (as was in fact the belief in the 1990s)? How does Brexit complicate matters? Finally, does Europe differ fundamentally from other regional defense alliance or organizations for economic cooperation? How, if at all, are armaments policy decisions discussed at regional levels elsewhere?

Acknowledgments

The author would like to thank Aude Fleurant, Ulrich Krotz, Çağlar Kurç, Stephanie Neumann and Yannick Queau for their helpful feedback on earlier versions of this article.

ORCID

Jocelyn Mawdsley http://orcid.org/0000-0002-1816-3161

Notes

1. Keith Krause, *Arms and the State: Patterns of Military Production and Trade* (Cambridge: Cambridge University Press, 1992).
2. Richard Bitzinger, "Asian Arms Industries and Impact on Military Capabilities," *Defence Studies* 17, no. 3 (2017): 295–311.
3. Krause, *Arms and the State.*
4. Pierre de Vestel, "The Future of Armament Cooperation in NATO and the WEU," in *Foreign and Security Policy in the European Union*, edited by Kjell Eliassen (London: Sage, 1998), 197–215.
5. Richard Bitzinger, "The European Defense Industry in the 21st Century: Challenges and Responses," in *The Modern Defense Industry: Political, Economic, and Technological Issues*, edited by Richard Bitzinger (Santa Barbara, CA: Praeger, 2009), 175–95.
6. Renaud Bellais, "Against the Odds: The Evolution of the European Naval Shipbuilding Industry," *Economics of Peace and Security Journal* 12, no. 1 (2017): 5–11.
7. European Defence Agency, "Aggregated Defence Data 2014 and 2015 (estimated)," www.eda.europa.eu/info-hub/press-centre/latest-news/2016/06/07/aggregated-defence-data-2014-and-2015-(estimated) (accessed June 7, 2016).
8. Judit Kiss, *Arms Industry, Transformation and Integration: The Choices of East Central Europe* (Oxford: Oxford University Press, 2014).
9. David Cooper, "New Trends in Defence Procurement: The Effect on European-Transatlantic Relations," in *European Defence Co-Operation: America, Britain, and NATO,* edited by Michael Clarke and Rod Hague (Manchester University Press, 1990); Keith Hartley, *The Economics of Defence Policy: A New Perspective* (London: Routledge, 2011); Ethan Kapstein, "Allies and Armaments." *Survival* 44, no. 2 (2002): 141–55; Todd Sandler and Keith Hartley, *The Political Economy of NATO: Past, Present and into the 21st Century* (Cambridge: Cambridge University Press, 1999).
10. Sandler and Hartley, *The Political Economy of NATO*; Hartley, *The Economics of Defence Policy.*
11. Ibid.
12. Arne Martin Fevolden and Kari Tvetbråten, "Defence Industrial Policy—a Sound Security Strategy or an Economic Fallacy?" *Defence Studies* 16, no. 2 (2016): 176–92.
13. Marc De Vore, "The Arms Collaboration Dilemma: Between Principal-Agent Dynamics and Collective Action Problems," *Security Studies* 20, no. 4 (2011): 624–62; Marc De Vore, "Organizing International Armaments Cooperation: Institutional Design and Path Dependencies in Europe," *European Security* 21, no. 3 (2012): 432–58; Marc De Vore, "Explaining European Armaments Cooperation: Interests, Institutional Design and Armaments Organizations," *European Foreign Affairs Review* 18 (2013): 1–27; Marc De Vore, "International Armaments Collaboration and the Limits of Reform." *Defence and Peace Economics* 25, no. 4 (2014): 415–43.
14. Krause, *Arms and the State.*
15. Terrence Guay, *At Arm's Length: The European Union and Europe's Defence Industry* (Basingstoke: Macmillan, 1998); Terrence Guay and Robert Callum, "The Transformation and Future Prospects of Europe's Defence Industry," *International Affairs* 78, no. 4 (2002): 757–76.
16. Michael Blauberger and Moritz Weiss, "'If You Can't Beat Me, Join Me!' How the Commission Pushed and Pulled Member States into Legislating Defence Procurement," *Journal of European Public Policy* 20, no. 8 (2013): 1120–38; Moritz Weiss and Michael Blauberger, "Judicialized Law-Making and Opportunistic Enforcement: Explaining the EU's Challenge of National Defence Offsets," *Journal of Common Market Studies* 54, no. 2 (2016): 444–62
17. Ulrika Morth, "Competing Frames in the European Commission—the Case of the Defence Industry and Equipment Issue," *Journal of European Public Policy* 7, no. 2 (2000): 173–89; Ulrika Mörth and Malena Britz, "European Integration as Organizing: The Case of Armaments," *Journal of Common Market Studies* 42, no. 5 (2004): 957–73.
18. Malena Britz, "The Role of Marketization in the Europeanization of Defense Industry Policy," *Bulletin of Science Technology Society* 30, no 3 (2010): 176–84.
19. Johanna Strikwerda, "Sovereignty at Stake? The European Commission's Proposal for a Defence and Security Procurement Directive," *European Security* 26, no. 1 (2017): 19–36.
20. Gordon Adams, *The Iron Triangle* (New Brunswick, NJ: Transaction Publishers, 1981).
21. Frédéric Mérand, *European Defence Policy: Beyond the Nation State* (Oxford: Oxford University, 2008).
22. Jean Joana and Andy Smith, "Changing French Military Procurement Policy: The State, Industry and 'Europe' in the Case of the A400m," *West European Politics* 29, no. 1 (2000): 71.
23. Hartley, *The Economics of Defence Policy*; Andrew Moravcsik, "Armaments among Allies: Franco-German Weapons Cooperation, 1975–1985," in *Double- edged Diplomacy: International Bargaining and Domestic*

Politics, edited by Peter Evans, Harold Jacobs, and Robert Putnam (Berkeley: University of California Press, 1993), 128–67.

24. Bastian Giegerich, "Budget Crunch: Implications for European Defence," *Survival* 52, no 4 (2010): 87–98.
25. Krause, *Arms and the State*, 31.
26. Ibid.
27. Jocelyn Mawdsley, "European Union Armaments Policy: Options for Small States?" *European Security* 17, no. 2–3 (2008): 367–85; De Vore, "Organizing International Armaments Cooperation"; De Vore, "Explaining European Armaments Cooperation."
28. Mawdsley, "European Union Armaments Policy."
29. Jocelyn Mawdsley, "The A400m Project: From Flagship Project to Warning for European Defence Cooperation," *Defence Studies* 13, no. 1 (2013): 14–32.
30. Kiss, *Arms Industry.*
31. Gordon Adams, *The Iron Triangle*; Moravcsik, "Armaments among Allies."
32. Jocelyn Mawdsley, "Arms, Agencies, and Accountability: The Case of OCCAR," *European Security* 12, no. 3-4 (2003): 95–111.
33. Britz, "The Role of Marketization."
34. Jan Joel Andersson, "A New Swedish Defence for a Brave New World," in *Denationalisation of Defence: Convergence and Diversity*, edited Janne Haaland Matlary and Øyvind Østerud (Farnham: Ashgate, 2007), 135–56; Britz, "The Role of Marketization."
35. Evy Berth and Serge Van Camp, *België En De Permanente Gestructureerde Samenwerking* (Brussels: Defensie studiecentrum, 2005).
36. Catherine Hoeffler, "European Armament Co-Operation and the Renewal of Industrial Policy Motives," Journal of European Public Policy 19, no. 3 (2012): 435–51.
37. Fulvio Castellacci, Arne Martin Fevolden, and Martin Lundmark, "How Are Defence Companies Responding to EU Defence and Security Market Liberalization? A Comparative Study of Norway and Sweden," *Journal of European Public Policy* 21, no. 8 (2014): 1218–35.
38. Jocelyn Mawdsley, "France, the UK and the European Defence Agency," in *The European Defence Agency—Arming Europe,* edited by Iraklis Oikonomou and Nikolaos Karampekios (London, Routledge, 2015), 139–54.
39. Michael Kluth, "European Defence Industry Consolidation and Domestic Procurement Bias," *Defense & Security Analysis* 33, no. 2 (2017): 158–73.
40. Ibid.
41. Kiss, *Arms Industry.*
42. Joana and Smith, "Changing French Military Procurement Policy."; Mawdsley, "The A400m Project."
43. SIPRI *Yearbook 2016: Armaments, Disarmament and International Security, SIPRI.* (Oxford: Oxford University Press, 2016).
44. Blauberger and Weiss, "'If You Can't Beat Me, Join Me!'"; Daniel Fiott, "Patriotism, Preferences and Serendipity: Understanding the Adoption of the Defence Transfers Directive," *Journal of Common Market Studies* 55, no. 5 (2017): 1045–61; Strikwerda, "Sovereignty at Stake?"; Weiss and Blauberger, "Judicialized Law-Making."
45. Fiott, "Patriotism, Preferences and Serendipity."
46. Strikwerda, "Sovereignty at Stake?"
47. In 2018, the European Commission launched infringement proceedings over national protectionism in defense procurement against Denmark, Italy, the Netherlands, Poland, and Portugal. Details can be found here at http://europa.eu/rapid/press-release_IP-18-357_en.htm (accessed March 10, 2018). The outcomes of these cases will be important.
48. Ron Smith, "Weapons Procurement and the Defence Industry," in *About Turn, Forward March with Europe: New Directions for Defence and Security Policy*, edited by Jane M. O. Sharp (London: Rivers Oram Press, 1996), 63–75, 69–70.
49. De Vore, "International Armaments Collaboration."
50. R. Smith, "Weapons Procurement and the Defence Industry."
51. On the failings of the EDA, see Nikolaos Karampekios and Iraklis Oikonomou, eds., *The European Defence Agency: Arming Europe* (London: Routledge, 2015); On NATO, see Hartley, *The Economics of Defence Policy.*
52. Giegerich, "Budget Crunch."
53. European Defence Agency, "Aggregated Defence Data."
54. European Commission, *Defence Action Plan COM(2016) 950 Final* (Brussels, November 30, 2016).
55. Daniel Fiott, "The EU, NATO and the European Defence Market: Do Institutional Responses to Defence Globalisation Matter?" *European Security* 26, no. 3 (2017): 398–414

56. Lucie Béraud-Sudreau, "The Extra-EU Defence Exports' Effects on European Armaments Cooperation," in *European Parliament, Directorate General for External Policies* (2015), www.europarl.europa.eu/thinktank/en/document.html?reference=EXPO_STU(2015)549043 (accessed June 2017).
57. Valerio Briani, "Armaments Duplication in Europe: A Quantitative Assessment." *CEPS No. 297* (2013), https://ssrn.com/abstract=2307853.
58. Gerhard Hegmann and Gesche Wüpper, "Wird der Leo ein Franzose?" *Die Welt*, October 27, 2014.
59. Bellais, "Against the Odds."
60. DGA, "Nouvelles étapes pour la coopération franco-britannique d'armement," Press release, November 25, 2016, Paris, www.defense.gouv.fr/actualites/economie-et-technologie/nouvelles-etapes-pour-la-cooperation-franco-britannique-d-armement (accessed October 2017).
61. Tomáš Valášek, *Surviving Austerity: The Case for a New Approach to EU Military Collaboration* (London: Centre for European Reform, 2011).
62. Mawdsley, "European Union Armaments Policy."
63. Krause, *Arms and the State.*
64. Béraud-Sudreau et al., "The Extra-EU Defence Exports' Effects."
65. Ibid.
66. Strikwerda, "Sovereignty at Stake?."
67. Valerio Briani and Nicolò Sartori, "Transatlantic Industrial Policies in the Security Sector," in *EU-US Security Strategies: Comparative Scenarios and Recommendations*," Issue 3 (2011): 156–66, http://csis.org/files/publication/110614_Conley_EUUSSecurity_WEB.pdf.
68. Kiss, *Arms Industry.*
69. Mawdsley, "European Union Armaments Policy."
70. Hartley, *The Economics of Defence Policy*; Bitzinger, "The European Defense Industry"
71. Karampekios and Oikonomou, eds., *The European Defence Agency.*
72. Kiss, *Arms Industry*; Kluth, "European Defence Industry Consolidation."
73. Carlos Escudé, "An Introduction to Peripheral Realism and Its Implications for the Interstate System: Argentina and the Condor II Missile Project," in *International Relations Theory and the Third World,* edited by Stephanie G. Neuman, (New York: St. Martin's Press, 1998), 55–75.

Defense industrialization in small countries: Policies in Czechia and Slovakia

Martin Chovančík

ABSTRACT
Small arms-producing countries on the global market and especially within NATO and the EU offer important insights into the selection of viable defense-industrial strategies. In two separate eras, Czechoslovakia was among the top three (1920s) or top ten (1980s) largest arms producers in the world. As successor states, the Czech and Slovak Republics have approached the transformation of their defense industrial sectors in dissimilar fashions, leading both through two extremely turbulent decades. The past few years have witnessed a renewed dedication of both countries to the defense sector. This article offers a comparative study of state policy developments in support of the sector, procurement practices, cooperation, and export considerations, relating said aspects to foreign policy. Special attention is dedicated to collaboration initiatives and the maneuvering of both countries within the bilateral, regional, European, and global defense economies.

Introduction

Our understanding of the defense-industrial policies of small states is often dictated by the perception of their preordained position within the globalized defense industry. Their study typically takes on the form of either regional studies or case studies utilized to examine a particular question—frequently in the language of origin. Due to their formidable defense-industrial legacy, Central and East European (CEE) countries have received commensurate attention in literature. However, almost all of said literature takes on the form of regional studies and focuses heavily on the period of conversion and transformation. Among the broadest and mostly comparative are the texts produced at SIPRI by Anthony[1] and Kiss,[2] with others including Kogan,[3] Gotkowska and Osica,[4] and most recently Jenkins et al.[5] The case study offered within this volume seeks to examine the decision making of both successor republics within their defense industries from a perspective of their maneuvering past these periods, especially in recent years. While the entire time frame allows for the illustration of links between defense-industrial and foreign policies, a closer examination of relatively recent decisions displays a new trend in Czechia and Slovakia. In the context of these decisions, both states are especially well-positioned to serve as test cases for the role of small states in the European and global defense industry as two most-similar cases which significantly diverged in their defense industrial policies only to recently realign.

As such, they offer the opportunity to investigate several questions. How do small states operate in the global defense industry, and specifically in the European Union? Are they protectionist and attempting to maintain security of supply, or are they willing to relinquish control of their defense sector to foreign investment, since within the EU and NATO national control presumably amounts to small gains?[6] Are they active in their foreign policies to acquire a role in the EDTIB, or have they resigned themselves to catering to developing nations, as postulated by Mawdsley?[7] Can nostalgia for a former top position and their legacy market standing be exploited to such an extent as to allow them to climb the arms-producer ladder? Which reaction to globalization and integration proves more viable for small states: is it better to prefer liberalization and foreign direct investment (FDI) at the cost of losing national security benefits[8] or to protect the industry, finding niche capabilities, and aggressively liberalizing exports and promotion?[9] What consequences have the combinatory choices of Czechia and Slovakia resulted in? What is the current production distribution among the potential Kapstein brackets (out of four: produce autonomously; co-develop; coproduce; import)?[10] Have both countries been able to integrate bilaterally or regionally to overcome joint challenges? How have their foreign policies during post–Cold War transformation and after joining NATO and the EU impacted the development of their Defense Industrial Base (DIB)? And finally, what has been the impact on military capabilities?

In examining these questions, the foreign policy of both countries on the bilateral level (especially between Czechia and Slovakia, with the U.S., Russia, Germany, and Israel), sub-regional level (within the Visegrad Four), regional level (EU), and globally is expected to have a clear impact on the defense-industrial policies of both countries and their recent alteration of state approaches to their development. The reverse relationship is not expected to be as strong due to the constraints of international commitments and the limited lobbying power of both industries within their respective countries. The impacts are examined in four key areas, domestic DIB support, procurement, bilateral and regional cooperation, and exports.

Domestic DIB support

The transformation of the global post–Cold War defense industry and its watershed version in the CEE have been described repeatedly and in great detail. As Czechoslovakia reached a peak position among global arms producers in 1987, the rapid decline between 1989 and 1993 has been a point of contention in national discourse ever since. This is mainly due to the role ascribed to the only president of post–Cold War Czechoslovakia, Václav Havel, and his pacifist dismantling of a prosperous defense industry. Albeit publicly most visible, Havel's role is severely overstated. While employing more than 80,000 workers directly and at least 90,000 indirectly in 1988, the Czechoslovak arms trade was profitable only in official numbers, offset by the aid to allied socialist countries and many defaults in trade with non-socialist countries. The CFE Treaty, although signed in 1990, had already produced an expected cap on the regional market in 1988. The dissolution of the Warsaw Pact eliminated the main markets, which became saturated by huge stockpiles across the postcommunist bloc and especially by more modern versions of the traded armaments directly from Russia and Ukraine.

Slovakia's focus on heavy weapons systems, especially its production of tanks, artillery, and large-caliber munitions, was decimated by global developments and Slovakia wasn't able to export T72 tanks despite outstanding contracts with, for example, Syria. While defense production accounted for 11 percent of Czechoslovak industrial production in 1987, the ratio was significantly higher for Slovakia alone. As a result, the conversion programs launched after the Cold War severely strained the federal and subsequently national budgets. Although less vulnerable due to advanced aviation, optics, and radar production, the Czech defense industry was left abandoned, with only one-fourth of the conversion funding flowing into Czechia during the federation years, followed by almost no funding after independence. The diverging path characterizing the following years is clearly established here.

Slovakia's more nationalist policies during the Mečiar era, closer ties to Russia, failed large-scale privatization projects, and the heavy industry–based defense production meant that Slovakia opted for a mix of government interventions (retaining control of strategic firms) and largely unsuccessful privatization (only to reverse it later and start it again) of the defense sector.

Meanwhile, Czechia liberalized and integrated its entire economy at a much quicker pace, showed little normative appetite for any support to the defense sector, and had the benefit of more technological and small arms–based defense production on its territory—hence, Czechia opted for liberalization and privatization with government withdrawal from the sector (save for a few exceptions). The detailed history of conversion and the first two decades of the post–Cold War defense industry in former Czechoslovakia is well documented by national[11] and international sources.[12] The impact of foreign policy on domestic DIBs and its effect on foreign policy may be illustrated with a few key moments.

The first may be seen in the disparate progress of both countries toward their integration into NATO and the EU. While Czech foreign policy in this period was extremely Atlanticist, Slovakia oscillated between the West and the East until the late 1990s,[13] resulting in a 1998 Czech joint venture between its flagship firm AERO Vodochody (producer of the indigenously developed high-performance trainer jet L-39 and fighter L-159) and Boeing, while at the same time Slovakia was forced to reverse the privatization of multiple large companies, still oriented toward the East, into a government holding, the DMD Group. The Czech 1998 joint venture with Boeing (which acquired 35 percent) was expected to elevate both the aviation and broader defense sector in the Czech Republic (CR). Unfortunately, a series of complications with the L-159 multipurpose combat fighter and the decision of the CR not to buy F/A-18 Super Hornets, but opt for JAS-39 Gripen (which, due to budget constraints in 2002, it continues to lease and not own), led to Boeing's loss of interest in the company and a government buyout. Despite this failure, Boeing's involvement helped integrate AERO into multiple international programs, including coproduction of S-76 components. AERO was privatized and fully acquired by the Czechoslovak investment group PENTA in 2007. During this period, and despite considerably more government attention devoted to the defense sector, the clearly pro-Western foreign policy of Czechia invited FDI, while Slovakia tried to maintain and support its ailing arms industry through government intervention and a long list of controversial arms trades.[14] Slovakia also opted for air force and other defense modernization through the often-criticized Russian debt unblocking by acquiring Mig-29A jets, S-300 SAMs, TU154 aircraft, and assorted helicopters from Russian production. As much of the equipment became operational in the Slovak arsenal in the early 2000s, this predetermined Slovakia's dependence on Russian service, upgrades, and spare parts, along with an orientation of much of the Slovak defense industry to the servicing, training, and overhauling of former Soviet and Russian platforms. The potential for FDI, as well as room for indigenous innovation for Western platforms, thus proved far more limited than in Czechia.

Czechia

Examining the current landscape of defense industries in both countries, the Czech DIB clearly continues to be more integrated, privately owned, and successful in exports. Dominant sectors in the Czech DIB are land systems, aviation, radar technologies, and small and light weapons. The state only controls five companies out of a 106 members of the National Defense Industry Association (NDIA) (LOM Praha, VOP CZ, Explosia, and two research institutes—approximately 3,000 employees altogether). Over 90 percent of defense production is thus privately owned and that is almost exclusively by domestic owners. Only the small arms munitions producer Sellier & Bellot (bought in 2009 by the Brazilian consortium CBC) and L410 aircraft producer Aircraft Industries (bought in 2008 by Russian UGMK) are foreign-owned defense companies. International cooperation is best developed with the U.S., Israel, Brazil, France, and Germany.

Land systems are dominated by Czechoslovak Group (CSG), which (like Polish PGZ) continues reintegrating defense companies in former Czechoslovakia and is currently the largest and most integrated defense actor in the CR, producing, among other products, Tatra vehicles and platforms, armoring, self-propelled howitzers (DANA-M1), and modernized IFV and APC platforms (Titus in collaboration with French Nexter). In 2015, CSG obtained a General Dynamics license for the production of Pandur II APCs and the Israeli RAFAEL license for the production of Samson weapon stations, plus other smaller-volume licenses. The strategic partnership with General Dynamics allows CSG to build on established markets based on the modernization and servicing of old systems (also carried out by state VOP CZ) and to produce new higher-tier vehicles also competitive on Western markets.[15] To this end, CSG has recently acquired a host of defense companies in the Czech Republic and Slovakia (Retia, Avia, MSM Group, etc. and most recently also in Serbia, IMK14)—aiming to also act as a systems integrator and improve its position as a supplier to both national armies. So far success has been mixed due to the governmental challenges discussed below, but CSG success on the international market is rapidly growing (with an annual turnover of 1.2 billion USD in 2017 including civilian production).

AERO Vodochody dominates the aviation sector. Under Penta ownership since 2007, AERO participates in a number of international projects including the full production of S-76 helicopters and UH-60M Black Hawk cockpits for Sikorsky, multiple KC-390 components in partnership with Embraer, as well as C-27J Spartan and F/A1-8E/F components, and civilian production for Airbus. Its international involvement is paralleled with the domestic development and production of the L-159 and L-39—currently L39NG aircraft. While the L-159 multipurpose combat fighter was a troublesome and overproduced project, AERO has finally been successful in exporting it to the U.S. for training (20 aircraft) and to Iraq (15 aircraft) for combat and training purposes (actively utilized against ISIS). Its current focus rests with restarting the production of the L-39 high-performance jet trainer in the L-39NG version. Having produced over 4000 L-39 aircraft since 1971 and with more than 800 still in operation across the world, AERO hopes to export primarily to the Middle East, North Africa, South America, and CIS countries. The most recent order by Senegal (March 2018) marks a restart of L-39 variant exports which had been null for two decades.

LOM Praha is the second-largest aviation company (owned by the state) focusing on maintenance and overhaul of Russian helicopters and aircraft, and it is also in partnership with Raytheon, training pilots, for example for Afghanistan. More crucially, in light of announced helicopter procurements, LOM Praha established a service contract with Bell helicopters in 2015.

In radar technologies, the successor company to the Czech Tesla conglomerate ERA has been successful with the VERA passive radio-location system, exported to many global markets including Europe and the U.S. and chosen by NATO tender for the NATO Deployable Passive ESM Tracker requirement. Its export to China, Pakistan, and Egypt has been repeatedly blocked by the U.S., but other Asian markets are growing (2016 turnover of 43 million USD). Retia (now part of CSG) produces successful primary and secondary surveillance radar.

In small arms, CZUB—Česká Zbrojovka Uherský Brod—has been a mainstay of production and innovation since 1936 and produces a wide range of rifles, submachine guns, grenade launchers, and pistols, expanding to Slovakia through a joint venture with MSM Martin and supplying both armies with their main service weapons (CZ BREN II and CZ 75). It has most recently also been successful in expanding to Hungary and increasing turnover to 190 million USD, supplying armies and civilian sectors in Europe, the U.S., Canada, Thailand, and others. Other key production includes Semtex explosives and ballistic protection from the state-owned Explosia, radio locators from MESIT, ammunition from Sellier & Bellot, optics from Meopta, and CBRN protection from B.O.I.S. As a common theme, all aforementioned companies have markedly increased their turnover and share of defense production in the last three years.

Slovakia

In comparison, Slovak production retains a larger share of state-owned companies and, except for Czech investments, remains almost completely unintegrated. The dominant reasons may be found in its small current scale, outdated focus of dominant heavy-armaments producers, transferal of major capacities to the automotive industry, and a lack of proactive policy on the part of successive governments. Dominant sectors in the Slovak DIB are artillery, large-caliber munitions, armored vehicles, mine clearance, and aviation C2 systems and communications. While the state currently only controls four companies out of 40 members of the NDIA (with over 112 companies active in Slovakia but not part of the NDIA), these represent a considerably larger portion of domestic production than in the case of Czechia (DMD Group, a holding of Konštrukta-Defence, ZTS Špeciál, and ZVS Holding; EVPÚ; and two institutes). Except for minor companies and Czech CSG ownership of MSM Group, CZ-Slovensko, 50 percent of ZVS Holding, MSM Martin, Vývoj Martin, and the lease of Military Repair Plants, the Slovak defense industry is rather devoid of FDI. Both CZUB and CSG acquisitions in Slovakia are recent (since 2014) and the pace of acquisitions is accelerating. Due to the close relationship of both countries, but also the personnel involved, the trend is very likely to continue beyond the current level of reintegration.

Heavy weaponry and munitions still dominate Slovak production, although more advanced technologies have started to achieve success, such as Aliter Technologies with over 17 NATO contracts on C4 systems to date (despite being a newcomer with only a 36 million USD turnover in 2017). In heavy weaponry, the state-owned DMD Group produces self-propelled howitzers ZUZANA and DIANA (both in cooperation with Poland) and a range of munitions and rockets (currently operating at a loss). Way Industries fields the BOZENA mine-clearance vehicle which saw success in Iraq. In armored vehicles, DMD Group, Kerametal, and EVPU all produce or coproduce 8 x 8 vehicles and EVPU specializes in weapons stations. Its Turra 30 remote-controlled turret is integrated into multiple systems, and currently also plays a crucial role in the modernization of Slovak armed forces, as the government chose Finish Patria AMVs to be mounted with said turret.

Military and aviation electronics companies have slowly been able to expand into markets with specific capabilities. Alongside Aliter, EVPU also produces a range of optoelectronics (at a turnover of 37 million USD in 2017). Virtual Reality Media offers synthetic training systems and simulators for Russian-based platforms, and Ales develops custom aviation C2 systems and mobile command posts. Progress of the Slovak DIB is currently severely hampered by the country's reorientation to vehicle production (Volkswagen, Peugeot, KIA, Jaguar), which directly employs over 127,000 people and is sapping potential workers as well as subcontractors. Lack of personnel is also an often-cited complaint of Czech defense firms.

A shift toward stronger support for the domestic DIBs can be observed in the strategic documents of both countries. Strategic documents continually reiterate the necessity to maintain security of supply, but have started to ascribe a more proactive role in the sector to government agencies—most often toward activity in the EU, where inadequate government support through the European Defense Agency (EDA) has repeatedly been criticized, while keeping the domination hypothesis set forth in this issue in mind.

New 2017 defense strategies in both countries (not yet approved in the Slovak Republic [SR]) offer unprecedented support to their DIBs in ensuring better continuity, predictability of military reform, foreign policy promotion, and increased support in integrating into NATO and EU acquisition processes. Previous strategic documents were not nearly as supportive, nor were they followed up by sector-specific strategies such as the *2025 Armaments and Defense Industry Development Support Strategy of the Czech Republic.*[16] Promotion of Czech defense products has risen sharply and the ministries are actively engaged, especially in Middle Eastern, South Asian, and African markets.

Nevertheless, longer-term defense planning and the possible designation of strategic capabilities and industries still remains a challenge. While both countries have produced multiple Concepts of the Armed Forces, Strategies of Research and Defense Industry Support, Army Models, white papers, and other strategic documents (the rate of production rising sharply of late, especially in the CR), both NDIAs stress the short-term nature of the documents, which are replaced even within the same election cycles.[17]

The aforementioned *2025 Armaments and Defense Industry Development Support Strategy of the Czech Republic,* while hailed by the NDIA, is already being altered at the political level. Greater continuity and the possible designation of strategic industrial partnerships would provide greater stability to domestic producers and allow them to invest more heavily in research and development. Concurrently, most domestic producers continue to perceive the Western European supply chain as closed, protected, and hard to penetrate even with quality products, despite a more active foreign policy abroad.[18] As shown in the analysis of exports, the increased activity in promotion and direct government support abroad is mostly oriented toward less-developed countries and still relies to a great extent on supporting Russian (especially with Slovakia, but also with Czechia) or second-tier platforms that are hard to integrate in the West. In attempting to bridge the gap, more Western imports are procured to transfer know-how, in turn diminishing the procurement from domestic producers. This cycle represents a primary concern for both DIBs, as supplying national armies with domestically innovated products would provide necessary references.[19]

Procurement

Procurements are at least as crucial to DIB development and foreign partnership selection as exports. While partnerships with export recipients and greater liberalization of exports increase revenue, viability, and therefore potential for innovation, procurements determine know-how transfer. Divergence between both countries can again be identified here, ranging from few procurements from domestic producers, through some joint-venture procurements, to a high portion of off-the-shelf procurements with no transfer. If government support of domestic DIBs were to be increasing, we would expect to see as few off-the-shelf purchases as possible. Furthermore, the choice of foreign partner would be heavily influenced by the ambitions of becoming further integrated into global, but particularly European, production chains, therefore prioritizing domestic companies capable, and at least already somewhat successful, in said integration.

While Czechia has been gradually modernizing, Slovakia has only truly approached modernization recently. According to EDA data, defense equipment procurement in Czechia averaged 240 million USD annually over a four-year period leading up to 2014. Slovakia averaged 77 million USD. For comparison, Belgium averaged 200 million USD annually.[20] Both countries have been only partially successful in avoiding off-the-shelf purchases and adequately developing domestic DIBs through offset and coproduction programs. National companies have also been only secondary participants in the modernizations, supplying as little as 30 percent of the armed forces modernizations; this ratio is currently increasing.

Czechia

Few procurements in Czech modernization were uncontroversial. Among the largest of these problematic CR procurements, either with contested tenders or completely without tenders, were the purchase of 588 TATRA trucks in 2006 (confirmed corruption by wiretaps); 199 Pandur APCs in 2006, with 40 percent of the production based in Czechia (indictment of the former minister of defense for a hugely overpriced contract that did not meet specifications); 90 IVECO trucks in 2008, with minor Czech participation on signal disruptors (severely overpriced through an intermediary); and 4 CASA EADS C-295M aircraft in 2009, which were purchased without tender and despite not fulfilling Ministry of Defense requirements (European Commission cited a breach of EU rules on public procurement, indictments followed). Based on leaked MoD documents, procurement has until recently been plagued by intermediaries such as Omnipol, MPI

Group, Praga Export, and others who dominate the import and export markets and diminish the role of direct state interaction with domestic and foreign defense companies.[21] DIB support in the CR has thus been damaged quite severely by multiple corruption scandals in acquisition as recently as in 2016, and multiple defense firms have stated a reluctance to enter into competition over possible government contracts due to either pressure for lower prices or prosecutions over the contracts.[22] Progress in strategic documents and a much more active role played by the NDIA aim to improve the procurement standards and transparency.

The Czech Republic is currently focusing on modernizing helicopters through a G2G contract and, although the choice seemed to have been made on 12 Bell UH-1Y Venoms from the U.S. with the active participation of LOM Praha in service and training, recent attention has turned to the S-70M Black Hawks which would include the active participation of AERO Vodochody—a choice that might be telling of government preferences for the future integration potential of both companies, as LOM Praha is a state-owned enterprise. It is worth noting that regionally, both Poland and Slovakia have opted for the UH-60 Black Hawk helicopters during the same modernization time frame.

The infantry vehicle pool will continue to be modernized with Pandur IIs as well as wheeled Titus armored vehicles, produced by Tatra in partnership with French Nexter. The largest announced tender is expected for new IFVs at the price of 2.6 billion USD and the choice of the so-far-preferred Puma from German PSM would be a strong indicator of government dedication for better integration into European production chains (as the involvement of the Czech DIB would be by far the largest and most technology-relevant). Tatra (CSG) has been successful in receiving a modernization contract for the DANA self-propelled artillery system. Most new contracts on ammunition, ballistic protection, service weapons, or logistical items like support cisterns are increasingly awarded to domestic producers (CSG, Sellier & Bellot, Argun, SVOS).

One of the most recent procurement choices better reflects growing government support for domestic industry integration and competitiveness in future development—the long-debated, but not yet concluded, contract for the ELM 2084 MMR ELTA Radar system.[23] Though originally a V4 project to coordinate procurement of 3-D radar with crucial roles for Czech and Slovak cooperation, Czechia has decided to pursue acquisition from Israel alone. Multiple sources have cited three critical advantages for this choice among the competition, other than the price. In foreign-policy terms, Czech affinity toward Israel and copious references to the replication of its defense-industrial prowess certainly come to the forefront. The existing domestic radar expertise and potential to develop know-how through domestic production of components (Retia/CSG) offers the best overlap with the modular design of the mobile air defense radar (MADR) system Israel is offering—the ambition to develop its further integration with various other systems through Czech production played a crucial role. Third, as larger Czech procurements loom in air and missile defense, the modular Israel-produced system allows joint companies to be best positioned for new contracts.[24] While trying to support the domestic DIB through a 30 percent participation in the production of the radar system, the Czech government has also been unduly protracting the procurement process and the outgoing minister of defense did not sign the extensive contract before leaving office, leaving the practically concluded matter to the new government. This will lead to sizeable delays and possible complications, as the new minister wishes to revise the contract.[25]

Slovakia

Slovak procurements have proven less controversial since they have until recently remained extremely modest. Nevertheless, they offer insight into the foreign policy preferences and DIB support of Slovakia. Unlike Czechia a year later, in modernizing its transport aircraft fleet after the tragic crash of its AN-24 while flying home from Kosovo, Slovakia opted for 2-C-27J Spartan aircraft in 2008—the first of which was delivered in November 2017. The expected arrival was accompanied by the prime minister's statement on the clear preference of European defense companies for future modernization.[26] This despite the fact that the most recent acquisition of nine helicopters resulted in the purchase of UH-60 M Black Hawks from the U.S. with very little participation on the part of the domestic DIB (VRM simulation center participation).

In infantry modernizations, with said exception, Slovakia has opted for new service rifles from the Czechoslovak CZUB, Swedish Carl Gustaf M4 recoilless rifles, and 40 Land Rover trucks. It also plans to replace its fleet of BVP IFVs with 485 Finnish Patria AMVs. The Patria AMV was selected as the preferred platform over the Pandur II 8 x 8 platform acquired and employed by the Czech Republic, due to the integration of the domestically produced EVPU Turra 30 remote turret, which supports technology transfer. The Patria AMV also won over the Polish Rosomak Scipio platform, after a deal for reciprocal modernization of Polish artillery by Slovak companies fell through. In modernizing its 4 x 4 fleet, Slovakia is opting for the home-produced Aligator Master II vehicle and has already purchased 180 AKTIS 4 x 4 1 R home-produced trucks.

Two large modernization projects are currently under discussion. After the failure of joint 3-D radar acquisition, Slovakia has yet to issue a tender for the replacement of its P37 radars and is currently selecting a replacement for its aged Mig-29A fleet. Due to budgetary constraints, the decision on MiG replacements had to be postponed to 2018, which means a renewal of the contract with Russia. Slovakia is very eager to find a European solution and most observers see the choice of the Czech and Hungarian-operated JAS-39 Gripen or the Poland-operated F-16 as most likely due to both the security situation, interoperability, and poor reliability of Russian deliveries of spare parts (fewer than four are fully operational at any time).

While both countries have pledged to increase their defense expenditures and focus those expenditures on modernization, neither of them is likely to reach the 2 percent commitment threshold by 2020 or even 2025. Procurement has, however, been increasing rapidly due to the security situation and displays both the greater involvement of domestic DIBs and a preference for cooperation with European companies (apart from helicopters). Due to the size difference and significant "modernization lag" in Slovakia, efforts to integrate in the European market can be seen more tangibly in the CR, whereas Slovakia does not seem to prioritize DIB development in procurement choices (Patria is a small exception).

Bilateral and regional cooperation in the V4

By far, the most significant development not reflected by any of the aforementioned literature is the quickly accelerating and expanding cross-border integration of Czech and Slovak defense industries under the umbrella of the privately owned Czechoslovak Group (CSG) holding. CSG, owned by Jaroslav Strnad, is reintegrating the defense industries of both countries to present a stronger partner for international cooperation, as well as a serving as a viable systems integrator for the armies of both republics. As mentioned before, CSG is coming to dominate both export markets and with the rapid growth of support for domestic DIBs represents a potential national champion that may attempt to succeed even in European supply chains—perhaps taking advantage of what is referred to as the European solidarity option in this issue.

An often-referenced frame of cooperation is the regional Visegrad Four Group (V4) of Central European countries (Poland, CR, Hungary, and SR), established in 1991 to serve as a coordination and cooperation forum on a range of political issues. However, and in spite of being an oft-repeated ambition, multilateral defense and security cooperation within the V4 has always been severely limited. Defense-industrial cooperation has been plagued by protectionism, competition, and lack of coordination, despite numerous proclamations to support mutual coordination in procurements, cooperation in development, and strategic partnerships. Until 2012 and the new EU directive, both Czechia and Slovakia (as landlocked countries requiring access to shipping

Table 1. Alignment of defense equipment needs by sub-region and sector.

	Land	*Air*	*C4ISTAR*	*Protection*	*Training*	*Average*
Visegrad	71%	54%	58%	38%	89%	62%
Baltic	38%	50%	30%	25%	29%	34%
South-East	40%	0%	58%	40%	0%	28%
Adriatic	60%	14%	50%	0%	0%	25%

Note. Adapted from Jenkins et al. (2016).[41]

routes) voiced repeated concerns that Germany and Poland had blocked a number of their transit licenses up to a fifth of annual turnover, while southern routes through Austria and Hungary were a priori unviable.[27]

Only in 2014 was the V4 capable of achieving a common vision and framework stemming from the Smart Defense and Pooling & Sharing initiatives.[28] As a result, only one V4 defense collaboration or procurement project has ever been executed. The project was between Czech Explosia (who owns the license), Slovak ZVS Dubnica nad Váhom, and Polish Dezamet Nowa Deba. The lack of production capacity in Hungary has stalled its involvement. The munition has been in use in Poland's Krab self-propelled 155 mm howitzer since 2016.

Projects on the joint development or procurement of IFVs and procurements of 3-D radar, and multipurpose as well as attack helicopters, have fallen by the wayside, with each country opting to pursue its own procurement process, securing a crucial position for its own DIB. Due to the size and relations of Poland's DIB in V4—with an intimate and dominant relationship with one country's defense sector (U.S.) mirrored by corresponding export recipients (nearly two-thirds of Polish defense exports are to the U.S.) - cooperation is significantly hindered by the gap between Poland and other members of the regional grouping. Poland's PGZ consolidation and dominance of the domestic market (having exported 500 million USD of defense materiel in 2015) with little need for partnering and a strong push to be the prime partner, hinders attempts. This reluctance is in turn reciprocated by other V4 countries through the cancellation of the 3-D radar procurement, cancellation of cooperation on the Slovak acquisition of Polish Rosomak IFVs, and the disregard for existing regional training and service centers for helicopters.

This is even though all V4 countries exhibit comparable foreign policies and more importantly share defense needs in land an air to an extent far greater than other CEE groupings (see Table 1).[29]

Perhaps most promising is the bilateral overcoming of a lack of defense-industrial cooperation with Germany. Although Germany is by far the largest Czech trade partner and the fourth-largest foreign direct investor in Czechia, engaged in very close military and security cooperation,[30] there are no cooperative programs between the two countries—neither are there any with Slovakia, where Germany is otherwise the second-largest investor. While Germany is known for its reservations in defense-industrial policy, active Czech and Slovak pursuance under the current conditions of Brexit, Permanently Structured Cooperation, and the EU Defense Fund may further a growing arms trade relationship. In November 2017, Czech firms were already invited to participate in developing a new generation of IFV Puma and associated land systems. Tellingly, the IFV is currently part of the largest procurement tender in Czechia, but was eliminated from the Slovak tender.

Export policies

In 2016, Czechia exported 823 million USD of military materiel, up 25percent from 2015, and 60 percent from 2014. Slovakia exported 30 million USD of military materiel in 2016, down 30percent from 40 million USD in 2015 (figures which are starting to reflect Slovakia's subcontracting role in CSG). Due to the size of both examined states, their position within NATO and the EU, and the dominance of a reactionary rather than a proactive foreign policy, many of the foreign policy drivers of arms sales—namely those associated with the power aspect of Krause's triangle—do not readily apply. Trade-volume and export-regime limitations within the EU also restrict the possible use of arms transfers out of CR/SR as extended-deterrence,[31] alliance-building measures,[32] or means of exerting influence.[33] As exports cannot feasibly be utilized to these ends, they are far more a reflection of the preexistent foreign policy and fulfill the advancement of wealth and prestige, rather than power. As a result, the similar foreign policy orientations of both countries conform their exports to European standards and policies. Thus, the main export destinations reflect global trends and converge with European policies. This includes (as elsewhere in Europe) controversial exports to markets deemed unsuitable by Common Position 2008/944/CFSP or ATT standards.

Following Marc DeVore's 2013 argument on coping with globalization and due to the dearth of foreign investment in Slovakia's defense industry prior to 2014, we would expect to see a higher incidence of controversial arms transfers out of Slovakia. This is certainly the case during the 1990s[34] and onward, most recently in arms transfer to Egypt (repeatedly, post-2013) or Saudi Arabia. Since ratifying the ATT, Slovakia has yet to make any of its reports publicly accessible, although most of the information may be pieced together from other public sources. While both countries were cited as funneling over 450 million USD worth of weapons to Syria[35] since 2012, Slovakia's exports contained more controversial items (MRLs and RPGs as opposed to truck components). Both have also been criticized for their trade to Saudi Arabia on account of its involvement in Yemen. We may thus readily illustrate how support for the domestic DIB influences existing foreign policy on export promotion[36] and results in greater leniency in the criticism of either human rights or international law abuses by recipient counties.[37]

This is mirrored by the altered composition of recipient countries—since 2005, the share of Middle East exports from the CR has gone up from 11 to 28 percent, while export to EU countries fell from 38 to 27 percent. Slovak exports in the same period experienced a further drop from few EU customers to none and a rising focus on the Middle East, South Asia, and African countries operating Soviet-era or Russian weaponry (in 2016, Saudi Arabia was the largest recipient, at a total of 6 million USD, followed by Iraq, Israel, and Mali). While the share of Czech exports to the EU fell relatively, in absolute numbers it has been steadily increasing for the past years. Although Slovakia accounts for one-fourth of Czech exports to the EU, the CR is experiencing some success in exporting its products to the European market, especially in small arms, ammunition, ballistic protection, and avionics. The Czech Republic has also been successful in expanding to the Vietnamese (VERA), Indonesian (IFVs and MRLs), and Indian (Tatra) markets.

Impact on foreign policy mostly takes on the form of export promotion and, as mentioned before, is more oriented to developing markets and legacy customers, who offer more opportunities for export, rather than toward Western and developed countries, where neither government has so far achieved great successes in OCCAR (Organisme Conjoint de Coopération en Matière ďArmement) or the EDA.

Impact on military capabilities

Due to post–Cold War history of both countries, establishing a clear impact of defense industrial relations on the military capabilities of both countries is somewhat problematic, as it presupposes longer-term, conscious decision-making on the role of the DIB in the defense of the state and the identification of ideal partners to help fulfill that role. Neither is characteristic of the covered period explicitly in defense production and is inferred more by overall foreign policy and economic transition choices. Nevertheless, certain impacts may be identified.

Most of the period since 1989 in both countries is characterized by an extremely sharp decline in military capabilities. From complete autarky, fully supplying the needs of the national armies with such an excess as to still export most of the production, both countries are now secondary suppliers to their militaries. The collapse of the defense industry through the first two decades was only able to maintain some systems which were becoming obsolete and the defense industry thus played a major role in prolonging the lifespan of multiple major systems (tanks, IFVs, artillery, missile systems, radio locators, and others). This allowed deferring modernization projects repeatedly, often to a point where no domestic company still had capacities to meaningfully participate on the procurement process—requiring systems which have been battle-tested and offer technologies which could not be domestically innovated to ensure military relevance. As a result, multiple military capabilities exist past-expectancy (such as BVP2 or repeatedly modernized T-72 variants in Czechia, or MiG-29s in Slovakia) and sustain mainly the state-owned part of the DIB (VOP CZ gained a contract in mid-2018 to maintain the T-72 M4CZ tanks for the Czech government for three years, for 22 million USD). A lack of long-term determination by either government of which military capabilities should be supported by domestic DIB production thus resulted in the bare necessity of maintenance and the belated (in case of Czechia) and long-overdue (Slovakia) modernization with little involvement of the domestic defense industry (apart from SALW). Furthermore, as most of the successful and exporting companies are privately owned and haven't enjoyed a great degree of support until recently, their export-oriented components/products add little to military capabilities.

The choice of defense industrial partners in the past only influenced this situation to the extent that Czechia decided to diversify away from Russian equipment sooner and was far more successful in attracting foreign investment along with its procurements (U.S., Brazil, Sweden) than Slovakia. Current partnership and procurement choices offer a more optimistic perception, as both countries have voiced support for diversified collaboration with European defense companies in tandem with the U.S. and specify in their latest documents the necessity to determine strategic domestic capacities which should be involved in these partnerships and thus contribute significantly to future military capabilities through international collaborative projects. Although multiple capacities and the companies that produce them have been named, as of yet no official designations exist.[38]

Conclusion

Having gone through an exceptionally turbulent quarter-century, the defense industrial policies of both examined countries seem to be reawakening thanks to three interwoven post-2014 phenomena: the global upswing of arms trade; the rapid deterioration of the regional security environment; and a bilateral reintegration of the two industries. Both political rhetoric and activity vis-à-vis domestic defense industries have reemerged and coincide with, but are not truly driven by, the potential opening up of defense cooperation opportunities in the European defense milieu.

Answers to the questions posed by this article and this special issue offer an optimistic assessment of the current position of the Czech defense industry especially and, due to reintegration, also to some extent that of Slovakia. Both countries display varied production across Kapstein's brackets but with few autonomously produced competitive products. Although the undertaken paths to build and promote their DIBs fall into two different categories under DeVore's approach—Czechia opting for stronger privatization, encouragement of FDI, and less-controversial export policies (with AERO being the most successfully integrated actor) and Slovakia trying to salvage crucial firms through state ownership, until recently without any FDI, and adapting foreign policy to more-controversial export policies—both countries still have similar obstacles to overcome, chief of which is a coherent long-term strategy and support for domestic DIBs through active coordination with the military. As shown in the procurement section, few procurements have been unproblematic, nor have they technologically developed domestic producers. The strategic documents in both countries are only now reacting to this deficit and adjusting procurement and foreign policy support.

Both economies are extremely export-oriented and NDIAs in both countries cite an 80–90 percent for-export designation of defense products. Foreign policy in promoting exports is hindered by lack of domestic references and frequent changes in procurement concepts and has to focus on maintaining a customer base, rather than proactive engagement in European discussions on CEE position in the European defense industry. While openly Euroskeptic only in choice areas—migration (V4) or common currency (CR)—both countries have offered full support to deeper European defense collaboration but remain rather passive in its advancement. Activity is certainly required if Czech defense companies are to collaborate within cooperative programs under the European Defense Action Plan (EDAP) or others, but as yet Czechia is perceived as passive and without clear capabilities. As the Czech senior policy officer in the EDA put it "Czechia doesn't seem like a smart customer in the eyes of Brussels. In the European format it doesn't know what it wants or really act with best value for money in mind."[39] Except for the reintegration between themselves, both republics thus continue to balance defense-industrial cooperation between Atlantic and European partners, leaning toward European preference only recently.

Despite common acquisition and security needs within the V4, the quadrilateral format has proven ineffective in defense-industrial cooperation and isn't likely to offer a viable format to engage dominant European players in adjusting EU policy toward more favorable terms for small and medium producers in CEE. Poland's focus on arming its own military and exporting primarily to the U.S., coupled with the comparably extremely small Slovak and Hungarian defense industries, seems to only leave room for bilateral cooperation, requiring proactive foreign policy engagement on the part of the CR or CR plus SR.

Export orientation allows both countries' DIB development to outpace their slowly increasing defense budgets, but the recent push on both fronts, coupled with bilateral reintegration, positions Czechia and Slovakia advantageously to potentially move from the periphery of European defense production to a more active role. Foreign political influence has not yet been proactively engaged in this direction. Especially the Czech defense sector is very well positioned, and according to most industry experts prepared, to engage in European collaborative projects without the necessity of significant restructuring and lacks perhaps only the government support and long-term designation of key capacities to be developed.[40] Without this, as NDIA members have stated repeatedly, the industry has to focus on prioritizing diverse exports to continue prospering, but cannot develop a significant innovation center (for example on CBRN, radar technology, or optics). Slovakia's defense industry remains only marginally promising in niche components and is likely to integrate further with the Czech defense industry. Major surgery is still required here, as multiple larger companies still operate on servicing or overhauling soviet-era systems with little innovation. The recent modernization push provides an excellent impetus for creating integrative opportunities.

Notes

1. Ian Anthony, "*The Future of the Defence Industries in Central and Eastern Europe*," in SIPRI Research Report No. 7, edited by Ian Anthony (Oxford: Oxford University Press, 1994), 1–15, www.sipri.org/sites/default/files/files/RR/SIPRIRR07.pdf (accessed January 2, 2018).
2. Her earlier works include Yudit Kiss, "Lost Illusions? Defence Industry Conversion in Czechoslovakia 1989–92," *Europe-Asia Studies* 45, no. 6 (1993): 1045–69; and "*Regional and Employment Consequences of the Defence Industry Transformation in East Central Europe*," International Labour Organisation, Employment and Training Papers No. 32 (1999), http://citeseerx.ist.psu.edu/viewdoc/download?doi=10.1.1.509.2039&rep=rep1&type=pdf (accessed January 2, 2018). Her later works focused heavily on Central Europe: Yudit Kiss, "Small Arms and Light Weapons Production in Eastern Central Europe," *Small Arms Survey*, Occasional Paper No. 13 (2004), www.smallarmssurvey.org/fileadmin/docs/B-Occasional-papers/SAS-OP13-SE-Europe-Production.pdf (accessed January 2, 2018); and *Arms Industry Transformation and Integration: The Choices of East Central Europe* (Oxford University Press, 2014).

3. Eugene Kogan, "European Union (EU) Enlargement and Its Consequences for Europe's Defence Industries and Markets," Bonn International Centre for Conversion, Occasional Paper 40 (2005); Eugene Kogan, *The State of Eastern European Defence Industries.* (RUSI Defence Systems, 2008). https://rusi.org/publication/rusi-defence-systems/state-eastern-european-defence-industries (accessed January 2, 2018)
4. Justyna Gotkowska and Olaf Osica, *Closing the Gap? Military Co-Operation from the Baltic Sea to the Black Sea* (Warsaw: OSW Centre for Eastern Studies, 2012).
5. Dan Jenkins, Giacomo Persi Paoli, James Black, Alexandros Kokkoris, and Marta Kepe, *Executive Summary. Central and Eastern European Countries: Measures to Enhance Balanced Defence Industry in Europe and to Address Barriers to Defence Cooperation across Europe* (RAND Europe, 2016), www.eda.europa.eu/docs/default-source/documents/rr-1459-eda-central-and-eastern-europe-report—executive-summary—final-22012016.pdf (accessed January 2, 2018).
6. Wally Struys, "The Future of the Defence Firm in Small and Medium Countries," *Defence and Peace Economics* 15, no. 6, (2004): 551–64.
7. Jocelyn Mawdsley, "European Union Armaments Policy: Options for Small States?" *European Security*, 17, no. 2–3 (2008): 367–385.
8. Marc DeVore, "Arms Production in the Global Village: Options for Adapting to Defense-Industrial Globalization," *Security Studies* 22, no. 3 (2013): 532–572, 542.
9. Ibid.; and Marc DeVore, "Defying Convergence: Globalisation and Varieties of Defence-Industrial Capitalism," *New Political Economy* 20, no. 4 (2015): 569–593.
10. Ethan Kapstein, *Global Arms Production: Policy Dilemmas for the 1990s* (New York: University Press of America, 1992).
11. Josef Procházka, Miroslav Krč, and Ladislav Ivánek, *Obranný Průmysl České Republiky po Rozpadu Bipolarity* (Brno: Military Academy, 2003); Zdeněk Kříž, "Army and Politics in the Czech Republic Twenty Years after the Velvet Revolution," *Armed Forces and Society* no. 4 (2010): 627–646.
12. Kiss, *Arms Industry Transformation and Integration.*
13. Martin Chovančík and Zdeněk Kříž, "Czech and Slovak Defense Policies since 1999: The Impact of Europeanization," *Problems of Post-Communism* 60, no. 3 (2012): 49–73.
14. Saferworld, *Arms Production, Exports and Decision-Making in Central and Eastern Europe,* 2002, www.saferworld.org.uk/resources/publications/68-arms-production-exports-and-decision-making-in-central-and-eastern-europe (accessed January 2, 2018); Human Rights Watch, "Ripe for Reform: Stemming Slovakia's Arms Trade with Human Rights Abusers," *HRW* 16, no. 2. (2004), www.hrw.org/reports/2004/slovakia0204/5.htm (accessed January 2, 2018).
15. Jiří Zatloukal, "Zbrojař Strnad: Nejsem překupník. Tatru Číňanům neprodám," Euro.cz, May 23, 2016, www.euro.cz/miliardari/zbrojar-strnad-nejsem-prekupnik-tatru-cinanum-neprodam-1290551 (accessed January 2, 2018).
16. Ministry of Defense of the Czech Republic (CR), *The 2025 Armaments and Defence Industry Development Support Strategy of the Czech Republic,* 2017, www.spsp.army.cz/sites/spsp.army.cz/files/dokumenty/nesmazatelna-stranka/industrial_support_strategy_eng.pdf (accessed January 2, 2018).
17. Martin Michelot and Milan Šuplata, "Defence and Industrial Policy in Slovakia and the Czech Republic: Drivers, Stakeholders, Influence," ARES Policy Paper No. 12, 2016, www.iris-france.org/wp-content/uploads/2016/12/Ares-Group-12-Policy-Paper-Slovakia-and-Czech-Republic-dec2016.pdf (accessed January 2, 2018).
18. Vilém Kolín, "Towards Balanced Defence Industry in Europe: Main Specificities of Central and Eastern European Defence Industries," IRIS Notes, 2015, www.eda.europa.eu/docs/default-source/documents/iris-note-march-2015-v-kolin1.pdf (accessed January 2, 2018).
19. Zdeňka Kuchyňová, "Interview with Jiří Hynek: Zbrojní Export Letos Překročí Rekordních 20 Miliard Korun," *Český rozhlas,* July 25, 2017, www.radio.cz/cz/rubrika/udalosti/zbrojni-export-letos-prekroci-rekordnich-20-miliard-korun (accessed January 2, 2018).
20. European Defense Agency, "National Breakdown of Defence Data," 2016, www.eda.europa.eu/info-hub/press-centre/latest-news/2016/06/20/national-breakdown-of-defence-data (accessed January 2, 2018).
21. CR Procurement Office, "Zpráva o přezkoumání akvizic vojenského materiálu v resortu obrany," http://docplayer.cz/4290127-Zprava-o-prezkoumani-akvizic-vojenskeho-materialu-v-resortu-obrany-faze-ii.html (accessed January 2, 2018).
22. Jiří Podpěra, "Interview for Europortal. Přežijeme i bez armády," Euro.cz, July 9, 2017, www.euro.cz/byznys/sef-omnipolu-podpera-prezijeme-i-bez-armady-1356775 (accessed January 2, 2018).
23. Jiri Kominek, "Czech MoD orders full review of Elta 3D radar contract." Jane's Defence Industry, January 19, 2018, https://www.janes.com/article/77192/czech-mod-orders-full-review-of-elta-3d-radar-contract (accessed August 20, 2018)
24. Ibid.

25. Oldřich Danda, "Šlechtová: Bez důvěry vládě miliardové nákupy nepodepíšu," December 23, 2017, www.mocr.army.cz/informacni-servis/for/slechtova:-bez-duvery-vlade-miliardove-nakupy-nepodepisu-139800/ (accessed January 2, 2018).
26. Jan Grohmann, "Slovakia Wants to Buy European Weapons," Armádní noviny, August 18, 2017, www.armadninoviny.cz/slovensko-chce-nakupovat-evropske-zbrane.html (accessed January 2, 2018).
27. CT24, *"Platí nová pravidla pro vývoz zbraní,"* 2012, www.ceskatelevize.cz/ct24/ekonomika/1160788-plati-nova-pravidla-pro-vyvoz-zbrani (accessed January 2, 2018).
28. Visegrad Group, *Long-Term Vision of the Visegrad Countries on Deepening their Defence Cooperation,* 2014 www.visegradgroup.eu/about/cooperation/defence (accessed January 2, 2018); Visegrad Group, *Framework for Enhanced Visegrad Defence Planning Cooperation,* 2014, www.visegradgroup.eu/about/cooperation/defence (accessed January 2, 2018).
29. Jenkins et al., *Executive Summary.*
30. Vladimir Handl, "Germany and Central Europe 2011. A Differentiated Dynamic Instead of Mitteleuropa," in *Regional and International Relations of Central Europe,* edited by Petr Drulák and Zlatko Šabič (Houndsmills: Palgrave Macmillan, 2012), 104–24; Jana Urbanovská and Zdeněk Kříž, "The Security Dimension of Czech-German Cooperation," in *Towards Partnership: The Third Decade of Czech-German Relations,* edited by Břetislav Dančák and Vít Hloušek (Brno: Muni PRESS, 2016), 178–212.
31. Curtis Signorino and Tarar Ahmer, "A Unified Theory and Test of Extended Immediate Deterrence," *American Journal of Political Science* 50, no. 3 (2006): 586–605; Christopher Sprecher and Volker Krause, "Alliances, Armed Conflict, and Cooperation: Theoretical Approaches and Empirical Evidence," *Journal of Peace Research* 43, no. 4 (2006): 363–369.
32. Shannon Blanton, "Instruments of Security or Tools of Repression? Arms Imports and Human Rights Conditions in Developing Countries," *Journal of Peace Research* 36, no. 2 (1999): 233–44; Shannon Blanton, "Foreign Policy in Transition? Human Rights, Democracy, and U.S. Arms Exports," *International Studies Quarterly* 49, no. 4 (2005): 647–68.
33. Richard Bitzinger, *Towards a Brave New Arms Industry* (London: Routledge, 2003).
34. Saferworld, *Arms Production; Human Rights Watch,* "Ripe for Reform."
35. Lawrence Marzouk, Ivan Angelovski, and Miranda Patrucic, "Making a Killing: The €1.2 Billion Arms Pipeline to Middle East," OCCRP Report, 2016, www.occrp.org/en/makingakilling/making-a-killing/ (accessed January 2, 2018).
36. Keith Hartley and Martin Stephen, "The Economics of UK Arms Exports," in *The Arms Trade, Security and Conflict,* edited by Paul Levine and Ron Smith (London: Routledge, 2003), 5–20.
37. Anna Stavrianakis, "Legitimizing Liberal Militarism: Politics, Law and War in the Arms Trade Treaty," *Third World Quarterly,* 37, no. 5, (2016): 840–865.
38. Jiří Hynek, "Připravenost českého obranného průmyslu na aktuální bezpečnostní rizika", Lidové noviny, November 11, 2016, https://www.lidovky.cz/byznys/eventy/pripravenost-ceskeho-obranneho-prumyslu-na-aktualni-bezpecnostni-rizika.A161130_104650_ln_byznys_eventy_hapa (accessed January 2, 2018).
39. Vilém Kolín, "Česká republika a „nová"Společná bezpečností a obranná politika EU: Čas zásadních rozhodnutí." *Vojenské rozhledy.* 26, no. 3, (2017):68–77. http://www.vojenskerozhledy.cz/kategorie-clanku/bezpecnostni-a-obranna-politika/cr-a-nova-sbop-eu (accessed January 2, 2018).
40. James Black et al., *Central and Eastern European Countries: Measures to Enhance Balanced Defence Industry in Europe and to Address Barriers to Defence Cooperation across Europe. Technical Annex.* RAND Europe, 2016, www.eda.europa.eu/docs/default-source/documents/rr-1459-eda-central-and-eastern-europe-report—technical-annex—final.pdf (accessed January 2, 2018).

Brazil's defense industry: Challenges and opportunities

Raul Gouvea

ABSTRACT
Brazil is reformatting its domestic defense industry. In the last three decades, Brazil has seen its defense industry go through a number of different phases: from being vibrant and export oriented in the 1980s, to a stagnant industry in the 1990s, with a resurgence in the 2000s. In the past three decades, Brazil built a dynamic and diversified defense industry. Successions of domestic political and economic policies, and international trends, have relegated Brazil's once-emerging defense industry to a marginal position in the global defense industry. This article analyzes future prospects, challenges, and growth strategies for Brazil's defense industry.

Introduction

In 2018, Brazil began reformatting its domestic defense industry. In the last three decades, Brazil has seen its defense industry go through a number of different growth and retrenchment phases. In the 1980s, Brazil had a vibrant, diversified and export-oriented defense industry. The industry was mostly driven by indigenous technology and innovation efforts, where the state, state-run companies, universities and research centers, and Brazil's private sector, domestic companies, and multinationals constituted the pillars of Brazil's defense industry. During this time, close to 80–90 percent of Brazil's defense-industry's production was exported to Latin America, Africa, and Arab and Asian countries. In the 1980s, Brazil was ranked the world's fifth-largest exporter of defense products and services, selling to more than 40 countries.[1]

In the 1980s, Brazil's domestic and a global matrix of motivations supported the industry as indicated below[2]:

(a) Initiative to become less reliant and dependent on foreign manufacturers of defense hardware and software;
(b) Desire to use its defense industry to expand its soft power over Latin American, African, and Middle Eastern nations;
(c) Diversification of its export portfolios of products and markets;
(d) Exports of defense hardware that could help Brazil address increasing trade deficits with oil-exporting countries, such as Iraq; and
(e) Solidifying a vibrant domestic defense industry for Brazil's military regime.

The period from 1990 to the early 2000s, on the other hand, saw a global reduction in defense expenditures. As a result, Brazil's defense industry saw a severe reduction in exports, forcing a dramatic downsizing of domestic production of defense hardware, and critically compromising its scope and capabilities. This new momentum in global defense markets deeply affected Brazil's export-oriented defense industry. As a result, a number of key players in Brazil's defense industry, such as Engesa, did not survive the new global defense-industry momentum.[3]

This new global defense momentum also propelled traditional defense exporters from developed countries to pressure emerging defense exporters, such as Brazil. For instance, a number of defense-technology transfer embargos from G-7 nations proved to be a major stumbling block for the further development and upgrade of Brazil's defense industry. The missile technology, and the supercomputer embargo from the G-7 nations, hampered Brazil's defense industry's ability to upgrade its defense hardware and software, which, in turn, compromised Brazil's global competitiveness in the defense industry. Brazil's defense exports and cooperation with a number of traditional markets for the U.S. and western European defense producers, such as Iraq, led to efforts to curb Brazil's penetration in these emerging markets. For traditional defense exporters, Brazil was also perceived as a proliferation risk, and it had yet not signed the Nuclear Non-Proliferation Treaty. Moreover, in the 1980s and early 1990s, Brazil was also developing a nuclear program that could eventually give Brazil the ability to develop a nuclear arsenal. In combination with its rocket technology, such as the Vertical Launching System (VLS), Brazil could have developed its first-generation nuclear missile. The missile and supercomputer embargo pressured and persuaded Brazilian policymakers to suspend its nuclear program. In 1998, Brazil signed the Nuclear Non-Proliferation Treaty, putting an end to a number of technology-transfer restrictions imposed on the country.[4]

Brazil was never able to fully recover from the missile and supercomputer embargo, which blocked the necessary upgrade in Brazil's defense technology and defense innovation. This would have allowed Brazil to remain competitive in global defense markets, yet this was not materialized. In less than three decades, Brazil was downgraded from the world's fifth-largest exporter of defense hardware to the twenty-seventh largest in 2016.[5]

Thus, in the 1990s, Brazil's defense industry faced not only a lack of internal support, as a result of a new political momentum, i.e., a leftist political regime not friendly to Brazil's armed forces, but also suffered from a global defense-exporting market facing declining sales. Moreover, traditional defense producers and exporters were more inclined to eliminate and impose restrictions on fast-growing, emerging defense producers. The G-7 nations' embargo on missile transfer technology and sales of supercomputers to Brazil illustrated the extension to which traditional defense producers and exporters would go to dismantle and weaken Brazil's defense industry. Thus, not only internal, but also external forces created the "perfect storm" to derail Brazil's expanding defense industry.

In addition, Brazil's defense industry was not able to design conversion, diversification, nor retrenchment strategies to endure downward trends in the global demand for its defense products. Brazil's defense industry's "do-or-die" strategy was not ineffective in face of a global inflection point, which was the global demand for defense hardware and software. This lack of forward thinking and vision inevitably led to the elimination of several of Brazil's primary defense companies, and also to the dismantlement of Brazil's defense "brain pool." The lack of a domestic-driven, i.e., "buy Brazilian-made defense hardware and software," strategy and policy to compensate for low levels of global demand further compromised the survival of Brazil's defense industry.[6]

After decades of a military regime, a democratic political environment was established in 1985. As a result, Brazil's defense forces and industry saw declining support and funds from Brasilia. In 1994, a new government headed by politicians that had opposed the military regime for decades took over. These new political forces did not want to support Brazil's military forces. These actions resulted in a steady decline in readiness resource allocations to the development of indigenous technology, and innovation. By the early 2000s, Brazil became a marginal player in the global defense industry. Furthermore, in 2011, Brazil ranked number twenty-seventh in the world as a global defense exporter, accounting for only 0.1% percent of global defense sales. In 2016, the United States, Russia, Germany, France, and China accounted for close to 74 percent of global defense sales.[7]

A new momentum for Brazil's defense industry

Since 2005, however, defense-related policy changes have been giving Brazil's defense industry a new momentum. For instance, in 2005 a combination of actions and policies by the Lula administration, such as the creation of the Military Commission for defense industry (CMID), the second edition of Brazil's *National Defense Policy*, and the establishment of Brazil's first National Policy for Brazil's defense industry (PNID) revived Brazil's defense industry. In 2008, the National Defense Strategy (END) laid the groundwork for Provisory Measure Number 511 of 2011. Years later, in 2012, Law 12.598 placed the defense industry back on the government's main policy agenda.[8]

The revival of Brazil's defense industry during the Lula administration, mainly during his second mandate, 2006–2011, was the result of a matrix of motivations. This matrix of motivations was shaped by active Lula and Labor Party (PT) supporters, and by other political allies that joined Lula's second administration support base after 2006, such as the PMDB political party. The Lula administration's belief in import-substitution industrialization strategies (ISI) and a strong perspective that defense expenditures may lead to further gains in economic growth and development, as well as political autonomy, acted as propellers for the revival of an "indigenous-driven" defense industry. The Lula administration was also seeking a greater role for Brazil in South America and in Africa. The defense industry, thus, was also perceived and rationalized as capable of projecting Brazil's "soft-power" in the Southern Hemisphere. This matrix of motivations led the Lula administration to develop an interest in supporting the revitalization of Brazil's defense industry.[9]

Moreover, Lula's "Mensalao" scandal in 2005 led him to develop a new political coalition, including a key partnership with Brazil's largest political party, the Party of the Brazilian Democratic Movement (PMDB). This new alignment of political forces allowed Lula to avoid impeachment and it changed the nature of Lula's government interaction with Brazil's armed forces. Clearly, these new political forces and parties that participated in Lula's administration after 2006 promoted a number of policies and programs to support the further growth and development of Brazil's defense industry. In addition, a number of new Brazilian-owned companies and defense multinationals joined the industry, further reinvigorating Brazil's defense industry. The combination of new political alliances, more aligned with Brazil's defense forces, participating in the second Lula mandate and in the Dilma administration, and the entry of new companies, both domestic and defense multinationals, reshaped Lula's and Dilma Rousseff's approach to Brazil's defense industry and provided a new domestic momentum for the industry.

It is important to note that Brazil's current President Michael Temer began to have an increasingly prominent political role in Lula's second term and eventually became Dilma Rousseff's vice president. In 2018, Temer developed a very close relationship to Brazil's defense forces. For instance, after twenty years, Temer appointed a general to be Brazil's defense minister.[10]

Brazil then designed a new strategy to regain prominence within the Southern Hemisphere and to increase its military leadership in the region. Brazil engaged in the direct purchase of defense hardware and software from countries such as Russia, and at the same time engaged in an aggressive strategy to lower its dependency on imported (OEMS) original equipment manufacturers by replacing imports of defense hardware and software with locally manufactured products. This ISI strategy followed four major strategic pillars: (a) provide incentives for technology transfer from foreign defense partners, (b) promote the expansion of Brazil's defense industry offerings, (c) promote the restructuring of Brazil's defense industry, and (d) promote the modernization of Brazil's defense hardware and software. In summary, these policies and strategies aim at placing a premium on promoting indigenous defense technologies in order to replace and compete with imported defense hardware and software.[11]

Brazil's drive to promote an indigenously grown defense industry relied heavily on an offset policy and on a strategy to force foreign defense companies to transfer technology and to use local Brazilian domestic companies to produce and assemble defense hardware and software.[12]

In the period from 2013 to 2019, it is anticipated that Brazil will spend close to US$190 billion in investments to upgrade its armed forces.[13] The main focus is to improve Brazil's defense capabilities, resulting in a more globally competitive defense industry. A number of defense projects will drive Brazil's defense industry in the next few years, such as: SIGAAZ (Amazonia Azul); SISFRON; the FX-2 programs; Brazil's nuclear submarine program; the modernization of its armored battle vehicles, and transport and attack helicopters; and cybernetics.[14]

In 2010, Brazil accounted for 60 percent of Latin America's defense spending. In 2016, Brazil's defense budget was ranked eleventh in the world.[15] In 2011, Brazil's defense budget was close to 1.5 percent of Brazil's GDP.[16] However, 73 percent of the allocated budget was designated to pay for military personnel wages and pensions, and only the remaining was available for the acquisition of new defense equipment, such as: (a) ships, 50percent, (b) sensors, 25 percent, (c) armored vehicles, 8 percent, (d) communications, 5 percent, and (e) AUVs, 1 percent.[17]

The taxonomy of Brazil's defense forces

In 2017, Brazil's defense industry reached a market size of US$6.8 billion, with exports accounting for US$3.8 billion and total imports of US$2.3 billion. The industry created 60,000 direct jobs and 240,000 jobs indirectly. Brazil's defense industry accounted for close to 1.4 percent of Brazil's GDP and has 220 companies associated directly with the industry.[18] It is important to note, however, that expenses with personnel and staff accounted for 64.6 percent of Brazil's armed forces expenditures, followed by 12 percent expenditures for upkeep, and investments of 9.2 percent. For the sake of comparison, in the United States, expenditures with personnel and staff account for only 25 percent of the defense budget, investments are close to 16 percent, and upkeep is around 40percent. It is clear that Brazil needs to increase the share of investments in its armed forces, lower the share of personnel and staff in its total budget, and enhance its overall readiness to become an effective defense force. Brazil's low investment on defense innovation and technology also compromises the country's ability to develop an indigenous-driven defense industry.[19]

In the meantime, the modernization of Brazil's defense systems will necessarily increase Brazilian defense hardware and software imports, as demonstrated by Brazil's US$2.3 billion in imports of defense hardware and software. Brazil still relies on imports of a number of different weapons systems by its armed forces.

A number of critical segments of Brazil's military capacities have been addressed by the aggressive ISI strategy. This strategy has resulted in Brazil manufacturing products locally, such as a number of its critical defense needs, from submarines and armored vehicles to fighter jets. However, Brazil still relies on imports of defense hardware and software to address a number of its defense needs. For instance, Brazil is still heavily dependent on imports of attack helicopters, missile systems, and cyber-warfare equipment, among other defense hardware and software. Thus, the import-substitution strategy implemented in the first decade of the 2000s has resulted in Brazil becoming more self-sufficient in a number of key areas of its defense needs. However, as a country, Brazil still relies on a number of foreign defense suppliers to address its total defense needs.[20]

In 2017, the proposed budget for the industry was US$30 billion. Brazil has elected six major defense projects as Brazil's defense main priorities: (a) Prosub, or Brazil's submarine program, (b) Brazil's nuclear submarine program—PNM, (c) armored vehicles—the Guarani program, d) SISFRON, Brazil's border-surveillance program, (e) the replacement of aging fighter jets, or FX-2 program, and (f) Brazil's multi-mission cargo plane—KC 390.[21]

Despite the recent commitments to upgrade Brazil's defense forces, the constant sequestration of funds for the defense industry not only has compromised the full implementation of key defense projects, but also compromises the readiness of Brazil's armed forces. Data from 2011–2014 indicates that, on average, 50 percent of Brazil's defense hardware was awaiting repair. For instance, Brazil's navy had half of its 98 ships out of commission and the air force had close to 50 percent of its planes and helicopters in operational condition.[22]

In 2018, the 17 percent budget cut deeply affected the ability for Brazil's defense forces ability to pursue its main projects. For instance, the PROSUB program will be delayed, as will acquisition of armored vehicles. The SISFRON program saw its budget cut in half. In 2018, SISFRON is only covering 4 percent of Brazil's 16.686 km of frontiers with 11 countries. The lack of funding will delay the full establishment of SISFRON from 2022 to 2035. It is expected that Brazil's deep recession of the last four years will considerably impact the government's ability to deliver Brazil's main defense projects on time.[23]

In comparison to neighboring countries, Brazil has the largest military personnel, army, navy, and air force. However, recent acquisitions by Chile, Peru, and Venezuela shed light on Brazil's aging defense hardware and defense software.[24]

Brazil's new defense projects

In the past few years, Brazil began slowly implementing a number of new defense programs and initiatives for all three of its defense branches. For some of the projects, Brazil is pursuing an offset-ISI strategy by inducing defense multinationals to manufacture their defense hardware and software in Brazil.[25]

Some of Brazil's new defense projects and programs include border surveillance systems, nuclear and conventional submarines, and a modern electronic warfare infrastructure.[26]

The main projects for Brazil's army in the next few years are: (a) Brazil's Borders Integrated Surveillance System, SISFRON, (b) air defense program, (c) armored vehicles, and (d) electronic warfare.

(a) SISFRON: Brazil's Integrated Border Monitoring System went into effect in 2008. The system will cover close to 17,000 kilometers, monitoring Brazil's borders with eleven countries. One of SISFRON's objectives is to integrate Brazil's armed forces programs and projects with other agencies in Brazil that monitor systems, such as the Amazon Protection System and Brazil's intelligence agency among other federal agencies. The further development of SISFRON will entail the acquisition of both air and land surveillance radars and sensors. Contrary to the monitoring and surveillance system initially implemented in Brazil's Amazon region (SIVAM), SISFRON has a high domestic valued-added content.[27]

(b) Air defense program: Brazil has developed an air defense program to increase its defense capabilities, relying on domestic defense companies and defense multinationals to expand its air defense capabilities. For instance, Avibras is developing a cruise missile, the MCT-300, with a 300 km range. Delivery of the MTC-300 is expected to take place in 2020. Brazil is also relying on foreign suppliers, and developing a number of defense projects with Russian defense companies. For instance, Brazil is interested in acquiring twelve Russia's Pantsir-S1 systems, an air defense missile, and an artillery system. The European company MBDA is also co-developing with Brazil's Avibras a medium-range air defense system. Russia has also delivered Igla-S shoulder-fired air defense missile systems to Brazil's army. Brazil has also ordered man-portable air defense systems, RBS 70 very-short-range air defense system, from the Swedish company Saab.[28]

(c) Armored vehicles: In December 2009, Brazil contracted the Italian defense multinational Iveco Defense Vehicles to supply Brazil's defense forces with wheeled armored personnel carriers. With the demise of Engesa in the 1990s, Brazil lost the capability of manufacturing its own armored vehicles and main battle tanks (MBTs). The VBTP-MR Guarani armored vehicle will replace the aging fleet of EE-11 Urutus manufactured by Engesa. The contract with Iveco foresees the local manufacturing of 2,044 vehicles by 2029.[29]

(d) Electronic warfare: Brazil has created a new unit within its army, the Cyber Defense Command (ComDCiber). The main purpose of this unit is to plan, coordinate, and integrate Brazil's cyber operations. The program will also foster the development of hardware, software, and supercomputers in order to foster the growth and development of Brazil's cyber capabilities. It will also integrate Brazil's army, navy, and air force electronic-warfare efforts. A National Cyber Defense Academy is being planned to supply local cyber talent. Meanwhile, Brazil is also relying on foreign defense multinationals to update its cyber-capabilities. For instance, Brazil has contracted the Israeli defense multinational Elbit Systems to supply electronic-warfare and communication systems to Brazil's Army. Elbit Systems will supply C4ISR electronic warfare, battle management systems (BMS), EW capabilities, and communications systems.[30]

Main projects for Brazil's air force for the next few years are: (a) F-X2, to replace aging jet fighters, (b) new cargo planes, and (c) new transport helicopters, and d) Alcantara Launch Center.

(a) FX-2, replacing aging jet fighters: Since the early 1990s, Brazil was looking to replace its aging jet fighter fleet. In 2013, Brazil selected Saab's Gripen NG jets. Several defense multinationals bid for the contract, including Boeing, Dassault, EADS, and Lockheed Martin. Saab won a contract for 36 aircraft, with an eventual 108 fighters in a three-cycle delivery program. Several factors, political and technical, influenced the bid in favor of Saab. For instance, Saab promised to offer local manufacturing partnerships, prompted engagement in technology-transfer agreements, and also offered to share integration source codes. Close to 70 percent of all the components will be manufactured in Brazil, Gripens will be serviced and repaired locally in Brazil, and Brazil will have choice of an independent array of weapons. Thus, the Gripen project may lead to the development of new defense supply chains in Brazil with a number of potential spillover effects for Brazil's defense industry, expanding its capabilities in different areas and segments. In addition to the 36 Gripen NG jets acquired by Brazil, 50 more, intended for foreign markets, could be produced. Future exports of Gripen jet fighters could open new defense markets for Brazil. Yet, Brazil would then have to comply with Sweden's foreign policy.[31] However, the selection of the Gripen NG has raised a number of national security issues: (a) the single-engine safety issue, (b) limited radar capability, (c) the shorter range than competitors, and d) the fact that it is not a true fighter jet. These issues have cast severe doubts about Brazil's decision to acquire the Saab JAS-39 Gripen.

(b) New cargo planes: Embraer has developed a new generation multi-mission aircraft, KC-390. The KC-390 is a medium size, twin-engine, jet-powered military transport aircraft. Delivery is scheduled to take place in 2018. The KC-390 opens new markets for Brazil's Embraer defense branch.[32]

(c) New helicopters: Brazil has been sourcing helicopters from a number of foreign multinational suppliers. In 2017, Brazil renewed its interest in acquiring additional Russian-made Mi-35 attack helicopters. The Mi-35 allows Brazil's air force to use guided and unguided weapons. Brazil has also acquired a number of modernized AugustaWestland Lynx helicopters from the UK. These multipurpose military helicopters with naval usage will be used in conjunction with Brazil's recently acquired helicopter carrier from the British Royal Navy. Brazil is also looking at increasing its share of U.S.-made attack helicopters. For instance, in 2018, Brazil's army is looking at acquiring surplus (USMC) Bell Super Cobra attack helicopters and Brazil's navy is working with CAE to supply S-70B Seahawk tactical training systems.[33]

(d) Alcantara Launch Center: The Temer government is negotiating with the U.S. government and companies, such as Space X and Boeing, for the use of Brazil's Alcantara launch center, located in Brazil's Amazon region, in Alcantara, Maranhao, d close to the equato. However, Brazil needs to sign a technological-safeguard agreement with the U.S. in order for negotiations to move forward. Space X and Boeing could develop partnerships with Brazil's space-program agency fostering ties with the U.S. space program and advancing Brazil's space program.[34]

Brazil's navy forces are also pursuing a number of projects, such as: (a) the Prosub Program, (b) nuclear-powered submarine, (c) The Blue Amazon Management System, and (d) Tamandare Class Corvette.

(a) Prosub Program: The Prosub Program calls for the production of four Scorpene diesel-electric submarines, S-BRs. The program started in 2008 by Brazilian Odebrecht Defesa and French defense multinational DCNS. The first Scorpene submarine produced in Brazil, the Riachuelo (S40) will join the Brazilian navy at the end of 2018.[35]

(b) Nuclear-powered submarine: Brazil is developing its own homegrown nuclear-propulsion capability. The nuclear submarine is being built with the French defense multinational DCNS's assistance. Brazil's nuclear submarine uses domestically developed reactor and uranium fuel-cycle technology. Brazil plans to build six nuclear-powered submarines.[36]

(c) Blue Amazon: Brazil is developing a sophisticated surveillance system to monitor its 8,500 km–long of seashore using satellites, radar systems, submarines, navy vessels, and drones. Brazil seeks to protect its marine resources and mineral resources offshore and along its coastline. The sea holds close to 90 percent of Brazil's hydrocarbon resources and 95 percent of its international trade is conducted by sea.[37]

(d) Tamandare-class corvette: Brazil's navy is planning to construct four Tamandare-class corvettes. The 2.7 thousand–ton warships will be constructed in Brazil by a state-owned or private shipbuilder. Construction will start in 2019. These corvettes will allow Brazil's navy to perform a wide array of tasks like patrolling Brazil's coastline.[38]

Challenges and opportunities

In 2018, the efforts of Michel Temer's administration to support the further growth and development of Brazil's defense industry will encounter a number of challenges and opportunities, as described below.

First, higher levels of scrutiny and budget constraints will impact a growth strategy for Brazil's defense forces, which may considerably delay the establishment of current and future defense programs and projects. In 2018, Brazil's defense budget will be reduced by 17 percent. This defense budget cut will deeply affect a number of defense projects. For instance, funds for Brazil's space program have been cut by 42 percent and Brazil's nuclear submarine (PROSUB) funds have been slashed by 40.5 percent. Moreover, many of these programs and projects are included in Brazil's federal Growth Acceleration Program (PAC) program. However, the large majority of PAC projects have not been implemented on time. Many are running years behind schedule. The global competitiveness and export performance, however, of an indigenous-driven defense industry in a very competitive global defense market were not main concerns for either the Lula or Dilma administration. Thus, the Lula and Dilma administrations created a defense-industry paradigm heavily dependent on the purchasing power of the Brazilian state. This defense paradigm is only feasible if Brazil's economy shows sustainable growth rates in years to come.[39]

Second, the entrance of new defense players in the global defense industry has resulted in a more contested global defense market, challenging a renewed export-driven growth strategy for Brazil's defense industry. As a result, defense exporters in Brazil will face a much fiercer global defense market than in the 1970s and 1980s. In 2018, traditional Western defense producers are entertaining the idea of defense contracts all over the world, and are considering concessions that a few years ago would not have ever been considered. Moreover, emerging defense exporters like South Korea, India, and Turkey are increasingly penetrating global defense markets. To make global defense markets even more contested, Russia and China are also more aggressively exploring these markets, offering more knowledge-intensive products and complete defense packages that are not currently available in Brazil's export-portfolio arsenal.[40]

Third, Brazil's ability to remain competitive in the global defense-industry market is closely related to its capability to innovate and to develop defense technologies. Brazil's defense-industry needs to become more R&D- and innovation-intensive, moving up the global innovation/R&D defense ladder. The low level of attention paid to R&D and innovation in Brazil may hinder and its ambitious objective to build a strong, indigenous defense industry. Increasingly, a number of technologies are permeating the future of defense industries, such as: (a) hypersonics, (b) machine learning and artificial intelligence (AI), (c) cyber and electronic warfare, and (d) human-machine collaboration. Brazil needs to embody these new frontier defense technologies or it will increasingly become marginalized in the global defense-industry marketplace. Low levels of expenditures on defense R&D and innovation may relegate Brazil's defense industry to a "copier and reproducer" status, thus jeopardizing Brazil's ability to develop a global competitive advantage in the defense industry.[41]

Fourth, the role of defense multinationals and foreign defense technology and innovation has changed the autarchic nature of Brazil's defense industry. It is clear that Brazil no longer has the momentum it did in the 1970s and 1980s, when domestic players dominated the defense industry. In 2018, many segments of Brazil's defense industry are now experiencing increased participation of multinational defense companies as final producers of defense equipment in Brazil. For instance, Helibras is now a subsidiary of Airbus Helicopters, and Iveco, the Italian defense multinational, is now supplying most of Brazil's medium-sized armored vehicles for transporting personnel. In the 1970s and 1980s, Engesa was the Brazilian-owned company supplying armored vehicles and MBTs to Brazil's defense forces. In 2016, Boeing and Embraer signed an agreement to jointly market and support the multi-mission and aerial-refueling plane, KC 390. Boeing has also proposed a partnership with Embraer, which would strengthen Embraer's technology and global presence. Brazil's nuclear submarine project is also being developed with the French company DCNS (Deputy Chief of Naval Staff).[42] In 2018, Boeing is developing a partnership with Embraer that will encompass not only civilian but also defense products.

Fifth, in addition to Embraer, Brazil's other key players in Brazil's BMD are: (a) Avibras, a producer of air defense systems, rockets, and missiles, (b) CBC, a producer of weapons and ammunitions, (c) Taurus, a producer of light weapons and safety equipment, and (d) Imbel, a producer of explosives and communication equipment. The Lula administration was also eager to attract Brazil's largest engineering companies to the newly revamped defense industry. These "four engineering sisters" had been involved in Brazil's largest infrastructure projects, from energy to telecommunications.

In 2008, Brazil's "four engineering sisters" were invited by the Lula administration to participate in Brazil's 2008 National Defense Strategy program. They were encouraged to develop partnerships with a variety of defense multinationals in order to accelerate the exchange of technology and production of Brazilian-made defense hardware and software. For instance: (a) Odebrecht Defesa e Tecnologia (ODT) designed a partnership with the French defense multinational DCNS to develop Brazil's Prosub Project and the nuclear submarine, (b) Andrade Gutierrez Defesa e Seguranca developed a partnership with the French defense multinational Thales to design complex monitoring systems for border control, (c) OAS Defesa developed a partnership with the Israeli defense company Rafael, aiming to developing monitoring systems for Brazil's SISFRON project, and (d) Queiroz Galvao has developed a partnership with U.S.'s defense multinational Northrop to create systems for the SISFRON project.[43]

Sixth, as Brazil embarks on making additional defense purchases, it is also important to address the nexus of corruption and defense acquisitions. As a result of the size of these defense contracts, technical complexity, secrecy, urgency, and lack of scrutiny, corruption tends to plague the relationship between governments and defense firms. "Buy national defense hardware and software" strategies are also likely to promote corruption schemes in defense industries controlled by populist regimes. In many instance, these industries are not competitive in global markets, leading to additional waste of resources and corruption. Brazil's overall defense capabilities and its abilities to respond to and address threats are weakened and compromised by corruption schemes. Countries need to design and implement transparency, enforcement, and accountability in addition to codes of integrity to curb defense-related corruption.[44]

Brazil is no stranger to corruption in its own defense industry. In the last few years, Brazil has seen an increasing number of reports on cases of corruption, permeating a number of key projects for the defense industry. For instance, Brazil's PROSUB's shipyard, being built by Odebrecht's subsidiary Itaguai Construcoes Navais, saw the cost of its construction inflated by 50 percent. Brazil's engineering company Norberto Odebrecht, involved in Brazil's Petrobras corruption scheme, is building the navy base and Brazil's first nuclear submarine in partnership with the French company DCNS. The same corruption scheme to inflate costs of infrastructure projects currently being investigated in several of Petrobras's projects are now being detected in Brazil's new defense projects. Embraer has also been accused of corruption and was fined US$205 million by the United States Department of Justice (DOJ) and SEC to resolve Foreign Corrupt Practices Act (FCPA) violations. Embraer bribed officials in Mozambique, Saudi Arabia, and the Dominican Republic. Prosecutors in Brazil are also investigating if Saab and members of Lula's and Dilma's administrations engaged in possible acts of corruption in the acquisition of the 36 Grippen fighters. The initial 2009 contract, estimated at US$4.5 billion, was increased to US$5.4 billion after Dilma Rousseff was reelected, raising a number of concerns by Brazilians prosecutors.[45]

Seventh, the increasing pressure from other emerging defense producers will force Brazil to reassess the costs and benefits of its defense programs and projects from a "make or buy" angle in order to address Brazil's increasing national defense strategies and objectives. Furthermore, Brazil will have to increase its specialization and narrow the scope of its domestic defense production. The degree of freedom experienced by the defense industry in the 1970s and 1980s is no longer present, since multinational defense companies have become active players in the industry.[46]

Eighth, policymakers in Brazil need to establish a national procurement policy in order to support the industry when international global markets experience cyclical downturns. The lack of such a policy was largely responsible for the elimination of key players in Brazil's defense industry such as Engesa, in the 1990s. Recent developments such as severe cuts in Brazil's defense budget are creating a similar scenario moving forward.[47]

Ninth, during the Lula and Dilma's administrations the expansion and diversification of Brazil's defense industry was perceived as an effort toward national autonomy. In 2018, the Temer administration, however, perceived the defense industry as an important industry that can help diversify Brazil's export portfolio and export volume. The Temer administration is putting a renewed effort to promote exports of Brazilian defense hardware and software by engaging Brazil's Bank of National Economic and Social Development (BNDEs) to finance

Brazilian defense exports and by enrolling the assistance of Brazil's Ministry of Foreign Affairs, through its embassies and consulates, to promote these defense sales. Temer's export drive of defense hardware and software will, however, be shaped by Brazil's manufacturing competitiveness and cost in addition to the technological competitiveness of defense hardware and software made in Brazil.

Final remarks

Currently, Brazil is taking steps to revitalize its indigenous defense industry. However, the 2000s' global defense environment is quite different from that of the 1980s, in both the internal and external dimensions. The globalization and consolidation of the global defense industry is shaping Brazil's defense industry, imposing closer ties to global defense producers. This, in turn, lowers Brazil's degree of freedom in becoming a meaningful and independent player in the defense industry. Defense manufacturers in Brazil are forming strategic alliances with foreign defense manufacturers at the production and technological levels, showcasing the new nature of defense projects and markets. Brazil's defense industry is now an extension of the global defense production cluster via: (a) market access, (b) joint production of defense hardware and software, (c) offsets, and (d) technology-transfer agreements. It is also important to mention that the political departure from the leftist foreign policies of Lula and Dilma may provide a new momentum in Brazil's defense realignment with the United States and traditional European suppliers of defense hardware. Brazil's defense policies and strategies, introduced by the Lula government and followed by the Dilma government, were designed to bring Brazil's defense industry closer to Russian and Chinese defense producers, and away from the U.S. and traditional European defense producers.

Politicians and policymakers in Brazil need to better understand the complexities involved in and the vital importance of building an indigenous defense-manufacturing policy and industry, from economic, national, and global perspectives. In the past few decades, Brazil's ministers of defense were political appointees with little knowledge of the complexities of national security on a global level and the dynamics of the global defense industry. Policymakers also need to understand the pressing issues threatening Brazil's borders, such as drug trafficking, weapons smuggling, and threats to its natural resources from third-party countries. Constant cuts in Brazil's defense budget, such as the one implemented in 2018, deeply affect the country's ability to address its main national security issues. Brazil's sequestration of defense resources could further threaten its national security and its overall ability to finalize a number of defense projects.

Notes

1. Patrice Franko-Jones, *The Brazilian Defense Industry* (New York: Westview Press, 1994); Patrice Franko, "The Defense Acquisition Trilemma: The Case of Brazil," Strategic Forum (Washington, DC: Institute for National Strategic Studies (INSS), January 2014), http://ndupress.ndu.edu/Media/News/News-Article-View/Article/718116/the-defense-acquisition-trilemma-the-case-of-brazil/; Igor Gielow, "Para Driblar Crise, Setor de Defesa Quer Mudar a Identidade," Folha de S. Paulo, April 4, 2017, www1.folha.uol.com.br/mercado/2017/04/1872392-para-driblar-crise-setor-de-defesa-quer-mudar-a-identidade.shtml; Raul Gouvea, "O Brasil No Mercado Mundial de Armamentos," *Estudos Economicos* 20, no. 3 (1990): 407–37; Raul Gouvea, "How Brazil Competes in the Global Defense Industry," *Latin American Research Review* 26, no. 3 (1991): 83–107; Raul Gouvea, "El Papel de Las Empresas Transnacionales En El Tripode de La Industria Militar Brasilena," *El Trimestre Economico* 58, no. 230 (Abril–Junio; 1991): 357–404.
2. James Everett Katz, *Arms Production in Developing Countries: An Analysis of Decision Making* (Lexington, MA: Lexington Books, 1984); Rodney W Jones and Steven A Hildreth, *Modern Weapons and Third World Powers* (Boulder: Westview Press, 1984); Steven D. Kahne, "Effect of the Brazilian Arms Industry on U.S. Strategy" (Maxwell AFB, AL: Air War College, May 1993), www.dtic.mil/docs/citations/

ADA283158; Helena Tuomi and Raimo Vayrynen, *Transnational Corporations, Armaments, and Development* (Hants: Gower, 1982); Stephen Williams, "Arming the Third World: The Role of Multinational Corporations," in *Multinational Corporations and the Third World*, edited by C. J. Dixon, D. Drakakis-Smith, and H. D. Watts (London: Croom Helm, 1986).

3. Raul Gouvea, "Brazil's New Defense Paradigm," *Defense & Security Analysis* 31, no. 2 (August 2015): 137–151; Raul Gouvea, "The Sinicization of Brazil's Defense Industry," *Journal of Defense Studies and Resource Management* 4, no. 1 (January 20, 2017): doi:2324-9315.1000125, https://doi.org/10.4172/2324-9315.1000125.
4. Sergio de Queiroz Duarte, "Brazil and the Nonproliferation Regime: A Historical Perspective," *The Nonproliferation Review* 23, no. 5–6 (November 1, 2016): 545–58, https://doi.org/10.1080/10736700.2017.1335901.
5. Gary Milhollin, "Testimony: Weak U.S. Export Controls Contribute to Iraqi WMD Efforts," *Wisconsin Project on Nuclear Arms Control* (blog), September 21, 1990, www.wisconsinproject.org/testimony-weak-u-s-export-controls-contribute-to-iraqi-wmd-efforts/; Reginaldo Santos, "O Programa Nacional de Atividade Espaciais Frente Aos Embargos Tecnologicos," Parcerias Estratégicas, 2009, http://seer.cgee.org.br/index.php/parcerias_estrategicas/article/viewFile/95/87.
6. Jurgen Brauer and John Tepper Marlin, "Converting Resources from Military to Non-Military Uses," *Journal of Economic Perspectives* 6, no. 4 (1992): 145–64; W. Burns, "Dismantling the Cold War's Arsenals," *Arms Control Today* 23, no. 7 (1993): 3–7; Jose Costa, *Analise Do Cenario Politico—Estrategico Que Favoreceu o Nascimento, Fortalecimento e Falencia Da Engesa* (Sao Paulo: Pontificia Universidade Catolica, 2013); Aloisio Goncalves Filho and Waldimir Pirro e Longo, "A Crise Fiscal Dos Estados Unidos: Implicacoes Para a Industria de Defesa Brasileira," Seminario Brasileiro de Estudos Estrategicos Internacionais, Porto Alegre, Brasil, 2013; Raul Gouvea and Sul Kassicieh, "From Defense Conversion to Globalization Strategies," *Journal of International Business and Entrepreneurship Development* 1, no. 2 (2003): 10–17; Raul Gouvea and Sul Kassicieh, "Shifting the Technology Paradigm: Moving Toward Commercialization: The Brazilian Experience," *Latin American Business Review* 4, no. 3 (2003): 91–109.
7. Christopher Cavas, "Lack of Strategy Plagues Brazil's Industry," *Defense News*, April 25, 2005; Marcio Rocha, "A Relacao Civil-Militar No Brasil: Uma Analise Do Reriodo de 1985 a 2006," in *Anais Do XV Encontro Nacional de Historia* (Rio de Janeiro: ANPUH, 2012); SIPRI, *SIPRI Yearbook 2017: Armaments, Disarmament and International Security*, SIPRI Yearbook Series (Oxford, New York: Oxford University Press, 2017); Center for Strategic and International Studies (CSIS), "U.S.–Brazil Relations and the Role of the Defense Industry," CSIS, 2012, www.csis.org.
8. Peterson Ferreira da Silva, "A política industrial de defesa no Brasil (1999–2014): intersetorialidade e dinâmica de seus principais atores" (Universidade de São Paulo, 2015), https://doi.org/10.11606/T.101.2015.tde-15092015-113930; Samuel Jesus, "O Livro Branco de Defesa do Brasil e suas Implicações Geopolíticas," *Revista Mundorama* (blog), June 1, 2013, www.mundorama.net/?p=11273; Ministerio da Defesa, *Estrategia Nacional de Defesa* (Brasilia: Ministerio da Defesa, 2008).
9. Octavio Amorim Neto, *De Dutra A Lula—A Condução E Os Determinantes Da Política Externa Brasileira* (Rio de Janerio: Elsevier Editora, 2011); Monica Herz, Layla Dawood, and Victor Coutinho Lage, "The Defense-Development Nexus: Brazilian Nuclear Policy under the Workers' Party Administrations," *Revista Brasileira de Política Internacional* 61, no. 1 (2018): 1–19, https://doi.org/10.1590/0034-7329201800105.
10. Juan Arias, "Por que tantos mimos de Temer aos militares?" EL PAÍS, February 27, 2018, https://brasil.elpais.com/brasil/2018/02/27/opinion/1519689207_346590.html; Luis Nassif, "Xadrez do governo Temer e o fator militar," GGN—O jornal de todos os brasis, May 7, 2016, https://jornalggn.com.br/noticia/xadrez-do-governo-temer-e-o-fator-militar.
11. Octavio Amorim Neto, "Democracy, Civil-Military Relations and Defense Policy in Brazil" (paper presented at the Annual Meeting of the American Political Science Association, New Orleans, LA: Social Science Research Network, July 4–5, 2012), https://papers.ssrn.com/abstract=2110718; Marco Cepik, "Politica de Defesa No Brasil: Instituicoes, Doutrina, Capacidade e Economia," 7, Note (Paris: Fondation pour la Reserche Estrategique, April 2, 2014); Steen Christensen, "Brazil's South Atlantic Strategy" (paper presented at International Studies Association (ISA) 2014: Spaces and Places, Toronto, Canada, July, 2014); Joe Leahy, "Foreign Defence Groups Drawn to Brazil," *Financial Times*, January 28, 2013, www.ft.com/content/c7e8e636-5f1c-11e2-8250-00144feab49a; Ministerio da Defesa, *Livro Branco de Defesa Nacional* (Brasilia: Ministerio da Defesa, 2012); Lucena Silva, "Globalização Militar, Segurança e Desenvolvimento: Comparação Entre as Indústrias Aeroespaciais de Defesa de Brasil, Índia e China," *Papel Politico* 15, no. 2 (December 2010): 667–90; Virginia Silveira, "Grupos Se Preparam Para a Disputa de Megalicitacao Da Marinha," *Valor*, January 14, 2014.
12. ASD Reports, "Future of the Brazilian Defense Industry: Market Attractiveness, Competitive Landscape and Forecasts to 2019" (Amsterdam: ASD Reports, 2014), www.asdreports.com; ASD Reports, "The Brazilian Defense Industry Is Expected to Positively Grow by Enhancing Its Domestic Defense

Capabilities" (Amsterdam: ASD Reports, 2014), www.asdreports.com; Pedro Casas and Rubia Rodrigues, "O Livro Branco de Defesa Nacional," Cenarios PUC Minas, 2011, www.pucminas.br/conjuntura; Salvador Raza, *Brazil's Defense Industry: The Emerging Transformational Role of C5I in Defense Industry's Cluster Formation* (Buenos Aires: Centro Argentino de Estudios Internacionales (CAEI), 2014); Marcos Degaut, "Brazil's Military Modernization: Is a New Strategic Culture Emerging?" *Rising Powers Quarterly* 2, no. 1 (2017): 271–97.

13. SIPRI, *SIPRI Yearbook 2017.*
14. "Brasil Adquire Helicopteros a Empresa Aeronautica Russa," *Base Militar Web Magazine,* 2012, www.alide.com.br; Tatiana Bautzer, "Avibras, Uma Guerra No Ar," *Isto E Dinheiro*, 2012; Samuel Cruz, Jr., "A Seguranca e Defesa Cibernetica No Brasil: E Uma Revisao Das Estrategias Dos Estados Unidos, Russia e India Para o Espaco Virtual," Texto Para Discussao (Rio de Janerio: Instituto de Pesquisa Economica Aplicada (IPEA), 2013); "Brazil's F-X2 Fighter Competition," *Defense Industry Daily,* December 13, 2012, www.defenseindustrydaily.com/brazil-embarking-upon-f-x2-fighter-program-04179/; Mario Cesar Flores, "A defesa nacional na sociedade e na política—Opinião," *Estadão*, July 30, 2012, https://opiniao.estadao.com.br/noticias/geral,a-defesa-nacional-na-sociedade-e-na-politica-imp-,893791; Chico Gois and Jailton Carvalho, "Brasil Escolhe Caca Sueco," *O Globo*, December 19, 2013; Ariela Leske, "Inovacao e Politicas Na Industria de Defesa Brasileira," Universidade Federal do Rio de Janeiro, Instituto de Economia, 2013; Sergio Lamucci, "Boeing Esta Otimista Com Licitacao Dos Cacas Da FAB," *Valor*, August 16, 2013.
15. Luke Heselden, "U.S.-Brazil Relations and the Role of the Defense Industry," Current Issues, CSIS, August 28, 2012; Leahy, "Foreign Defence Groups Drawn to Brazil"; SIPRI, *SIPRI Yearbook 2017.*
16. Igor Gielow, "Politizacao e Verba Escassa Freiam Renovacao Militar," *Folha de Sao Paulo*, February 20, 2012.
17. Jamil Chade, "'Saab fará do Brasil um produtor de caças', diz executivo de companhia sueca," Estadão, January 11, 2014, https://politica.estadao.com.br/noticias/geral,saab-fara-do-brasil-um-produtor-de-cacas-diz-executivo-de-companhia-sueca,1117422; Gielow, "Politizacao e Verba Escassa Freiam Renovacao Militar"; ASD Reports, "Future of the Brazilian Defense Industry"; ASD Reports, "The Brazilian Defense Industry"; CSIS, "U.S.-Brazil Relations and the Role of the Defense Industry."
18. Gielow, "Para Driblar Crise, Setor de Defesa Quer Mudar a Identidade"; Igor Gielow and Gustavo Patu, "Temer Retoma Investimentos Em Programas Militares," *Folha de Sao Paulo*, March 13, 2017.
19. Gielow and Patu, "Temer Retoma Investimentos Em Programas Militares."
20. Gouvea, "The Sinicization of Brazil's Defense Industry."
21. *ExportGov,* "Brazil Commercial Guide: Brazil—Defense," August 10, 2017, http://apps.export.gov/article?id=Brazil-Defense.
22. Fernando Rodrigues and Igor Gielow, "Metade Dos Armamentos Do Pais Esta Indisponivel," *Folha de Sao Paulo*, March 13, 2011.
23. Roberto Caiafa, "Proposta de Orçamento 2018: Defesa sofre cortes expressivos," *Tecnologia & Defensa,* November 2, 2017, http://tecnodefesa.com.br/proposta-de-orcamento-2018-defesa-sofre-cortes-expressivos/; Leandro Prazeres and Wellington Ramalhoso, "Governo corta pela metade investimento em monitoramento de fronteiras," Cotidiano, March 5, 2018, https://noticias.uol.com.br/cotidiano/ultimas-noticias/2018/03/05/governo-corta-pela-metade-investimento-em-monitoramento-de-fronteiras.htm.
24. Lucena S. Silva, "Conselho de Defesa Sul Americano: Possibilidade de Integracao Efetiva na America do Sul," Brasilia: Universidade Nacional de Brasilia (UNB), 2012; Strategic Defence Intelligence (SDI), "Future of the Brazilian Defense Industry—Market Attractiveness, Competitive Landscape and Forecasts to 2018" (London: SDI, 2013); Paul Taylor, "Why Does Brazil Need Nuclear Submarines?" *Proceeding Magazine*, 2009; Marianne Wiesebron, "Blue Amazon: Thinking the Defense of Brazilian Maritime Territory," *Brazilian Journal of Strategy & International Relations* 2, no. 3 (2013): 101–24.
25. Flavia Squeff and Lucas Assis, "The Defence Industry in Brazil: Characteristics and Involvement of Supplier Firms," Discussion Paper, Rio de Janeiro: IPEA, 2014.
26. Bautzer, "Avibras, Uma Guerra No Ar"; *Defesabr,* "Os Exportadores Brasileiros de Defesa," 2013, www.defesabr.com; Danilo Fariello, "Superbelicas Verde-Amarelas," *O Globo*, July 15, 2012; Ministerio da Defesa, *Livro Branco de Defesa Nacional*; Gielow, "Politizacao e Verba Escassa Freiam Renovacao Militar"; Roberto Godoy, "Iveco Leva Guarani Ao Exterior," *O Estado de Sao Paulo*, September 9, 2012; Roberto Godoy, "Brasileira Avibras Fecha Contrato de US$400 Milhoes Com a Indonesia," *O Estado de Sao Paulo*, November 21, 2012; Silvana Mautone, "Embraer Entrega Nova Proposta Para Licitacao Nos EUA," O Estado de Sao Paulo, 2012, www.estadao.com.br; Grant Turnbull, "Rethinking Defence: Naval Modernisation in South America," *Naval Technology* (blog), October 27, 2013, https://www.naval-technology.com/features/feature-rethinking-defence-naval-modernisation-south-america/; Raul Gouvea, "US–Latin America's Security: Moving through an Inflection Point?," *Defense & Security Analysis* 33, no. 3 (July 3, 2017): 223–41, https://doi.org/10.1080/14751798.2017.1351138; Strategic Defence Intelligence,

"The Brazilian Defense Industry—Market Opportunities and Entry Strategies Analyses and Forecasts to 2017" (London: SDI, 2017).

27. Roberto Caiafa, "A Look at SISFRON, Brazil's Integrated Border Monitoring System," *Dialogo Americas,* February 22, 2017, https://dialogo-americas.com/en/articles/look-sisfron-brazils-integrated-border-monitoring-system; Marco Cepik and Frederico Licks Bertol, "Defense Policy in Brazil: Bridging the Gap between Ends and Means?" *Defence Studies* 16, no. 3 (July 2, 2016): 229–47, https://doi.org/10.1080/14702436.2016.1180959; Prazeres and Ramalhoso, "Governo corta pela metade investimento."
28. "Brazil interested in purchasing air defense missile systems from Russia," *TASS,* April 4, 2017, http://tass.com/defense/939212; Richard Tomkins, "Brazil Orders Man-Portable Air Defense System from Saab," *UPI,* October 30, 2017, https://www.upi.com/Defense-News/2017/10/30/Brazil-orders-man-portable-air-defense-system-from-Saab/4491509371680/; Dylan Malyasov, "Brazil's Cruise Missile Development Program Enters Final Phase," *Defence Blog* (blog), March 28, 2018, http://defence-blog.com/news/brazils-cruise-missile-development-program-enters-final-phase.html.
29. "Brazilian Army Takes Delivery of the 300th Guarani Armored Vehicle," *Army Recognition,* March 16, 2018, https://www.armyrecognition.com/march_2018_global_defense_security_army_news_industry/brazilian_army_takes_delivery_of_the_300th_guarani_armored_vehicle.html.
30. "Elbit Systems to Supply Electronic Warfare and Communication Systems to Brazilian Marine Corps," *Defense World,* May 10, 2017, www.defenseworld.net/news/19245/Elbit_Systems_To_Supply_Electronic_Warfare_and_Communication_Systems_To_Brazilian_Marine_Corps#.WxD2aMi-l0w; Taciana Moury, "Brazilian Army Invests in Cyber Defense," *Dialogo Americas,* May 12, 2017, https://dialogo-americas.com/en/articles/brazilian-army-invests-cyber-defense.
31. Carlos Federico Domínguez Avila, Deywisson Ronaldo de Souza, and Marcos Aurélio Guedes, "Arms Transfer Policies and International Security: The Case of Brazilian-Swedish Co-Operation," *Contexto Internacional* 39, no. 1 (April 2017): 135–56, https://doi.org/10.1590/s0102-8529.2017390100007.
32. "Brazilian KC-390 Achieves Initial Operational Capability," *Defense Update,* December 20, 2017, http://defense-update.com/20171220_kc390-2.html; Marcelo Sakate, "Impulso para novos voos," *Veja,* 2018.
33. "Brazil Conducts First Training Flight of Updated Lynx Helicopter," Defense-Aerospace, April 24, 2018, http://www.defense-aerospace.com/articles-view/release/3/192754/brazil-conducts-first-training-flight-of-updated-lynx-helicopter.html; Victor Barreira, "Brazilian Army Eyes US SuperCobra Helicopters," *Jane's 360,* March 8, 2018, www.janes.com/article/78455/brazilian-army-eyes-us-supercobra-helicopters; *Sputnik,* "Brazil Interested in Extra Batch of Russian Mi-35 Helicopters - FSMTC," April 6, 2017, https://sputniknews.com/military/201704061052359193-russia-helicopter-mi35-brazil/.
34. Cleide Carvalho, "Base espacial no Maranhão esbarra em disputa histórica," *DefesaNet,* December 24, 2017, www.defesanet.com.br/space/noticia/28037/CLA—Base-espacial-no-Maranhao-esbarra-em-disputa-historica/; Aluri Rebello, "Brasil tenta parceria com SpaceX e Boeing para lançar foguetes no Maranhão," *UOL Economia,* February 22, 2018, https://economia.uol.com.br/noticias/redacao/2018/02/22/brasil-tenta-parceria-com-space-x-e-boeing-para-lancar-foguetes-no-ma.htm.
35. Vincent Groizeleau, "Update on Brazil's Submarine Programme," *Mer et Marine,* July 21, 2017, www.meretmarine.com/fr/content/update-brazils-submarine-programme; Guilherme Wiltegen, "Prosub: Submarino 'Riachuelo' é transferido para Base Naval de Itaguaí," *Defesa Aérea & Naval* (blog), January 13, 2018, www.defesaaereanaval.com.br/prosub-submarino-riachuelo-e-transferido-para-base-naval-de-itaguai/.
36. Eugenio Pacelli Lazzarotti Diniz Costa, "Brazil's Nuclear Submarine: A Broader Approach to the Safeguards Issue," *Revista Brasileira de Política Internacional* 60, no. 2 (2017): 1–20, https://doi.org/10.1590/0034-7329201700205; Herz, Dawood, and Lage, "The Defense-Development Nexus."
37. Beatriz Rodrigues Bessa Mattos, Francisco Eduardo Lemos de Matos, and Kai Michael Kenkel, "Brazilian Policy and the Creation of a Regional Security Complex in the South Atlantic: Pax Brasiliana?" *Contexto Internacional* 39, no. 2 (August 2017): 263–80, https://doi.org/10.1590/s0102-8529.2017390200004; Wiesebron, "Blue Amazon."
38. Andréa Barretto, "The Brazilian Navy Begins Process of Acquiring New Warships," *Dialogo Americas,* June 15, 2017, https://dialogo-americas.com/en/articles/brazilian-navy-begins-process-acquiring-new-warships.
39. Caiafa, "Proposta de Orçamento 2018"; Diego Silva, "How Brazil's Political and Economic Crisis Affects Its Military Spending," SIPRI, June 22, 2017, https://sipri.org/commentary/blog/2017/how-brazils-political-and-economic-crisis-affects-its-military-spending.
40. Gouvea, "US–Latin America's Security"; Zachary Keck, "South Korea: Arms Dealer to the World?" *The National Interest,* December 16, 2017, http://nationalinterest.org/blog/the-buzz/south-korea-arms-dealer-the-world-23690.
41. Luciana Amaral, "Defesa vê pouco estímulo do governo à pesquisa e inovação e projeta 'dependência,'" Folha de Sao Paulo, January 20, 2018, https://noticias.uol.com.br/politica/ultimas-noticias/2018/01/20/defesa-ve-pouco-estimulo-do-governo-a-pesquisa-e-inovacao-e-projeta-dependencia.htm; Luciana Amaral, "Orçamento limitado por teto pode ampliar obsolescência das Forças Armadas e preocupa militares,"

Política, January 20, 2018, https://noticias.uol.com.br/politica/ultimas-noticias/2018/01/20/orcamento-limitado-por-teto-pode-ampliar-obsolescencia-das-forcas-armadas-e-preocupa-oficiais.htm; Virginia Silveira, "Exército planeja aplicar conceitos de inovação da Suécia," *DefesaNet,* September 19, 2012, http://www.defesanet.com.br/terrestre/noticia/7812/Exercito-planeja-aplicar-conceitos-de-inovacao-da-Suecia; Virginia Silveira, "Centro de Tecnologia Atrai Boeing e Airbus," *Valor,* August 13, 2013; Valtteri Vuorisalo, "Five Technology Trends Reveal a New Future for Defence," *UK Defence Journal* (blog), June 1, 2017, https://ukdefencejournal.org.uk/five-technology-trends-reveal-a-new-future-for-defence/; "Technology Trends for 2018," Lockheed Martin, 2018, https://www.lockheedmartin.com/en-us/news/features/innovations.html.

42. Joao Neto and Ana Ribeiro, "Presidente Da Embraer Defende Negociacao Com a Boeing," *O Globo,* December 28, 2017.
43. Kristina Mani, "Military Entrepreneurs: Patterns in Latin America," *Latin American Politics and Society* 53, no. 3 (2011): 25–55; Andre Mileski, "As 'Cinco Irmãs' No Setor de Defesa [e Espaço]," *Panorama Espacial* (blog), July 28, 2013, https://panoramaespacial.blogspot.com/2013/07/as-cinco-irmas-no-setor-de-defesa-e.html.
44. Tehmina Abbas, "Defence Procurment—Understanding, Identifying and Addressing Corruption Risks," in *Public Procurement 2014,* edited by Hans-Joachim Preiß (London: Getting the Deal Through, 2014), 8–10, http://ti-defence.org/wp-content/uploads/2016/03/2014-06_DefenceProc_PublicProc_Chapter.pdf; Sam Perlo-Freeman, "Transparency and Accountability in Military Spending," SIPRI, August 3, 2016, https://www.sipri.org/commentary/topical-backgrounder/2016/transparency-and-accountability-military-spending.
45. Felipe Amorim, "Lula e mais três são denunciados pelo MPF por tráfico de influência," *Política,* December 9, 2016, https://noticias.uol.com.br/politica/ultimas-noticias/2016/12/09/lula-e-mais-tres-pessoas-sao-denunciadas-pelo-mpf-no-ambito-da-zelotes.htm; Fabio Serapiao and Beatriz Bulla, "Odebrecht relata propina para projeto de submarino nuclear da Marinha—Política," *Estadão,* December 15, 2016, https://politica.estadao.com.br/noticias/geral,odebrecht-relata-propina-para-projeto-de-submarino-nuclear-da-marinha,10000094692; Richard L. Cassin, "Former Embraer Sales VP Pleads Guilty to Aramco Bribes," The FCPA Blog, December 21, 2017, http://fcpablog.squarespace.com/blog/2017/12/21/former-embraer-sales-vp-pleads-guilty-to-aramco-bribes.html;jsessionid=5FE2EF4DD722CC789DF59F76CDB8C3AF.v5-web016; Leandro Prazeres, "MPF aponta superfaturamento de R$2,8 bilhões em programa de submarinos," *Folha de Sao Paulo,* March 24, 2018, https://noticias.uol.com.br/politica/ultimas-noticias/2018/03/24/mpf-encontra-superfaturamento-de-r-28-bilhoes-em-programa-de-submarinos.htm; Silva, "A política industrial de defesa no Brasil (1999-2014)"; Mario Simas Filho, "Propina a Jato," ISTOÉ Independente, June 3, 2016, https://istoe.com.br/propina-a-jato/; Julia Affonso, Fausto Macedo, and Mateus Coutinho, "Lula é denunciado na Zelotes por tráfico de influência na compra dos caças Gripen," Estado de Sao Paulo, December 9, 2016, http://politica.estadao.com.br/blogs/fausto-macedo/ex-presidente-lula-e-filho-sao-denunciados/.
46. Julio Ottoboni, "Russos buscam espaço da defesa nacional," DefesaNet, March 7, 2013, http://www.defesanet.com.br/br_ru/noticia/9971/Russos-buscam-espaco-da-defesa-nacional; Atila Roque and Mauricio Santoro, "O Brasil e o Comercio de Armas," *Folha de Sao Paulo,* August 1, 2012; Fernando Valduga, "Russian Technologies e Odebrecht Defesa e Tecnologia fecham acordo para montagem de helicópteros Mi-171 no Brasil," *Cavok Brasil* (blog), December 17, 2012, http://www.cavok.com.br/blog/russian-technologies-e-odebrecht-defesa-e-tecnologia-fecham-acordo-para-montagem-de-helicopteros-mi-171-no-brasil/.
47. Amaral, "Orçamento limitado"; ASD Reports, "Future of the Brazilian Defense Industry"; ASD Reports, "The Brazilian Defense Industry Is Expected to Positively Grow"; Merval Pereira, "Além dos caças," O Globo, December 28, 2013, https://blogs.oglobo.globo.com/merval-pereira/post/alem-dos-cacas-519416.html; Ottoboni, "Russos buscam espaço da defesa nacional"; Silveira, "Grupos Se Preparam"; Squeff and Assis, "The Defence Industry in Brazil."

Defense industrialization in Latin America

Patrice M. Franko and Mônica Herz

ABSTRACT
This article analyzes contrasting approaches to defense modernization in the Latin American region focusing on Brazil, Chile, Colombia, and Argentina. Three variables of autonomy, spending, and integration highlight the tradeoffs in each country's strategy while facing the pressure of rising costs of technologically sophisticated systems. We show that these countries' responses to the defense trilemma between autonomy, technology, and economic sustainability differ according to geographic, economic, and political conditions. Finally, we suggest that regional cooperation in this field is one possible response to the trilemma.

Overview: Contrasting approaches to defense modernization in Latin America

Modern defense acquisition is framed by tradeoffs between autonomy, technology, and economic sustainability. Sovereignty for superpower nations has traditionally been grounded in the autonomous decisions regarding the structure of military equipment without constraints on system design or supplier. Nations with robust defense industries can develop systems that address specific national needs; with significant technological capacities, they are not dependent on export controls of supplier nations. Nations dependent on arms imports are constrained by policies determined outside their capitals, circumscribing activities for human rights or geopolitical concerns. Rising powers, however, may not have the access to industry and technology for autonomous defense production. This idealized state of autonomy is practically constrained by budgets—resources further stretched by exponentially rising costs in computerized weaponry. With limited resources for defense, nations must cede pure autonomy to purchase systems from the most economical source.[1] A limited autarky may emerge with varying degrees of freedom in the international system.[2] Technology and budgets therefore limit choice.

The tradeoffs in defense production—with increasingly sophisticated systems commanding high price tags—pushes nations to collaborate with defense-production partners in a global value chain.[3] As DeVore notes, small- and medium-size states can calibrate options to develop defense-industrial capabilities by engaging with foreign producers.[4] Amortizing the high costs of defense technologies requires a scale of purchase outside the budgets of most individual nations.[5] European defense industries offer important examples of the benefits of partnerships to overcome economies of scale and address security needs. Even great powers may no longer be able to pursue autarkic strategies in defense production.[6] Internationalization has become necessary even for the United States.[7] Global sales become a survival mechanism for private producers to capture economies of scale.

But partnerships can compromise autonomy. National needs might differ on a joint project or strategic aims may not always coincide. Nations are caught in the trilemma of having to choose

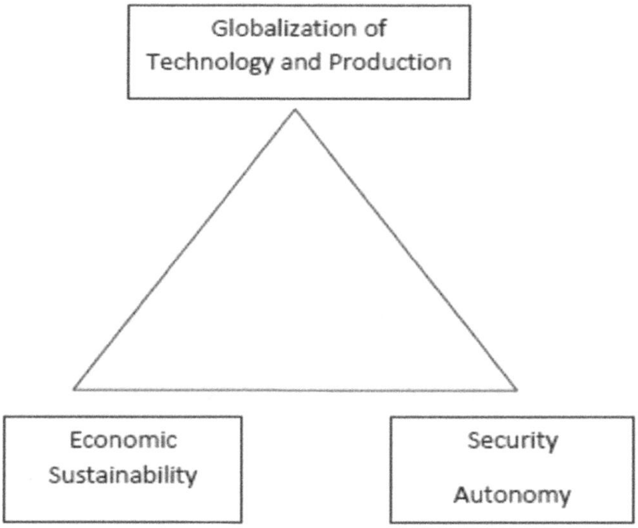

Figure 1. The defense trilemma.

between sustainable defense budgets, autonomy, and access to sophisticated technologies. This defense trilemma, depicted in Figure 1, can be used to characterize choices made in Latin American defense modernization.[8] Countries are forced to one point or another by virtue of dominant constraints.

Latin American nations offer contrasts in ordering two of the three points on the triangle. As summarized in Table 1, this article analyzes four country cases in the Latin American region that illustrate different tradeoffs: Brazil, Chile, Colombia, and Argentina. Brazil has historically prioritized autonomy. As the regional power with global ambitions, Brazil identified its continental reach as positioning it to act without the restrictions that might be imposed by the United States. Although economic crises have limited its procurement designs, it has prioritized developing domestic defense capabilities. Technological sophistication and economies of scale, however, have forced Brazil—like nearly all nations—into cooperative agreements in the global value chain. Like other small and medium producers, the high cost of sophisticated armaments, the size of multinational competitors, and the globalization of production structures have forced a globalization of its defense sector.[9]

Chile pursued the opposite path. With dedicated financing through its copper fund, the Chilean armed forces have been less constrained in acquisitions. Yet, as a small and internationally open country, it decided to accept limitations on sovereignty in exchange for off-the-shelf purchases of more sophisticated technologies. Colombia was a bit of a hybrid. Tightly bound to the United States through American initiatives in counter-narcotics—and fighting a fifty-year civil war—Colombia ceded autonomy by integrating into the global value chain. Its defense production has been at a lower technological level—which it is now expanding in a time of relative peace in Central America and Andean countries. Although in the last decades of the twentieth century Argentina dedicated the largest portion of GDP to defense production, its force capabilities have been decimated in recent years by economic crises. Its defense modernization has stalled; it now struggles with operational capabilities across its three forces. As it modernizes during a period of greater defense-value chain globalization worldwide, Argentina is taking advantage of global linkages to acquire technologies and systems.

This article analyzes these contrasting approaches to defense modernization in the Latin American region. Acknowledging within-country differences among the different branches of the

Table 1. Tradeoffs between autonomy, spending and integration in Latin America.

	Brazil	Chile	Colombia	Argentina
Autonomy	High	Low	Low/medium	High yet isolated
Milex	Variable	Strong	High and declining	Low
Integration	Increasing	BOTS*	Growing	Low but rising

Note. *Buy off the Shelf.

armed forces, it teases out lessons for defense-industrial policies. We show that with rising costs of technologically sophisticated systems, countries are forced into the global value chain to moderate the economic pressures on defense budgets. Detailed case studies across these three variables of autonomy, spending, and integration highlight the tradeoffs in each country's strategy.

Autonomy: Prioritizing strategic independence or promoting interdependence in arms production?

Table 2 compares the strategic objectives of Brazil, Chile, Colombia, and Argentina. Brazil's National Defense Strategy situates defense as central to national development.[10] The strategy places the mastery of strategic technologies as key to "autonomy" and Brazil's ability to leverage international influence. Military power and a robust state afford the nation greater freedom of action; a weak country can be bullied, but intimidating a stronger nation is a tall order. The Brazilian goal has deep geostrategic roots; the work of General Meira Mattos of Brazil as a country with continental reach continues to find resonance today. Security and development have long been intertwined with the national vision. With the exception of Ecuador and Chile, Brazil shares borders with ten South American neighbors. With national frontiers and long, exposed coastlines, Brazil maintains traditional objectives of territorial and maritime control. As illicit networks have expanded globally, it has developed regional and extra-regional partnerships to promote national security. Brazil's professionalized foreign service, Itamaraty, has used this regional platform to enhance its global standing. As the point nearest to Africa, and sharing Portuguese with several African nations, its South Atlantic projection also figures prominently in its global design.[11]

Chile is strategically isolated—or perhaps protected—by the Andean mountain chain and a challenging Pacific coastline. Rather than the power projection sought by Brazil, Chile's smaller size leads to more modest roles on the global stage. Along with Brazil and Argentina, it participates in international peace missions and promotes cooperative solutions with regional neighbors. Its national security policy, ENSYD, promotes the protection of Chilean resources and territorial integrity as a top strategic priority. Resources shortages and environmental change along with earthquakes and tsunamis are very present in the national consciousness; the mission of the armed forces is therefore aligned with disaster management and humanitarian intervention. Chile recognizes the role of transnational actors their threat to domestic security. Its smaller size has positioned Chile as an outward-looking internationalist. Rather than seeking to project power, Chile emphasizes international peace missions and cooperative efforts, linking increased participation to increased influence or soft power in global institutions. Its recent engagement with the Pacific Alliance and the TPP (Transpacific Partnership) symbolize its external orientation. Chileans point to their "special" relationship with the United States, viewing the benefits of American military sales and assistance as outweighing the downsides of dependency. Combined with this special (although not uncomplicated) relationship with the United States, a kind of isolated internationalism—rather than a quest for autonomy—positions Chile in the global arena.[12]

Like Chile, Argentina's strategic reach is limited by its geography. Although it shares borders with Bolivia, Brazil, Chile, Paraguay, and Uruguay, natural borders of the Andean mountain range and its long coastline historically provided protection. After a highly contested transition

Table 2. National security objectives.

Brazil	Argentina	Chile	Colombia
• Autonomy & development - Domination of strategic technologies of cyber, nuclear, and space sectors - Defense industry with capabilities in the most vital/strategic military technologies - Transnational criminality & territorial control • Dissuasion • Regional defense integration	• Defense of national territory and international commitments • Strategic interests - International peace and security - Limitation of mass destruction weapons - Regional integration and security - Scientific and technological development - Protection of the nation from the drug trafficking and international terrorism - Renewable and nonrenewable resources - Environmental protection - Maritime, insular, and fluvial spaces of national interest - Argentine air space - Inter-ocean passages - Preservation of geopolitically empty areas (unpopulated and with no government presence) - Preservation of the Argentine position in the Antarctic system (1999)	Chile's defense policy is founded on: • The principle of cooperation in the international system • Respect for international rights • Promotion of peaceful relations among states • Promotion of democracy • A responsibility to cooperate • Dissuasion	• Combat of transnational non-state actors • Contribute to international peace/regional initiatives • Cooperation against mutual threats • Training Latam armies • Dissuasion

from military rule, modern Argentina distanced its political space from defense-related endeavors. It defines its maritime and air spaces as critical to national security, has promoted international regime participation for antinuclear and other proliferation concerns, and is vested in preserving the Argentine position in the Antarctic system. With greater recognition of climate change, renewable energy has come into national focus and, like others in the region, the domestic effects of narco-trafficking have made slowing the movement of illicit goods a priority.[13]

Colombia connects Mexico to North America through a narrow isthmus containing the Northern Triangle countries of Guatemala, Honduras, and El Salvador—places of intense internal violence. Central America's integration into global drug trafficking—and Colombia's own role—create imminent security threats in a context of fragile democratic governance and rule of law. Colombia's national security objectives are undergoing a radical reorientation as the nation's focus shifts from more than fifty years of civil war to a new regional role. The interlacing of narco-trafficking with both the insurgent and government forces has complicated the strategic transition in Colombia. Colombia also suffers from the human exodus from Venezuela—the nearly one million who entered Colombia in 2017.

Unlike the isolation of Chile and Argentina, Colombia's regional neighborhood pushes it toward collaboration to address pressing security concerns. Its legacy of cooperation with the United States connects it to North American defense producers. It does not have the choice of autonomy, but rather must actively coordinate on a bilateral and multilateral basis to confront transnational crime. Its strategic experience in confronting internal tensions is now being repositioned as leadership in regional efforts confronting common threats and natural disasters.[14]

Regional defense spending: Highly constrained

Defense spending in Latin America is modest. Whether using the metric of percent of government spending (a measure of the direction of defense policy) or percent of gross domestic product, regional spending falls below global averages. SIPRI shows Latin American as the lowest expenditures of all regions.[15] With Colombia, emerging from a fifty-year civil war as the exception, spending in the region is around or below 2 percent of GDP. Spending is also heavily directed toward personnel, eating up 76 percent of the budget in Brazil, 64 percent in Chile, and 79.4 percent in Argentina.[16] The ratio for the U.S. is roughly inverted, with personnel consuming approximately a quarter of the defense budget. Brazil, the largest absolute spender in the region, only clocks 4 percent of the U.S. total.[17] With low spending largely for personnel and maintenance, the size of the defense-equipment market in Latin America is relatively miniscule.

Budgets were also limited during the global financial crisis, significantly slowing acquisition.[18] In Brazil, the defense budget was capped, along with all other department budgets, under the 2017 law implemented by President Temer that placed a ceiling on overall government expenditures growing at the rate of inflation for the next twenty years. According to the Brazilian ministry (Defense Scenario 2020–2039), the new fiscal regime, layered on top of unmet needs from the past decades, is limiting the modernization plans of the Brazilian armed forces. In no uncertain terms, the ministry warned that the available resources are not sufficient to control the airspace, maintain territorial control, or patrol the sea.[19] Year-to-year budgets are also highly uncertain, varying 15–25 percent. With this type of unpredictable spending policy, defense companies find themselves in a difficult environment for long-term planning and investment needed for complex projects. For firms requiring expensive research and development (R&D) and skilled labor, the variation is immobilizing. As the cost of high-technology programs continues to outpace inflation, this results in an overall weakening of the buying power of regional militaries. Scheetz calls this demilitarization.[20]

Constrained defense spending in Argentina has resulted in operational incapacities. In the period of democratic turnover between 1983 and 2003, the Argentine defense budget was cut 58.7 percent, restricting its share in the national budget from 13.78 to 7.7 percent—less than 1 percent of GDP. By late 2015, the operational capabilities of the Argentine armed forces had declined significantly due to resource constraints; the very public loss of its submarine put pressure on the government to realign priorities.[21] In January 2016, Defense Minister Julio Martinez announced that the new government's plans for the country did not include "an Air Force which could not fly or a Navy that could not sail" and reiterated that the Macri administration would seek to remedy operational deficiencies. Martinez emphasized wide-ranging equipment needs from a lack of attention that predated the Kirchner administrations. The 2016 defense budget for Argentina included financing for Fabricaciones Militares, the state armaments company; shipbuilding; and Antarctic security.[22] President Macri plans to spend US $2 billion in major platforms, largely from the U.S., Italy, and Israel, making it the largest weapons acquisition since the country's Malvinas War.[23] But binding economic constraints make this plans unrealistic.

Chilean modernization spending has been a far smoother process. The Chilean military benefits from Chilean legislation called the Ley Reservada del Cobre, a law that transfers 10 percent of exports from the state copper company to the Chilean military. The Copper Law allows for more consistent military spending than in Brazil, but even still Chilean spending (adjusted for exchange rate changes) slowly decreased between 2012 and 2015. Furthermore, like Brazil, Chilean military expenditure is heavily hampered by personnel concerns, chewing up 70 percent of the annual budget. Chilean defense producers also contest the image that the copper fund creates unconstrained spending.[24] Although the fund exists, branches of the armed forces are also constrained by overall macroeconomic caps on spending to manage the aggregate fiscal stimulus. One might think of the fund more as a trust than a bank account; spending caps are enforced to smooth

Table 3. Defense-production capabilities in the region.

Defense Production in Latin America: Four Country Cases								
	Aerospace		Naval		Armament		Other	
	Public	Private	Public	Private	Public	Private	Public	Private
Brazil		Embraer;* Avibras; Helibras (wholly owned subsid of Airbus Helicop)	AMAZUL - Amazônia Azul Tecnologias de Defesa S.A; EMGEPRON - Empresa Gerencial de Projetos Navais	SIEM Offshore do Brasil(Consub)	IMBEL	Iveco (Brazil subsid)		Taurus; Brazil has a large number of smaller supplier firms (see ABIMDE)
Colombia	CIAC		Cotecmar***		INDUMIL		Codaltec	
Chile	ENAER		Asmar**; ASENAV		FAMAE			Fabricaciones Militares (FABMIL electronics) ; SISDEF
Argentina	Fábrica Argentina de Aviones (FAdeA), INVAP		Argentine Naval Industrial Complex (CINAR) (includes Tanador)		Fabricaciones Militares		Institute of Scientific and Technical Research for Defense (CITEDEF)	Nostromo Defensa (UAV)

Note. *Government holds a share; **Asmar is an autonomous state-owned enterprise, off budget; ***mixed state-private.

expenditures over time. While this helped in post-tsunami reconstruction, it does not provide an open checkbook for procurement.

Defense spending in Colombia has largely been directed toward its internal security needs; the current period is one of rationalization of spending and a reorientation toward external defense. The 2017 defense budget received a 2 percent annual increase to support the peace process with the FARC, replace aging equipment, build police stations, and upgrade communications equipment. Of the USD $10.2 billion budget (approximately 13.1 percent of the Colombian government budget), only 3 percent is directed toward the procurement of new systems, with the balance tied to operations, payroll, and pensions.[25] Preferential purchases also help support defense industries. Colombian Law N. 816, 2003, created a margin of 10 percent and 20 percent for national goods or services to encourage procurement through domestic industries. Under the Colombia-U.S. Free Trade Agreement, goods procured from the United States are treated as if of national origin; overall products originating from the U.S. account for about half of Colombia's strategic arsenal.[26]

From autonomy to production under budget constraints

Our four Latin American cases evidence different responses to the defense trilemma. Table 3 summarizes defense production capabilities over our four countries in the region. As introduced above in Table 1, Brazil has historically focused on autonomous capabilities. Despite budget constraints, it has continued to focus on the development of national capabilities. This strategic posture and a larger economy have resulted in stronger autonomous production across a mix of public and private producers. Chile's profile reflects the diametrical position: externally oriented, with smaller and larger state-controlled enterprises. Argentina is in the middle; its geographic isolation and political distance from military spending has limited domestic capabilities. Colombia's fifty-year civil war created external partners; as it now pivots to regional threats, it is embracing stronger relationships with international producers. Let us turn to consider distinctive elements of each case. Despite the difference in autonomy and economic resources, we find that all four nations are looking to the global value chain to expand production.

Brazil's priority on autonomy of action has shifted under economic constraints. Although the budget ceiling hasn't fundamentally altered its ambitious primary strategic programs—developing nuclear-submarine capabilities, strengthening naval presence in the South Atlantic, expanding sophisticated terrestrial abilities (especially in the Amazon), and improved air abilities (evidenced in the Gripen fighter jet program)—it has slowed down the rate of acquisition. There has also been a subtler switch in its defense-industrial ambitions: a move toward technological autonomy over production independence. That is, rather than retain the capabilities to produce systems within national supply chains, investments are targeted toward maintaining access to the knowledge of how to produce. Technological reach has come to overshadow productive capacity. This capabilities approach is consistent with other medium-sized defense producers; very few outside China, Russia, and the U.S. can support national production. The Brazilian industry now engages "technologies that are domestically mastered."[27] Rather than direct ownership (with the exception of the small munitions firm IMBEL), Brazil incentivizes this production through a margin of preference in acquisitions of 25 percent to promote national development.[28] The National Defense Strategy (NDS) denotes Brazilian firms as "strategic: to qualify the national defense industry so that it conquers the necessary autonomy in indispensable technologies to defense purposes." With preferences in purchases, these firms also become attractive partners to foreign producers looking for a foothold in the Brazilian market. The earlier concept of self-reliance on domestic sources for equipment has been reframed to emphasize technological superiority through research and development.[29] Unlike the old paradigm of needing to export to create economies of scale, today's strategy prioritizes defense-related industrial capabilities. Brazil is reluctantly embracing integration in the global value chain that brings the technology crucial to continued strategic capabilities.

Brazilian firms are also developing domestic alliances to operate internationally. Embraer, as a major systems integrator, has spurred the development of a set of smaller providers such as Akaer solutions that works with Brazilian Avibras, Pratt Whitney Boeing Helibras, Ael, Elbit, and the Brazilian Aerospace Technical Center, CTA. The integration work carried out by Akaer for the Saab-Embraer Gripen fighter-aircraft project provides an example of a higher value-chain product than simple raw-material exports. The project was extremely successful for Akaer, resulting in the augmentation of its work force from 70 to 300 employees and significant investment in the company.[30]

Some successful firms are targets for takeover: For example, the company responsible for the REMAX automated weapon system, Ares, was sold to the Israeli firm Elbit (despite maintaining 100 percent Brazilian army intellectual property rights to the product). The Swiss multinational Saab, in partnership with Embraer, is promoting technological development in areas such as São Bernardo, where Saab invested in the creation of a parts subsidiary along with CISB (the Swiss-Brazilian Center of Research and Innovation) as part of the offset in the purchase of the Gripen strike fighter.[31] Brazil also utilized offsets with the German KMW's Santa Maria, RS plant; KMW agreed to use local suppliers and create economic/industrial relationships, such as with the Federal University of Santa Maria for research. Italian truck manufacturer IVECO followed a similar bid in the Guarani armored-vehicle project when it signed an agreement for nationalization index of 60 percent at its Sete Lagoas plant. In these projects, Brazil imported know-how, creating linkages and capacity for Brazilian firms to ultimately replace foreign companies.

Chile is the counterpoint to Brazil's model of global integration production. The Chilean forces, though the most technologically advanced in Latin America, are small in numbers and rely heavily on the "buy off-the-shelf" (BOTS) procurement strategy for advanced products rather than on developing capabilities needed for defense-procurement independence. MOTS (military off-the-shelf) purchases have several advantages. Cost is known (no need to plan for overruns) and acquisition is faster. Users may also benefit from the experience of other forces, potentially accessing training; for paired users, interoperability is enhanced.[32]

The role of Chilean firms such as Enaer, Asmar, and Famae is largely to provide maintenance to the armed forces. The importance of this, however, should not be underestimated. During the 20–30-year lifespan of a major weapons platform, the communications and electronics may undergo several generations of change. Maintenance is therefore more than changing oil; rather, it is working with suppliers to maintain modern warfare capabilities. The Chilean government has put a premium on technologically advanced hardware, with its firms working to retain a technological edge.

The linkages in a BOTS + maintenance model are thinner than in integrated production. Beyond replacement parts, the upgrades tend to be more software-systems changes over full production overhaul. Another drawback of the BOTS method is that if supplier nations are not diversified enough, security autonomy is sacrificed due to the fact that the exporting countries hold leverage over the purchaser. In the unlikely event that Chile's national interests were to conflict with those of the United States, all arms purchases between the two nations could be halted, and the Chilean fleet of vehicles of American origin would be irreplaceable/irreparable (in the absence of any tech transfers). Mitigating this is a wide array of second-tier defense firms that work with nations to upgrade capabilities. The Israelis, for example, are agile collaborators in upgrading electronics and communication systems. With multiple suppliers on their own production chain, a purchasing nation is rarely left isolated—especially one as globally integrated as Chile.

In contrast to Brazilian naval acquisition, all large vessels of the Chilean navy are imported. Although Chile did not create any large-scale linkages through its naval programs, the nation still fields the most capable fleet in the area. The development of an offshore patrol boat is an exception to the Chilean maintenance focus. The Chilean naval shipyard Asmar has taken initiative in technology transfers, buying a design from German Fassmer for domestic production, with export potential already realized (sold to Iceland). However, this transfer was only on the OPV scale and pales in comparison to the Brazilian PROSUB project. Asmar relies on its external sales to generate profits for reinvestment. Its maintenance and upgrade capabilities are widely sought by international partners in both the military and civilian spheres. Chile prefers to address domestic security issues, such as transnational crime and smuggling, with a coastal defense force, rather than seek the ability to create a long-range naval force that would allow for autonomous defense of interests abroad. Initiative has been taken to utilize local production, but thus far it has remained on a small scale and not extended to truly advanced technologies that would provide for lucrative export and power projection.

The Chilean army is one of the most technically advanced in the region, and is even equipped with a higher quantity and quality of armored corps than Brazil, with over 300 tanks to Brazil's 219. The majority of the hardware, especially the most advanced, has been purchased from foreign makers. Furthermore, the most potent challenge facing the Chilean high command is the aging of its fleet of vehicles (even the Leopard 2s are in desperate need of modernization) and the increasing difficulty in finding replacement parts for maintaining the old systems. The Chileans are presented the twofold challenge of not only developing a modernization strategy, but also a procurement strategy that will allow for continued maintenance in the longer run. For example, a 2011 contract with BAE Systems for the modernization of the M-109s, worth $15.6 million, saw twelve of the vehicles modernized and significantly overhauled, but the process itself would take place at BAE Systems locations in the United States, rather than utilizing domestic production infrastructures in Chile.

Chile chose to prioritize a more limited type of joint venture, specifically in the realm of maintenance of existing systems. However, Chile has utilized smaller-scale partnerships to allow for domestic dominance of maintenance regimes. For example, the state-owned FAMAE is currently responsible for the maintenance of Chilean Leopards and other armored vehicles, providing repairs and logistical support for the mechanized units. FAMAE closed an agreement with the German firm Diehl Remscheid for a technology transfer regarding tracks for the Leopard tanks, allowing Chile to domestically provide for the needs of its tank corps without the need to turn to sources abroad for the resolution of common problems. With such agreements, Chilean firms are tasked with the responsibility for systems the military purchases, created linkages, though more limited, with the local economy.

With the exception of its trainer aircraft the T-35 Pillan, the Chilean Air Force also largely relies on a BOTS strategy.[33] ENAER has produced the T-35 Pillan trainer for export to various regional countries, and ENAER further carries out maintenance for its products in foreign markets.[34] ENAER provides servicing (including part production, maintenance, and overhauls) for not only the Chilean Air Force, but also that of Colombia, Ecuador, Uruguay, and Bangladesh. Furthermore, Eurocopter Chile serves as the firm's distribution hub for the region, providing products, services, and support for Chile, Argentina, Peru, Bolivia, and Uruguay.[35] While Chile does not have the same ambitious vision as Brazil in the aviation sector, Chilean firms, especially ENAER, have found a profitable regional niche in lower levels of the global value chain such as servicing and part production.

Colombia is a bit of a hybrid of Brazil and Chile. Its firms to date have largely been engaged in the maintenance and modernization goals of Chile—but looking forward it appears to be opening its producers, especially in armored vehicles and ships, to more ambitious development. Indumil's exports increased 71.5 percent in 2016 over the previous year; 2017 was headed for a similar gain.[36] The nation appears able to leverage its past experience in engaged combat to work with regional militaries on upgrading capabilities. Unlike Brazil (and much like Chile), the firms are lodged within the state as autonomous enterprises. This largely means that they must generate their own revenues to cover costs, and not be dependent on federal budget outlays. Colombia's domestic linkages are less robust than those of Brazil, necessitating the import of subsystems. But as a strong political and economic partner of the United States, it faces fewer obstacles under ITAR, the U.S. export control regime for military products.

The interesting movements in the Argentine defense industry are taking place at the edges of defense, security, and environment. The traditional defense providers Fábrica Argentina de Aviones (FAdeA), Fabricaciones Militares, and the Argentine Naval Industrial Complex (CINAR) have been severely debilitated under budgetary pressures. The aircraft facilities in Cordoba leased under concession to the American Lockheed in 1995 was returned to the government ownership in 2009. The defense ministry now holds 99 percent of FAdeA's shares; its workforce of 1,000 (down from its peak of 9,000) is mostly engaged in maintenance.

Argentina's strong technological base expresses itself more strongly in semiautonomous and private firms outside the traditional defense providers. Its highly globalized production reflects the new outward orientation of President Macri. INVAP, a government firm that survives off-budget on its own earnings, is aggressively penetrating a variety of sectors: satellite, nuclear, wind, solar energy. It operates as a local integrator of subsystems sold primarily on the global market.[37] Private Nostromo Defensa is investing in UAVs—key instruments in environmental protection. Investment in the sector is supported by CITEDEF (Institute of Scientific and Technical Research for Defense) and Law N. 25.551, 2001, preferences goods and services of national origin whenever prices are equal to or lower than the foreign plus a band of 5–7 percent.[38]

Tensions along the trilemma

The armament strategies of the four nations respond to their orientation on the defense trilemma. Brazil, with autonomy as its primary objective, is on a far more expensive and resource-intensive course, to support its global reach. But the turbulent state of Brazilian politics, wracked with the impeachment of Dilma Roussef in 2016 and high-profile government scandals, makes the future of Brazilian military programs unpredictable. The market-oriented government of acting president Michel Temer encourages increased globalization over internal defense-industrial policy—but the direction after the 2018 election is uncertain. The Chileans, content with a more limited position in global politics, engage in global value chains from the modest demands of maintenance, neglecting security autonomy. Colombia's close ties with the United States and its substantial security expertise from its civil war position its peacetime trajectory as deeply rooted in the global defense-industrial chain. Argentina, looking to rectify decades of neglect in military systems, will also turn toward global partners. Macri's market approaches along with significant budget pressures are pushing firms toward the external market to promote economies of scale. For all, the economic constraints in the face of the rising costs of technology push firms to the global value chain.

Regional cooperation and the defense industry

One release from the constraining nature of the trilemma would be to conceptualize security on a regional level. South American elites understand that security cooperation is crucial for enhancing state capacities to deal with regional threats, particularly growing criminality; maintain peace and security; reproduce the image of a peaceful region; and enhance participation in international security mechanisms, such as peace operations. The region has invested in considerable confidence-building measures that might act as a foundation for cooperation. We turn to recap this history of regional security cooperation, coordination, and common socialization among regional military establishments as a possible exit from the trilemma.

Although defense integration in the region may seem improbable, advances have already taken place. One of the most important geopolitical changes in South America in the 1990s was the move from intense rivalry between Argentina and Brazil to regional cooperation in the security and defense areas. Re-democratized states created the Argentine-Brazilian Agency for Accounting and Control of Nuclear Materials (ABACC) in 1991, to apply full-scope safeguards to all nuclear activities covering all nuclear materials in both countries, and the Quadripartite Agreement (Brazil, Argentina, ABACC, IAEA) was signed, which placed all nuclear installations in both countries under the supervision of the IAEA. The ABACC, which verifies both countries' pledges to use nuclear energy for exclusively peaceful purposes, is considered a model of success in terms of confidence building and nonproliferation.

Peace operations have offered militaries unique opportunities to develop collective operational experience; MINUSTAH, the UN operation in Haiti involving Brazilian, Chilean, Bolivian, and Peruvian soldiers, has been particularly important. Collective military training is a further expression and crucial reproduction mechanism of regional interaction. In 2016 alone, South Americans took part in fifteen different multilateral exercises, with two of these involving only Latin American forces.[39] South American air forces performed several joint aerial-combat training exercises, including Cruzex (Exercício Cruzeiro do Sul) hosted by the Brazil, Salitre (Saltpeter) hosted by the Chile, and Ceibo (Erythrina crista-galli flower) hosted by Argentina.

The Conference of Defense Ministers of the Americas was part of a broader attempt to revitalize the Inter-American System in the 1990s; it is a highly institutionalized confidence-building mechanism allowing for the meeting of thirty-four ministers on a biannual basis. Since the 1990s, the Organization of American States has also organized and sponsored conferences on confidence- and security-building measures designed to strengthen military-to-military relations, deal with historic rivalries, and create an environment that permits the governments of the region to modernize defense forces without triggering tensions between them or leading to an arms race.

UNASUR emerged from a regional process since the first meeting in Brasilia in 2000 that defined needs and potential for hemispheric cooperation. UNASUR offered a vision of a South American region with specific needs and potential. [40] The council aims to generate a "South American defense identity," "consolidate South America as a zone of peace," and stimulate defense cooperation. UNASUR's Defense Council promoted confidence building in the region, including a common methodology for the assessment of military spending and procedures. Since 2010, the council has created mechanisms for coordination of peace operation activities. This progress, however, was stalled, as the organization has been deeply impacted by the Venezuelan crisis and the division created among countries in the region over appropriate steps. Ernesto Samper, general secretary between 2014 and 2017, has not yet been replaced. In April 2018, six countries (Argentina, Brazil, Chile, Colombia, Paraguay, and Peru) decided to temporarily leave the organization.

UNASUR's Defense Council is a collaborative space where a common defense industry project might be devised.[41] The council created a system of information on the region's defense industry, has kept track of defense fairs, and organized seminars on regional security needs. The *South America Defense Observatory* is published monthly and the *South American Registry of Defense Spending* is published annually. One of the specific objectives of UNASUR's Defense Council is to promote interchange and cooperation in the defense-industry arena;[42] its plan identifies possible forms of cooperation in research, technology transfer, and technical cooperation.

Although these defense-industry plans have not yet come to fruition, the intense interaction between military establishments is a crucial social base for further cooperation in the defense-industry sphere. Two institutions have been playing a central role in creating a common culture and generating a common expertise in the field of defense. In 2011 the Center of Strategic Studies on Defense was launched in Buenos Aires. The work plan for 2017 included interoperability of the defense forces in the region.[43] The center has begun preliminary work, embodied in

South America 2025, which identifies regional security and defense potential, opportunities, challenges, and possible risks. In April 2015, the South American Defense College under the UNASUR umbrella was inaugurated in Quito; its mission is to serve as a think tank, formulate a coherent South American view of defense policies, and coordinate with other military and academic centers. The college's research agenda includes cyber defense, strategic vision, and the development of a common military doctrine for the region. This regional socialization may foster the development of a South American defense embedded in a coordinated military network.

Before UNASUR was put on pause due to the Venezuela crisis, the organization was stewarding three projects. One objective was to develop a single-platform training system attuned to South American training-aircraft needs. The IA-73 UNASUR I project included Argentina, Brazil, Ecuador, and Venezuela; it planned to start production of 92 aircraft in 2020 divided over 50 in Argentina, 24 in Venezuela, and 18 in Ecuador.[44] Brazil and Argentina reached an initial agreement on the terms of Argentina's participation in the design and production through FAdeA (Fábrica Argentina de Aviones). In 2014, a new firm called UNASUR Aereo was created through firms in Argentina (FAdeA), Brasil (NOVAER, AVIONCIF y AKAER), Venezuela (CAVIM), and Ecuador (DIAF). This project, however, has been tabled. In addition to the crisis dividing UNASUR, it became difficult for national militaries to appropriate fiscal resources that would flow to extra-national partners.[45]

The private sphere holds more promise for regional integration. Argentina, Brazil, Chile, Colombia, and Uruguay are also partners in a more advanced tactical transport plan being developed by the Brazilian aviation giant Embraer. Embraer KC-390 is a medium-size, twin-engine, jet-powered military transport aircraft capable of aerial refueling. Embraer's KC-390 tactical transport plane project has been securing international partners as part of a strategy to take on bigger rivals, including Lockheed Martin. Embraer sees its KC-390 filling the gap left by a global phasing out of Lockheed Martin's C-130 Hercules. Embraer as an integrator is working with partner countries to produce parts and subsystems. Regional air forces plan to purchase the KC390—the benefit for Embraer as it facilitates technological transfer in the region. The KC-390 has demonstrated that it can refuel low-speed aircraft, such as helicopters and transport aircraft. Despite a crash in test flights in May 2018, The Brazilian air force intends to bring the KC-390 to initial operating capability in late 2018.[46]

Shared environmental and border concerns have also led to collaboration. Brazil and Argentina have been collaborating in the space and nuclear fields since the 1990s; although these endeavors do not involve the defense industry, they constitute a base for further cooperation in science and technology development. Brazil and Argentina successfully carried out their first joint space mission in December 2007.[47] A product of a 1998 bilateral agreement for space cooperation, the Angicos Operation consisted of the launch from Brazil of a suborbital sounding rocket carrying microgravity experiments from both Brazil and Argentina. Since 2010, Argentina's CONAE (comissão nacional de atividades espaciais) and Brazil's INPE (instituto nacional de pesquisas espaciais) have been developing Sabiá-Mar, a satellite for the observation of the oceans.

Collaboration, of course, has limitations. More partners can lead to greater production complexity, increasing transactions costs and project-management overhead. Nations may have different strategic needs. More partner nations add to transaction costs by increasing the complexity of procurement, project management, and the industrial supply-side arrangements. Work-sharing becomes more complex and costlier with more nations. A smaller number of players is less complex; bilateral collaborations may therefore offer the best value for money.[48] As weighed against high R&D costs, however, regional cooperation is a promising mechanism to appropriate economies of scale. As militaries increase regional interaction, production may follow, loosening the economic constraints in the defense trilemma. With national strategies increasingly focused on regional goals of addressing illicit trafficking, violence, and the dislocations created by climate change, regional production approaches could well align with security needs.

Acknowledgments

This article was researched with the support of CNPq (National Council for Scientific and Technological Development- Brazilian government) and FAPERJ (Foundation for the Support of Research of the state of Rio de Janeiro) as well as the Grossman Chair at Colby College.

Notes

1. Richard A. Bitzinger, "Chapter 2: Transition and Readjustment in Second-Tier Defence Industries: Five Case Studies," *The Adelphi Papers* 43, no. 356 (2003): 39–62, https://doi.org/10.1080/714027875.
2. Richard A. Bitzinger, "New Ways of Thinking about the Global Arms Industry: Dealing with 'Limited Autarky,'" Strategic Insight (Barton: Australian Strategic Policy Institute [ASPI], November 5, 2015).
3. Stephanie G. Neuman, "Power, Influence and Hierarchy: Defence Industries in a Unipolar World," *Defence and Peace Economics* 21, no. 1 (2010): 105–134, https://doi.org/10.1080/10242690903105398.
4. Marc R DeVore, "Arms Production in the Global Village: Options for Adapting to Defense-Industrial Globalization," *Security Studies* 22, no. 3 (2013): 532–572.
5. Keith Hartley, "The Economics of Smart Defense," *Connections: The Quarterly Journal* 12, no. 3 (2013): 1–8, http://dx.doi.org/10.11610/Connections.12.3.01.
6. Stephen Brooks, *Producing Security: Multinational Corporations, Globalization, and the Changing Calculus of Conflict* (Princeton, NJ: Princeton University Press, 2005).
7. Masako Ikegami, "The End of a 'National' Defence Industry? Impacts of Globalization on the Swedish Defence Industry," *Scandinavian Journal of History* 38, no. 4 (2013): 436–57, https://doi.org/10.1080/03468755.2013.823536.
8. Patrice Franko, "The Defense Acquisition Trilemma: The Case of Brazil," *Strategic Forum* (Washington, DC: Institute for National Security Studies [INSS], January 2014), http://ndupress.ndu.edu/Media/News/News-Article-View/Article/718116/the-defense-acquisition-trilemma-the-case-of-brazil/; Jose Carlos Albano Amarante and Patrice Franko, "Defense Transformation in Latin America: Will It Transform the Technological Base?" *Democracy and Security* 13, no. 3 (2017): 173–95, https://doi.org/10.1080/17419166.2017.1290527.
9. DeVore, "Arms Production in the Global Village."
10. Brazil's White Paper of 2012 is under revision but has not been released by Congress.
11. Monica Herz, Layla Dawood, and Victor Coutinho Lage, "The Defense-Development Nexus: Brazilian Nuclear Policy under the Workers' Party Administrations," *Revista Brasileira de Política Internacional* 61, no. 1 (2018): 1–19, https://doi.org/10.1590/0034-7329201800105; Rafael Duarte Villa, "Brazilian Hybrid Security in South America," *Revista Brasileira de Política Internacional* 60, no. 2 (2017): 1–22, https://doi.org/10.1590/0034-7329201700203.
12. Joaquín Fermandois, "Pragmatism, Ideology, and Tradition in Chilean Foreign Policy Since 1990 Latin American Foreign Policies," in *Latin American Foreign Policies*, edited by Gian Luca Gardini and Peter Lambert (New York: Palgrave, 2011), 35–52; Miguel Navarro Meza, "La Conduccion Politica de La Defensa: Algunas Consisderaciones Politicas y Juridicas," in *Desafíos de La Seguridad y Defensa En El Mundo Contemporáneo*, vol. 39 (Academia Nacional de Estudios Políticos y Estratégicos [ANEPE], 2016), 117–52.
13. Jorge Battaglino, "The Politics of Defense Revival in Argentina," *Defense & Security Analysis* 29, no. 1 (2013): 3–15, https://doi.org/10.1080/14751798.2013.760251; Mark P. Jones, "Strategic Posture Review: Argentina," *World Politics Review*, March 15, 2011, www.worldpoliticsreview.com/articles/8191/strategic-posture-review-argentina.
14. Michael Martelle, "Colombian Defense After FARC," *Offiziere.ch*, May 24, 2017, www.offiziere.ch/?p=30199; Geraldine Cook, "Colombian Armed Forces Prepare to Take on New Security Challenges," *Dialogo Americas*, August 22, 2016, https://dialogo-americas.com/en/articles/colombian-armed-forces-prepare-take-new-security-challenges.
15. *SIPRI Yearbook 2017: Armaments, Disarmament and International Security*, SIPRI Yearbook Series (Oxford, New York: Oxford University Press, 2017).
16. Thomas Scheetz, "El Impacto de La Crisis Financiera En El Gasto Militar Sudamericano," *Tecnología militar* 34, no. Extra 5 (2012): 8–10; no data for Colombia.
17. Vitelio Marcos Brustolin, "Dimensões e Aplicações do Orçamento de Defesa do Brasil/Dimensions and Executions of the Defense Budget of Brazil," *Mural Internacional* 5, no. 1 (2013): 38–45, https://doi.org/10.12957/rmi.2014.7574.
18. Scheetz, "El Impacto de La Crisis Financiera en el Gasto Militar Sudamericano."

19. "O Ministério Da Defesa No Sumário Executivo Do Document—Cenário Defesa 2020–2039," *DefesaNet,* January 21, 2018, www.defesanet.com.br/bid/noticia/28224/Cenario-Defesa-2020-2039—Orcamento-limitado-por-teto-pode-deixar-Forcas-Armadas-mais-obsoletas-e-preocupa-militares-/.
20. Thomas Scheetz, "O Ministério Da Defesa No Sumário Executivo Do Documento 'Cenário de Defesa 2020–2039,'" *Tecnología militar,* December 1, 2014, www.defesanet.com.br/bid/noticia/28224/Cenario-Defesa-2020-2039—Orcamento-limitado-por-teto-pode-deixar-Forcas-Armadas-mais-obsoletas-e-preocupa-militares-/.
21. The Economist, "New Thinking on the Armed Forces after Argentina Loses a Submarine," *The Economist,* December 2, 2017, www.economist.com/news/americas/21731879-waste-corruption-and-austerity-plague-countrys-army-navy-and-air-force-new-thinking.
22. *SIPRI Yearbook 2017.*
23. *Global Security,* "Argentina—Military Spending," April 30, 2017, www.globalsecurity.org/military/world/argentina/budget.htm.
24. FIDAE (Feria Internacional del Aire y del Espacio), April 2018. Conversations with firm representatives.
25. "Colombia—Defense," *Colombia Country Commercial Guide,* July 31, 2017, www.export.gov/article?id=Colombia-Defense.
26. "Colombia— Defense."
27. Flávia de Holanda Schmidt Squeff and Lucas Rocha Soares de Assis, "The Defense Industry in Brazil: Characteristics and Involvement of Supplier Firms," Discussion Paper (Brasilia: Instituto de Pesquisa Econômica Aplicada (IPEA), January 2014), www.en.ipea.gov.br/agencia/images/stories/PDFs/TDs/ingles/dp_195.pdf.
28. Ibid.
29. Ibid.
30. FIDAE, April 2018. Conversations with firm representatives.
31. "Saab Vai Instalar Fábrica de Componentes No Bairro Cooperativa Em São Bernardo," *DefesaNet,* April 25, 2018, twww.defesanet.com.br/br_se/noticia/29107/Saab-vai-instalar-fabrica-de-componentes-no-bairro-Cooperativa-em-Sao-Bernardo/.
32. Andrew Davies and Peter Layton, "We'll Have Six of Them and Four of Those: Off-the-Shelf Procurement and Its Strategic Implications," Special Report (Burton: ASPI, November 24, 2009), https://www.aspi.org.au/report/special-report-issue-25-well-have-six-them-and-four-those-shelf-procurement-and-its.
33. Ibid.
34. Dieter Hanel, "The Defense Industry in Latin America," *Military Technology* 3 (2010):22.
35. Ibid.
36. Yudy Alexandra Garcia Montealegre, "El Comercio Electrónico Como Herramienta Para Fortalecer Las Dinámicas Comerciales de La Industria Militar a Nivel Global: A Partir de La Caracterización de Las Industrias de Colombia, Brasil y Estados Unidos" (Universidad Militar Nueva Granada, 2017), https://repository.unimilitar.edu.co/bitstream/10654/16633/3/Garc%c3%adaMontealegreYudyAlexandra2017.pdf.
37. FIDAE, April 2018. Conversations with firm representatives.
38. Brazilian Government, n.d., www.planalto.gov.br/ccivil_03/_Ato2007-2010/2010/Exm/EMI-104-MP-MF-MEC-MCT-MPV-495-10.
39. Marcela Donadio, *A Comparative Atlas of Defence in Latin America and Caribbean* (Beunos Aires: RESDAL, 2010), www.resdal.org/atlas/atlas-completo2010-ingles.pdf; Kai Michael Kenkel, "Multilateralism and Concepts of Security in South America," *International Studies Review* 17, no. 1 (2015): 150–52, https://doi.org/10.1111/misr.12192.
40. Oscar Medeiros Filho, "A South American Defence Structure: Problems and Prospects," *Contexto Internacional* 39, no. 3 (December 2017): 673–89; T. G. Galvão, "América do Sul: Construção pela reinvenção (2000–2008)." *Revista Brasileira de Política Internacional* 52, no. 2, (2009): 63–80.
41. J. Battaglino, "Defence in a Post-Hegemonic Regional Agenda: The Case of the South American Defence Council," in *The Rise of Post-Hegemonic Regionalism: the Case of Latin America,* edited by P. Riggirozzi and D. Tussie (London: Springer, 2012); B. Weiffen, L. Wehner, & D. Nolte, "Overlapping Regional Security Institutions in South America: The Case of OAS and UNASUR." *International Area Studies Review* 16, no. 4 (2013): 370–389.
42. "Estatuto Do Conselho de Defesa Sul-Americano," 2017, www.defesa.gov.br/arquivos/relacoes_internacionais/unasul/normativa_unasul_2017.pdf.
43. CEEDCDS, 2017, www.ceedcds.org.ar/Espanol/03-Planes_de_Trabajo/PLAN-TRABAJO-2017.pdf.
44. Villa, "Brazilian Hybrid Security in South America," 11.
45. FIDAE, April 2018. Conversations with firm representatives.
46. "O Ministério da Defesa no sumário executivo do document."

47. Robert C. Harding, "Emerging Space Powers of Latin America: Argentina and Brazil," in *Yearbook on Space Policy 2012/2013*, edited by Cenan Al-Ekabi et al., *Yearbook on Space Policy* (Springer, Vienna, 2015), 221–31, https://doi.org/10.1007/978-3-7091-1827-6_6.
48. Derek Braddon and Keith Hartley, "More for Less? Exploring the Economic Dimensions of Multilateral Collaboration in Military Aerospace Projects," *Defense Studies and Resource Management*, no. 2 (2013): 2–12, https://doi.org/10.4172/2324-9315.1000110.

The puzzle: Multi-vector foreign policy and defense industrialization in Central Asia

Çağlar Kurç

ABSTRACT

The multi-vector policy adopted by the Central Asian countries provides a basis for a flexible approach in their relations with competing international actors to acquire payoffs from economic and military affiliations or partnerships. Consequently, we expect that the defense-industrialization and procurement practices in the region would follow a similar path. However, a closer look reveals that Russia is still the dominant actor in the security and defense-industrial relations in the region. This article argues that perceived threats to regime security, the patrimonial system of rule, and weak industrial bases push Central Asian countries toward Russia as well as hindering the development of capable defense industry.

Introduction

Following their independence, Central Asian countries adopted the multi-vector foreign policy, which has become a guiding principle of their foreign, economic, and security relations. Although each state implemented their own versions of multi-vectorism, according to the official discourse, it aims to balance Russian influence through establishing relations with different international actors based on a non-ideological and pragmatic basis to pursue economic and security benefits. Departing from the multi-vector principle, we expect that the Central Asian countries would be motivated to pursue defense industrialization to balance the influence of Russia, especially the ones that have natural resources and some industrial base.

For emerging countries, the goal of an independent foreign policy is one of the core motivations behind defense industrialization. Dependency on foreign suppliers enables the supplier state to have control over both the military capabilities of the recipient military power and its foreign policy[1] by controlling the supply of weapons systems and technologies. The supplier state, therefore, has the ability to shape the recipient state's foreign policy through arms embargoes and restrictions on the usage of supplied weapons systems.[2] Consequently, defense industrialization becomes a tool for making substitute weapon systems, indigenous systems, accessing high-technology systems through both domestic and collaborative research and development (R&D), and decreasing the influence of supplier states while enabling a guaranteed supply of arms.[3] At the outset, despite variance in the processes and desires, the defense-industrial and procurement policies of Central Asian countries, except for Tajikistan, resemble the other emerging countries. However, a closer investigation reveals that Russia is still an important partner in defense-industrial relations and the industrialization process is unlikely to challenge Russia's presence in this sector.

The transformation of the global defense market and the increased number of suppliers and partners who are willing to invest should have eased establishing defense-industrial relations[4] with many different suppliers. However, the main investment in the Central Asian defense industries predominantly comes from Russia, even for Kazakhstan, which was able to draw foreign direct investments and establish partnerships with many different actors. Therefore, defense-industrialization and procurement practices in Central Asia present a puzzle. How could we explain the dissonance between the multi-vector policy and Russia's dominance in Central Asian defense industries?

This article argues that multi-vector foreign policy is primarily geared toward regime survival rather than construct an overall balance in all policy areas. The perceived threats to regime security, both from terrorist groups and democratization moves, push Central Asian countries closer to Russia, thus de-linking defense industrialization and security policies from the foreign policy desire to balance Russia. Second, the patrimonial system of rule and weak industrial bases, which still reflect the old Soviet structures, hinder the development of sustainable defense industries. In the end, defense industrialization is secondary to regime-security concerns in Central Asian countries.

Multi-vector foreign policy as a survival strategy

When independence came, Central Asian countries, as Martha Brill Olcott argues, were catapulted to independence.[5] These states were lacking the "necessary fiscal, military, political, or economic framework to deal with this newly gained status of independence."[6] As Olcott contends, "technological and diplomatic expertise was sorely lacking in these new states."[7] For example, at the time of independence Central Asian states had only a handful of trained senior diplomats, most of whom worked in the foreign ministry of the Soviet Union.[8] However, technical issues aside, the most pressing issues for Central Asian ruling elites, many of whom rose to power through community party ranks (with the exception of Kyrgyzstan's Askar Akaev), are to maintain power, entrench one-party patrimonial systems, and eliminate threats to their authority.[9]

The political void was filled by both Soviet informal networks and Central Asian clan politics. During the Soviet times, the region was highly integrated with the union-wide economic system and the region's ruling elites enjoyed spoils of the informal patronage networks within the Soviet system.[10] To maintain their rule, Central Asian rulers had to restructure their economies and reap the benefits from Western assistance, thereby keeping power through using state resources for private gain, especially for the ruling elite, amassing personal fortunes and sustaining loyalties through informal patronage and distributive networks.[11] To this end, "presidents use their position to engage in corruption, asset-stripping, and nepotism with impunity, often making their decisions under the guise of using a strong hand to further the 'national interest.'"[12] The formulation of the foreign policy, therefore, was based on the interests of the ruling elites and conceptualized in "multi-vectorism."

All Central Asian countries adopted their version of multi-vector foreign policy as a survival strategy but presented it as an attempt at self-reliance. Kazakhstan is one of the first states to pursue and name its policy a "multi-vector" foreign policy. Uzbekistan defined its foreign policy around the principle of *musqallik*, which aims for "a sort of genuine independence through legal, economic and cultural forms of non-dependency,"[13] with the future goal of becoming a "great state."[14] Turkmenistan adopted a strict neutrality, and, thus, refuses to join any sort of alliance or union schemes. Kyrgyzstan, while seeking to have cooperative relations with Russia, also seeks good relations with neighboring countries and other external partners based on the principle of equality and mutual respect.[15] Tajikistan embraced an "open door" policy that seeks friendly relations with all countries based on reciprocal respect, equality, and mutually beneficial cooperation.[16] In simple terms, multi-vector foreign policy is about developing relations that are based on non-ideological and pragmatic foundations, which are shaped by the interplay of external and domestic dynamics, to foster short- or long-term benefits.[17]

Multi-vector foreign policy opens up an avenue by which states pursue flexibility in their relations to acquire payoffs from economic and military affiliations or partnerships with competing international actors in the region.[18] Such behavior is highly visible in Central Asian state behavior, while each state adopts its own version the multi-vector foreign policy depending on its unique weaknesses and strengths, natural resources, international interests, domestic structures, and security problems.

In general, Central Asian rulers initially tended to formulate their foreign policy behaviors in terms of prevailing norms and practices during the 1990s, mainly to acquire economic benefits from cooperating with Western countries and companies as the issue of NATO expansion became the priority, while Russia was distracted and distanced from the region. For states that had natural resources, the quickest way to acquire wealth was cooperating with the West. As Anna Matveeva states, the "desire to cooperate with the West… was determined in large part by the need to secure financial assistance and investment in order to develop the natural resources."[19] For example, Kazakhstan has in-depth cooperation with Western institutions such as NATO, the European Union, and the Organization for Security and Cooperation in Europe (OSCE), as well as good relations with the Collective Security Treaty Organization (CSTO), Shanghai Cooperation Organization (SCO), and Eurasian Economic Union (EEU). Yet, the international actor's level of interest determines what can be achieved and how it could be achieved in the foreign, economic, and security activities of the Central Asian states.

The intensification of U.S., Russian, and Chinese engagement in the 2000s empowered regional elites to leverage Central Asia's geopolitical position more to their advantage.[20] This is mainly because the acquisition of economic and security benefits through international cooperation enables state elites to have control over the domestic population.[21] The changes in the international system and the major-actor interests in the region facilitated "pick-and-choose" strategies and band-wagoning-for-profit policies.[22] Driven by the desire to secure and sustain the regime, the concept of multi-vectorism provided the basis and ability to play off the external powers against one another, or finding a balance between Russia and China, and between these actors and Western states and institutions.[23] For example, Turkmenistan sought to diversify its exports options and draw foreign investments. However, it showed little interest in companies associated with the Nabucco project, which aimed to diversify European natural-gas suppliers. In practice, Turkmenistan's export strategy showed a clear preference to China.[24] Such preference is the main result of both China's increasing economic power and the failures of Western-initiated projects. China uses its economic potential and the demand for energy to lure Central Asian countries into bilateral cooperation that also includes regional trade and joint investments.[25] Another example is Uzbekistan's erratic foreign policy behavior in establishing partnerships. It reorients its alignment when one alliance presents greater benefit at little or no cost.[26] Uzbekistan, in cooperation with Georgia, Ukraine, Azerbaijan, and Moldova, formed GUUAM in 1999 for boosting economic and security cooperation with the Western alliance.[27] However, relations with the West, which were established to gain access to investments and aid, soured over the U.S. decision to suspend aid following the Andijon crisis and led to realignment with Russia.[28] In the end, foreign policy behaviors are manifestations of Central Asian ruling elites' survival strategies. However, as we will discuss below, multi-vectorism does not necessarily lead to a balancing of all actors in every policy issue or a true attempt for self-reliance.

The effect of governance and overall economy on state behavior

Under the Soviet Union, the economies of Central Asia were integrated into the other constituent states and the central planning of Moscow. Within the integrated all-union economic system, production in the Central Asian states was based on monoculture of cotton and various heavy industrial projects, but mineral wealth remained largely underdeveloped. Following the collapse of the Soviet Union, Central Asian countries were cut off from their vital supply chains and left with industries that cannot operate outside the all-union system. Central Asian countries embarked on restructuring of their economies, though each has followed a different path. Kazakhstan initially focused on the country's energy resources for economic restructuring. This strategy is aimed at decreasing the political significance of former Russian Soviet elites, who derived their power from their role in the former industries. However, this policy paved the way for the dissolution of Kazakhstan industries.[29] Kazakhstan suffered from this choice and experienced a decrease in GDP. Having realized that dependency on energy sources alone would not create a stable economy, Kazakhstan began to invest in industrialization. However, as Pomfret argues, "poor institutions, characterized by red tape and corruption, distorted financial sector development and lack of competition are the fundamental obstacles to new enterprise formation and efficient restructuring of existing enterprises."[30]

Uzbekistan struggles to implement an economic reform that would support industrialization. Although still under the shadow of the Soviet economic system, Uzbekistan chose a gradual reform of the economy rather than the "shock therapy" model.[31] The government maintained strict control over the key sectors of economy and reallocating resources from one sector to another through various administrative means. This has resulted in misallocation of scarce resources, reduction in the market incentive mechanism in both private and public-sector production, and damages in private property rights, thus breeding inefficiency.[32] While the idea of relying exclusively on the production of raw materials is disliked,[33] Uzbekistan saw the agricultural and energy sectors as potential sources to fund industrialization.[34] Although the government was able to appropriate significant rent from the agricultural and energy sectors, the investable surplus accumulated was not enough to finance the government's ambitious development programs. Uzbekistan had to borrow considerable amounts, reaching nearly 55 percent of GDP[35] from external sources, thus further weakening the economy.

Turkmenistan, despite its energy resources, failed to direct its resources to create sustainable economy in which non-energy sectors could thrive. Given the interest of foreign investors in Turkmenistan's oil and gas industry and the anticipated gains from exports in the 1990s, Turkmenistan initiated an economic program similar to that of many newly independent states of the 1950s and 1960s.[36] However, the difficult business climate and lack of export opportunities hindered development. The murky legal environment, favoritism in awarding contracts, and extensive bribe taking and kickbacks further alienated many investors, resulting in their avoidance of Turkmenistan.[37] A very few Turkish, Iranian, and Western companies managed to negotiate their way through Turkmenistan's bureaucracy, while accepting Russia as the only real export route. The situation worsened when Turkmenistan's main partners for gas, Russia, Ukraine, and Belarus continued to pay below world prices or through barter arrangements.[38]

Kyrgyzstan and Tajikistan have the weakest economies in the region. Tajikistan is one of the poorest countries in Central Asia and, having suffered from a civil war, it did not have valuable resources (except water, which is gradually becoming the most needed resource in Central Asia) to attract significant investments. Similarly, Kyrgyzstan's problems with corruption (one of the main problems in the region) and weak economy are compounded by its lack of energy resources. As the International Crisis Group reports, virtual monopolies with major branches under the control of members of the presidential family dominate the economy, and lack of legal guarantees, corruption, and few resources put off all but the bravest investors.[39] According to the UN Development Program, annual corruption in Kyrgyzstan is estimated at $700 million (11 percent of GDP).[40] Kyrgyzstan is losing more resources than it puts into the defense budget, which is between 2.3–3.5 percent of GDP since 2000.

National security concerns strengthen Russia's influence

Russia continues to be the dominant actor in the security field, despite the ebbs and flows of the relations since the independence. The preeminence of Russia could be seen as contradictory to the multi-vector policies in the region. However, Strakes argues that the concept of "security-autonomy tradeoffs" has to be integrated into the analysis of multi-vector policies.[41] Since small states lack necessary resources and opportunities to expand their power, they seek asymmetric alliances with larger states for enhanced protection and resources. In return, small states give up a degree of their political self-determination. The decision to accept or reject the dominance of the larger state depends on how small states evaluate the desirability of the imposed limitations on their autonomy relative to the other domestic and international priorities.[42] In the case of Central Asia, ruling elites' perceptions of the threats to their regime determines their level of cooperation with Russia.

Since their independence, Central Asian countries have wrestled with threats, with varying degrees and forms, emanating from the desire to sustain elite power and prevent internal instability.[43] Local leaders resort to authoritarian and clientelistic polices to hold onto power. Although their authoritarian and rent-seeking form of government is one of the main sources of security problems, Central Asian governments also resented Western initiatives to strengthen governance and what they perceive as the encouragement of democracy. This has been the main fallout between the Central Asian governments and the West. For example, the United States was adamant in stressing human rights, democracy, and political reform in Kyrgyzstan, which led to disaffection with the U.S. as a partner in the government. [44] Central Asian countries chose to clamp down on Western-sponsored NGOs, the domestic political opposition, and remnants of the free media,[45] as they increasingly adopted Russian ideas on legitimacy, authority, respect, order, and sovereignty as opposed to Western ideals.[46] Their desire to keep the power and continuation of rent-seeking and authoritarian and clientelistic policies also translated into the proliferation of multiple military, intelligence, and police forces (which receive more resources than their regular armies).[47] Central Asian elites opted for coercive means rather than addressing the weaknesses in state institutions and the economy. The continuing economic weakness and patrimonial rule also seem to be providing a breeding ground for religious extremism in Central Asian countries, especially after the Syrian civil war and the U.S. drawdown in Afghanistan.

The common concern is that this religious extremism could spill over from Afghanistan into Central Asia, where there is already a considerable potential for radicalization.[48] As the International Crisis Group reports, there have been increasing reports of Central Asian guerrillas operating within an ethnically diverse movement in the northern provinces of Afghanistan.[49] Furthermore, the defection of the head of Tajikistan's Special Assignment Police Unit (OMON), General Gulmurod Khamilov, to Islamic State in Syria[50] shows that the radicalization also has roots in the Central Asian states. Hizb-ut Tahrir is also argued to be gaining foothold in the region through recruiting highly ideological and psychologically manipulated young men who are committed to overthrowing Central Asian governments and establishing an Islamist order.[51] Although the immediacy of the religious extremism, as Kim, Blank, and Ordabek argue, is substantially over-hyped, it nevertheless shapes the behaviors of local governments and drives closer relationships with Russia.[52]

The lack of military capabilities compounds the fears of Central Asian governments, which in turn pushes them to seek increased cooperation with Russia. Central Asian militaries generally are in poor condition and lack training and adequate equipment, which make them ill-fitted to counter terrorism and guerrilla warfare in mountainous areas.[53] Yet, each state faces different levels of threats. Therefore, the impact of military weaknesses for overall security shows variance. For example, the threat of religious extremism remains low in Turkmenistan; therefore, the effects of having a weak military force do not severely affect the security of the state.[54] On the other hand, Tajikistan's army and security services' weakness make it more prone to destabilization.[55]

As Central Asian governments became more threatened by religious extremism and regime change, especially after the colored revolutions, they began to seek more cooperation with Russia.

Russia is willing to capitalize on the insecurity of Central Asian ruling elites. It has already become more active in the region following Putin's ascendance to the presidency. The increased threat perceptions from terrorism and the colored revolutions, especially after the Tulip Revolution in Kyrgyzstan, provided an invaluable opportunity for Russia to assert its influence in the region and counter the diffusion of democracy. Through regional security organizations[56] and military support, especially to Tajikistan against commonly perceived external threats,[57] Russia capitalized on this opportunity and established good relations with Central Asian regimes in the security field. Through CSTO, Russia cements its position in Kazakhstan, Kyrgyzstan, and Tajikistan. While Uzbekistan and Turkmenistan remain outside of regional security organizations, Russia continues to be a major actor in their security relationships. Uzbekistan joins regional security organizations when it feels the most threatened, as showcased by its admission to CSTO between 1994–1999 and 2006–2012. Yet, as the Uzbek Defense Minister Kabul Berdiyev said "Maybe there were some periods when our cooperation was not that active but we have always been with Russia, and Russia is our main strategic partner."[58] Only in Turkmenistan is Russia the second major arms provider, following Turkey. In the end, Central Asian governments are willing to cooperate with Russia and accept its hegemony when their threat perception emanating from either religious extremism or spread of democracy is heightened.

Virtual defense industries

Except for Turkmenistan, Central Asian states inherited some defense-industrial capabilities from the Soviet Union. During the Soviet period, non-Slavic republics, on average, accounted for a little more than half of defense production in Russia.[59] Among the Central Asian states, Kazakhstan inherited a significant amount of defense-industrial production capabilities. These capabilities have included the production of missiles, mines, control systems, navigational equipment, radar, armaments for tanks, infantry weapons, air defense system components, radio-electronic equipment, and howitzers.[60] Uzbekistan inherited one of the largest military aircraft production plants that is outside of the Russian Federation. The Chkalov Tashkent Aviation Production Association (TAPO) assembled Il-76 transport planes, Il-78 aerial refueling planes and Il-114 reconnaissance planes in the 1980s.[61] Kyrgyzstan's legacy defense industries could produce a number of products which do not have any impact on the country's military capability but are viable for export, such as VA-111 Shkval rocket torpedo, proximity fuses, and guidance and homing systems.[62] Tajikistan's inheritance was primarily in the processing and enrichment of locally mined uranium for the Soviet nuclear industry (the Vostokredmet plant in Chkalovsk, the successor of the Soviet Leninabad Mining and Chemical Combine) and missile fuel (the Zaria Vostoka plant), none of which was useful for producing weapons or equipment for Tajikistan's military.[63] However, as was the case with economic structures, these defense-industrial capabilities were viable as long as they were part of the all-union planning and production networks.

The military-industrial complex of the Soviet Union developed according to the needs of the Cold War and in line with its economic structure. Consequently, its defense production network exhibited similar characteristics: "Goods and services were channeled throughout this network by central planners in Moscow, and, of equal importance, through the informal networks of personal relations that plant managers had developed."[64] The dissolution of the Soviet Union took away the administrative hierarchies of the defense production network and the primary customer for the weapons and components, leaving the Central Asian states in possession of random elements of former-union industrial and research systems without any coordination through plans or markets.[65] Therefore, this resulted in the loss of defense-industrial production capabilities.

Today, Central Asian governments, with the exception of Tajikistan, declare that they want to build up their defense industries. But all them are seeking to strengthen their militaries. The level of investment and development of defense industries shows a great variance, depending on the number of willing partners and political and economic structures.

Kazakhstan

Kazakhstan's defense-industrialization policy follows a path similar to other industrializing countries and adopts similar policy goals, such as seeing defense industrialization as the locomotive of the overall economy and a possible avenue for exports. Similar to others, Kazakhstan demands technology transfers and production licenses not only in joint-production agreements but also for direct procurements. For example, in 2008, Kazakhstan Defense Minister Daniyal Akhmetov explained defense-industry policy in the following words: "As the main condition for purchasing new samples of military hardware, we demand that all technical documentation be handed over. Under the money in exchange for technology scheme, for example, we purchased the new Nayza missile system from Israel and obtained all technical documentation for manufacturing this system."[66] In parallel for the demand for technology transfer, the defense minister also ordered that 80 percent of defense purchases is to come from domestic suppliers.[67] Consequently, establishment of joint ventures is the main gateway for the Kazakh defense market.

The key to Kazakhstan's defense industries is Kazakhstan Engineering (KE), the state-owned defense management holding. It forms the core of industrial development. The company commands many of the defense companies, including the surviving factories such as the Kirov plant (communications equipment), the Zenit plant (ships, including minesweepers and patrol boats), the Ziksto plant (anti-ship missiles), the Metalist plant (high-caliber machine guns), the Petropavlosk heavy machine-building plant (targeting systems and parts of ballistic missiles), the Granit plant (air defense systems) and the Kirov machine-building plant (torpedoes).[68] Aviamaster Aircraft, West Kazakhstan Engineering, and Burundaivia are the only companies that remain outside of KE ownership. KE handles international cooperation through establishing joint ventures with foreign companies, such as Airbus Group (EU), Aselsan (TUR), Thales (EU), Indra (ESP), Safran (FRA), Rheinmetall (DEU), Paramount Group (ZAF), ST Engineering (SGP), Kamaz (RUS), Russian Helicopters, and Uralvagonzavod (RUS). Although Kazakh defense industries depend heavily on foreign partnerships, which are realized through joint ventures, in acquiring modern technologies and inputs, officials argue that Kazakhstan has reached a 50 percent local production rate and hope to increase this to 80 percent by 2020.[69] However, investment in the defense industry has not translated into indigenous system production. For example, Barys 8 x 8 Wheeled Armored Vehicle is the localized version of the South African Mbombe 8.[70] Overall, Kazakhstan has a modicum of production capacity in the areas of aerospace, land systems, weapon systems, naval systems, and Command, Control, Communications, Computers, Intelligence, Surveillance and Reconnaissance (C4ISR). But, this production capability is not enough to break the dependence on Russia.

Russia continues to be the most significant partner in arms trade and industrial relations despite the interest of other countries. Despite international interest in the Kazakh market,[71] there has not been a significant change in Kazakhstan's defense procurement. Russia continues to dwarf the other suppliers such as Spain, Germany, Israel, and Turkey. As the backbone of the Kazakh military is still composed of Russian materiel, defense procurement also shows a bias toward Russian systems, with exceptions of Lynx self-propelled multiple rocket launchers on Russian truck chassis, C-295 transport aircraft, Sea Dolphin patrol craft, the EC145 light helicopter, and the EC725 transport helicopter. EC145 and EC725 were assembled in Kazakhstan, while Marauder and Mbombe-6 were produced by Kazakhstan Paramount Engineering, a joint venture between Kazakhstan Engineering and the South African Paramount Group. Despite the nascent nature of Kazakh defense industries and continuation of significant dependency on Russia, the investment in defense industries will continue in the foreseeable future.

Defense industrialization for Kazakhstan is not only about increasing military capabilities, but also is seen as an opportunity for overall industrial development and exports; a desire similar to that exhibited by other emerging countries as well. Kazakhstan is seeking to diversify its economy; thus, it seeks to decrease its dependency on oil and gas production. The arms industry is one of the sectors it chooses to promote, although its products are far from cutting edge.[72] Kazakhstan does not have major arms exports.[73] However, it formed a joint venture, Kyrgyztechnoexport, which upgrades armored vehicles. In 2008, Defense Minister Akhmetov also argued that Kazakhstan wants to become the leading regional exporter of arms in Central Asia and hopefully increase its international exports .[74] According to the recent statement of Kazakh Minister of Defense and Aerospace industry Beibut Atamkulov, Kazakhstan's defense exports reached USD $49 million in 2017. The most notable export success is the export of night-vision devices to Turkey and Uzbekistan by the joint venture Kazakhstan Aselsan Engineering.[75] While, this is good news for Kazakh officials, at the current levels of defense industrialization, dependence on foreign partnerships for production, and Russia's market dominance in the region, the goal of becoming the leading regional exporter of arms seems to be a distant goal.

Uzbekistan

In January 2017, President Shavkat Mirziyoyev declared the new Defense Doctrine of Uzbekistan, which focused on three areas of development: rearming of the military with modern weapons, launching a local military industry, and reorganizing the armed forces. The priority for the period 2017–2021 is on procurement of military goods and repair and modernization of available military equipment while ensuring their purposeful financing. To this end, Uzbekistan established the State Committee for Defense Industry on November 2017, which is tasked with organizing the defense industry and defense procurement. The current goal for the defense industries remains modest: providing maintenance and decreasing the cost of import agreements[76]. This represents a significant shift from the past, when the unorganized management of defense industries resulted in the exit of one of the most promising factories from defense production. Consequently, building the new defense industrial base would be a herculean task.

Currently, Uzbekistan's defense industrial base is weak, mainly focused on civilian production and dependent on international collaboration. Its defense industry is composed of a mix of private companies, largely producing electronics, and state companies in electronics, aerospace, and land systems. International collaboration is important for increasing and sustaining defense-industrial capabilities. UzAvtosanoat (UzAuto), the state-owned auto factory, established joint ventures with South Korean Daewoo and U.S. General Motors to locally produce cars, while its cooperation with German MAN enables production of heavy-duty commercial vehicles.[77] Furthermore, Uzbek Heat Resistant and Refractory Materials Integrated Plant, which produced hard alloys, powders, and rolled metals for the defense industry during the Soviet era, entered a joint venture with South Korean Shindong Resources for manufacturing automobile components. These partnerships are important for increasing capabilities in maintenance, repair and overhaul, and manufacturing of military vehicles, yet there have been no signs of their impact on defense-industrial production. A direct impact on defense-production cooperation comes from the recent agreement between Uzbekistan's UzAuto and Turkey's Nurol Makina on the joint production of 1,000 Ejder Yalçın III armored vehicles.[78] Despite cooperation with other countries, this did not have an impact on Uzbekistan's dependency on Russia.

Russia is the dominant partner for Uzbekistan both in defense-industrial cooperation and procurement. Although Uzbekistan suspended its CSTO membership in 2012, it maintains bilateral defense ties with Russia and uses predominantly Soviet-era weapon systems.[79] Russia is also highly visible in defense-industrial cooperation. Uzmashprom, which is a machine-building corporation, produces Russian-licensed small arms, including the AK-74M and the SVD-7 sniper rifle. Russia also invested in Uzbekistan's aerospace industry through the UsRosAvia joint venture, which was founded in 2007 to create a regional service and repair center for Mi-8, Mi-17, and Mi-24 helicopters.[80] In 2016, Russia and Uzbekistan signed a military-technical cooperation agreement, and negotiations for closer military cooperation resulted in a contract for the sale of a dozen Mi-35 attack helicopters to Uzbekistan.[81] However, the case of TAPO shows how the rent-seeking behavior of Uzbek elites hinders Uzbekistan's defense-industrial capabilities.

TAPO, which relied heavily on Russian research, expertise, and goods,[82] began to deteriorate with the decline of orders, lack of cooperation with Russia and neighboring countries, and corruption in the 1990s. Between 1996 and 1999, nearly 50 to 65 percent of specialists left the company[83] due to poor working conditions. The only way to survive was to cooperate with Russia and become integrated into the Russian production network. In 2007, the Russian government wanted to take over TAPO and make it a part of the newly established United Aircraft Corporation (UAC). According to the Russian plans, TAPO would become the only plant for the production of the Il-114. The negotiations with the Uzbek government failed because Uzbekistan wanted to acquire a 10 percent share of UAC, an offer which Russia declined.[84] Based on the views of local analysts, Omar Sharifov reports that "the authorities of Tashkent were eager to get a better participation in making a profit from the sale of a promising aircraft as a whole [since] neither the share in the UAC, nor the share in joint venture, suited them, given the potential Il-114 sales market and possible profits."[85] As the bargaining failed, Uzbekistan could not have kept the company afloat; it went bankrupt in 2010, thus resulting in the loss of any capability for aircraft manufacture. The company was relaunched as a manufacturer of building structures, household products, car components, and spare parts for farm machinery.[86]

Kyrgyzstan

Kyrgyzstan also seeks to increase its defense-industrial capabilities; defense-industrial production is limited to production of torpedoes. The development of defense-industrial capabilities is dependent on cooperation with foreign companies, which shows some signs of improvement. Kyrgyzstan established a joint venture with Kazakhstan for the upgrade and maintenance of armored vehicles and procured secondhand Mi-8MT/Mi-17 from Kazakhstan, which was financed by the United States. Kyrgyzstan also signed a military-technical cooperation agreement with India in 2015.[87] As usual, Russia is the most interested party in developing defense-industrial relations with Kyrgyzstan. In 2005, two countries agreed to set up a joint venture for the production of special communication equipment.[88] However, the jewels of the Kyrgyz defense industry are Dastan Joint Stock Company, which produces the strategically important VA-111 Shkval rocket torpedo for the Russian navy, and the Kyrgyz-Russian joint venture the Ozero Company, which develops new torpedoes. Yet, elite rent-seeking behavior ended in the loss of production capability in the Kyrgyz defense industries.

The negotiations between Russia and Kyrgyzstan on the ownership and the future of Dastan were plagued with inconsistencies and the rent-seeking behavior of the ruling elites in Kyrgyzstan, similar to the case of TAPO in Uzbekistan. Due to its strategic significance for itself, the Dastan Company has been the center of attention for Russia. In 2006, Russia proposed to assume a 37 percent of share of Dastan, in return for providing $30 million. The negotiations failed in 2008. According to the official explanations, the reason was that members of the national parliament of the previous convocation hindered privatization of the company for their own personal reasons. It is alleged that the parties failed to reach an agreement on the size of the "kickback."[89] Yet, Russia placed a major order at Dastan in 2008. In 2009, then-President

Kurmanbek Bakiyev reached an agreement with then-President Dmitry Medvedev for the deletion of Kyrgyz debt to Russia in exchange for 48 percent of Dastan, which would make Russia the controlling shareholder. However, the Kyrgyz authorities later revealed that the state had only 37 percent of the shares and the rest belonged to private shareholders who were affiliated with the Kyrgyz president's son, Maxim[90]. In 2010, then-President Roza Otunbayeva claimed that Kyrgyzstan was ready for negotiations with Russia on Dastan. In this round, Russia was interested in acquiring at least 51 percent of the shares, which Kyrgyzstan was not ready to honor due to, as Kyrgyz Temporary Charge d'Affairs in Russia Ulukbek Chinaliyev argued, the legal collisions and violations regarding the legislation during privatization. Again, it was alleged that the Kyrgyz authorities foiled negotiations with Moscow in the hope to secure additional preferences.[91] In 2012, Russia and Kyrgyzstan entered one last negotiation under then-President Almazbek Atambayev. This time, Russia demanded 75 percent of the shares, while President Atambayev insisted on 48 percent of shares in exchange for the deletion of Kyrgyzstan's $180 million debt.[92] As the negotiations continued, President Almazbek Atambayev insinuated that Turkey might obtain shares of the Dastan Company.[93] While Turkey declared that it would help Kyrgyzstan to build up its defense industry,[94] Turkish investment in Kyrgyzstan's defense industry has not happened yet. In the end, the negotiations failed, this time for good. Following the crisis in Ukraine, Russia backed away from buying Dastan in 2015.[95] The disappearance of Russian interest in the company resulted in significant losses for it, which stopped its production in 2017, while Kyrgyzstan continues to search for new investors and tries to get orders from Russia.[96] Kyrgyzstan has squandered its chance to make Dastan a viable defense company while remaining dependent on Russia.

Turkmenistan

Turkmenistan does not have any form of defense industry, and has not officially declared any intentions yet. The 2016 Military Doctrine, however, aims to increase defense capability in order to safeguard national interests and territorial integrity.[97] Although it is very difficult to find reliable information, Turkmenistan spared between 1.8–4.0 percent of its GDP for military expenditure. It is striving to modernize its armed forces, mainly through direct procurement.[98] While the military is equipped with Soviet-era weapons and Russia is an important supplier, Turkmenistan has been diversifying its suppliers. Between 2011 and 2017, Turkmenistan procured 34 percent of its new equipment from Turkey, 26 percent from Russia, and 20 percent from China. These purchases include CH-3 and WJ-600 UAV/UCAVs from China, a T-90S tank from Russia, and Cobra APVs and Kirpi APCs from Turkey.[99] In addition to direct procurement, there are some indications of the desire to invest in defense-production capabilities.

President Saparmurat Niyazov was believed to be particularly interested in developing a capacity for production of personal weapons, including cartridges and spare parts; upgrading and repairing tanks and armored vehicles; building an aircraft repair facility; and repairing and modernizing naval vessels.[100] However, as Gorenburg argues, these plans had not materialized by the time of Niyazov's passing in 2006. There were some attempts to initiate defense industrialization. In 2013, Ukraine declared that it was ready for military-technical cooperation with Turkmenistan. Although Turkmenistan sought defense-industrial cooperation with India, the talks were inconclusive.[101] In 2013, Belarus and Turkmenistan reached an agreement for procurement and local production of Grif-1 tactical UAV.[102] Apart from these attempts, there have not been serious investment in defense-production capability. In the end, Turkmenistan continues to depend on direct procurement.

Tajikistan

Tajikistan, the poorest of all Central Asian countries, does not have the desire to invest in the defense industry. The inherited defense-production capabilities are unsuitable for becoming the foundation of a defense-industrialization process. Given economic, military, and industrial weaknesses, Tajikistan does not have capabilities to diversify its suppliers. Consequently, Russia continues to be the main provider of its security, with its military force deployed in Tajikistan, and the main supplier of arms as well. In 2014, Russia and Tajikistan concluded a deal on modernization of the Tajik military forces, followed by the signing of the 2017 Military Cooperation Plan in late 2016.[103] Furthermore, Russia is considering building up Tajikistan's defense industries with mediation from CSTO. In 2015, CSTO Secretary-General Nikolai Bordyuzha said:

> The CSTO is considering the possibility of establishing cooperation between Tajik and Russian enterprises to make military-purpose products... First we need to decide if the enterprises that have changed their area of operation have potential and find points of contact with the Russian enterprises... We also need to evaluate the current needs of Russian defense industry enterprises. If we can do it, we will organize joint ventures to ensure interaction between these enterprises.[104]

During the 14th Session of the CSTO Inter-State Commission for Military-Economic Cooperation in Dushanbe, Russia and Tajikistan agreed to integrate their defense-industrial enterprises.[105] These declarations show Russian interest in integrating the former Soviet production capabilities in Tajikistan. However, building up a defense-industrial capacity that could meet Tajik military needs is still questionable.

Conclusion

Defense industrialization in Central Asia shows variance according to the unique factors in each country. Among countries that inherited some defense-production capabilities from the Soviet Union, Kazakhstan showed the most progress in defense industrialization which is based on the surviving defense factories and research centers. Kazakhstan managed to increase its defense-industrial capabilities with the help of various foreign companies, was able to invest its energy resources in overall industrialization, and was able to institutionalize defense industrialization. Yet, the process was limited. Kazakh products are largely modified versions of foreign systems and depend on foreign inputs, mostly Russian. Defense industrialization, therefore, is not enough to break the dependence on Russia, as Russia still continues to be an important partner in Kazakhstan's defense industries, both through direct procurements and industrial partnerships. Because of its relative progress in the defense industrialization, Kazakhstan could serve as gateway to enter Central Asian markets, which makes the country a viable option for investment and defense-industrial cooperation as Turkish Aselsan did with its joint venture.

Other countries were not as successful as Kazakhstan because of their structural and economic problems. Uzbekistan is also investing in defense industrialization, though not on the remnants of former Soviet defense industries, which were lost due to the rent-seeking behavior of its elites. Uzbekistan's transient relations with the West and inefficient economic structures result in an inability to draw much-needed foreign investment in defense industries. Consequently, Uzbekistan could not capitalize on its inherited defense-industrial capability in the past due to the lack of a consistent outlook on defense industrialization and rent seeking. What remains is the basic capability for communication-systems manufacturing, vehicle maintenance, and metal and alloy production.

Kyrgyzstan has weak defense-industrial capability but shows signs of a desire to build it up. However, Kyrgyzstan suffers from a rampant corruption, which leads to losing both precious resources and investors. Thus, for Uzbekistan and Kyrgyzstan, Russia remains the only partner who is willing to support these regimes and invest in defense industries.

Turkmenistan is adamant in sustaining its neutral status and spares a significant amount of its GDP for its defense budget; however, the country was unsuccessful in initiating defense industrialization. The country is unable to draw investments to its economy mainly due to the difficult business climate, which is plagued by corruption, and its inability to diversify its exports.

Financial power is further crippled when its main partners for natural gas either make payments below world prices or through barter agreements. Thanks to the reflection of its weak economy and rampant corruption, Turkmenistan is also unable to draw partners for defense industrialization and spends its very limited resources for direct procurement. Despite its insistence on neutrality and increased relations with Turkey, Russian military hardware continues to form the backbone of Turkmenistan's military.

Finally, Tajikistan remains uninterested in investing in defense production because of its weak economy and very limited resources, although it aims to increase its military capability. Therefore, only Kazakhstan is able to benefit, though in a limited way, from the increased suppliers in the global arms market, while others suffered from their internal structures and prioritizing national security concerns over declared self-reliance policies.

In the end, defense industrialization in these countries, at its current state, does not provide an opportunity to balance Russia. Central Asian countries present a dissonance between their declared foreign policy goals, balancing Russia, and their security concerns, which results in increased cooperation with Russia. Internal structures significantly shaped the character and the process of defense industrialization. Although the impact varies, threats to regime security and economic structures, coupled with corruption, hinder the development of defense industries that could usher in true self-reliance.

ORCID

Çağlar Kurç http://orcid.org/0000-0001-6191-1834

Notes

1. Stephanie G. Neuman, "Arms, Aid and the Superpowers," *Foreign Affairs* 66, no. 4 (1988): 1044–66.
2. Kenneth J. D. Boutin, "Emerging Defense Industries: Prospects and Implications," in *The Modern Defense Industry: Political, Economic, and Technological Issues*, edited by Richard A. Bitzinger (Santa Barbara, CA: Praeger Security International/ABC-CLIO, 2009), 229; David Kinsella, "Arms Transfer Dependence and Foreign Policy Conflict," *Journal of Peace Research* 35 (January 1, 1998): 35.
3. Carol Evans, "Reappraising Third World Arms Production," *Survival* 28, no. 2 (1986): 99–118.
4. Richard A. Bitzinger, "The Globalization of the Arms Industry: The Next Proliferation Challenge," *International Security* 19, no. 2 (1994): 170–98; Richard A. Bitzinger, *Towards a Brave New Arms Industry*, Adelphi Paper 356 (New York & London: Routledge, 2003); Stephanie G Neuman, "Power, Influence and Hierarchy: Defence Industries in a Unipolar World," *Defence and Peace Economics* 21, no. 1 (2010): 105–34.
5. Martha Brill Olcott, "Central Asia's Catapult to Independence," *Foreign Affairs* 71, no. 3 (1992): 108–13, https://doi.org/10.2307/20045233.
6. Pınar Akçalı, "Nation-State Building in Central Asia: A Lost Cause?" in *Central Eurasia in Global Politics: Conflict, Security, and Development*, edited by Mehdi Parvizi Amineh and Henk Houweling, 2nd ed. (Leiden & Boston: Brill, 2005), 96.
7. "Central Asia's Catapult to Independence," 109.
8. Olcott, 120.
9. Cooley, *Great Games, Local Rules: The New Great Power Contest in Central Asia* (Oxford, New York: Oxford University Press, 2012), 21.
10. Ibid., 17.
11. Ibid., 25–26.
12. Kathleen Collins, "Economic and Security Regionalism among Patrimonial Authoritarian Regimes: The Case of Central Asia," *Europe-Asia Studies* 61, no. 2 (February 2009): 262.
13. Bernardo da Silva Relva Teles Fazendeiro, "Uzbekistan's 'Spirit' of Self-Reliance and the Logic of Appropriateness: TAPOich and Interaction with Russia," *Central Asian Survey* 34, no. 4 (2015): 487.
14. Bernardo da Silva Relva Teles Fazendeiro, "Keeping Face in the Public Sphere: Recognition, Discretion and Uzbekistan's Relations with the United States and Germany, 1991–2006," *Central Asian Survey* 34, no. 3 (2015): 344.

15. "New Understanding of Foreign Policy," Ministry of Foreign Affairs of the Kyrgyz Republic, www.mfa.gov.kg/contents/view/id/125 (accessed January 26, 2017),
16. "Concept of the Foreign Policy of the Republic of Tajikistan," The Ministry of Foreign Affairs of the Republic of Tajikistan, January 27, 2015, http://mfa.tj/en/law-base-fp/concept-of-the-foreign-policy-of-the-republic-of-tajikistan.html.
17. Reuel R Hanks, "'Multi-Vector Politics' and Kazakhstan's Emerging Role as a Geo-Strategic Player in Central Asia," *Journal of Balkan and Near Eastern Studies* 11, no. 3 (September 2009): 259.
18. Jason E Strakes, "Situating the 'Balanced Foreign Policy': The Role of System Structure in Azerbaijan's Multi-Vector Diplomacy," *Journal of Balkan and Near Eastern Studies* 15, no. 1 (March 2013): 47.
19. Anna Matveeva, "Democratization, Legitimacy and Political Change in Central Asia," *International Affairs* 75, no. 1 (1999): 30.
20. Cooley, *Great Games, Local Rules*, 21.
21. Christopher Clapham, 1998, cited in Emilian Kavalski, "The International Politics of Fusion and Fissure in the Awkward States of Post-Soviet Central Asia," in *Stable Outside, Fragile Inside? Post-Soviet Statehood in Central Asia*, edited by Kavalski (Farnham & Burlington: Ashgate, 2010), 11.
22. Kavalski, "The International Politics of Fusion and Fissure." 11.
23. Alyson J. K. Bailes and Pál Dunay, "The Shanghai Cooperation Organization as a Regional Security Institution," in *The Shanghai Cooperation Organization*, edited by Bailes et al., SIPRI Policy Papers 17 (Bromma: CM Gruppen, 2007), 14.
24. F. Stephen Larrabee, "Turkey's Eurasian Agenda," *The Washington Quarterly* 34, no. 1 (February 2011): 114.
25. Georgiy Voloshin, "Kazakhstan and Central Asia Security: Ensuring Regional Stability in the Eurasian Balkans," *Fletcher Forum of World Affairs* 36, no. 1 (2012): 92.
26. Aleksandr Pikalov, "Uzbekistan between the Great Powers: A Balancing Act or a Multi-Vectorial Approach?" *Central Asian Survey* 33, no. 3 (September 2014): 298.
27. Gregory Gleason, "Inter-State Cooperation in Central Asia from the CIS to the Shanghai Forum," *Europe-Asia Studies* 53, no. 7 (2001): 1089.
28. Pikalov, "Uzbekistan between the Great Powers," 305.
29. Matveeva, "Democratization, Legitimacy and Political Change in Central Asia," 28.
30. Richard Pomfret, "Kazakhstan's Economy Since Independence: Does the Oil Boom Offer a Second Chance for Sustainable Development?" *Europe-Asia Studies* 57, no. 6 (September 2005): 870.
31. Pikalov, "Uzbekistan between the Great Powers," 304.
32. Kobil Ruziev, Dipak Ghosh, and Sheila C Dow, "The Uzbek Puzzle Revisited: An Analysis of Economic Performance in Uzbekistan Since 1991," *Central Asian Survey* 26, no. 1 (March 2007): 27.
33. Fazendeiro, "Uzbekistan's 'Spirit,'" 488.
34. Ruziev et al., "The Uzbek Puzzle," 19.
35. Ibid., 21.
36. Richard Pomfret, "Turkmenistan: From Communism to Nationalism by Gradual Economic Reform," *MOST: Economic Policy in Transitional Economies* 11, no. 2 (2001): 166.
37. *Repression and Regression in Turkmenistan: A New International Strategy,* Asia Report (Osh/Brussels: International Crisis Group, November 4, 2004), 17, www.crisisgroup.org/europe-central-asia/central-asia/turkmenistan/repression-and-regression-turkmenistan-new-international-strategy.
38. *Cracks in the Marble: Turkmenistan's Failing Dictatorship,* Asia Report (Osh/Brussels: International Crisis Group, January 17, 2003), 15, www.crisisgroup.org/europe-central-asia/central-asia/turkmenistan/cracks-marble-turkmenistans-failing-dictatorship.
39. *Kyrgyzstan's Political Crisis: An Exit Strategy,* Asia Report (Osh/Brussels: International Crisis Group, August 20, 2002), 2, www.crisisgroup.org/europe-central-asia/central-asia/kyrgyzstan/kyrgyzstans-political-crisis-exit-strategy.
40. *Kyrgyzstan: State Fragility and Radicalisation,* Europe and Central Asia Briefing (Osh/Bishkek/Brussels: International Crisis Group, October 3, 2016), 4, www.crisisgroup.org/europe-central-asia/central-asia/kyrgyzstan/kyrgyzstan-state-fragility-and-radicalisation.
41. Strakes, "Situating the 'Balanced Foreign Policy,'" 47.
42. Ibid., 47–48.
43. Dmitri Gorenburg, "External Support for Central Asian Military and Security Forces," SIPRI-OSF Policy Brief (Stockholm: SIPRI, January 2014), 2.
44. *Kyrgyzstan's Political Crisis,* 19–20.
45. Collins, "Economic and Security Regionalism," 274.
46. Nicole J Jackson, "The Role of External Factors in Advancing Non-Liberal Democratic Forms of Political Rule: A Case Study of Russia's Influence on Central Asian Regimes," *Contemporary Politics* 16, no. 1 (March 2010): 104.

47. Stephen Blank, "Rethinking Central Asia and Its Security Issues," *UNISCI Discussion Papers*, no. 28 (January 2012): 26.
48. Nargis Kassenova, *Relations between Afghanistan and Central Asian States After 2014* (Sweden: SIPRI, 2014), 9.
49. "Tajikistan: The Changing Insurgent Threats," Asia Report (Bishkek/Brussels: International Crisis Group, May 24, 2011), 10, www.crisisgroup.org/europe-central-asia/central-asia/tajikistan/tajikistan-changing-insurgent-threats.
50. "Tajikistan Early Warning: Internal Pressures, External Threats," Europe and Central Asia Briefing (Bishkek/Brussels: International Crisis Group, January 11, 2016), 1, www.crisisgroup.org/europe-central-asia/central-asia/tajikistan/tajikistan-early-warning-internal-pressures-external.
51. "Radical Islam in Central Asia: Responding to Hizb Ut-Tahrir," Asia Report (Osh/Brussels: International Crisis Group, June 30, 2003), 33, www.crisisgroup.org/europe-central-asia/central-asia/uzbekistan/radical-islam-central-asia-responding-hizb-ut-tahrir.
52. Younkyoo Kim, Stephen Blank, and Erden Ordabek, "Central Asia and Post-2014 Afghanistan: A New Turn in Russia's Military Policy in Central Asia," *Korean Journal of Defense Analysis* 27, no. 4 (2015): 526.
53. Sam Perlo-Freeman and Petter Stalenheim, "Military Expenditure in the South Caucasus and Central Asia," in *Armament and Disarmament in the Caucasus and Central Asia*, edited by Bailes et al. (Stockholm: SIPRI, 2003), 17.
54. Vitaly Gelfgat, "Central Asian States: Matching Military Means to Strategic Ends," *Connections: The Quarterly Journal* 13, no. 3 (2014): 14.
55. "Tajikistan Early Warning," 7–8.
56. Roy Allison, "Virtual Regionalism, Regional Structures and Regime Security in Central Asia," *Central Asian Survey* 27, no. 2 (June 2008): 190.
57. Jackson, "The Role of External Factors," 111.
58. BBC Monitoring Central Asia, "Uzbekistan Says Military Ties with Russia Increasing," *BBC Monitoring Central Asia*, November 30, 2016, http://ezproxy.cul.columbia.edu/login?url=http://search.proquest.com/docview/1844596776?accountid=10226.
59. Ilya Bass and Leslie Dienes, "Defense Industry Legacies and Conversion in the Post-Soviet Realm," *Post-Soviet Geography* 34, no. 5 (1993): 303–8.
60. Gorenburg, "External Support for Central Asian Military and Security Forces," 7.
61. Ibid., 11; Bass and Dienes, "Defense Industry Legacies," 309–10.
62. Gorenburg, "External Support for Central Asian Military and Security Forces," 19.
63. Ibid., 23.
64. Ethan Kapstein, "The Economic Transition in Defence-Dependent Regions of Russia," *Defence and Peace Economics* 6, no. 3 (November 1995): 256.
65. Julian Cooper, "The Economies of the Former Soviet Union: Structural Issues," *Diplomacy & Statecraft* 5, no. 3 (November 1994): 455; Igor Filatotchev, Trevor Buck, and Mike Wright, "The Military-Industrial Complex of the Former USSR: Asset or Liability?" *Communist Economies and Economic Transformation* 5, no. 2 (December 2007): 195.
66. Roger N McDermott, "Kazakhstan Emerging as an Arms Exporter," News, Jamestown, May 20, 2008, https://jamestown.org/program/kazakhstan-emerging-as-an-arms-exporter/.
67. Gorenburg, "External Support for Central Asian Military and Security Forces," 8.
68. Ibid., 7–8.
69. Interfax, "Military Goods Reach 50% of All Output Produced by Kazakh Defense Industry," February 13, 2012, https://search.proquest.com/docview/921299698.
70. Army Recognition, "Barys 8 x 8 Armored Vehicle Fitted with Sarbaz Turret Unveiled at KADEX 2018," *Army Recognition*, May 23, 2018, http://armyrecognition.com/kadex_2018_news_official_show_daily/barys_8x8_armored_vehicle_fitted_with_sarbaz_turret_unveiled_at_kadex_2018.html.
71. Joshua Kucera, "Kazakhstan: Weapons on Parade, But Army Band Steals the Show," Pulitzer Center, May 10, 2012, http://pulitzercenter.org/reporting/kazakhstan-kadex-astana-weapons-army-band-dancing-queen.
72. Ibid.
73. SIPRI, "Arms Transfers Database," Stockholm International Peace Research Institute, 2018, https://www.sipri.org/databases/armstransfers.
74. McDermott, "Kazakhstan Emerging."
75. Charles Forrester, "Kazakh Government Reports Increase in Defence Exports," *Jane's 360,* May 16, 2018, www.janes.com/article/80125/kazakh-government-reports-increase-in-defence-exports.
76. "Uzbekistan Aims to Boost Its Military Capabilities," *Forecast International* (blog), December 22, 2017, https://blog.forecastinternational.com/wordpress/uzbekistan-aims-to-boost-its-military-capabilities/.
77. IHS Jane's, "Uzbekistan—Defence Industry," *Jane's Defence Industry,* August 8, 2016, https://janes.ihs.com.ezproxy.cul.columbia.edu.

78. "Uzbekistan Aims to Boost Its Military Capabilities."
79. IISS, "Chapter Five: Russia and Eurasia," *The Military Balance* 118, no. 1 (February 2018): 214–15.
80. Gorenburg, "External Support for Central Asian Military and Security Forces," 11.
81. "Uzbekistan Aims to Boost Its Military Capabilities."
82. Fazendeiro, "Uzbekistan's 'Spirit,'" 485.
83. Omar Sharifov, "Мертвая Петля Для ТАПОиЧ [Dead Loop for TAPOiCh]," Фергана - международное агентство новостеЙ, November 15, 2010, http://www.fergananews.com//article.php?id=6798.
84. Fazendeiro, "Uzbekistan's 'Spirit.'"
85. Sharifov, "Мертвая Петля Для ТАПОиЧ [Dead Loop for TAPOiCh]."
86. Sputnik News, "Uzbek Aircraft Plant Ends 70 Years of Plane Building," https://sputniknews.com/business/20120613174001250/ (accessed February 15, 2018).
87. Jon Grevatt, "India Signs Defence Deals with Central Asian States," *Jane's Defence Industry*, July 13, 2015.
88. BBC, "Russian-Kyrgyz Joint Venture to Produce Army Communication Equipment," March 3, 2005, http://ezproxy.cul.columbia.edu/login?url=http://search.proquest.com/docview/460351489?accountid=10226.
89. Grigory Mikhailov, "Russia Gave up Shkval," *Defense and Security* (Russia), May 16, 2008, http://www.lexisnexis.com/lnacui2api/api/version1/getDocCui?lni=4SHM-5X30-TX4V-P12P&csi=8411%2C270077%2C11059%2C270944&hl=t&hv=t&hnsd=f&hns=t&hgn=t&oc=00240&perma=true&secondRedirectIndicator=true.
90. Kabai Karabekov and Gennady Sysoev, "Squandering Russian Interests," *Defense and Security* (Russia), February 21, 2011, http://www.lexisnexis.com/lnacui2api/api/version1/getDocCui?lni=5276-R4M1-JCBG-D2HV&csi=8411,270077,11059,270944&hl=t&hv=t&hnsd=f&hns=t&hgn=t&oc=00240&perma=true.
91. Vladimir Mukhin, "Torpedoed Friendship: Bishkek Refuses to Part with Ownership of the Factory that Makes Unique Weapons," *What the Papers Say* (Russia), July 23, 2010, http://www.lexisnexis.com/lnacui2api/api/version1/getDocCui?lni=800T-NWM1-2R6R-8337&csi=8411,270077,11059,270944&hl=t&hv=t&hnsd=f&hns=t&hgn=t&oc=00240&perma=true.
92. "Media: Kyrgyzstan Does Not Agree with Russia's Dastan Terms," *Trend News Agency*, April 16, 2012, https://en.trend.az/casia/kyrgyzstan/2014770.html.
93. Dmitry Shlapentokh, "Turkey and Kyrgyzstan Deepen Ties," *CACI Analyst*, March 21, 2012, www.cacianalyst.org/publications/analytical-articles/item/12464-analytical-articles-caci-analyst-2012-3-21-art-12464.html?tmpl=component&print=1.
94. Gelfgat, "Central Asian States," 9.
95. "Russia Changes Mind to but Kyrgyz Plant Due to Ukraine Crisis -Minister," *BBC Monitoring Central Asia*, February 13, 2015, http://www.lexisnexis.com/lnacui2api/api/version1/getDocCui?lni=5F94-3XG1-DYRV-3328&csi=8411,270077,11059,270944&hl=t&hv=t&hnsd=f&hns=t&hgn=t&oc=00240&perma=true.
96. "Atambayev: Kyrgyzstan Not Ready for Import Substitution Yet," *Central Asian News Service*, June 22, 2017, http://www.lexisnexis.com/lnacui2api/api/version1/getDocCui?lni=5NVH-DN51-F11P-X1GN&csi=8411,270077,11059,270944&hl=t&hv=t&hnsd=f&hns=t&hgn=t&oc=00240&perma=true.
97. IISS, "Chapter Five: Russia and Eurasia," 208.
98. Perlo-Freeman and Stalenheim, "Military Expenditure in the South Caucasus and Central Asia," 16, 18.
99. SIPRI, "Arms Transfers Database."
100. IHS Jane's, "Turkmenistan—Defence Production and R&D," *Jane's Sentinel Security Assessment—Russia and the CIS*, November 2, 2016, https://janes-ihs-com.ezproxy.cul.columbia.edu/RussiaCIS/Display/1302993.
101. "Turkmenistan Seeks Military Aid from Russia," *EurasiaNet*, June 9, 2016, http://www.eurasianet.org/node/79151.
102. IHS Jane's, "Turkmenistan—Defence Production and R&D."
103. IISS, "Chapter Five: Russia and Eurasia," 207.
104. Interfax, "CSTO Suggest Rebuilding Defense Enterprises in Tajikistan," *Interfax: Central Asia General Newswire*, March 16, 2015, https://search.proquest.com/docview/1663832159.
105. Interfax, "Russia, Tajikistan Decide to Revive Relations between Their Defense Companies," *Interfax: Russia & CIS Business and Financial Newswire*, May 20, 2016, https://search.proquest.com/docview/1790187916.

Conclusion

Çağlar Kurç, Richard A. Bitzinger and Stephanie G. Neuman

The manufacture of arms predates history. More importantly, the emergence, development and spread of civilization took place simultaneously with advances in weaponry and warfighting. Indeed, civilization would probably not be possible without armaments. And yet, before World War II, there was no real arms industry to speak of, or certainly not on the same scale as today. To be sure, factories and armouries produced rifles and cannon, and shipyards constructed all manner and classes of warships. Moreover, during the interwar period (1918–1939) there was a rapid growth in aviation, and aircraft companies around the world competed to manufacture fighter planes and bombers. And yet, until the early 20th century, arms manufacturing was historically a minor business, one that rose and fell as wars and conflict waxed and waned. In the United States, for example, the huge, technologically innovative arms industry that arose out of the Civil War soon collapsed following the Confederates' surrender, and it did not recover for several decades.

Less than a hundred years later, this has all changed. The manufacture of arms has dramatically grown in terms of size, scope and technological sophistication, while at the same time spreading out geographically, as countries on every continent have created indigenous defence industries manufacturing a variety of weapons systems. Today, therefore, the defence industrial base has become a critical sector in many nations' economies, either for its current economic and technological benefits, or for its potential to contribute to the future economic and scientific development (or both). Despite the shared motivations for defence industrialization, states do not necessarily follow the same policies and development paths.

As the authors of this volume have shown, there exists a considerable variance when it comes to formulating national defence industrialization policies and development paths. Although most of the countries addressed in this volume initiated their defence industrialization efforts with the goal of self-sufficiency – mainly to break their dependence on foreign suppliers and to gain more independence in foreign policy-making – some states acquiesced to more limited expectations when it came to defence industrialization. These countries accepted their limitations in terms of constrained financial resources, fewer research and development (R&D) capabilities and smaller domestic markets, and most pursued defence-industrial strategies that integrated them into global arms production chains while also sustaining some indigenous arms-producing capabilities in critical areas. Rather than seeking overarching self-sufficiency, these countries instead opted on focusing on niche markets. For some scholars, this is the expected outcome of the defence-industrial globalization. On the other hand, another group of states have persisted in their quest for self-sufficiency, despite the high entry costs and penalties involved in such an effort. This begs of the question: all things being equal (especially when it comes to resources), why do we observe different approaches, strategies and goals when it comes to these two broad groups? Furthermore, why do we observe differences in success and failure *within* the grouping of countries that pursue similar policies?

Whether a state has followed a more limited defence industrialization path or whether it has pursued more aggressive efforts at self-sufficiency, there exist some general, observable patterns. For example, most less-developed states or relatively recent entrants into the arms-producing business have tended to defy the "convergence" effects of globalization. Even if a state decides to integrate itself into global production chains, its defence industry policies can often differ from others (Kurç and Bitzinger 2018, p. 256). In addition, some states rely heavily on private firms to carry out arms development and production, where contracts are distributed by competitive bidding and formal contracting, while other countries are notable for their considerably more direct state participation in defence production and negotiated contracting (DeVore 2015). This critical difference in production bases – public versus private – tends in turn to greatly determine the priority given to pursuing the domestic development and production of certain types of armaments or technologies. Finally, there also exists a variance between states that, while pursuing autarky, are more open to international collaborations and encourage the participation of foreign companies, while others seek to restrict the participation of foreign companies as much as possible. These differences in policies direct us to look into state-specific factors.

To understand this variance in defence industrialization strategies and its implications for the international security, the chapters in this volume presented a series of in-depth case studies and comparative analyses in order to shed empirical light on the defence-industrial decision-making process in new and emerging arms-producing states and the political, economic and the military factors that have shaped this process. Our focus has been on the inner workings of the process: why certain policies were adopted, what the productive capabilities of selected emerging defence industries are and how they are changing in response to transformations in the global defence industrial base. As this volume has shown, this variance is the result of a unique balance between domestic and international factors that have shaped the defence industrialization behaviour and policies of the less or newly industrialized states. The dialogue between domestic and international factors has clearly influenced the variations in these states' defence industrialization policies, as well as their success or failure. While international factors have created opportunities, they have also tended to limit the options available to emerging economies. Domestic economic, technological and political factors have also played an important role in shaping the policy choices of the states' decision-makers.

Understanding the Motivations

Particularly in newly industrialized countries – many of whom were addressed in this volume of chapters – arms manufacturing is seen as a locomotive of growth and innovation when it comes to new industries and new technologies, particularly in the areas of aerospace, electronics and information technologies. For example, Gulf Cooperation Council (GCC) countries, such as Qatar, Saudi Arabia and the UAE, see the defence industrialization as a mean to advance the local technology base (Borchert 2018, p. 299). Similarly, Brazil, in the both 1980s and 2000s, supported defence industrialization because it could help Brazil to address increasing trade deficits and may lead to further gains in economic growth and development (Gouvea 2018, pp. 346, 348). Some Asian countries, such as

China, India, South Korea and Indonesia, view arms manufacturing as a critical component in the national economy, encouraging economic growth and development (Bitzinger 2017, pp. 297, 303). However, this is not the only motivation. The effect of defence industrialization on the national economy represents only one side of the coin.

The other side of the arms-manufacturing coin is the security-driven imperative for self-reliance in armaments. Nation-states, in seeking to shore up their capacities for self-defence, often seek to locate arms industries within their own borders, and subsequently reduce or even eliminate the need for arms imports. This autarky in arms acquisition is often a critical national security objective. Reducing dependencies on foreign weapons system can reinforce national political independence, and also lessens the ability of a foreign supplier to use supplier-based restrictions (such as arms embargoes or third-party sales) as a diplomatic-economic cudgel to extract concessions or political behaviour on the part of the buyer. Beyond this "security of supply," indigenous arms industries are supposed to support the particular needs of a country's military to adequately defend against likely adversaries. Simply put, domestic defence industries are intended to "deliver the goods" to their national armed forces, by supplying essential capabilities to these forces.

Desire for security of supply is present in every state at the initial stages of defence industrialization mainly because of the bad experiences with their suppliers and/or desires to increase their influence at the international arena. In the 1980s and later in the 2000s, Brazil attempted to expand its soft power over Latin America, Africa and the Middle East through its defence industry by making itself less reliant and dependent on foreign manufacturers (Gouvea 2018, pp. 346, 348). Egypt perceived defence industrialization as a mean to build strong military to defend itself and to expand its Arab nationalist and socialist ideology in the Middle East (Abul-Magd 2019, p. 2). GCC nations perceived development of the indigenous defence industry as a tool to support their increasing assertive foreign policy in the region (Borchert 2018, p. 299). China's search for security of supply was reinforced following the abrupt cut-off of Soviet military aid in the early 1960s, and then by the Western arms embargo following the 1989 Tiananmen Square crackdown (Bitzinger 2017, p. 300). Turkey initiated its defence industrialization after experiencing US arms embargo following the Cyprus operation in 1974 (Mevlutoglu 2017, p. 284). Similarly, Israel's defence industrialization focus changed from limited production to munitions independence, self-sufficiency in major systems, following the French arms embargo in 1967 that severed Israel's access to advanced armaments (Rubin 2017, p. 231). South Korea's defence industrialization gained momentum because of the fear of abandonment after the promulgation of the Nixon Doctrine, which reduced US defence commitments to Asia (Bitzinger 2017, p. 302). Countries, such as India, Kazakhstan, Uzbekistan, Turkmenistan, Kyrgyzstan and Tajikistan, see the defence industrialization as a mean to sustain their non-aligned foreign policy (Bitzinger 2017, p. 301, Kurç 2018, pp. 317–8, Weiss 2018, p. 287).

Apart from the perceived economic benefits and desire for independent foreign policy-making, defence industrialization has also been a matter of prestige for many emerging states. Particularly in the cases of aspiring regional or great powers, such as China and India, an independent defence industry not only increased national military power, but attempted to demonstrate the country's industrial and technological prowess and therefore elevate the country's international standing in the broadest sense (Bitzinger 2017, p. 297). However, defence industries are not only about the prestige and status. There is also an important domestic dimension to investing in indigenous defence industries, which can be clearly seen in the case of Turkey and the Gulf states. For them, defence industrialization and the production of indigenous arms permitted ruling elites to gain legitimacy in the eyes of public by portraying themselves "as smart stewards that are able to steer the respective nations into the twenty-first century, where high technology exemplifies economic diversification and promises alternative sources of economic growth" (Borchert 2018, p. 301). Thus, defence industrialization has become a tool not only for increasing military capabilities and following independent foreign policy but also for stroking nationalism and national pride in order to garner legitimacy and support for the ruling elites.

Explaining the Variance: The Impact of International and Domestic Factors on Defence Industrialization

Ultimately, the big question is, is the process of defence industrialization and indigenization worth the effort? In other words, do they meet some particular metric of cost versus benefits? This is a highly debatable point. For too many countries, the effort to build national defence industrial bases is similar to Dr. Samuel Johnson's famous saying about a dog walking on its hind legs, to wit (and to paraphrase), it may be not done well, but one is surprised to find it done at all. In many cases, it is arguably cheaper to import foreign weapons, while these systems generally function better and are more capable than most domestically produced arms. To understand this behaviour, we need to look into how domestic and international factors affect the decision-making process of different countries and how decision-makers negotiate the trade-offs.

The transformation of the global arms production has created both opportunities and challenges for emerging arms producers. While determining their defence industrialization policies, they are faced with trade-offs between autonomy, technology and economic sustainability – a defence-industrial "trilemma". Nations seeking autonomy must have independent defence production capabilities and not be exposed to the exports controls of supplier states. As already argued, this is one of the key considerations driving defence industrialization in many emerging or newly industrialized countries. However, these countries' access to military technology and production know-how is limited. They could choose to pour money into R&D and try to produce indigenous technology by themselves. Yet, their capacities for doing so are determined by available financial resources, which also determine the sustainability of the defence budget (budget to sustain defence industrialization). Since many emerging countries lack the necessary resources to produce every necessary type of weapon system, they have to either opt for limited defence industrialization or engage in collaboration with foreign companies as a stepping-stone for establishing independent defence industries. Limited defence industrialization approaches can provide varying degrees of autonomy in the international system and decrease the cost of defence procurement, but they must also cede pure autonomy (Franko and Herz 2018, pp. 331–2).

When states decide to engage in cooperative relations with the foreign companies, they can amortize the high cost of defence production and reduce the technological and economic burdens of development and/or reaching economies of scale. However, international partnerships also compromise autonomy, since national needs might differ on a joint project or strategic aims may not always coincide (Franko and Herz 2018, pp. 331–2). As the case studies in this volume show, states tend to have different priorities while making these trade-offs (or in some cases, they are forced to make these trade-offs), which leads to variation in the defence industrialization paths.

Departing from the above framework, the countries that historically valued independent foreign policy and had regional and international ambitions have tended to prioritize the pursuit of autarky in armaments. These countries – e.g., Brazil, Argentina, China, India, South

Korea and Turkey – are often willing to spend significant amounts of money on defence industrialization. On the other hand, countries, that are already bound to another country for its security, such as Colombia, Slovakia and Czechia, have tended to cede their autonomy by integrating into the global value chains (integration to global arms production). Yet, the need to cooperate with foreign companies and integration to global value chains are not restricted to the countries with limited defence industrialization capacities. Technological and financial limitations tend to force countries that are seeking self-sufficiency to nevertheless cooperate with foreign companies in order to acquire technology transfers and know-how. At same time, many emerging countries still believe that such cooperation with foreign players can be a stepping-stone on their path for self-sufficiency.

However, while collaboration with foreign suppliers can be an important mechanism for increasing defence industrial capacity, how these cooperative relations operate can show significant variation among player, even if they possess similar end-goals. We would expect that countries with the high expectations for autarky would limit the participation of foreign suppliers, perhaps not in the short-run but definitely over the long term. As Heiko Borchert argues, "the long-term ambition of any policy aimed at defence-industrial independence is to limit – if not stop – outside influence" (Borchert 2018, p. 309). This exactly what the Gulf and Asian states are doing. South Korea, for example, continues to be very protective of its defence industries, and the participation of foreign companies in terms of direct investment remains limited (Bitzinger 2017, Neuman and Kurç 2017, p. 320). In India, participation of foreign suppliers is negligible (Weiss 2018, p. 290). On the other hand, some states operate in a completely opposite manner. Turkey, for example, is such an outlier; it actively seeks integration into the global arms production chains while seeking self-sufficiency. Foreign companies have been and still are deeply involved in Turkey's defence industrial sector, setting up joint ventures and establishing subsidiaries through direct investments (Kurç 2017, Neuman and Kurç 2017, p. 321). For Turkey, international cooperation is not only a means by which to acquire technology and know-how, but it is also an opportunity for Turkish defence companies to enter new export markets. Thus, Ankara actively seeks workshares in multinational projects, especially under the auspices of European and NATO agencies (Kurç 2017, p. 271).

When difficulties in accessing technology and know-how are coupled with financial constraints, states have tended to scale back their defence industrialization ambitions, sometimes drastically. The cases of Brazil, Israel and Egypt illustrate this problem. Brazil, despite its long-term emphasis on autarky, was forced by economic difficulties to significantly downsize its defence industries during the 1980s and 1990s. Rather than seeking self-reliance, Brazil shifted its focus to attaining technological autonomy in key niches, such as aviation. As such, maintaining access to foreign know-how has become more important than retaining the capacity to produce systems within strictly national supply chains (Franko and Herz 2018, p. 337). The result was a more open domestic market and increased cooperation with the foreign suppliers.

The same has also been true for Israel. Rubin described the painful reality that the Israeli government was forced to accept, beginning in the late 1980s. Although cost overruns and the escalating expense of Israel's three major programmes (the Lavi fighter aircraft, the Sholef self-propelled artillery system and the next-generation warship) contributed to Israel's policy crisis, it was Israel's persistent dependence on US and European key technologies that forced the government to accept that across-the-board autarky in defence production was beyond the country's industrial capabilities. It was simply cheaper and more efficient to buy foreign advanced systems off-the-shelf, rather than produce them indigenously. As we have seen, the Israeli government instead decided to focus its resources on creating a robust R&D base and on producing weapons that could address Israel's strategic needs. Israel became a niche producer, manufacturing electronics, intelligence and communication technologies, missiles, anti-missile systems and protection systems for armoured vehicles (Neuman and Kurç 2017, p. 320, Rubin 2017).

Egypt's defence industrialization goes back to the 1950s. Defence industrialization in Egypt started within context of a socialist state and the Cold War, with a goal of establishing a strong military to defend Egypt from perceived Western and Israeli aggression and to expand its influence in the Middle East. At the initial stages, Egypt followed an import-substitution defence industrialization approach, but armaments production remained heavily dependent on Soviet technology. Following its defeat in the 1967 Arab-Israeli war and the subsequent economic crisis, several indigenous weapons programmes had to be shut down and Egypt was forced to scale back defence industrialization plans. Egyptian defence industries gained new momentum during the 1980s and entered into another expansion cycle, although, this time, the United States acted as Egypt's main partner in armaments production. Nevertheless, by the end of the 1980s, Egyptian defence industries had once more begun to contract, and recent attempts to diversify and increase defence production capabilities have remained limited (Abul-Magd 2019).

Management styles, resource limitations and the structure and organization of national defence industrial bases have also exacerbated inefficiencies in defence production in some emerging states. Mevlutogglu maintains that inadequate human resources explain the weaknesses in Turkey's defence industrial production. Turkey's human resources, he argues, are both overstretched and overwhelmed by the plethora of technologies that Turkey has tried to master with too-few R&D personnel and engineers. As a result, Turkish defence industries continue to be ineffective, lacking the focus and vertical expertise to produce advanced weapons systems (Mevlutoglu 2017, Neuman and Kurç 2017, p. 319).

Kurç goes further, arguing that Turkey's defence industrial problems go deeper than just the lack of human resources. He particularly emphasizes institutional and political factors, such as the country's chaotic defence industrial decision-making process and dysfunctional civil–military relations. Turkey, he points out, is still struggling to construct a medium to long-term procurement plan and a prioritized strategy to advance its defence production capabilities. Moreover, a drawn out decision-making process has delayed funding for R&D and ongoing weapons programmes. In the end, the ever-shifting priorities of the decision-makers and their divergent goals have inhibited industrial progress and agreement on a coherent defence industrial policy (Kurç 2017, Neuman and Kurç 2017, p. 319).

Similarly, India's defence industry also suffers from ineffective and over-complicated state-run management of its defence procurement process. The Indian arms industry remains dominated by government-owned defence public sector undertakings (DPSUs), which have significantly impaired the integration of foreign contractors and limited technology transfer. Furthermore, these DPSUs are generally inefficient when it comes to production, with bloated workforces, excess productive capacity and little concern paid to meeting development or production milestones. Finally, the defence bureaucracy is dominated by civilian technocrats, rather than the military end-users, resulting in procurement decisions often being made at the expense of the armed forces' specific requirements (Weiss 2018, pp. 286, 290–5).

Problematic civil–military relations and corruption are an added hurdle. Tensions between Turkey's civil and military personnel have delayed important defence development decisions, particularly when it comes to determining the structure of procurement agencies and their respective lines of authority. Instead, much of the decision-makers' attention and energy is directed at resolving quarrels as to who controls what, rather than at improving the quality of human resources or facilitating the flow of information and experience from the military to defence industrial personnel (Kurç 2017, Neuman and Kurç 2017, p. 319). Defence industrialization of Uzbekistan, Kyrgyzstan and Turkmenistan suffers from rampant corruption, which hinders foreign partnerships in these countries and prevents them from participating in global production chains (Kurç 2018).

Given the changing nature of the global defence industrial landscape and the limitations that emerging countries face in their pursuit of becoming significant arms producers, many states have turned to establishing regional cooperative structures in order to make their existing defence production sustainable. In Latin America, for example, regional security organizations such as the Union of South American Nations (UNASUR) are attempting to counter regional threats, maintain peace and security and enhance participation in international security mechanisms. As such, UNASUR could facilitate the emergence of South American defence identity, which could also promote common defence industrial projects, such as the Brazilian-Chilean-Argentine C-390 military transport aircraft (Franko and Herz 2018, pp. 340–2).

Similarly, in Europe, there appears to be a behavioural change, in that many EU member states are tolerating both the European Defence Agency's (EDA) and the European Commission's efforts to regulate the sector and encourage the establishment of a European Defence Equipment Market (EDEM) and a European Defence Technological and Industrial Base (EDTIB). Some European states are even abandoning their domestic suppliers in favour of other European firms and leaning increasingly toward pan-European countries cooperation, either multilaterally or bilaterally, because, as Mawdsley argues, "most states are effectively constrained by the system in which they operate" (Mawdsley 2018, p. 267). The dominance of the large arms-producing states, in terms of defence production, budget and R&D, has tended to limit the export opportunities of smaller or lesser arms-producing states (Mawdsley 2018, p. 267). Since these smaller arms-producing states do not possess domestic defence markets large enough to support a broad-based defence industrial base, the structure of the market forces them to cooperate and integrate even if they would like to pursue protectionist policies, thus their attempts to achieve defence autarky have been mostly unrealizable.

And yet these arguments have not dissuaded countries around the world from continuing their endeavours to develop and manufacture their own armaments. The depth and breadth of the regional cooperative structures remained problematic. Despite the increased interactions between the military establishments in South America, the defence industry plans have not yet come to fruition mainly because of the Venezuela crisis (Franko and Herz 2018, p. 342). The regional cooperation in Europe is, also, far from perfect and has not met earlier high expectations. Despite the defence industrial consolidation in the 1990s and emergence of regional organizations, such as the Organization for Joint Armament Co-operation (OCCAR) and EDA, the European defence industrial landscape has failed to become truly integrated. The European defense business continues to be beset with fragmentation and protectionism, despite the general acceptance in establishing an EDEM or EDTIB. States' desires to maximize their own national interests and to protect their defence industrial base are the main culprits in the continuing fragmentation of the European defence market, which also results in the suboptimal defence capabilities of all European states (Mawdsley 2018, p. 268). For example, Slovakia and Czechia continues to reiterate the necessity of maintaining security of supply, while engaging in regional and Europe-wide cooperation. Even in the case of Central

European countries, regional cooperation is limited and plagued by protectionism, competition and lack of coordination (Chovančík 2018, p. 279).

Indeed, if anything, more and more countries are jumping into the business of arms manufacturing (such as Abu Dhabi and Saudi Arabia), or are attempting to expand the range and sophistication of their defence industries (such as Iran, Turkey and Brazil). If so, and if the reasons have less to do with economics, security of supply or even military capabilities, then these countries could be embarking on a very expensive and not very productive (from a standpoint of developing critical military systems) fool's errand.

Marc DeVore offers an alternative line of reasoning (DeVore 2017). He argues that maintaining the capacity for military-technological adaptation is perhaps even more important than the security of supply. Domestic defence industries, even if they are narrowly focused, can nevertheless be valuable assets when a state needs to deal with "technological and tactical surprises" and "adapt to unanticipated military challenges" (DeVore 2017, p. 243). As such, possessing even limited proficiencies when it comes to innovation can reap important benefits: "Even small defence industries", he argues, are "strategically valuable because they cultivate engineers that understand weapons-related technologies". In addition, these industries possess a "second skill set", that is, "the tacit knowledge" needed to work with their militaries to "address battlefield needs" (DeVore 2017, p. 256). DeVore has particularly focused on Israel's capacities for adaptive innovation, and he argued that Israeli defence firms, due to the continued closeness to their key stakeholders, i.e., the Israel Defense Forces (IDF) and the Israeli defence ministry, have "played critical roles" in helping the IDF adapt to technological surprises. DeVore makes some intriguing points, which opens the door for further research.

Conclusion

The global arms industry is a dynamic phenomenon, a constantly moving target. It expands and contracts, it undergoes phases of growth and prosperity and phases of crisis and decline, both on a historical and on a regional basis, and often the two are not in sync with each other. Nevertheless, for a variety of reasons, countries will continue to manufacture weapons, and the family of arms-producing nations will continue to expand. Despite technological hurdles and high entry costs, other factors – national security imperatives, projected technology benefits, jobs and even national pride – continue to be very strong impulses acting on most arms-producing states, especially smaller states or new entrants. The quest for autarky in armaments will likely remain the singular, prevailing tendency among these states. At the same time, it is equally likely that many of these arms-producing countries will continue to experience great difficulties and considerable expense in their endeavours to produce arms, while gaining relatively little when it comes to improving their military capabilities.

The questions the issues raised in these series symposiums suggest the need for further in-depth single-case and comparative studies to decode the decision-making process in emerging states and to give greater analytic attention to the proliferation of defence industrial capabilities and its consequences. One of the most important conclusions of this volume is that the dialogue between domestic and international factors clearly influences the variation in defence industrialization policies, as well as their success or failure. While international factors create opportunities, they also limit the options available to emerging economies. Domestic factors also play an important role by shaping the policy choices of the states' decision-makers. The interplay between international and domestic economic, technological and political factors will increasingly affect decision-making when it comes defence industrial strategies among emerging and new arms produces, and even more established arms industrial bases, such as Western Europe. We hope this volume will help spur further study of defence industrial transformation and arms proliferation and their implications for the national security interests of countries around the world (Neuman and Kurç 2017, pp. 324–5).

References

Abul-Magd, Z., 2019. Egypt's Defense Industry: Dependency, Civilian Production, and Attempts at Autonomy. *All Azimuth: A Journal of Foreign Policy and Peace*, 0 (0), 1–23.

Bitzinger, R.A., 2017. Asian Arms Industries and Impact on Military Capabilities. *Defence Studies*, 17 (3), 295–311.

Borchert, H., 2018. The Arab Gulf Defense Pivot: Defense Industrial Policy in a Changing Geostrategic Context. *Comparative Strategy*, 37 (4), 299–315.

Chovančík, M., 2018. Defense Industrialization in Small Countries: Policies in Czechia and Slovakia. *Comparative Strategy*, 37 (4), 272–285.

DeVore, M.R., 2015. Defying Convergence: Globalisation and Varieties of Defence-Industrial Capitalism. *New Political Economy*, 20 (4), 569–593.

DeVore, M.R., 2017. Commentary on the Value of Domestic Arms Industries: Security of Supply or Military Adaptation? *Defence Studies*, 17 (3), 242–259.

Franko, P.M. and Herz, M., 2018. Defense Industrialization in Latin America. *Comparative Strategy*, 37 (4), 331–345.

Gouvea, R., 2018. Brazil's Defense Industry: Challenges and Opportunities. *Comparative Strategy*, 37 (4), 346–359.

Kurç, Ç., 2017. Between Defence Autarky and Dependency: The Dynamics of Turkish Defence Industrialization. *Defence Studies*, 17 (3), 260–281.

Kurç, Ç., 2018. The Puzzle: Multi-Vector Foreign Policy and Defense Industrialization in Central Asia. *Comparative Strategy*, 37 (4), 316–330.

Kurç, Ç. and Bitzinger, R.A., 2018. Defense Industries in the 21st Century: A Comparative Analysis—The Second E-Workshop. *Comparative Strategy*, 37 (4), 255–259.

Mawdsley, J., 2018. Armaments Decision-Making: Are European States Really Different? *Comparative Strategy*, 37 (4), 260–271.

Mevlutoglu, A., 2017. Commentary on Assessing the Turkish Defense Industry: Structural Issues and Major Challenges. *Defence Studies*, 17 (3), 282–294.

Neuman, S.G. and Kurç, Ç., 2017. Conclusion: The Need for Continuous In-Depth and Comparative Study. *Defence Studies*, 17 (3), 317–325.

Rubin, U., 2017. Israel's Defence Industries–An Overview. *Defence Studies*, 17 (3), 228–241.

Weiss, M., 2018. State vs. Market in India: How (Not) to Integrate Foreign Contractors in the Domestic Defense-Industrial Sector. *Comparative Strategy*, 37 (4), 286–298.

Index

Note: **Bold** page numbers refer to tables and *italic* page numbers refer to figures.

For Product Safety Concerns and Information please contact our EU representative GPSR@taylorandfrancis.com Taylor & Francis Verlag GmbH, Kaufingerstraße 24, 80331 München, Germany